T0393114

Rethinking Post-Disaster Recovery

This book presents an original interdisciplinary approach to the study of the so-called recovery phase in disaster management, centred on the notion of repairing.

The volume advances thinking on disaster recovery that goes beyond institutional and managerial challenges, descriptions and analyses. It encourages socially, politically and ethically engaged questioning of what it means to recover after disaster. At the centre of this analysis, contributions examine the diversity of processes of repairing through which recovery can take place, and the varied meanings actors attribute to repair at different times and scales of such processes. It also analyses the multiple arenas (juridical, expert, political) in which actors struggle to make sense of the "what-ness" of a disaster and the paths for recovery. These struggles are interlinked with interest-based and power-based struggles which maintain structural inequality and exploitation, existing social hierarchies and established forms of marginality. The work uses case studies from all over the world, cutting-edge theoretical discussions and original empirical research to put critical and interpretative approaches in social sciences into dialogue, opening the venue for innovative approaches in the study of environmental disasters.

This book will be of much interest to students of disaster management, sociology, anthropology, law and philosophy.

Laura Centemeri is Senior Researcher in Environmental Sociology at the French National Centre for Scientific Research, and a member of the Centre for the Study of Social Movements (CEMS-EHESS), France.

Sezin Topçu is Senior Researcher in Science and Technology Studies at the French National Centre for Scientific Research, and a member of the Centre for the Study of Social Movements (CEMS-EHESS), France.

J. Peter Burgess is Professor and Director of the Chair in Geopolitics of Risk at École Normale Supérieure, France.

Series: Routledge New Security Studies

Series Editor: J. Peter Burgess,
École Normale Superieur (ENS), Paris

The aim of this book series is to gather state-of-the-art theoretical reflection and empirical research into a core set of volumes that respond vigorously and dynamically to new challenges to security studies scholarship. Routledge New Security Studies is a continuation of the PRIO New Security Studies series.

Crypto-Politics
Encryption and Democratic Practices in the Digital Era
Linda Monsees

Negotiating Intractable Conflicts
Readiness Theory Revisited
Amira Schiff

Standardization and Risk Governance
A Multi-Disciplinary Approach
Edited by Odd Einar Olsen, Kirsten Juhl, Preben Lindøe and Ole Andreas Engen

Nordic Societal Security
Convergence and Divergence
Edited by Sebastian Larsson and Mark Rhinard

The Molecularisation of Security
Medical Countermeasures, Stockpiling and the Governance of Biological Threats
Christopher Long

Translations of Security
A Framework for the Study of Unwanted Futures
Trine Villumsen Berling, Ulrik Pram Gad, Karen Lund Petersen, and Ole Wæver

Rethinking Post-Disaster Recovery
Socio-Anthropological Perspectives on Repairing Environments
Edited by Laura Centemeri, Sezin Topçu and J. Peter Burgess

For more information about this series, please visit: www.routledge.com/Routledge-New-Security-Studies/book-series/RNSS

Rethinking Post-Disaster Recovery

Socio-Anthropological Perspectives on Repairing Environments

Edited by Laura Centemeri, Sezin Topçu and J. Peter Burgess

Routledge
Taylor & Francis Group

LONDON AND NEW YORK

First published 2022
by Routledge
2 Park Square, Milton Park, Abingdon, Oxon OX14 4RN

and by Routledge
605 Third Avenue, New York, NY 10158

Routledge is an imprint of the Taylor & Francis Group, an informa business

British Library Cataloguing-in-Publication Data
A catalogue record for this book is available from the British Library

Library of Congress Cataloging-in-Publication Data
A catalog record for this book has been requested

ISBN: 978-1-032-02713-5 (hbk)
ISBN: 978-1-032-02715-9 (pbk)
ISBN: 978-1-003-18478-2 (ebk)

DOI: 10.4324/9781003184782

Typeset in Times New Roman
by Apex CoVantage, LLC

Contents

Figures

Contributors

Marco Armiero, Research Director, Institute for Studies on the Mediterranean (ISMED), CNR, Naples (Italy) and Director, Environmental Humanities Laboratory, KTH, Stockholm (Sweden)

Janine Barbot, Research Director INSERM in Sociology, Center for the Study of Social Movements (CEMS), Ecole des Hautes Etudes en Sciences Sociales, Paris (France)

J. Peter Burgess, Professor and Chair of Geopolitics of Risk at the Ecole Normale Supérieure, Paris, and Adjunct Professor at the Center for Advanced Security Theory (CAST), University of Copenhagen

Laura Centemeri, Senior Researcher CNRS in Environmental Sociology, Centre for the Study of Social Movements (CEMS), Ecole des Hautes Etudes en Sciences Sociales, Paris (France)

Francis Chateauraynaud, Professor of Sociology, Groupe de Sociologie Pragmatique et Réflexive, Ecole des Hautes Etudes en Sciences Sociales, Paris (France)

Josquin Debaz, Researcher in Sociology, Groupe de Sociologie Pragmatique et Réflexive, Ecole des Hautes Etudes en Sciences Sociales, Paris (France)

Daniel Delatin Rodrigues, PhD student in Sociology, University of Milano-Bicocca (Italy)

Nicolas Dodier, Research Director INSERM and Professor of Sociology, Center for the Study of Social Movements (CEMS), Ecole des Hautes Etudes en Sciences Sociales, Paris (France)

Santiago Gorostiza, Postdoctoral Researcher in History, Centre d'Histoire de Sciences Po, Sciences Po Paris (France)

Matthew Hall, Professor of Law and Criminal Justice, Lincoln Law School (UK)

Paul Jobin, Associate Research Fellow in Sociology, Institute of Sociology, Academia Sinica (Taiwan)

Frédéric Keck, Senior Researcher CNRS in Anthropology, Laboratoire d'Anthropologie Sociale, Collège de France and Ecole des Hautes Etudes en Sciences Sociales (France)

Lorenzo Natali, Associate Professor in Criminology, School of Law, University of Milano-Bicocca (Italy)

Sandrine Revet, Senior Researcher FNSP in Anthropology, CERI, Sciences Po/ CNRS (France)

Line Marie Thorsen, DFF Postdoc in Anthropology, Center for Environmental Humanities, Aarhus University (Denmark)

Sezin Topçu, Senior Researcher CNRS in Science and Technology Studies, Center for the Study of Social Movements (CEMS), Ecole des Hautes Etudes en Sciences Sociales, Paris (France)

Acknowledgements

This edited volume benefited from financial support from the research group Risk, Violence and Reparation coordinated by Janine Barbot within the Center for the Study of Social Movements (EHESS/CNRS UMR8044/INSERM U1276). Financial support was also granted by the research project Humanités environnementales à l'heure de l'Anthropocène (SHS-ENV) coordinated by Christophe Bonneuil and funded by PSL University (Paris Sciences Lettres) (2016–2018). It allowed the organisation of the international workshop 'Repairing Environments: Post-disaster Mobilisations, Experiences, Tensions' (28 September 2018, Paris) which helped to prepare this book. We are grateful to Franky Demoulin for his help with the editing of the manuscript, and to Clare Ferguson and Joséphine Blount for their help with the copyediting.

Introduction

Recovery, resilience and repairing: for a non-reductionist approach to the complexity of post-disaster situations

Laura Centemeri, Sezin Topçu and J. Peter Burgess

As a young girl growing up in Poland during World War II, the Polish poet and Nobel Prize winner Wislawa Szymborska experienced first-hand the dilemmas of a return to normal life after a catastrophe. In her acclaimed poem 'The End and the Beginning' (Szymborska 2001), she draws a pointed, penetrating picture of post-war social conditions, recalling how the mundane need 'to push the rubble/to the side of the road,/so the corpse-filled wagons/can pass' and to 'prop up a wall', 'glaze a window', 'rehang a door' and rebuild the bridges slowly but inexorably undermined the quest for responsibility and any examination of causes and effects. Showing how the people became progressively caught up in everyday matters and preoccupations and lost interest in the 'dull' discourses about the past, Szymborska's poem enacts the emotional, moral, social and political tensions between forgetting and remembering that are strewn across the paths forged by damaged communities as they endeavour to 'remake a world' (Das *et al.* 2001) after a catastrophe.

Striking a different tone, the author, film-maker and climate activist Naomi Klein denounced, in her best-selling book *The Shock Doctrine* (2007), the way in which certain proponents of neoliberalism, in particular in its earliest form, in the Chicago School movement led by Milton Friedman, envisaged exploiting major catastrophes (from wars to 'natural' disasters like the tsunami in Sri Lanka in 2004 and Hurricane Katrina, in the United States, in 2005) in order to implement radical free market reforms. Klein argued that the logic of neoliberalism sees post-disaster situations less as catastrophic breakdowns in need of repair than as windows of opportunity for socio-economic change that are rife with interest-based struggles. The notion of 'disaster capitalism', despite questions over its lack of analytical clarity (see Wisner 2009), has since gained currency amongst critical disaster researchers and social movement activists (see Gunewardena and Schuller 2008; Fletcher 2012; Schuller and Maldonado 2016).

Albeit in very different ways, Szymborska and Klein thus both touch upon the same fundamental sociological, political and ethical questions. How is a social fabric preserved – or challenged – during a disruptive event? What is indispensable to the continuity of a society's values, the cohesion of its communities and the minimum functioning of its institutions? What can be left behind, replaced or remodelled? More fundamentally, who decides these things? Who has the

DOI: 10.4324/9781003184782-1

legitimacy and authority to determine what is critical and non-critical, essential and non-essential? And once this is determined, who is responsible for organizing the complex task of repairing?

In this volume, we propose a perspective on disaster recovery that goes beyond the institutional and managerial challenges, definitions, descriptions, analyses and prescriptions to present a more socially, politically and ethically engaged questioning of what it can and should mean to repair a society that has been struck by disaster. Throughout the book, we try to enrich an approach to recovery that centres on resilience, while discussing some of its limitations. The work takes as its starting point the diversity of motivations, means, strategies and tools that are brought into play to cope with situations of socio-ecological disruption. This diversity, as the volume will show, is not immediately compatible with an approach to recovery that sees a community disaster as just a technical, logistical or infrastructure problem. In an attempt to revolutionize this monolithic view of human vulnerability and provide it with colour and texture, this book will mobilize the notion of 'repair' and show how it offers the possibility of addressing post-disaster recovery in all its complexity, sociality and humanity.

In the broad and diverse field of disaster research and management,[1] *recovery* is defined as the process of a return to normalcy, or the 'period of time where deliberate actions are undertaken to routinize everyday activities of those individuals and groups whose daily routines have been disrupted. These activities may restore old patterns and/or institute new ones' (Quarantelli 1999: 3).

Traditional approaches to recovery have been criticized for being limited in their temporal scope and for being poorly equipped theoretically (Berke *et al.* 1993; Passerini 2000; Weidner 2009; Tierney and Oliver-Smith 2012; Aijazi 2015). While disaster research on recovery initially centred mainly on questions relating to the appropriate reconstruction of housing, shelter, resettlement, relocation, displacement and psychological and psychosocial recovery, the field began in the 1990s to address issues such as the roles of institutions, the state and civil society actors in recovery policy-making and implementation. The focus has been on coping strategies, adaptation mechanisms and more recently resilience building. However, the research has rarely addressed questions of social change after disasters through long-term studies on recovery outcomes, including the role played by pre-existing socio-economic conditions in shaping post-disaster trajectories. This reveals a still largely dominant understanding of disasters as *temporally delimitated phenomena.*[2]

This book aims at challenging such an approach. In so doing, it aligns itself with a tradition of research on disaster that first emerged in anthropology and then, more recently, in STS studies and that requires us to *expand time frames in the study of disasters*, to problematize assumptions about the onset of crises and to recalibrate assumptions about the scope and duration of their aftermath (see Oliver-Smith 1986; Oliver-Smith and Hoffman 1999; Dowty and Allen 2011; Revet and Langumier 2015; Fortun *et al.* 2017). The book focuses on this process of recalibration as a way to fully understand, on the one hand, the pervasive, longlasting, 'slow' (see Nixon 2011; Knowles 2014) nature of the impact of disaster on both societal or community life and on individuals' environments and their bodies and, on the other, how diverse forms of injustice structurally inscribed in a social fabric can contribute to increasing vulnerability to disastrous events. In addition to social injustice, the recent research on disasters has shown that questions of environmental (Schlosberg 2007), epistemic (Allen 2018; Frickel 2008) and narrative (Barca 2014) injustice are of crucial importance to understand the specific trajectories of recovery after disaster.

Consequently, the approach to recovery developed in this volume connects with the current debates and recent developments in social theory and takes into serious account the fact that the ways in which we think about disaster have 'profound operational and political consequences' (Fortun *et al.* 2017: 1008; see also Kreps and Drabek 1996).

Recovery and the disputed 'what-ness' of disaster

There is a general agreement in the literature that disasters are social phenomena, regardless of the hazardous agents involved. Phenotypic classifications that distinguish disasters according to agent – separating, for example, natural disasters from technical disasters and public health disasters from ecological disasters – have been increasingly contested for their lack of analytical clarity. In line with Perry (2018: 14), a consensus has formed around the definition of disaster as a 'fundamental disruption in the social system (of whatever size) that renders ineffective whatever patterns of social intercourse prevail'. Its 'causes rest in the *social structure*, *social interactions* and the *environment* as a whole' (*ibid.*: 15, our emphasis). With regard to its disruption of patterns, a disaster can trigger a 'chain of occurrences' that can potentially result in the long-lasting transformation of previous structures and practices, a defining trait of what Sewell (1996) called 'historical events'. 'Historical events' here refer to temporally extended situations that reveal the interplay between action, culture and structures (including material infrastructures and the environment) in the production of social transformation. This book aims at exploring, through a focus on repair processes and *dispositifs*, how social structures and patterns undergo this transformation, what the causes and correlates of the transformation are and the multilevel reach of its aftermath.[3]

In her literature review of 'what we know, or think we know, about long term disaster recovery', Passerini (2000: 67) argued that the transformative potential of disasters is more often than not defused by 'a myriad of structural and cultural forces that keep people from considering or embracing change', while, at the same time, disasters can sometimes overwhelm the capacity of communities to recover. Moreover, when change does occur, it happens on different scales, in a variety of forms, at different rates and in a time span that is impossible to predetermine. Indeed, the transformative potential of a disaster can stay latent until broader conditions for change are in place.

Similarly, the issue of scale is often debated in the literature on recovery, where it is understood in terms of the social level, or unit, from which the 'success of recovery' should be assessed (Quarantelli 1999). Disaster recovery is in this sense understood as a finite objective that can be achieved and subsequently dispensed with. It is a measure that remains external to the process, a measure that is determined and imposed by the observer. As a consequence of the focus on 'success' at the expense of 'social change', there is often a lack of perspective and clarity in the assessment. The historical situation and the observer's value projections silently shape the normative underpinnings of disaster management as well as the specific meanings attributed to 'success'. Successful for whom? According to whom? Such questions are often neglected in the managerial approaches to recovery.

This same lack of reflexivity on normative assumptions can be found in the currently fashionable idea of recovery as 'Building Back Better'. This catchphrase was coined by the former US president Bill Clinton in the aftermath of the 2004 Indian Ocean earthquake and tsunami, and was developed into a list of 10 propositions conceived as operational guidelines for the humanitarian post-disaster intervention. As shown by Benadusi, in the case of Sri Lanka (2015: 93), however, the direct importation of this idea, with no public discussion of its assumptions and aim, has encouraged the proliferation of conflicting interpretations of the slogan.

An analysis of the epistemic, cognitive, normative, financial and judiciary tensions that pervade the process of recovery are at the core of the contributions gathered in this book. The focus is not on developing tools and means for measuring disaster impact and recovery but on providing analytical tools to explore 'the cultural, social-organizational, and political-economic conditions/options that affect how reconstruction occurs (for better or worse)' (Passerini 2000: 71). The matter of whether or not recovery from a disaster is possible, or even desirable, at least for some actors, is also a salient question given serious consideration by the contributors to the volume. The analytical frameworks mobilized are grounded in the assumption that any disaster situation is marked by the uncertainty of the 'what-ness' (Quéré and Terzi 2014) of the disaster, which depends on the diversity of actors experiencing its consequences and their involvement in a variety of processes of acknowledging, evaluating and managing these consequences at different scales. Disasters can be sociologically analyzed as 'problematic situations' in which, following the pragmatist philosopher John Dewey, the usual ways of making sense and doing things do not work. Actors deal with this practical and existential uncertainty by engaging in the contentious process of 'inquiry' in order to cognitively and normatively describe the situation in terms of attributing causes and responsibilities and identifying damages and victims (see Cefaï 2016).

The contributors to this volume share a similar approach in researching processes of recovery that consists in following how the disaster and its consequences are made the object of a variety of *sense-making struggles*, that is, struggles around the meaning of what happened and how it affected the given order of things and the possible future (Centemeri 2010; 2015; see Chapter 7). These struggles are interlinked with interest-based struggles and power-based struggles that more often than not reproduce the pre-existing social hierarchy and forms of marginality, as shown by feminist and postcolonial scholars in disaster studies on the Global South (see Fortun 2001; Choi 2015). There is evidence, however, that disasters in the Global North also usually intensify pre-existing conditions of inequality in the long term (Passerini 2000). We believe that in order to explain the dynamics through which such inequalities are maintained and reinforced, it is crucial to understand how a shared sense of the 'what-ness' of the disaster is generated and stabilized, at least temporarily because we know that this stability is always potentially open to future revision (see Chapter 4).

These sense-making struggles take place in a variety of 'arenas' (Cefaï 2002; see also Hilgartner and Bosk 1988) where the actors concerned come into contact with one another. An 'arena' can be defined in general terms as a *dispositif* that brings together speakers and their audiences and that defines a mode of confrontation either between the speakers or between the speakers and their audience (Dodier 1999). Arenas organize a form of collective reflexivity – and 'reflexivity loops'. They are specialized to varying degrees according to the rules that define the conditions for access (Dodier and Barbot 2016). We can therefore distinguish between technical-expert arenas, judiciary arenas, media arenas, parliamentary arenas and other arenas of public or expert debate. In such arenas, actors express conflicting understandings of the disaster and conflicting normative expectations about what should be done to recover, what is worth recovering and what types of processes can be considered to be a 'good' recovery.

The contributors to this book also examine sense-making struggles in the context of 'governing (by) disasters' *dispostifs*. As highlighted by Revet and Langumier (2015) in their anthropological approach to *dispositifs* in disaster situations, 'frictions' (Tsing 2005) are ubiquitous between, on the one hand, the variety of *dispositifs* that are meant to govern disasters and, on the other, the actors' 'normative expectations' (Dodier and Barbot 2016) and the diversity of their practical 'modes of engagement' (Thévenot 2007) in the situation. This shows 'the fundamental heterogeneity of the resources that allow individuals and groups to assess risks and position themselves relative to them' (Dodier 2015: 224).

The fact that governing by disasters is now a distinctive feature of contemporary societies should not lead us to assume that the integration of disasters into a 'general economy' is a smooth process (Dodier 2015: 226). If we assume that the power of *dispositifs* automatically lies in ensuring that the actors' practices and normative expectations align with one another, there is the risk we overlook any frictions or ignore their importance, both in the making and in the unmaking of hegemony (Tsing 2005: 6). Conflicts of interest and power struggles are thus constantly interwoven with processes that aim at defining a shared 'sense of things' across a variety of arenas, *dispositifs*, scales and temporalities (Chateauraynaud 2016).

These processes are of crucial importance in explaining the specific observable path to recovery after a disaster, and they cannot be properly understood if the fact that disasters also disrupt everyday life space by affecting people's 'attachments' (in the sense of Hennion 2004) is not taken into account.

Direct experiences of death, destruction, toxicity and displacements present the victims of disaster with three vastly different but intertwined needs. They have to find ways of meeting basic physiological requirements, rebuild familiarity with people and places and deal with the irreversibility of loss. Revet and Langumier (2015: 5) noted that:

> The everyday life of 'disaster victims' and those 'displaced' by catastrophe cannot be summarized solely in terms of the management of a day-to-day existence that has been impacted by these events. Far from the cameras and in unspectacular fashion, life very quickly resumes its course on the ruins and traces of disaster. [. . .] The issue is therefore no longer to recognize and account for what disaster destroys but what it contributes to producing, the social recompositions it brings about.

From a different perspective but with a similar focus, Aijazi (2015:16) introduced into disaster studies, or more specifically recovery studies, the perspective of social repair developed by Das in her work on and with survivors of violence (Das 2007). Das' approach reveals that the process of reoccupying the same spaces of daily life that once experienced disruption is peppered with 'acts of self-creation', meaning a renewal and revitalization of oneself, one's social relationships and one's relationship to the place. 'Generative spaces for social remaking' (Das 2007) can thus emerge that are centred on the ordinary activities necessary to keep life going, like providing food and shelter and taking care of children and elderly people.

Initiatives for 'grassroots recovery' can occasionally overlap with 'interstitial initiatives' that aim at reclaiming a form of autonomy from dominant economic and political logics and structures (Monticelli 2018), as in the case of the post-earthquake ecovillage of Pescomaggiore (L'Aquila, Italy) discussed by Tomassi and Forino (2019).[4] However, as shown by Benadusi (2013; 2015), grassroots initiatives in contexts heavily exposed to international aid are systematically instrumentalized to support a rhetoric of resilience that reinforces deeply entrenched local power dynamics and the reproduction of conditions of inequality.

The resilience framework and its limitations

Today, 'resilience' is a key concept guiding not only the analysis of but also public interventions in recovery after disaster, and it has generated a vast body of literature (see Alexander 2013). It has prompted researchers to explore the inherent qualities and internal factors that affect a community's ability to recover, or 'bounce back', from disaster and how to translate these factors into quantifiable indicators in order to help design more effective mitigation strategies (amongst such pioneering work, see Mileti 1999). Social capital and a variety of other 'capitals' (including community and economic capitals) and capacities (from improvisation to infrastructure resources) are thus identified as 'elements of resilience' that can be operationalized (Kendra *et al.* 2018). The concept of resilience and its use as a diagnostic and prognostic tool in recovery after disaster is also highly contested (see Aguirre and Best 2015; Tierney 2015). In particular, it has met with considerable criticism from researchers attempting to clarify its relationship to the logic of neoliberalism (Walker and Cooper 2011; Chandler and Reid 2016; Revet 2020). Efforts to operationalize resilience through a list of standardized indicators have to face the fact that responses to disaster are closely connected with socio-historical and cultural dimensions that are specific to each locality and that contribute to shaping the sense of what counts as a 'good' recovery.

Beyond the criticism of the implicit normative assumptions of the resilience metrics that have been developed with the aim of defining a universally valid model of resilience building, resilience has often been 'co-opted' as a justification put forward by neoliberal projects for withdrawing government support for universalistic welfare measures and, more generally, public infrastructure investments. Communities are then forced to compete for public and also increasingly private funding to support resilience building, with the result that: 'Resilience, paradoxically, is not for everyone, but for those who are best equipped to compete in the demanding *milieu* of government and philanthropic funding mechanisms' (Kendra *et al.* 2018: 101). On a similar note, Benadusi (2013: 434) highlighted the fact that in post-disaster situations, actors confronted with international aid *dispositifs* have to appear 'just resilient enough [. . .], but not so resilient as to tarnish the image of vulnerability still required to intercept aid'. In post-Chernobyl Ukraine (Petryna 2013), post-Fukushima Japan (Hasegawa 2013) and post-Hurricane Katrina New Orleans (Adams 2013), individuals had to compete in order to 'prove' that their victimized conditions justified state assistance or compensation and that they qualified for it by showing that they were learning to become 'resilient' as a community of (acknowledged) victims. All these cases show how the 'social resilience' framework (see Hall and Lamont 2013) promotes a specific normativity that is sustained by neoliberal policies and narratives and is based on individual and collective capacities to cope and 'creatively' adapt to unavoidable catastrophes. From this perspective, resilience has been defined as the new 'social morphology' of our societies, which are 'insecure by design' (Evans and Reid 2014).

However, it is important to distinguish between resilience as a governance tool, resilience as a justificatory argument that can be mobilized by a variety of actors in concrete situations and resilience as an analytical framework that can be used to approach the way in which societies respond to disruptions. In this latter case, resilience has the merit of drawing attention to the need for an interdisciplinary approach to the study of recovery after disasters that takes into account the systemic dimension of interwoven ecological, technical, socio-cultural and political factors at different scales. Indeed, the resilience framework invites us to develop an approach to disasters in which social dynamics are analyzed in their interdependences with the specific environment in which the disaster occurs. From the perspective of resilience, disasters can be considered as 'interactive phenomena of social and technical systems distributed over geographic space' (Kendra *et al.* 2018: 104).

The implicit reference in the resilience framework to the mutually constitutive dynamics of systems and places invites us to include the dimension of *milieu* (see Chapter 7) in order to understand how 'nested systems' can produce 'injurious outcomes that cannot be straightforwardly confined in time or space, nor adequately addressed with standard operating procedures and established modes of thought' (Fortun *et al.* 2017: 1004). However, we believe that the technocratic reduction of resilience to a tool that can be mobilized by a larger form of neoliberal 'governing through standards' (Ponte *et al.* 2011) as well as the community-based focus that this framework implicitly supports and the social morphology it encourages profoundly hinder the potential of such a notion as a tool that can be used to explore the dynamics of post-disaster initiatives and the diversity of patterns towards social change.

The aim of this book is to clear the way for the development of an alternative perspective on researching recovery after disasters that is based on the socially, culturally, politically, ecologically and ethically informed notion of *repairing environments*. It consists in analyzing *how a variety of socio-technical, socio-ecological and socio-cultural repairing issues are defined and dealt with in arenas,* dispositifs *and practices that together shape the possible paths of recovery after disaster.*

From resilience to the multiple meanings of the 'repairing environments' notion

The contributions assembled in this book show how the resilience discourse is displaced, reshaped, enhanced and challenged by introducing a 'repairing' perspective into researching recovery after disasters.

Before going any further, we need to clear up a possible misunderstanding. At the core of the notion of 'repairing' as discussed in this book is a partial distancing from the common understanding of 'repairing' as restoring a being, object, situation or environment that has been impaired to its original state. Our approach is based on considering 'the repair' as an ambivalent social phenomenon that is both transformative and aimed at maintaining a continuity with the past condition through transformation (see Attia 2018). Therefore, the effects of the repair will manifest in an undetermined way in an unforeseeable future with an unknown spatial scope. From this perspective, 'repair' is a notion that can be useful in exploring human communities' relationships with their environment.

Disasters, in all their different forms, remind us of human interdependences with the material world and societies' dependence on material infrastructures and 'infrastructuring practices' (Star 1999; Bowker and Star 1999; Edwards 2003). Moreover, major chemical and nuclear disasters have contributed at least since the 1960s to the emergence of a form of environmental reflexivity on the global dimension of the ecological crisis epitomized by the sociological 'risk society' category (Lagadec 1981; Amoore 2013; Amoore and de Goede 2008; Beck 1992) and, more recently, to the notion of 'Anthropocene' (Bonneuil and Fressoz 2017; Blok and Jensen 2019). This implies that it is increasingly hard to draw a clear line – if indeed this were ever possible – between what can be considered a natural environment and what can be considered a socially and culturally shaped environment (Latour 1993). In addition, it has become even more difficult to address issues of social change in isolation from larger processes of ecological and techni-cal transformations.

In contrast to the general propensity to speak in terms of an undifferentiated global environment, disaster situations force us to pay attention to 'the activities, materialities, and concepts through which an environment is performed in always situated and contested ways', which reveal 'an array of environments, themselves heterogeneous and differently organized' (Blok *et al.* 2016). In fact, disasters dis-rupt a variety of ecologies that shape environments, thus triggering a multiplicity of repairing processes that account for the emergence, or not, of new patterns of socio-ecological organization (see also Oliver-Smith 1998).

Consequently, this reference to environments points to the need to address the analysis of disaster recovery through a consideration of the variety of material ecologies that become visible as a result of their misfunctioning and the efforts to repair them (see also Frickel *et al.* 2009). With regard to the notion of 'environ-ments', we would like to stress the importance of paying attention in the analysis of disaster recovery, on the one hand, to social phenomena as embedded in socio-ecosystems and, on the other, to their place-based nature as phenomena that are geographically located and shaped in a material 'web of life' that is culturally invested with meaning and value (Gieryn 2000).

By connecting disasters and environments, the objective of this book is to emphasize that disasters potentially reconfigure not only societies but also ontolo-gies through the variety of processes of repairing that actors engage in to return to normalcy. Recent developments in the field of environmental law, like the creation of legal rights for rivers (O'Donnell and Talbot-Jones 2018), point to evolutions in this direction.

Furthermore, while the notion of recovery (in both its institutional and scien-tific conceptualizations) implicitly focuses on the physical-material dimension of disrupted environments at that *present* time and optimistically assumes that these environments can be restored (or at least recovered or made invisible), the repair perspective takes into account the causes of the disruption, those responsible for it and those suffering from or victimized by it. It thus takes seriously both the past and the present in its approach to (build) the future. Finally, it is our understanding that the notion of 'repair' points, much more so than the notion of 'recovery', to a process rather than a finality, which means that the very possibility that certain disaster situations or conditions are unrepairable (although individuals most often seek to repair them – as a preliminary condition for survival) is incorporated in it.

As discussed in the chapters of this volume, observing actual processes of recovery after disaster reveals the coexistence of a 'multiplicity' (Law and Mol 2002) of possible understandings of repairing that guide actors' conduct as part of the recovery after a disaster.

Repairing, understood here as *asking for reparation*, can point to the right-ing of a wrong, typically through means of making amends to those who have been wronged. Thus, the juridical term 'reparation' performs an 'accusatory function, invoking a kind of repair that entails identifying the actor who caused the damage in question, denouncing the formal injustice of damages suffered and determining corresponding faults, crimes, victims and perpetrators' (Dodier 1995 – translated from French). In this case, the disaster is framed as a moral or juridical crisis requiring reparation through remuneration or other assistance to the party that has been wronged. This implies resorting to the legal or moral code and to the *dispositif* of the trial (Dodier and Barbot 2016). Legal procedure is, however, not always well adapted to meeting the objectives implied in resolving moral questions. Feelings of injustice can persist when victims or their representatives contest the appropriateness or adequacy of the form of compensation made. The valuation and evaluation of damages to body, life and environment imply a series of complex and contentious processes that can bring about important transformations in legal systems (Fourcade 2011; Petryna 2013). Beyond monetary compensation, victims or their representatives can ask for symbolic forms of reparation, such as an apology, especially from state actors (Mihai 2012), the importance of which can vary significantly according to the cultural context.

Depending on the nature of disasters and their destructive potential, these contentious processes can also reveal the power of industrial actors and practices of 'ignorance production' or of strategic (non)production and use of knowledge in the context of the evaluation of damages (Oreskes and Conway 2010; see also Chapter 1). A variety of factors influences these reparation processes and their potential to trigger social change, including the existence of national liability mechanisms, juridical and environmental protection systems and the lobbying capacity of collective mobilizations.

During the recovery process, however, actors have to deal not only with a moral crisis but also with the re-establishment and then improvement of the functionalities of the various infrastructures (including the ecological, economic and technical infrastructures) that the disaster has disrupted. The focus of this *functional understanding of repairing* is not on the past and the identification of crimes but on the future and the discovery and anticipation of dysfunctions (Dodier 1995). 'To repair' means, in this sense, *to fix a systemic breakdown* so as to avoid its repetition. In this case, too, law and regulations play an important role because they should guarantee, at least formally, the conditions for safety and the prevention of future accidents. This implies the mobilization of specific devices such as technical protocols, 'stress tests', maintenance procedures, preparedness measures (see Chapter 5), ecological restoration programmes (including revegetation, habitat enhancement, remediation) and insurance or liability systems. Furthermore, such devices are increasingly being conceived and organized at an international level, especially in very high-risk sectors such as the nuclear sector (see Chapter 2), where the cross-border nature of radioactive fallout has been a major concern since the Chernobyl accident.

These devices are intended to deal with technical issues, but they have a huge impact on the trajectories of recovery. They can be contested on technical grounds (controversies) as well as on the grounds of the social consequences of their design with regard to exclusion and injustice (conflicts). As Klein's *Shock Doctrine* reminds us, the repairing of infrastructures can present not only an economic opportunity for interest groups but also a political opportunity to advance a vision of how the society in question should function.

The technical fixing of infrastructures inevitably crosses over with the practices that actors engage in individually and collectively to maintain and repair their own environments, which is understood as the everyday activities of taking care of people, objects, places and non-human beings. The reference here is to the notion of 'repair' as discussed by feminist scholars and activists in relation to the concept of *care*, which was defined by Fisher and Tronto (1990: 40) as:

> a species activity that includes everything that we do to maintain, continue, and repair our 'world' so that we can live in it as well as possible. That world includes our bodies, our selves, and our environment, all of which we seek to interweave in a complex, life-sustaining web.

As Jackson argued when discussing his 'broken world thinking' perspective: 'Care [. . .] reconnects the necessary work of maintenance with the forms of attachment that so often (but invisibly, at least to analysts) sustain it' (2014: 232). Haraway (2016: 55) referred instead to 'precarious times' and advocated an intense human-nonhuman interplay to 'renew the biodiverse powers of terra' within the 'Chthulucene', which is:

> made up of ongoing multispecies stories and practices of becoming-with in times that remain at stake, in precarious times, in which the world is not finished and the sky has not fallen – yet. We are at stake to each other. Unlike the dominant dramas of Anthropocene and Capitalocene discourse, human beings are not the only important actors in the Chthulucene, with all other beings able simply to react. The order is reknitted: human beings are with and of the Earth, and the biotic and abiotic powers of this Earth are the main story.

Repairing can thus also be understood as a focus on individual and collective practices of reflexively maintaining one's own world in material, multispecies, experiential and emotional terms. As an expression of care, repair after disasters involves engaging in maintaining, as far as possible, the ordinary activities and experiences (such as providing food, sleeping, taking care of children and spending time with friends and family) that are necessary to support the texture of everyday life. Disasters reveal the importance of such ordinary practices for the preservation of the 'human life form' (Lovell *et al.* 2013).

This sense of repairing thus refers to the embodied and 'emplaced' (Pink 2011) experience of the catastrophe and points to forms of self-organization that emerge as part of the response to the disaster and recovery process. These practices respond to the need to recreate, at the levels of meaning, attachments and everyday life, close relationships between human beings, on the one hand, and between human beings, other living beings and places, on the other. These repair practices rely on the mobilization of a form of 'negative capability', which is defined as the ability to maintain the continuity of everyday life in the face of the loss of meaning (Lanzara 1993). The scope of such repair practices and their contribution to recovery can be understood only through taking into account the importance of the 'familiar environment' as a space in which individual capacities are rooted (Breviglieri 2012). In order to grasp repairing at the level of everyday life, ethnography is therefore a fundamental complement to other methodologies of inquiry.

With this third understanding of repair, our aim is to bring to disaster studies recent developments that have emerged in the field of repair studies (see Graziano and Trogal 2019). Repair studies focuses on the activities of 'maintaining the world' as a potential 'site of altering'; that is, as a potential site of 'contingent political change without relying upon the myth of ex-nihilo creation' (Graziano and Trogal 2019: 214). Far removed from the idea of re-establishing the *status quo*, repairing as caring thus refers to the work of maintaining interdependences as a potentially transformative process. Repairing practices can therefore be linked to the construction of a collective demand and can sustain struggles for reparation. However, analyses of the processes of recovery after major nuclear accidents (like Chernobyl and Fukushima) have revealed the instrumentalization of this kind of ordinary repairing through the resilience narrative in order to mask conditions of irreparability and to prove nuclear risk is socially acceptable, thus contributing to the maintenance of the *status quo*. As discussed by Ribault (2019: 4) in the case of resilience narratives after the Fukushima catastrophe:

> As individuals are called upon to act upon themselves hygienically to measure and mitigate radiation exposure after catastrophic levels of contamination, the proposed responses consist in shifting the target for resilience from biology to individual psychology and to society. Resilience is thus operating as a governing technology – more specifically as a technology of consent – that displaces some problems – here the irreversible biological effects induced by radiation exposure – by offering substitute problems such as empowering individual [sic] and rebuilding communities.

In the same way, 'nuclearists' in Chernobyl and Fukushima have been promoting a 'radiological culture' (e.g., the use of a Geiger counter on a daily basis to govern everyday activities in such a way as to reduce exposure to radiation) aimed at turning radioactivity into an 'ordinary' feature of the everyday life experience, *de facto* producing a form of collective ignorance (Topçu 2013; Kimura 2017).

In this case, the human capacity for 'maintaining one's own world' is instrumentalized in order to sustain a vision of repairing that is exclusively focused on the recovery of systemic functionalities. This vision of functional repairing imposes a technocratic, non-negotiable reconfiguration of ordinary human-environment interdependences that are oriented towards future technoscientific achievements. As Ribault showed in the case of Fukushima, these achievements can include 'robotic, agronomic [. . .], biological, and medical experiments' as well as 'architectural and urban planning experiments including land deregulation, smart cities, and other smart communities projects' (2019: 6). Ribault's (2019) notion of the 'incantatory' mechanism that is sustained by resilience narratives contributes, in the case of Fukushima, to silencing present experiences of irreparable losses – including the invisibility of remediation workers – and to hampering collective efforts to transform these harms into damages in need of reparation.

Repairing environments: the contributions

This volume contains 10 contributions (and a concluding chapter) from scholars of diverse disciplinary backgrounds, including sociology, criminology, anthropology, history and philosophy. The majority of the contributions are based on case studies located in different parts of the world, such as France, Spain, Taiwan, Hong Kong, Brazil and Japan. The contributions are organized into three sections, which focus on (1) the challenges of repairing slow disasters; (2) an analysis of processes of repairing as an expression of collective efforts to remake liveable worlds; and (3) the role of law and judicial processes in repairing environmental harms. Of course, there are common theoretical and analytical concerns running through the three sections, which reflects the integration of these perspectives on recovery from the vantage point of repairing.

Collectively, the contributions seek to enhance our knowledge and understanding of the ways in which the different repair logics interact in *dispositifs*, practices and arenas, where the interplay of normative expectations around recovery and the struggles over sense-making in relation to disaster situations can be analysed as part of larger interest-based struggles within a power-laden framework. They also raise relevant issues for critically assessing the heuristic potential of the repairing perspective and address broader theoretical questions, especially concerning the contribution of the social sciences to the analysis of transformative dynamics of complex systems.

Part I opens with Paul Jobin's discussion of the 'economy of compensation' and struggle for reparation in the case of Formosa Plastics in Taiwan. The author explores the reparation issues in the case of chronic pollution caused by the activities of a major petrochemical industry. In particular, Jobin highlights how monetary compensation for the damage is consolidating a local economy that ends up legitimising polluting activities. At the same time, his research shows the efforts of the victims, who are gathered together in a class action, to make monetary compensation an opportunity to denounce the polluting practices of industry. These collective mobilisation experiences allow the participants to develop forms of agency that are worthy of consideration for their potential to ultimately translate into concrete forms of environmental repair.

In Chapter 2, Sezin Topçu analyses the strategies, doctrines and tools that nuclear states and agencies have elaborated to deal with post-accident recovery. Focussing on the problem of contaminated land, she explores how plans were made for the land to be managed and how it was or is effectively managed in regions victimized by the Chernobyl and Fukushima accidents. She analyzes the contexts, policies and discourses that, instead of tackling the contaminated zones as a social and political problem, led to the formulation of the problem in terms of the 'technical' modalities of evacuation. In particular, her contribution sheds light on three managerial strategies of recovery (geological, biological and psychosocial) that conflict with the multiple forms of reparation demanded or trialled by activists and victim groups.

This section on slow disasters ends with Daniel Delatin Rodrigues' contribution on attempts to repair the ecological disaster caused by the industrialization of agriculture in the Brazilian region of Pontal do Paranapanema. This disaster resulted from a *de facto* alliance between local elite landowner groups and global modernization processes. The ecological reparation promoted by an agro-ecology project, which is a collaboration between the Sem Terra movement and local university technicians and academics, cannot therefore be separated from the larger social goal to propose a model of agricultural organization that is more respectful of social and ecological justice. However, this case study shows the difficulties of implementing such a project when most farmers are still totally dependent on globalized economic circuits. These conditions appear quite unfavourable in terms of the experiments that are necessary in order to find effective socio-ecological reparative *agencements* between humans and non-humans.

Part II begins with Santiago Gorostiza and Marco Armiero's historical investigation of the long-term consequences of the catastrophic collapse of the Vega da Tera dam, in Spain. At around midnight on 9 January 1959, the Vega de Tera dam broke, releasing approximately 8 million cubic metres of water. It destroyed the Spanish town of Ribadelago and killed 144 people. To this day, it remains the worst dam-related failure in the past two centuries of Spanish history. In the aftermath of the disaster, the efforts of the Francoist dictatorship prioritized anticipating similar disasters and avoiding a repetition rather than identifying who was responsible or repairing the victims. In this context, memory emerged as a strategic tool for the recovery of the survivors' individual and collective agency as part of a wider process to achieve social repair. The authors' analysis of the aftermath of the disaster in the long term reveals that the survivors fought to achieve both a judicial and a narrative reparation, which were intertwined.

The next contribution, by Frédéric Keck, explores a topic of growing centrality in a context of increasingly globalized disasters, which is the processes of repairing following a pandemic. Focusing on pandemic preparedness in Hong Kong in the aftermath of the 1997 bird flu outbreak, Keck shows that this influenza pandemic was an event that Hong Kong had been preparing for through sentinels, simulation and stockpiling but that it was also a disaster that had already happened in the mass culling of poultry to eradicate the reservoir of the disease. He explores the disjunction between a disaster that actually affected this bird species and a disaster that could have potentially affected the human species by describing how the mass death of poultry in Hong Kong was perceived as a signal of human extinction. This multispecies approach questions the nature of a community that recovers from a disaster. In particular, Keck discusses how the decision to cull or cure the birds can be understood as a signal of what could happen to humans. He examines the grounds for justifying this decision by looking at the fabric of memory and heritage in the narrative of a collective disaster as a traumatic event.

Following on from this multispecies questioning, Line Marie Thorsen discusses how groups of artists in Japan have been turning towards natural farming and permaculture practices as a way of grappling with environmental and ecological issues after the triple disaster known as 3.11 – that is the earthquake, tsunami and Fukushima Daiichi nuclear power plant meltdown of 11 March 2011. The author argues that agricultural artists have a particular potential for reworking aesthetic imaginaries both of life after and of life combatting complex disastrous events through reworking and mending the soil to farm without the use of risky energy forms.

The section ends with Francis Chateauraynaud and Josquin Debaz's contribution on the consequences of the Mariana dam disaster, also known as the Samarco dam disaster. It occurred on 5 November 2015, when a tailings dam at the iron ore mine in the Samarco Mariana mining complex, near Mariana, in the Brazilian state of Minas Gerais, suffered a catastrophic failure. Adopting a pragmatist approach to study the long-running critical processes in relation to the Mariana catastrophe, the authors examine how different actors evaluated the multiple ecological, health and socio-economic consequences of the disaster and how they engaged in a variety of processes of reparation. These processes tackled a wide range of conflicting issues related to extractivism and environmental justice, including scientific controversies around the extension of the damage to the coral reef of the Abrolhos Islands. This contribution aims at exploring how actors deal with the question of the (ir)reversibility of damage; how they identify, represent and argue for the possibility, or impossibility, of repairing, restoring and compensating; and how these processes shape the dynamics of reconstructing liveable worlds.

The final section, on the role of law in repairing environmental harms, begins with Lorenzo Natali and Matthew Hall's contribution on green criminology and the case for environmental restorative justice. The chapter approaches the notion of repairing from the manifold perspective of green criminology, presenting some of the theoretical frameworks that appear best suited to support the interdisciplinary debate on recovery after disaster and highlighting the importance of paying attention to the perspectives of human and non-human victims. The authors make the case for restorative justice and mediation-based approaches as a means to provide alternative or parallel justice mechanisms for victims of environmental crimes and harms. In so doing, they highlight innovative directions for future research that might contribute to collectively devise new ways of repairing environmental harm.

In Chapter 9, Sandrine Revet explores, from an anthropological perspective, the possibilities and limitations of a specific judicial *dispositif* as a way to repair that goes beyond the accusatory understanding of reparation. In particular, she analyzes a specific event in the criminal trials that took place after Storm Xynthia, which caused 29 deaths and extensive destruction in the French municipality of La Faute-sur-Mer in 2010. During the first trial, the court transported the proceedings to the scene of the disaster and organized a walk through the site that had been destroyed by the flood. Based on an ethnographic observation,

Revet analyzes the walk not just as a judicial tool of reenactment but also as a means to commemorate the disaster and as a ritual of making amends. She suggests that the notion of reparation in a criminal trial can encompass other dimensions than a mere accusatory one, depending on how the participants make use of the judicial *dispositif*.

The section ends with Janine Barbot and Nicolas Dodier's contribution, which introduces the notion of the 'ecology of reparation *dispositifs*' to address the reparation of a health catastrophe. The authors define as 'normative work' the evaluations victims have to carry out with regard to both legal *dispositifs* (civil or criminal) and other reparation *dispositifs* (associative, compensatory, medical, media-based, etc.) that contribute to the local ecology of repairing in each disaster. Through the conflicting evaluations that this normative work reveals, victims explicitly show what they value in one judicial strategy over another. These explanations make it possible for the victims to reconstruct their experiences of the different procedures and to analyze how the judicial reparation processes bring them together or divide them and how the strategies they implement fit more broadly into the ecology of the reparation *dispositifs* that they face. By comparing the ways in which different countries dealt with the same disaster (the growth hormone health disaster), the authors suggest the existence of contrasting national reparation trajectories in relation to the existing ecologies of *dispositifs*. This contribution extends the approach proposed in the book to the case of health disasters by showing its heuristic potential beyond the analysis of environmental damage that is at the heart of the other chapters. Through the notion of ecologies of *dispositifs*, the authors also identify a promising path for the development of systematic diachronic and synchronic comparative analyses of recovery trajectories.

In the concluding chapter, we enrich the discussion on the repair perspective, between theory and practice, insisting on the importance of taking into account a plurality not only of normative expectations but also of forms of knowledge and mechanisms of exclusion. In addition, we emphasize the need to highlight the systemic causes of disasters while paying attention to the experience of actors directly affected and their struggles to turn recovery into a process of designing liveable worlds.

While we acknowledge that our book does not outline a 'theory of recovery', we think that it does provide a theoretically informed approach to the study of socio-ecological change that takes into account the interaction between the socio-technical, environmental and cultural dimensions. Finally, as the contributions show, the standpoint of repair adopted in this volume is less normative-laden and politically connoted than resilience and more alert to the contentious nature of recovery processes. Our hope is that in articulating a research agenda centred on the notion of repair, this book will contribute to what Fortun *et al.* (2017: 1018) hoped would progressively become a shared objective in the community of disaster research, namely the development of 'methodologically and theoretically inventive, empirically rich' ways to study disasters that pay attention 'to the acute problems of representations that beset disaster (and disaster studies)'.

Notes

1 For a historical reconstruction see Tierney (2007), Cabane and Revet (2015), Dahlberg *et al.* (2016), Fortun *et al.* (2017).
2 As a consequence, there has been less research conducted on mitigation and recovery after disaster than on preparedness and response. This focus on preparedness and response has not necessarily been accompanied by practical or political actions. In the management of flu epidemics, for instance, regimes of preparedness and unpreparedness co-exist or operate in a complementary way (Lakoff 2017).
3 *Dispositifs* are conceived here as 'a prepared concatenation of sequences, intended to qualify or transform a state of affairs through the medium of an assemblage of material or language elements' (Dodier and Barbot 2016: 301).
4 A research field that has recently emerged in disaster studies is that of 'self-recovery', which is meant to provide tools to support the process whereby disaster-affected households repair, build or rebuild their shelters either themselves or with the help of local builders while trying to avoid some of the pitfalls that have emerged in the actual practice of resilience-building initiatives (see Twigg *et al.* 2017).

References

Adams, V. (2013) *Markets of Sorrow, Labors of Faith: New Orleans in the Wake of Katrina*, Durham, NC: Duke University Press.

Aguirre, B.E. and Best, E. (2015) 'How Not to Learn: Resilience in the Study of Disaster', in H. Egner, M. Schorch and M. Voss (eds) *Learning and Calamities: Practice, Interpretations, Patterns*, London and New York: Routledge.

Aijazi, O. (2015) 'Theorizing a Social Repair Orientation to Disaster Recovery: Developing Insights for Disaster Recovery Policy and Programming', *Global Social Welfare*, 2: 15–28. <https://doi.org/10.1007/s40609-014-0013-x>.

Alexander, D.E. (2013) 'Resilience and Disaster Risk Reduction: An Etymological Journey', *Natural Hazards and Earth System Sciences*, 13(11): 2707–2716.

Allen, B. (2018) 'Strongly Participatory Science and Knowledge Justice in an Environmentally Contested Region', *Science, Technology & Human Values*, 43(6): 947–971.

Amoore, L. (2013) *The Politics of Possibility: Risk and Security beyond Probability*, Durham, NC: Duke University Press.

Amoore, L. and de Goede, M. (2008) *Risk and the War on Terror*, London: Routledge.

Attia, K. (2018) 'Open Your Eyes!', *Third Text*, 32(1): 16–31.

Barca, S. (2014) 'Telling the Right Story: Environmental Violence and Liberation Narratives', *Environment and History*, 20(4): 535–546.

Beck, U. (1992) *Risk Society: Towards a New Modernity*, London and New York: Sage.

Benadusi, M. (2013) 'The Two-Faced Janus of Disaster Management: Still Vulnerable Yet already Resilient', *South East Asia Research*, 21(3): 419–438.

Benadusi, M. (2015) 'Cultivating Communities after Disaster: A Whirlwind of Generosity on the Coasts of Sri Lanka', in S. Revet and J. Langumier (eds) *Governing Disasters: Beyond Risk Culture*, London: Palgrave Macmillan.

Berke, P.R., Kartez, J. and Wenger, D. (1993) 'Recovery after Disaster: Achieving Sustainable Development, Mitigation and Equity', *Disasters*, 17(2): 93–109.

Blok, A. and Jensen, C.B. (2019) 'The Anthropocene Event in Social Theory: On Ways of Problematizing Nonhuman Materiality Differently', *The Sociological Review*, 67(6): 1195–1211.

Blok, A., Nakazora, M. and Winthereik, B.R. (2016) 'Infrastructuring Environments', *Science as Culture*, 25(1): 1–22.

Bonneuil, C. and Fressoz, J.-B. (2017) *The Shock of the Anthropocene: The World, History and Us*, London: Verso.

Bowker, G.C. and Star, S.L. (1999) *Sorting Things Out: Classification and Its Consequences*, Cambridge, MA: MIT Press.

Breviglieri, M. (2012) 'L'espace habité que réclame l'assurance intime de pouvoir: Un essai d'approfondissement sociologique de l'anthropologie capacitaire de Paul Ricoeur', *Études Ricoeuriennes/Ricoeur Studies*, 3(1): 34–52.

Cabane, L. and Revet, S. (2015) 'La cause des catastrophes. Concurrences scientifiques et actions politiques dans un monde transnational', *Politix*, 111(3): 47–67.

Cefaï, D. (2002) 'Qu'est-ce qu'une arène publique? Quelques pistes pour une approche pragmatiste', in D. Cefaï and I. Joseph (eds) *L'Héritage du pragmatisme*, La Tour d'Aigues: Éd. de l'Aube, 51–82.

Cefaï, D. (2016) 'Publics, problèmes publics, arènes publiques . . . Que nous apprend le pragmatisme?', *Questions de communication*, 30: 25–64.

Centemeri, L. (2010) 'The Seveso Disaster's Legacy', in M. Armiero and M. Hall (eds) *Nature and History in Modern Italy*, Athens, OH: Ohio University Press & Swallow Press.

Centemeri, L. (2015) 'Investigating the "Discrete Memory" of the Seveso Disaster in Italy', in S. Revet and J. Langumier (eds) *Governing Disasters: Beyond Risk Culture*, London: Palgrave Macmillan.

Chandler, D. and Reid, J. (2016) *The Neoliberal Subject: Resilience, Adaptation and Vulnerability*, London: Routledge.

Chateauraynaud, F. (2016) 'Pragmatique des transformations et sociologie des controverses. Les logiques d'enquête face au temps long des processus', in Y. Cohen and F. Chateauraynaud (eds) *Histoires pragmatiques*, Paris: EHESS, 349–385.

Choi, V.Y. (2015) 'Anticipatory States: Tsunami, War and Insecurity in Sri Lanka', *Cultural Anthropology*, 30(2): 286–389.

Dahlberg, R., Rubin, O. and Vendelø, M.T. (eds) (2016) *Disaster Research: Multidisciplinary and International Perspectives*, London and New York: Routledge.

Das, V. (2007) *Life and Worlds: Violence and the Descent into the Ordinary*, Berkeley: University of California Press.

Das, V., Kleinman, A., Lock, M., Ramphele, M. and Reynolds, P. (eds) (2001) *Remaking a World: Violence, Social Suffering, and Recovery*, Berkeley: University of California Press.

Dodier, N. (1995) *Les hommes et les machines. La conscience collective dans les sociétés technicisées*, Paris: Métailié.

Dodier, N. (1999) 'L'espace public de la recherche médicale. Autour de l'affaire de la ciclosporine', *Réseaux. Communication, technologie, société*, 95: 107–154.

Dodier, N. (2015) 'Postscript: Thinking (by way of) Disaster' in S. Revet and J. Langumier (eds) *Governing Disasters: Beyond Risk Culture*, London: Palgrave Macmillan.

Dodier, N. and Barbot, J. (2016) 'The Force of dispositifs', *Annales. Histoire et Sciences Sociales* (English edition), 71(2): 291–317.

Dowty, R.A. and Allen, B.L. (eds) (2011) *Dynamics of Disaster: Lessons on Risk, Response and Recovery*, London: Routledge.

Edwards, P.N. (2003) 'Infrastructure and Modernity: Force, Time and Social Organization in the History of Sociotechnical Systems', in T.J. Misa, P. Brey and A. Feenberg (eds) *Modernity and Technology*, Cambridge, MA: The MIT Press, 185–225.

Evans, B. and Reid, J. (2014) *Resilient Life: The Art of Living Dangerously*, Oxford: Polity Press.

Fisher, B. and Tronto, J.C. (1990) 'Toward a Feminist Theory of Caring', in E. Abel and M. Nelson (eds) *Circles of Care: Work and Identity in Women's Lives*, Albany: State University of New York Press.

Fletcher, R. (2012) 'Capitalizing on Chaos: Climate Change and Disaster Capitalism', *Ephemera*, 12(1/2): 97–112.

Fortun, K. (2001) *Advocacy after Bhopal: Environmentalism, Disaster, New Global Orders*, Chicago: University of Chicago Press.

Fortun, K., Knowles, S.G., Choi, V., Jobin, P., Matsumoto, M., de la Torre III, P., Liboiron, M. and Murillo, L.F.R. (2017) 'Researching Disaster from an STS Perspective', in U. Felt, R. Fouche, C.A. Miller and L. Smith-Doerr (eds) *The Handbook of Science and Technology Studies*, 4th edition, Cambridge, MA: The MIT Press, 1003–1028.

Fourcade, M. (2011) 'Cents and Sensibility: Economic Valuation and the Nature of "Nature"', *American Journal of Sociology*, 116(6): 1721–1777.

Frickel, S. (2008) 'On Missing New Orleans: Lost Knowledge and Knowledge Gaps in an Urban Hazardscape', *Environmental History*, 13(4): 643–650.

Frickel, S., Campanella, R. and Vincent, M.B. (2009) 'Mapping Knowledge Investments in the Aftermath of Hurricane Katrina: A New Approach for Assessing Regulatory Agency Responses to Environmental Disaster', *Environmental Science & Policy*, 12: 119–133.

Gieryn, T. (2000) 'A Space for Place in Sociology', *Annual Review of Sociology*, 26: 463–495.

Graziano, V. and Trogal, K. (2019) 'Repair Matters', in *Ephemera. Theory and Politics in Organization*, 19(2): 203–227.

Gunewardena, N., and Schuller, M. (eds) (2008) *Capitalizing on Catastrophe: Neoliberal Strategies in Disaster Reconstruction*, Lanham, New York, Toronto and Plymouth: AltaMira Press.

Hall, P.A. and Lamont, M. (2013) *Social Resilience in the Neoliberal Era*, Cambridge, MA: Cambridge University Press.

Haraway, D.J. (2016) *Staying with the Trouble: Making Kin in the Chthulucene*, Durham, NC: Duke University Press.

Hasegawa, R. (2013) 'Disaster Evacuation from Japan's 2011 Tsunami Disaster and the Fukushima Nuclear Accident', *IDDRI Study*, n°5. <www.iddri.org/sites/default/files/import/publications/study0513_rh_devast-report.pdf>.

Hennion, A. (2004) 'Une sociologie des attachements. D'une sociologie de la culture à une pragmatique de l'amateur', *Sociétés*, 85(3): 9–24.

Hilgartner, S. and Bosk, C.L. (1988) 'The Rise and Fall of Social Problems: A Public Arenas Model', *American Journal of Sociology*, 94(1): 53–78.

Jackson, S.J. (2014) 'Rethinking Repair', in T. Gillespie, P. Boczkowski and K. Foot (eds) *Media Technologies: Essays on Communication, Materiality and Society*, Cambridge, MA: MIT Press.

Kendra, J.M., Clay, L.A., and Gill, K.B. (2018) 'Resilience and Disasters', in H. Rodríguez, W. Donner and J.E. Trainor (eds) *Handbook of Disaster Research*, 2nd edition, New York: Springer.

Kimura, A.H. (2017) 'Fukushima ETHOS: Post-Disaster Risk Communication, Affect, and Shifting Risks', *Science as Culture*, 27(1): 98–117.

Klein, N. (2007) *The Shock Doctrine: The Rise of Disaster Capitalism*, New York: Metropolitan Books.

Knowles, S.G. (2014) 'Learning from Disaster? The History of Technology and the Future of Disaster Research', *Technology and Culture*, 55(4): 773–784.

Kreps, G.A. and Drabek, T.E. (1996) 'Disasters Are Non-Routine Social Problems', *International Journal of Mass Emergencies and Disasters*, 14: 129–153.

Lagadec, P. (1981) *La Civilisation du risque*, Paris: Seuil.

Lakoff, A. (2017) *Unprepared: Global Health in a Time of Emergency*, Oakland, CA: University of California Press.

Lanzara, G.F. (1993) *Capacità negativa: competenza progettuale e modelli di intervento nelle organizzazioni*, Bologna: Il Mulino.

Latour, B. (1993) *We were Never Modern*, Cambridge, MA: Harvard University Press.

Law, J. and Mol, A. (eds) (2002) *Complexities: Social Studies of Knowledge Practices*, Durham, NC: Duke University Press.

Lovell, M., Pandolfo, S., Das, V., and Laugier, S. (2013) *Face aux désastres. Une conversation à quatre voix sur la folie, le care et les grandes détresses collectives*, Paris: Editions d'Ithaque.

Mihai, M. (2012) 'When the State Says "Sorry": State Apologies as Exemplary Political Judgments', *The Journal of Political Philosophy*, 21(2): 200–220.

Mileti, D. (1999) *Disasters by Design: A Reassessment of Natural Hazards in the United States*, Washington, DC: Joseph Henry Press.

Monticelli, L. (2018) 'Embodying Alternatives to Capitalism in the 21st Century', *tripleC: Communication, Capitalism & Critique*, 16(2): 501–517.

Nixon, R. (2011) *Slow Violence and the Environmentalism of the Poor*, Cambridge and Oxford: Oxford University Press.

O'Donnell, E.L. and Talbot-Jones, J. (2018) 'Creating Legal Rights for Rivers: Lessons from Australia, New Zealand, and India', *Ecology and Society*, 23(1). <https://doi.org/10.5751/ES-09854-230107>.

Oliver-Smith, A. (1986) *The Martyred City: Death and Rebirth in the Peruvian Andes*, Prospect Heights, IL: Waveland.

Oliver-Smith, A. (1998) 'Global Changes and the Definition of Disaster', in E.L. Quarantelli (ed.) *What Is a Disaster? A Dozen Perspectives on the Question*, London and New York: Routledge.

Oliver-Smith, A. and Hoffman, S. (eds) (1999) *The Angry Earth: Disaster in Anthropological Perspective*, Abingdon and New York: Routledge.

Oreskes, N. and Conway, E. (2010) *Merchants of Doubt: How a Handful of Scientists Obscured the Truth on Issues from Tobacco Smoke to Global Warming*, New York: Bloomsbury Press.

Passerini, E. (2000) 'Disasters as Agents of Social Change in Recovery and Reconstruction', *Natural Hazards Review*, 1(2): 67–72.

Perry, R.W. (2018) 'Defining Disaster: An Evolving Concept', in H. Rodríguez, W. Donner and J.E. Trainor (eds) *Handbook of Disaster Research*, 2nd edition, New York: Springer.

Petryna, A. (2013) 'How Did They Survive?' in A. Petryna (ed.) *Life Exposed: Biological Citizens after Chernobyl*, 10th anniversary edition, Princeton, NJ: Princeton University Press.

Pink, S. (2011) 'From Embodiment to Emplacement: Re-thinking Competing Bodies, Senses and Spatialities', *Sport, Education and Society*, 16(3): 343–355.

Ponte, S., Gibbon, P. and Vestergaard, J. (eds) (2011) *Governing through Standards: Origins, Drivers and Limitations*, Basingstoke: Palgrave Macmillan.

Quarantelli, E.L. (1999) *The Disaster Recovery Process: What We Know and Do Not Know From Research*, Newark: University of Delaware Disaster Research Centre.

Quéré, L. and Terzi, C. (2014) 'Did you say Pragmatic? Luc Boltanski's Sociology from a Pragmatist Perspective', in S. Susen and B. Turner (eds) *The Spirit of Luc Boltanski: Essays on the Pragmatic Sociology of Critique*, London and New York: Anthem Press.

Revet, S. (2020) *Disasterland: An Ethnography of the International Disaster Community*, London: Palgrave Macmillan.

Revet, S. and Langumier, J. (eds) (2015) *Governing Disasters: Beyond Risk Culture*, London: Palgrave Macmillan.

Ribault, T. (2019) 'Resilience in Fukushima: Contribution to a Political Economy of Consent', *Alternatives: Global, Local, Political*, 44(2–4): 94–118.

Schlosberg, D. (2007) *Defining Environmental Justice: Theories, Movements, and Nature*, New York: Oxford University Press.

Schuller, M. and Maldonado, J.K. (2016) 'Disaster Capitalism', *Annals of Anthropological Practice*, 40(1): 61–72.

Sewell, W. (1996) 'Historical Events as Transformations of Structure: Inventing Revolution at the Bastille', *Theory and Society*, 25(6): 841–881.

Star, S.L. (1999) 'The Ethnography of Infrastructure', *American Behavioral Scientist*, 43(3): 377–391.

Szymborska, W. (2001) *Miracle Fair: Selected Poems of Wisława Szymborska*, trans. Joanna Trzeciak, New York: W.W. Norton & Company.

Thévenot, L. (2007) 'The Plurality of Cognitive Formats and Engagements: Moving between the Familiar and the Public', *European Journal of Social Theory*, 10(3): 409–423.

Tierney, K.J. (2007) 'From the Margins to the Mainstream? Disaster Research at the Crossroads', *Annual Review of Sociology*, 33(1): 503–525.

Tierney, K.J. (2015) 'Resilience and the Neoliberal Project: Discourses, Critiques, Practices – and Katrina', *American Behavioral Scientist*, 59(10): 1327–1342.

Tierney, K.J. and Oliver-Smith, A. (2012) 'Social Dimensions of Disaster Recovery', *International Journal of Mass Emergencies and Disasters*, 30(2): 123–146.

Tomassi, I. and Forino, G. (2019) 'The Ecovillage of Pescomaggiore (L'Aquila): Birth and Death of a Self-determined Post-disaster Community (2009–2014)', *Disaster Prevention and Management: An International Journal*. <https://doi.org/10.1108/DPM-09-2018-0305>.

Topçu, S. (2013) 'Chernobyl Empowerment? Exporting Participatory Governance to Contaminated Territories', in S. Boudia and N. Jas (eds) *Toxicants, Health and Regulation since 1945*, London: Routledge.

Tsing, A.L. (2005) *Friction: An Ethnography of Global Connections*, Princeton, NJ: Princeton University Press.

Twigg, J., Lovell, E., Schofield, H., Morel, L.M., Flinn, B., Sargeant, S., Finlayson, A., Dijkstra, T., Stephenson, V., Albuerne, A., Rossetto, T. and D'Ayala, D. (2017) 'Self-recovery from Disasters. An Interdisciplinary Perspective', Working Paper No. 523, Overseas Development Institute, London.

Walker, J. and Cooper, M. (2011) 'Genealogies of Resilience: From Systems Ecology to the Political Economy of Crisis Adaptation', *Security Dialogue*, 2(42): 143–160.

Weidner, J.S. (2009) 'Review of Disaster Recovery', *Journal of Homeland Security and Emergency Management*, 6(1): 1–2.

Wisner, B. (2009) 'The Grocer's Daughter and the Men in Suits: Who Exactly Capitalizes on Catastrophe? And Why the Question Matters', *Capitalism Nature Socialism*, 20(3): 104–112.

Part I

Repairing slow disasters

1 The economy of compensation and struggle for reparation

The case of Formosa Plastics in Taiwan

Paul Jobin

On Sunday, 7 April 2019, at 2 pm, in the vicinity of a petrochemical complex on the west coast of central Taiwan, a blast shattered the windows of houses and cracked or displaced brick walls. The explosion was heard within a perimeter of six kilometres around the site. In the days that followed, tons of clams, shrimp, mullet and perch died. One year later, those who suffered losses were still waiting to be paid compensation. This kind of explosion has been recurrent since the zone's start of operations some 20 years ago. In the meantime, the fence-line populations have been struck by a high rate of cancer mortality. Despite a solid corpus of epidemiological and environmental studies showing evidence of adverse health effects for the neighbouring townships, the state has failed to implement policies that would stop or reduce chronic pollution and enforce stricter safety controls. Left with no other option, a group of 30 families have launched a lawsuit seeking damages. The petrochemical complex is owned by the Formosa Plastics Group (FPG), one of the ten largest chemical companies in the world (Tullo 2019).

The firm has also been under legal attack in the United States for the marine pollution from plastic pellets discharged by its plants near Houston, Texas. In a recent court decision, federal judges described the company as a 'serial offender' (Collier 2019). Another lawsuit is in preparation to prevent the construction of a new complex, in Louisiana's 'Cancer Alley', that is set to become the US's biggest plastic producer. Although the communities around the site are already overexposed to toxicants, Formosa Plastics has asked permission to release double the legal amount of air pollutants there; the plant is, moreover, expected to emit a staggering level of greenhouse gases (Mitchell 2019; Einhorn and Carroll 2019; McConnaughey 2020).

Formosa Plastics is just one amongst many petrochemical firms that have been the source of a multi-scale disaster. At the global level, the petrochemical industry bears a large share of the responsibility for the climate crisis and the million tons of plastic waste that have turned our epoch into a 'Plasticene', the plastic facet of the Anthropocene (Reed 2015; Haram *et al.* 2020). Far from stopping this worldwide disaster, and despite a continuous increase in sales, the petrochemical industry instead laments the diminution of its profit margin (Tullo 2019). Worse, since the late 1970s, the petrochemical industry has pursued intensive lobbying to deny global warming (Oreskes and Conway 2010; Rich 2019; see also Michaels 2008).

DOI: 10.4324/9781003184782-3

At the same time, along with claiming to invest in the production of 'more sustainable plastics' (IEA 2018), the major firms have launched green-washing programmes, ostensibly to 'end plastic waste' (Brown 2019), or to develop organic vegetables and environmental education (as in the case of Formosa Plastics). But behind this facade, the petrochemical industry has demonstrated its willingness to carry on with business as usual (Lerner 2019; Hamilton *et al.* 2019).

At the local level, petrochemical plants are regularly subject to recurrent explosions. Furthermore, they discharge a long list of toxic by-products with all kinds of adverse effects for both ecosystems and public health. This 'chronic technical disaster' (Couch and Kroll-Smith 1985; Zavestoski *et al.* 2002) constitutes a 'slow violence' (Nixon 2011) for fence-line communities, which are – not coincidentally – disadvantaged in terms of social and economic capital (Davies 2019). Quantitative studies have highlighted the burden for public health, in particular amongst communities on the fence-line of petrochemical plants (*e.g.* Lin *et al.* 2017; Jephcote and Mah 2019). Qualitative studies have further emphasized the problems of epistemic injustice, and the importance of lay knowledge to redress the lacunae from 'undone science' (Allen *et al.* 2017; Ottinger 2013; cf. Frickel *et al.* 2010; Hess 2016).

A majority of these case studies are located in the US, starting with Louisiana's chemical corridor, the infamous 'Cancer Alley' (Allen 2003; Lerner 2005; Ottinger 2013; Davies 2019). But recent research has extended further over a greater variety of cultural and economic contexts, from the mobilized fence-line communities of Italy, France and Taiwan (Allen 2011; Allen *et al.* 2017; Ho 2014; Grano 2015), to the more compliant population of China (Mah and Wang 2019).

Through the class action launched by the communities bordering Formosa Plastics' petrochemical zone in Taiwan, this chapter focuses on the ambiguous role of money in disputes over the recognition of the damage to the environment and the public health. By 'money', I mean the funds either requested or effectively paid in compensation or punitive damages. As the editors of this book note in their introduction, reparation is associated with a juridical repertoire, which performs what they call an 'accusatory function' vis-à-vis an injustice. In the plural form, 'reparations' denotes compensation for war damage, slavery, genocide and other transformational happenings. In toxic torts and other civil actions, 'damages' is another word for compensation, as if such payment might offset the actual damage incurred. In different legal environments, class actions and other forms of collective lawsuits have indeed been a salient expression of challenging industrial polluters (George 2001; Allen 2011; Jobin and Tseng 2014; Marichalar 2019), even in countries lacking an independent judiciary system, such as China (van Rooij 2010; Stern 2013).

The communities that are ready to take the risk of filing a case require support from lawyers and citizen groups, and considerable patience as lawsuits can last a very long time. Moreover, many plaintiffs might die before the ruling is reached, the judges might dismiss the case or the amounts of compensation might ultimately be very low. This moral cost for the victims is often quite heavy. More problematically, even if the suit ends with a positive decision for the plaintiffs, the whole effort might be in vain if it does not compel the petrochemical firm in question to take serious measures to stop its chronic pollution and prevent recurrent explosions (a common hazard within the industry).

Further complicating matters is the widespread practice of regular company payments to nearby residents, as a sort of nuisance fee. As van Rooij *et al.* (2012) have shown in the case of China, the resultant economic dependency between the polluters and fence-line communities often creates what they call a 'compensation trap': the distribution of money becomes a social habit that tends to normalize the pollution, thus allowing companies to postpone efforts to prevent it. In other words, reparation does not repair the environment in the various meanings of repair as defined by the editors in the introduction to this volume – rather, it implies a tacit agreement to pursue business as usual. This mechanism also applies to the case of Taiwan, despite its radically different political context – democratic, as opposed to China's authoritarianism.

However, since civil actions necessarily involve the question of compensation, it is essential to examine the nature of compensation itself. Although the compensation trap is likely to continue as long as the plant is operational, what we might call the 'economy of compensation' does not necessarily dampen the various expressions of critique. I therefore consider compensation in dialectical terms and posit that, despite procedural slowness and uncertain outcomes, class actions can offer an opportunity to redefine the meaning of compensation for industrial damage.

This chapter is mainly based on a four-year research project conducted in Taiwan (2016 through 2019), which included observation of court hearings, in-depth interviews and group meetings with the plaintiffs, their lawyers and local sources.

Environmental justice and money

Oil and its related industries hold a central role in the monetary flow of contemporary capitalism. Mitchell (2011) has demonstrated how this 'fuel economy' and its 'fuel money' have weakened unions of Western democracies and strengthened authoritarian regimes in the Middle East. In a similar way, oil refineries and petrochemical firms make regular payments to the population surrounding their plants, in order to undermine opposition to their persistent pollution.

A number of historical and sociological studies on chemical plants have shown the pernicious role of such patronage payments. For example, the Japanese chemical factory that provoked the infamous Minamata disease in the 1950s had been the source of recurrent fish loss long before that disaster. As early as the 1920s, the company established the habit of paying what it called a sympathy payment (*mimaikin*) to evade responsibility and compel the fishermen's submission; this practice set a standard for the later treatment of Minamata disease victims (George 2001: 72–73). As analyzed by Ottinger (2013), programmes of corporate social responsibility in Louisiana's 'Cancer Alley' can be seen as the last avatar of such 'chemical patronage'.

In their study of a case of industrial pollution in rural China, van Rooij *et al.* (2012) have conducted a fine-grained analysis of the compensation trap. They show that citizen grievances and demands are shaped by compensation rather than the control or prevention of pollution. Eventually, compensation becomes a licence to pollute, and the polluter labels the victims as greedy opportunists, thus adding insult to injury. Mah and Wang's (2019) interviews with workers and inhabitants of fence-line communities in the petrochemical area of Nanjing find similar results; the authors emphasize that uneven and generally low compensation bears witness to neglect, not only by petrochemical enterprises, but also by the Chinese state. Although these conclusions can apply to Taiwan as well as to many cases around the world, I think we need to further understand the role of money in issues of environmental damage. The economy of compensation, as I use the term, includes resistance to the fuel economy and its compensation trap and further considers the cultural meanings of money.

The victims of public health hazards entertain different expectations when confronted with reparation schemes, such as insurance systems or lawsuits (Barbot and Dodier 2015). Heterodox economists have described the 'languages of valuation' through which vulnerable communities denounce the incommensurability of environmental damage (Martínez Alier 2002; Anguelovski and Martínez Alier 2014). Temper and Martinez-Alier (2013: 85–86) posit a clear-cut distinction between those who are 'fighting for higher compensation and those who refuse to give their land at any price'. Comparing litigations over two oil spill cases, in France and the US, Fourcade (2011) shows how different cultural perceptions of 'nature' resulted in different legal valuations of the disaster. Centemeri (2015: 307) further argues that, in these disputes, the focus is most often on 'how to commensurate, but not *whether* to commensurate', but for those who lost what she calls a 'dwelled-in environment', the damage means a radical incommensurable loss. As Chateauraynaud and Debaz (2017: 597) define incommensurability, the loss has no *equivalent* measure, for it 'emerges from the comparison of heterogeneous orders of magnitude and valuation'.

Communities that are victims of environmental damage may nevertheless be right to seek compensation. Some indigenous cultures do not exclude monetary payments in compensation for a crime or an offense (Hu 2012; Guo 2011; 2014). However, it is not money in the Western sense, *i.e*, commensurable on a universal scale and convertible at variable rates set by global financial markets. Moreover, in Taiwan and China, money is not necessarily tainted with modern utilitarianism but involves all sorts of social interactions and intergenerational transmissions, such as the red envelopes offered at weddings, white envelopes at funerals and paper money burnt for the dead (Martin 2015).

Departing from early analyses by Marx and Simmel, the sociology of money in modern Western cultures has also shown that allocations of money often mingle with intimacy, affective investments and a large range of symbolic meanings (Zelizer 1994; Bandelj *et al.* 2017). Ng and He (2017) further show that compared to the US, where the commensuration of 'blood money' (*e.g.* damages for the loss of a parent) is largely determined by a legal and technical discourse, in China, the judges and the litigants attach more importance to the moral meaning of compensation. These analyses encourage us to suspend our own moral judgements about money and consider how the victims of industrial harm themselves perceive it. In other words, they invite us to look at demands for justice and compensation as two sides of the same coin.

Furthermore, in collective lawsuits, unless the case is filed in a criminal court, civil actions over toxic torts necessarily target the payment of compensation or punitive damages. It may thus be counterproductive, both for mobilizing and for seeking a remedial policy, to divide the movements of victims into two clearly distinct groups: those seeking compensation (who 'are in it for the money'), and those indifferent or radically opposed to it (who 'won't accept it at any price').

In this chapter, I therefore reconsider how problems of commensurability and incommensurability are entangled, forging a web of motivations and expectations amongst the victims of petrochemical damage, whether from chronic pollution or recurrent explosions. I further argue that problems of reparation are a central issue for analyzing the risk perception and motivations of fence-line communities engaged in disputes over environmental damage persisting over the long term.

Formosa Plastics in Taiwan

The case presented in this chapter deals with one of the world's biggest petrochemical complexes.[1] Located in Yunlin County, on the southwest coast of central Taiwan, it covers an area of 2,000 hectares of reclaimed land over the sea (see Figures 1.1 and 1.2). The complex comprises approximately 50 plants, which developed around Taiwan's Number Six Naphtha Cracker. The Formosa Plastics Group (FPG), which controls the zone, had initially planned to build the cracker in Ilan County (in the northeast of the island), but strong opposition by the local population succeeded in blocking the project (Hsu 1995). After another project, in Taoyuan County, similarly failed, a compromise was finally reached with the authorities of Yunlin County, despite protests by local fishermen (Ho 2014). Since the start of operations in 1998, FPG has made huge profits from it; in 2010, only 12 years after the start of operations, its total output already accounted for 10.6 per cent of Taiwan's GDP.[2]

The complex has been heavily polluting the air, sea and soil with all sorts of chemical by-products. The 400 chimneys in the zone eject a wide range of chemicals, such as nitrogen, sulphur oxides, fine particulate matters such as PM2.5, heavy metals and volatile organic compounds which transform into fine particles with proven carcinogenic effects, resulting in a significant increase in cancer incidence (Yuan *et al.* 2018). Moreover, explosions release considerable levels of air pollutants, which entail further health hazards (Shie and Chan 2013). But the Taiwanese state has so far failed to implement effective controls to prevent or

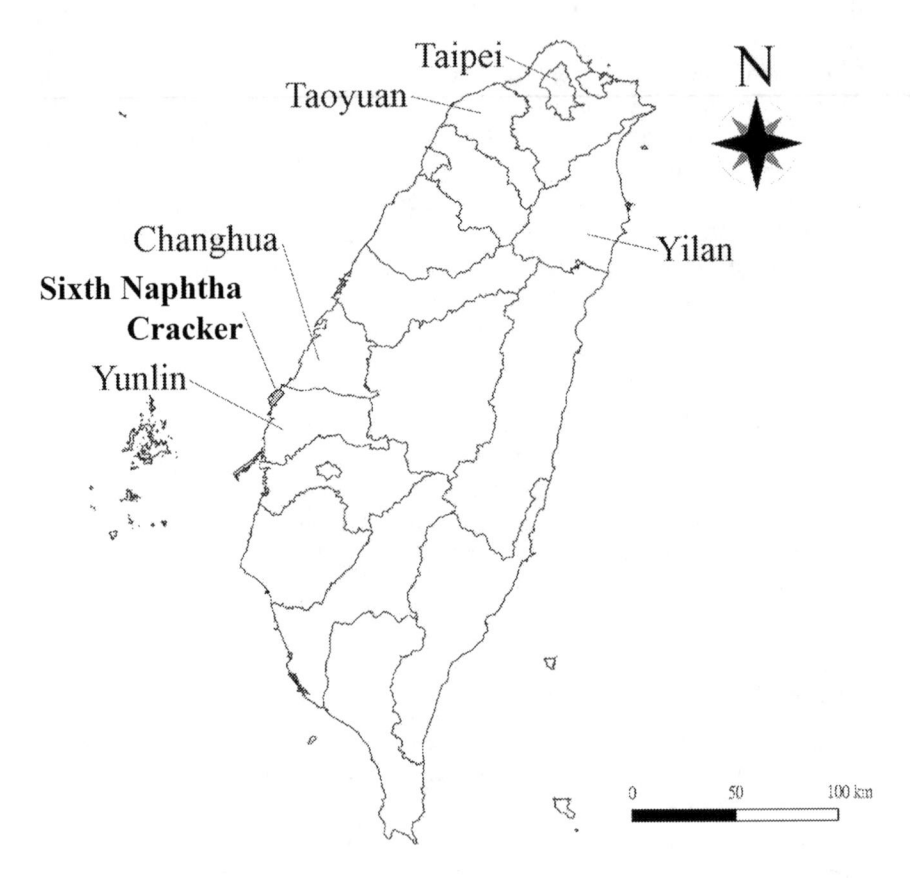

Figure 1.1 Taiwan and the Sixth Naphtha Cracker petrochemical zone (Map design by
     Shih-hao Jheng)

Source: QGIS and Natural Earth (used with permission)

reduce this pollution (Tu *et al.* 2014; Shih and Tu 2017); the fence-line population
has tended to accept this chronic pollution, the rare protests coming only in the
wake of explosions (Jobin 2010; Lin 2019).

In 2015, however, 30 families of the fence-line township of Taisi decided to
sue Formosa Plastic Group and four related companies. The goal was to stop
the chronic pollution and recurrent explosions and obtain some compensation
for their illnesses, like cancer, or the premature death of their parents. With the
help of research assistants (see Acknowledgements), I have conducted research
on this lawsuit since March 2016. In addition to attending the court hearings (16
as of August 2021) and numerous discussions with the plaintiffs' lawyers and
the key local organizer of the lawsuit, we have interviewed 25 of the 30 families

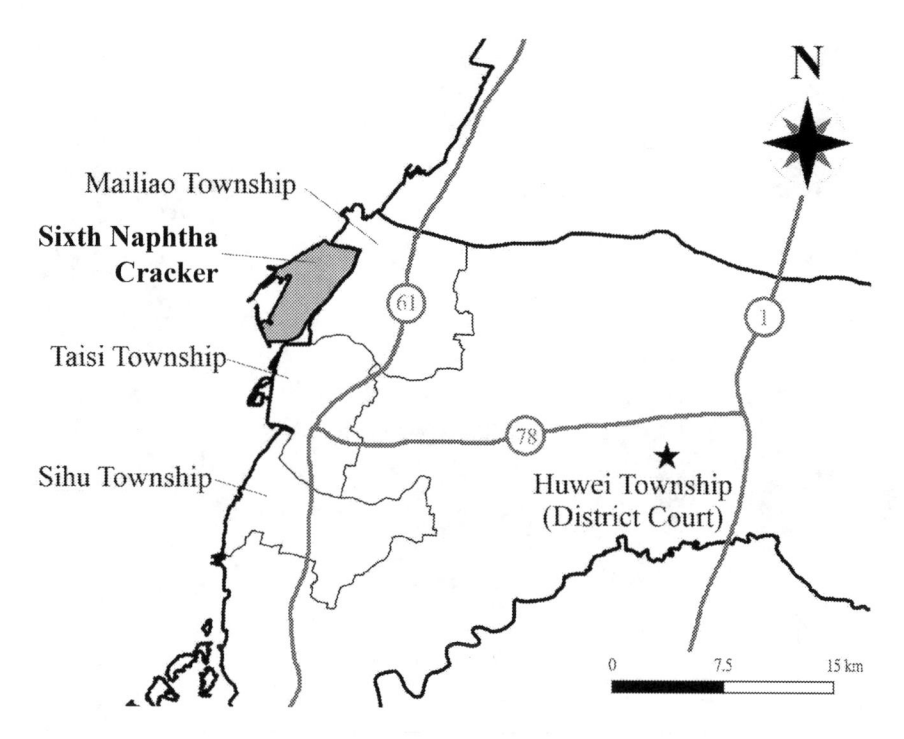

Figure 1.2 The Sixth Naphtha Cracker petrochemical zone and fence-line townships (Map design by Shih-hao Jheng)

Source: QGIS and Natural Earth (used with permission)

involved in order to understand their motivations as plaintiffs in the case. More-over, we interviewed a dozen local actors, including labour and environmental activists, politicians, a mayor, physicians, social workers, a pharmacist, members of the clam and oyster farmers' union, and two senior technicians working at the petrochemical plant.

As observed in other studies on fence-line communities of petrochemical zones (Allen 2003; Lerner 2005; Davies 2019; Mah and Wang 2019), risk perception starts with damage to the environment. In Taiwan, in the area around Yunlin's petrochemical zone, fish have become scarce, seagulls have disappeared and the sea is now covered with oil. Fruits and vegetables, like watermelons and cabbage, show stunted growth. Farming of milkfish, shrimp, oysters and clams, which used to be the pride of the region, has been shrinking from year to year.[3]

No one dares to drink water from wells or the tap. Each village has several water stations where residents may fill cans with local water filtered to meet certain standards. The owner of the first water station used to have a petrol station; he says that water does not pay as much, but it is less of a hassle.[4] Acrid odours irritate the nose and the throat and cause headaches. Black smoke from the factories'

Figure 1.3 The petrochemical zone seen from Taisi, October 2016
Source: Chia-shuo Tang (used with permission)

chimneys is sometimes visible during the daytime (see Figure 1.3), but most of it is discharged at night. When very noxious toxicants are to be released, workers at the petrochemical site discreetly send warning messages to relatives and neighbours to shut their windows.[5]

Twenty years after the start of operations, cancer has become the most common cause of death in the region. For instance, in one family of interviewees, the father died of liver cancer, while the daughter and the sister-in-law both suffer from lung cancer.[6] Death by cancer is readily apparent, for funerals are usually visible rituals in Taiwan. Starting with a mourning period of one to two weeks, a tent is installed in front of the house to host a picture of the deceased, along with flowers and offerings; people passing by can come in to burn incense and pray for the dead, and express sympathy to the family. At such a communal event, the cause of the death rapidly becomes common knowledge. On two occasions, while we were conducting interviews, a funeral procession passed by. One of our interviewees further mentioned: 'The current mayor has a funeral parlour business. So did the former mayor. Funerals have become the best business in town in recent years!'[7]

In rural China, Anna Lora-Wainwright (2013: 91–116) observed that a traditional aetiology of cancer being a result of hard work is now competing with an aetiology giving more importance to exposure to farm chemicals. She defines cancer as a form of social suffering, or what she calls 'the moral economy of cancer'. In Taiwan also, in places like Yunlin, this moral economy of cancer has been deeply disrupted, as one victim explains:

> When I was young, my father had a friend who was selling insurance, one type of which was against cancer. But he would meet with angry rejection when he tried to propose it. At that time, cancer was like a curse, the result of wrongdoings. Nowadays, it is banal. Around here, everyone dies of cancer![8]

As indicated here, in contrast to the process described by Lora-Wainwright in China, in Taiwan, interpretive categories of cancer causes did not include hard work, but treated it instead as a curse or the result of misdeeds. However, the dramatic change in the environment has transformed the traditional aetiology of cancer in a comparable manner.

This lay perception of damage to health and the environment has been confirmed by the epidemiological studies of the team led by Dr. Chang-chuan Chan (hereinafter 'C.C. Chan'), a specialist in air pollution, graduate of Harvard University and dean of the School of Public Health at National Taiwan University. These studies, which were requested in 2008 by the Yunlin office of the Environmental Protection Administration, highlight that after one decade of operation (1998–2008), the cancer rates had already multiplied fourfold in the three townships near the petrochemical zone of Formosa Plastics. The results were presented in five reports (in Chinese), and a dozen peer-reviewed articles have been published in international journals (*e.g.* Shie and Chan 2013; Yuan *et al.* 2018).

However, this academic research addresses only the problem of air pollution; the pollution of the rivers, underground waters and seas remains largely unknown. Furthermore, equivalent research could not be done for occupational hazards and injuries, which, as our interviewees explain, also affect many of those employed in the zone. For instance, the elder son of one plaintiff died at the age of 40 from an accident at the complex, which was never reported as an occupational injury.[9] Another plaintiff, whose younger brother died of colorectal cancer, suspects the cause of his death might have been his chronic exposure to chemicals while working in the zone.[10]

The invisible cost of explosions and other 'normal accidents'

Another related issue is the normalization of recurrent explosions. The blast of April 2019 mentioned in the introduction was the last such major incident to date. According to the company, at 9 AM, the control room of the aromatic hydrocarbon plant number three of Formosa Chemicals and Fiber Corp. noticed a possible leak from a pipeline for propylene or liquefied petroleum gas (LPG). Ding, a veteran worker, further explains the possible chain of events:

> If I was there and I saw a propylene pipe leaking, I would have immediately dispatched two men to help me collect the equipment. In an emergency, to

> stop the leak, I would first use a special wet bandage. Actually, when it dries, it's even harder than iron, so it can prevent the pipe from further cracking. This can be fixed in 30 minutes. [. . .] So I asked the manager: 'What did you do during those three hours!?'

At first, the manager used the pretext that this occurred on a Sunday, so it was difficult to find subcontractors to fix it. But as Ding kept questioning, the manager finally confessed:

> He told me: 'Brother Ding, you know, after two more years, I will retire. This leakage scared me to death, I dare not go there'. The office was about 500 metres away from the spot, but when the manager noticed the leak, he didn't dare to stay around, so he found an excuse to run away. Those left there were local employees and contract workers. But he is not a local.

For Ding, who is a local: 'This kind of job is not only for earning money; it is also about saving lives. Our family has a fish farm next to the zone. So I have done my best to keep studying how it works.'[11]

As Ding further elucidated, if the estimated budget to conduct indispensable maintenance or repair is greater than TWD 10 million, it must go through a lengthy procedure of collecting signatures. So, in case of an emergency such as a leak, the manager tries to keep it below TWD 10 million and look for a subcontractor who will agree to that price (or preferably one even lower). Ding assumed that, as he was constrained by this procedure, the manager probably lost precious time making phone calls, trying to obtain the cheapest price possible, until he realized that it was too late, and that he had better run away.

The constant search for cutting costs, even in case of emergency, is entangled with two other problems. The first is corruption, as Ding explained:

> Take, for example, a pipeline 10 miles long [which needs to be replaced]. It should have a thickness of 6 centimetres, for a total cost of [TWD] 1 million for each 10 metres. But the supervisor wants to earn extra money from this, so he orders pipes of 5 centimetres for a total of 900,000, and he keeps the difference of 100,000 for himself. And if another guy wants his share, they will reduce the pipe by another centimetre.

And when the company is visited by state inspectors, 'the safety managers always guide them for a quick visit, then they invite them for lunch', Ding added.

Secondly comes a conflict between real and prescribed tasks (Montmayeul *et al.* 1994). Office managers assign to workers a range of tasks based on norms and prescriptions such as those set by ISO, the International Organization for Standardization. These norms transform safety into nice-looking manuals and presentation slides. Of course, in practice, things never happen exactly as predicted in a slideshow. So the real task is what the workers effectively do to cope with thousands of conflicting parameters.

When Ding was looking for a plausible explanation of what *really* happened on 7 April, he had an argument with the manager and his staff who provided him with what sounded like ready-to-serve answers. Before the explosion that day, the deputy general manager of Formosa Plastics had asked Ding for advice on the plant's safety. Ding recommended that he launch a task force of twelve workers across the different companies in the zone. This could be done with a reasonable annual budget of TWD 100 million (around USD 3.3 million). But the manager refused the plan, arguing that it wasn't worth the money. However, according to a discussion Ding had with the same manager after the explosion, the total cost to repair the damage could reach a total of NTD 100 *billion*. This structural safety failure belongs to what Charles Perrow (1999; 1st edn 1984) summed up with the oxymoronic term 'normal accidents'.

Like the normalization of explosions and other accidents, the invisibility of occupational hazards is another consequence of the structural 'non-safety' of the petrochemical zone, as experienced by Tsai. In June 2019, Tsai and his colleague were asked to change a pipe section. But when they cut the pipe, a chemical liquid poured out onto Tsai's legs, causing him a serious chemical burn. He was transported to an office where he was given some basic emergency care, but then, instead of going to the nearest hospital, his colleague took him to another hospital in Huwei Township, a 40-minute drive away.

This was to avoid his boss getting into trouble with FPG. As a matter of fact, Tsai never reported the injury; his boss gave him the equivalent of a month's wages and asked him to rest. 'Otherwise, I could not be reemployed', he added, to explain the unwritten rule prevailing in the zone. The law would normally require the workers and their employer to conduct a systematic reporting of occupational injuries. But Formosa Plastics has launched a different code of conduct in the zone. Even regular employees in charge of safety do not dare report injuries. Ding also gave detailed accounts of other accidents and working injuries, which, he emphasized, were only the tip of the iceberg.

Ms. Wu, the person who arranged our meeting with Ding and Tsai, commented that such a corporate culture was difficult to reform. Even an explosion as severe as the one of 7 April was not sufficient to awaken the board of managers to the fact that there was something going wrong. Formosa Plastics even compelled many local workers whose houses were damaged by the explosion to sign a pledge that they would not apply to the government for compensation. The workers were furious about it, but they did not dare say it publicly.

Yunlin people *vs.* Formosa plastics

In August 2015, despite this prevailing fatalism amongst the population, 30 families decided to file a lawsuit against the petrochemical complex. Two residents supported this initiative: one is Huang Yuan-ho, a professor of English literature at a local university, and Wu Jih-hui, who lives on odd jobs, such as planting trees along the petrochemical zone. 'Brother Wu', as he is familiarly called, is not himself a plaintiff, but 10 years ago, after having enjoyed a stable job in Taipei, he came back to his homeland of Taisi in the hope that he could help do something for the damaged environment.

Huang and Wu were encouraged by C.C. Chan and a team of lawyers led by Thomas Chan, who has been involved in environmental issues for the past two decades. In May 2016, after the election of Tsai Ying-wen as president of the Republic of China (Taiwan), Thomas Chan was appointed Deputy Minister of the Environmental Protection Administration (EPA); although he had to give up his activity as a lawyer, he kept an eye on this lawsuit.

In September 2018, he resigned his EPA post due to a disagreement with Prime Minister William Lai, who was eager to push forward the construction of a coal-burning thermal plant despite promises to reduce air pollution. Since August 2019, Thomas Chan has been back at the court hearings in Yunlin. Meanwhile, the plaintiffs have received the support of an additional group of seven lawyers from the Legal Aid Foundation (a public institution launched in 2003 to provide legal assistance to those with lower incomes). Some of these lawyers acquired valuable experience during one of the first collective pollution lawsuits in Taiwan, a case of dioxin and mercury pollution in Tainan, which ran from 2008 to 2018 (Jobin and Tseng 2014; Chang and Hsiao 2018).

The suit in Yunlin seeks damages for premature deaths and severe diseases (mainly cancers) due to air pollution from the petrochemical zones. Instead of damage to human health, whose causation vis-à-vis environmental pollution is always difficult to prove, suing the company for economic loss due to the diminishing harvests of clams and oysters could be thought a more pragmatic option. The lawyers, however, explained that they were compelled to sidestep property damages for lack of sufficient proof and rely on the science that was already available. Based on the robust studies conducted by C.C. Chan and his team (*e.g.* Shie and Chan 2013; Yuan *et al.* 2018) that clearly show a sharp increase in cancer incidence, they hope that legally proving damage to human health will act as leverage toward enforcing drastic measures to stop the pollution, which is a priority to be accomplished before the severely damaged environment around the zone can be restored.

From the first hearing in January 2016 until April 2020, the defendants have constantly denied the legitimacy of the scientific evidence presented by the plaintiffs, such as the epidemiological studies conducted by C.C. Chan (*supra*). Despite the fact that these studies were published in well-known international journals, the defendants' lawyers argued that Chan had an obvious bias in favor of the plaintiffs. The plaintiffs' lawyers, for their part, have been trying to obtain from the judge a confrontation between C.C. Chan (or other experts chosen by the victims), and the experts the defendants are expected to call to testify in court. But so far, Formosa Plastics' lawyers have succeeded in postponing such a confrontation. The debate has thus been going around in circles for three years now (see Figure 1.4).

However, a window of opportunity opened for the plaintiffs when the judge asked the two sides to present their own definition of danger, as regards article

Figure 1.4 The litigants' lawyers at a hearing, Yunlin District Court, 12 January 2017
Source: P. Jobin (used with permission)

191–3 of the Taiwanese civil code on the damage liability caused by business activity:

The Judge:	'What exactly is the content of those emissions? What sort of dangerous substances do they contain? We often see smoke coming from the plants and don't know what they are . . .'
Defendants' lawyer 1:	'This is water vapor.'
The judge:	'Could be, I don't know.'
Defendants' lawyer 2:	'If it is black smoke, it's not good, but the white smoke is OK!'

The defendants further argued that the criteria for estimating the level of hazards contained in the plants' emissions should be limited to those that went beyond the levels permitted by law. Thomas Chan, the head of the plaintiffs' lawyers, challenged this statement:

Emissions do not necessarily need to go beyond permissible levels to be dangerous. Besides, big accidents occur frequently in the defendants' plants, and in these moments, the norms are certainly bypassed, but we haven't yet obtained the proof from the local authorities. The big fire that occurred at Formosa Plastics on 25 July 2010 kept on burning for three days. This year, there was another explosion on 7 April. The calculation of the damage is still being processed. [. . .] In addition, they discharged a lot of pollutants over a long period. If this is not a dangerous business, I wonder which company can be defined as such![12]

The plaintiffs are split into two groups: 10 plaintiffs are suing the companies for their own cancer, and around 65 plaintiffs are suing them for the premature death of their parents (20 cases), making a total of about 75 plaintiffs.

The main pathologies at issue are lung and liver cancers. According to Brother Wu, the number of plaintiffs could increase up to 500 if the Legal Aid Foundation step in to provide help and cover the litigation costs. In March and April 2019, the foundation launched public meetings in Taisi to evaluate how many more plaintiffs would be interested in joining the action under these conditions. Only a few dozen people showed up, outnumbered by employees from Formosa Plastics who came only to check the level of mobilization (see Figure 1.5).

Figure 1.5 The plaintiffs and their lawyers after a court hearing at the Yunlin District Court, 9 September 2016

Source: P. Jobin (used with permission)

The lawyers set the amounts of compensation between TWD 1 and 3 million (or between approximately USD 33,000 and 100,000). It is composed mainly of mental anguish compensation (*jingshen weifujin*) of TWD 2 million (USD 66,000) for plaintiffs still alive, and a half million (USD 16,500) for the beneficiaries of the dead, to which can be added indemnification for an incapacity to work, as well as for medical and funeral expenses.

Five of the plaintiffs, who are suing on behalf of their dead parents, do not live in Yunlin but in Taipei or Kaohsiung. The sudden death of their parents shocked them and made them aware that many people in Taisi had been stricken with cancer. Compared to those still living in Taisi, these plaintiffs have relatively stable earnings. For these plaintiffs, the lawsuit protesting against this massive chronic pollution is a way to remember and pay a moral tribute to their parents, while keeping a link with their region and their attachment to a lost 'dwelled-in environment' (Centemeri 2015).

Valuating the loss: cancers and oysters

For all other plaintiffs, the reparation of the damage is entangled in a complex mix of moral indignation and a political economy of dependency at the petrochemical complex. As one of the plaintiffs, Ms. Wu, explains: 'One of our neighbours works for a subcontractor in the zone. There isn't much other choice around here [. . .], as we can't go fishing in the sea [due to the pollution].'[13]

Almost all of the plaintiffs have parents or neighbours working in the zone, but only a few of them are regular employees. The total workforce in the zone consists of approximately 12,000 regular employees and an additional flexible labour population of around 25,000 contract workers; although the latter are paid in daily wages and have no health insurance, many consider themselves lucky just to have found a job in the zone.[14]

Amongst the plaintiffs is one such worker. He more or less manages to earn a monthly income of around TWD 30,000 (approximately USD 1,000). He must take care of his wife and two children, and, since the death of his father (from lung cancer, at the age of 65), he also supports his mother, who is a diabetic. Of his three younger sisters who live nearby, two have uterine tumours and one has a chronic cough. Of his role in suing the complex, he says:

> I would just like the company to compensate us a little bit for all this pollution. Money, it's what the company gets, and it earns a lot. But the pollution, see, it's for us! So it's natural that we look for a way to get some compensation, don't you think so?[15]

Around a third of the plaintiffs live off fishing or farming. Ms. Wu's husband died of prostate cancer at the age of 64. Since then, she and her daughter have tried to continue farming mussels and clams. But harvests have diminished from once yearly to once every two years. Mussels are selling poorly because they are too stunted and have a taste of mud. As for the oysters, the fishermen themselves do not dare to eat them anymore. Ms. Wu and her daughter are so sceptical of their chances to win this suit that they call it a battle of 'small shrimps against the whale', a Chinese equivalent of David versus Goliath. But they want to try, hoping that such an action can help stop the pollution, or at least bring some improvements (*gaishan*). Their decision does not result from a rational calculation of what the death of Mr. Wu has meant for the family. Given their current economic difficulties, if Formosa Plastics was forced to pay them compensation, it would certainly be helpful. But cash is not their main standard of wealth; what matters, rather, is the number of baskets of clams collected at each harvest (see Figure 1.6). Ms. Wu further expresses her main goal and indignation: 'Around here in town, what we say is that factories pay reimbursement for oysters. But if people die, it does not count, there is no compensation!'[16]

The local clam farmers union has been through several contentious episodes involving the petrochemical zone. When we asked if they would consider launching a civil action, the head of the union answered with a similar moral argument: 'Yes, perhaps, we should do that. But if you mean asking for reimbursement [*buchang*], I don't want a penny. What I would ask for is compensation [*peichang*], because they are guilty.'[17]

Figure 1.6 Harvest of clams, with the petrochemical zone in the background, 1 August 2017

Source: P. Jobin (used with permission)

Tu *et al.* (2014: 79) noted that when Formosa Plastics pays for damage to crops, the company emphasizes that these are not *peichang* but *buchang*, in support of stable agricultural development. Both words can be translated as 'compensation', and though not technically correct from a Taiwanese legal angle, it is generally believed that only *peichang* implies moral and legal liability (like the English 'damages'), whereas *buchang* is perceived rather as a reimbursement, as in an insurance payment.

A 'good neighbour'

The union head and Ms. Wu indirectly pointed to the political economy shaped by the petrochemical complex. Over two decades of operation, the company has learnt how to dampen protest against environmental damage and all kinds of hazards, including numerous road fatalities caused by truck traffic. Protests have not been repressed by the police force, as has been seen in China (van Rooij 2010). Rather, money has been a tool for buying public peace. In 2018, the Formosa Plastics Group, the main shareholder of the complex, had an annual turnover of TWD 1.7 trillion (USD 52 billion), which accounted for 9.6 per cent of Taiwan's GDP.

Such large earnings allow the company to pay for all kinds of local patronage. The company calls it 'good neighbour relations' (*dunqin mulin*), and most people consider it as just recompense for the various nuisances, such as truck traffic in and out of the zone, and a means to share the wealth. In addition, a hospital launched by the company provides free health care, the public elementary school delivers free meals to children, the elderly can benefit from home service care, and so forth. Furthermore, households receive monthly allocations, with amounts that depend on the township of residency. The total amount of all this expense so far is estimated to be around TWD 10 billion (around USD 330 million). Perhaps not surprisingly, according to investigative reporter Yu-iou Lim, local township and village leaders have been involved in corruption scandals more frequently than elsewhere in Taiwan (Fang *et al.* 2019: 109–129). It seems to be commonplace for Formosa Plastics to distribute 'red envelopes' to local politicians: according to one of our interviewees, for a county delegate, the standard amount varies between TWD 1 and 2 million (USD 33,000 and 66,000).[18]

In 2010, a series of explosions stirred a wave of local protests and was instrumental in a nationwide opposition movement against the extension of the petrochemical complex to the north (Jobin 2010; Ho 2014; Grano 2015; Shih and Tu 2017). Thereafter, the firm reinforced its 'good neighbour' policy, by for instance, more than doubling the monthly allowance of TWD 293 per household in Mailiao Township. The town's former mayor claimed that this was the result of his efforts to convince the leaders of Formosa Plastics that to build a 'peaceful coexistence' with the local communities, the firm had to provide more substantial services and economic incentives (Lin Y.-I., in Fang *et al.* 2019: 118–119).

But this was a preferential treatment for Mailiao Township, where the petro-chemical zone's administration is registered (see Figure 1.2). The other fence-line townships of Taisi and Sihu are treated differently. Moreover, in sharp contrast with the intense activity in Mailiao, which has seen its population grow, Taisi appears economically devastated, with many houses standing empty. In addition to the hospital built by Formosa Plastics, Mailiao residents benefit from care for the elderly, lunchboxes for schoolchildren and a monthly allowance of about TWD 600 per capita (about USD 20), compared to only TWD 100 (USD 3) for the residents of Taisi and Sihu. For residents of Taisi and Sihu, even though these amounts are quite modest, it is a matter of principle: the difference between them is a concrete sign of unfair discrimination.

This discrepancy, and what Zelizer (1994) defines as the 'social meaning of money', may therefore explain why all the plaintiffs are from Taisi (and one family from Sihu) and none are from Mailiao. Inhabitants of Taisi share the assumption that the petrochemical zone is the main cause of their cancers, whereas, in Mailiao, most people prefer not to think about that. The lawsuit can be interpreted partly as a demand for a more equal distribution of 'good neighbour' practices. But if this were the only goal, instead of stopping the pollution and restoring the devastated environ-ment, the lawsuit would just entail asking for additional patronage payments.

Only a small minority rejects this economy of compensation. However, as we have seen, some refuse to call it 'compensation', for these payments lack moral responsibility. Brother Wu, the local organizer of the lawsuit, wants to believe that money is not the main motivation of the plaintiffs. During our private discussions, he has often expressed his disgust with the local elite and politicians who have become spoiled by Formosa Plastics' 'good neighbour' policy: 'If these people who have benefited from a better education resign and accept this farce, how can simple farmers resist against it?'[19]

During group meetings and press conferences in Taipei, Brother Wu has care-fully avoided this problem, for fear that it would harm the mobilization and bring further prejudice to his township. During one of our academic presentations on this lawsuit, a graduate student commented: 'You know, what they want above all is money'. This remark is not unusual. The demand for damages is often subject to doubt, as if it were simply a function of greed. 'Thus, the compensation trap springs shut', concluded van Rooij et al. (2012: 742). And this trap includes a moral condemnation of all forms of compensation.

Brother Wu summed up the challenge of resisting the company's 'good neigh-bour' policy this way: 'Formosa Plastics has succeeded in imposing such a rotten culture. . . . It leads everybody to accept massive chronic pollution, provided the company distributes regular payments. Changing such a culture is so difficult, almost impossible'.[20]

Looking for another way of changing that culture, Brother Wu decided to go to northern India, near Nepal, for one or two years to study Buddhist sutras with a lama.

Formosa Plastics' domination of local and national politics has forged a culture of postponing effective environmental measures, as if the pollution were bound to continue. The flow of 'fuel money' (Mitchell 2011) tends to legitimize the pollution, or at least make it tolerable. Some, like Brother Wu, firmly reject this money. For the other plaintiffs, although their motivations do not exclude a moral and symbolic component, the incommensurable dimensions of the suffered harm tend to be swallowed up by the firm's system of regular allocations and welfare patronage. As narrowly defined by the company, the economy of compensation therefore reduces the valuation of environmental damages to a very low price, another form of what Jason Moore (2015) calls 'cheap nature'.

Conclusion

In addition to its responsibility for the climate crisis and the 'Plasticene' (*i.e.* enormous amounts of plastic waste), the petrochemical industry harms local communities with recurrent explosions and chronic pollution. Moreover, despite evidence that this pollution is the most likely cause of their high incidence of cancer and other serious illnesses, the industry's main response, as with global warming, consists in the further production of doubt (Michaels 2008: 72–78, 198–202). Despite NGOs' efforts to stop this ongoing multi-level petrochemical disaster, international solidarity from civil society remains limited. At the local and national levels, the degree of contention depends on the reaction of local communities, their economic dependency on the industry and the support they can find from national NGOs, as well as political and scientific elites.

In the case of Formosa Plastics' petrochemical zone in central Taiwan, specialists in environmental science and public health studies have been able to conduct research and show evidence of a significant increase of cancer resulting from chronic exposure and the side effects from explosions. In addition, activists and lawyers have collected a lot of evidence of the illegal chronic air pollution. Despite some significant deficiencies – or problems of 'undone science' – regarding pollution of the sea and occupational hazards, this research and data were sufficient to launch a collective lawsuit. A decisive motivation for the majority of the plaintiffs was the discrepancy in the financial treatment delivered by the firm, according to the township of residency – Mailiao or Taisi. Although modest, the discrepancy in payments has become a symbol of geographical discrimination, one that has influenced the perception of both the damage and its narratives. Feeling justifiably dissatisfied with the company's 'good neighbour' practices has made it easier for these residents to start to challenge Formosa Plastics on other, larger issues. Through the lawsuit, the victims are requesting an exceptional payment of money – clearly denoted as 'compensation' (*peichang*) – as a sign of the firm's liability.

Shocked by the 'slow violence' of this economy of compensation, as defined by the firm, the most radical plaintiffs and activists would like the state to impose drastic reforms or even close the plants. But economic dependency contains the conflicts between inhabitants and the firm into a state of low-level intensity, and this situation postpones the prevention of further explosions and chronic pollution. Yet, in the face of overwhelming capitalist domination and the constraints of civil suits (which compel the lawyers to translate damage into damages), the collective lawsuit has encouraged some inhabitants and workers to start formulating a critique of the economy of compensation within which they are confined. The goal is not to exclude compensation, but rather to rethink the various meanings of money in issues of industrial damage. So do such awards contribute to repairing toxic environments? From this particular case in Taiwan, and the petrochemical industry in general, the answer clearly inclines toward the negative. Nevertheless, the people involved in the demands for reparation develop certain forms of agency that are worthy of consideration for their potential to eventually transform into concrete forms of environmental repair.

Acknowledgements

Attorney Thomas Chan and his colleagues Aslan Hung and Shu-fang Huang welcomed and encouraged me in this research. I also owe many thanks to Brother Wu, Hao-chung Chan, Robin Yuan-ho Huang, and Ming-yi Wu for their help and generosity. My research assistants Chia-shuo Tang, Chee-Wei Ying, Fei-hsin Chang, Shih-hao Jheng and Yi-ying Tsai aided in conducting and transcribing interviews. Pei-yi Hsieh and Hung-yang Lin offered further notes and transcriptions. Discussions with Wenling Tu, Kanlin Hsu, Xavier Sun, Yen-ting Lin and other participants of the Citizen Platform on Formosa's Sixth Naphtha Cracker proved quite fruitful. The editors of this book and Rebecca Fite helped to improve the initial manuscript. Shih-hao Jheng made the maps with QGIS software, an open source Geographic Information System.

Notes

1 Some of the results of the research discussed in this chapter have been published previously in Jobin (2021).
2 Ministry of Economic Affairs, Republic of China (Taiwan), 16 January 2012.
3 Interview with Ms. Wu and her daughter, Taisi, 16 August 2016 (see also Tu *et al.* 2014; Lin 2019).
4 Interview with Mr. Lin Zh-C., Taisi, 1 September 2017.
5 Interview with Mr. and Ms. Lin C., Taisi, 20 May 2016.
6 Family of Mr. Lin C. First interview, 20 May 2016.
7 Interview with Mr. Huang, August 2016.
8 First interview with Mr. Wu B., Taipei, 6 September 2016.
9 Interview with Mr. Lin Z.C., Taisi, 19 May 2016.
10 Interview with Mr. Ding, Taisi, 20 May 2016.
11 Interview with Mr. Ding, Mailiao, 30 August 2019.
12 Idem.
13 Interview with Ms. Wu and her daughter, Taisi, 16 August 2016.
14 Interview with Ding and Wu M.Y., Mailiao, 30 August 2019. A previous source, Wu S.L. (Mailiao, 22 March 2016) estimated regular employees to number around 10,000, and contract workers between 10,000 and 20,000. The company does not disclose data.
15 Interview with Lin X. and his mother, Taisi, 20 May 2016.
16 Interview with Ms. Wu and her daughter, Taisi, 16 August 2016.
17 Interview with three union members, Taisi, 1 September 2017.

18 Interview with Mr. Wu W.J., Taipei, 16 December 2017.
19 Discussion with Wu Ri-hui in Taisi, 24 November 2017.
20 Discussion with Wu Ri-hui in Taipei, 27 August 2018.

References

Allen, B. (2003) *Uneasy Alchemy: Citizens and Experts in Louisiana's Chemical Corridor Disputes*, Cambridge, MA: MIT Press.

Allen, B. (2011) 'A Tale of Two Lawsuits: Making Policy-Relevant Environmental Health Knowledge in Italian and U.S. Chemical Regions', in C. Sellers and J. Melling (eds) *Dangerous Trade: Histories of Industrial Hazard across a Globalizing World*, Philadelphia: Temple University.

Allen, B., Ferrier, Y. and Cohen, A.K. (2017) 'Through a Maze of Studies: Health Questions and "Undone Science" in a French Industrial Region', *Environmental Sociology*, 3: 134–144.

Anguelovski, I. and Martínez Alier, J. (2014) 'The "Environmentalism of the Poor" Revisited: Territory and Place in Disconnected Global Struggles', *Ecological Economics*, 102: 167–176.

Bandelj, N., Wherry, F. and Zelizer, V. (eds) (2017) *Money Talks: Explaining How Money Really Works*, Princeton, NJ: Princeton University Press.

Barbot, J. and Dodier, N. (2015) 'Victims' Normative Repertoire of Financial Compensation: The Tainted hGH Case', *Human Studies*, 38: 81–96.

Brown, D. (2019) 'The Existential Crisis of the Petrochemical Industry and Discourses of Sustainability: Reflections from the 34th World Petrochemical Conference', *Toxic News*, 28 May (online).

Centemeri, L. (2015) 'Reframing Problems of Incommensurability in Environmental Conflicts through Pragmatic Sociology: From Value Pluralism to the Plurality of Modes of Engagement with the Environment', *Environmental Values*, 24: 299–320.

Chang, W.-C. and Hsiao, S. (2018) 'CPDC Ordered to Compensate Contamination Victims', *Taipei Times*, 29 November.

Chateauraynaud, F. and Debaz, J. (2017) *Aux bords de l'irréversible. Sociologie pragmatique des transformations*, Paris: Editions Pétra.

Collier, K. (2019) 'Federal Judge Rules against Formosa Plastics in Pollution Case, Calling Company a "Serial Offender"', *The Texas Tribune*, 28 June.

Couch, S.R. and Kroll-Smith, J.S. (1985) 'The Chronic Technical Disaster: Toward a Social Scientific Perspective', *Social Science Quarterly*, 66: 564–575.

Davies, T. (2019) 'Slow Violence and Toxic Geographies: "Out of Sight" to Whom?', *Environment and Planning C: Politics and Space*. <https://doi.org/10.1177/2399654419841063>

Einhorn, B. and Carroll, J. (2019) 'A Plastics Giant that Pollutes Too Much for Taiwan is Turning to America', *Bloomberg*, 13 December.

Fang, H.-C., Ho, J.-H., Lin, Y.-Y. and Chiang, I.-C. (2019) *Yancong zhi dao: women yu shihua gongcun de liangwan ge rizi* (A Smoking Island: Petrochemical Industry, Our Dangerous Companion for Fifty Years), Taipei: Spring Hill.

Fourcade, M. (2011) 'Cents and Sensibility: Economic Values and the Nature of "Nature"', *American Journal of Sociology*, 116: 1721–1777.

Frickel, S., Gibbon, S., Howard, J., Kempner, J., Ottinger, G. and Hess, D. (2010) 'Undone Science: Charting Social Movement and Civil Society Challenges to Research Agenda Setting', *Science, Technology, & Human Values*, 35(4): 444–473.

George, T. (2001) *Minamata: Pollution and the Struggle for Democracy in Postwar Japan*, Cambridge, MA: Harvard University Press.

Grano, S. (2015) *Environmental Governance in Taiwan: A New Generation of Activists and Stakeholders*, London: Routledge.

Guo, P. (2014) 'The Aesthetics of "Justice" among the Langalanga, Solomon Islands', *Taiwan Journal of Anthropology*, 12(1): 87–130. (in Chinese)

Guo, P.-Y. (2011) 'Law as Discourse: Land Disputes and the Changing Imagination of Relations among the Langalanga, Solomon Islands', *Pacific Studies*, 34(2/3): 223–248.

Hamilton, L., Feit, S. *et al.* (2019) *Plastic and Climate: The Hidden Costs of a Plastic Plane*, Washington, DC: Center for International Environmental Law. <www.ciel.org/plasticandclimate>.

Haram, L., Carlton, J., Ruiz, G. and Maximenko, N. (2020) 'A Plasticene Lexicon', *Marine Pollution Bulletin*, 150. doi.org/10.1016/j.marpolbul.2019.110714.

Hess, D. (2016) *Undone Science: Social Movements, Mobilized Publics, and Industrial Transition*, Cambridge, MA: MIT Press.

Ho, M.-S. (2014) 'Resisting Naphtha Crackers: A Historical Survey of Environmental Politics in Taiwan', *China Perspectives*, 3: 5–14.

Hsu, J.-Y. (1995) 'The Struggle Over Local Space: A Case Study of the Environmental Movement in Taiwan', *Capitalism Nature Socialism*, 6(1): 113–124.

Hu, C.-Y. (2012) 'Comparative Analysis of Glass Beads Used among Austronesian Groups in Taiwan: Some Thoughts on Forms, Values and Materiality', *Journal of Archaeology and Anthropology*, 76: 97–133. (in Chinese)

International Energy Agency (IEA). (2018) *The Future of Petrochemicals Towards More Sustainable Plastics and Fertilisers*, Paris: IEA.

Jephcote, C. and Mah, A. (2019) 'Regional Inequalities in Benzene Exposures across the European Petrochemical Industry: A Bayesian Multilevel Modelling Approach', *Environment International*, 132: 104812.

Jobin, P. (2010) 'Hazards and Protest in the "Green Silicon Island." The Struggle for Visibility of Industrial Hazards in Contemporary Taiwan', *China Perspectives*, 3: 46–62.

Jobin, P. (2021) 'Our "Good Neighbor" Formosa Plastics: Petrochemical Damage(s) and the Meanings of Money', *Environmental Sociology*, 7(1): 40–53.

Jobin, P. and Tseng, Y. (2014) 'Guinea Pigs Go to Court: Epidemiology and Class Actions in Taiwan', in S. Boudia and N. Jas (eds) *Powerless Science? Science and Politics in a Toxic World*, Oxford: Berghahn, 170–191.

Lerner, S. (2005) *Diamond: A Struggle for Environmental Justice in Louisiana's Chemical Corridor*, Cambridge, MA: The MIT Press.

Lerner, S. (2019) 'Waste Only: How the Plastics Industry Is Fighting to Keep Polluting the World', *The Intercept*, 20 July (online).

Lin, C.-K., Hung, H.-Y., Christiani, D.C., Forastiere, F. and Lin, R.-T. (2017) 'Lung Cancer Mortality of Residents Living Near Petrochemical Industrial Complexes: A Meta-analysis', *Environmental Health*, 16: 101.

Lin, H.-Y. (2019) *Industrial Pollutions, Environmental Controversies, and Local Movements: A Case Study of Mailiao, Yunlin*, Master thesis, Department of Geography College of Science, National Taiwan University.

Lora-Wainwright, A. (2013) *Fighting for Breath: Living Morally and Dying of Cancer in a Chinese Village*, Honolulu, HI: University of Hawaii Press.

Mah, A. and Wang, X. (2019) 'Accumulated Injuries of Environmental Injustice: Living and Working with Petrochemical Pollution in Nanjing, China', *Annals of the American Association of Geographers*, 109(6): 1961–1977.

Marichalar, P. (2019) 'How to Judge Safety Crime: Lessons From the Eternit Asbestos Maxi – Trials', *New Solutions: A Journal of Environmental and Occupational Health Policy*, 29(2).

Martin, E. (2015) *The Meaning of Money in China and the United States*, Chicago, IL: Hau Books.

Martínez Alier, J. (2002) *Environmentalism of the Poor: A Study of Ecological Conflicts and Valuation*, Cheltenham, UK: Edward Elgar.

McConnaughey, J. (2020) 'Groups Challenge Louisiana Permits for Plastics Plant', *New York Times*, 14 February.

Michaels, D. (2008) *Doubt is Their Product: How Industry's Assault on Science Threatens Your Health*, Oxford: Oxford University Press.

Mitchell, D. (2019) 'For Massive New Plants, Formosa Wants OK to Double Amount of Chemicals Released into St. James', *The Advocate*, 8 July (online).

Mitchell, T. (2011) *Carbon Democracy: Political Power in the Age of Oil*, London: Verso.

Montmayeul, R., Mosneron-Dupin, F. and Llory, M. (1994) 'The Managerial Dilemma between the Prescribed Tasks and the Real Activity of Operators: Some Trends for Research on Human Factors', *Reliability Engineering & System Safety*, 45(1–2): 67–73.

Moore, J. (2015) *Capitalism in the Web of Life: Ecology and the Accumulation of Capital*, London: Verso.

Ng, K.H. and He, X. (2017) 'The Institutional and Cultural Logics of Legal Commensuration: Blood Money and Negotiated Justice in China', *American Journal of Sociology*, 122(4): 1104–1143.

Nixon, R. (2011) *Slow Violence and the Environmentalism of the Poor*, Cambridge, MA: Harvard University Press.

Oreskes, N. and Conway, E. (2010) *Merchants of Doubts: How a Handful of Scientists Obscured the Truth on Issues from Tobacco Smoke to Global Warming*, London: Bloomsbury.

Ottinger, G. (2013) *Refined Expertise: How Responsible Engineers Subvert Environmental Justice Challenges*, New York: New York University Press.

Perrow, C. (1999; 1st edition 1984) *Normal Accidents: Living with High-Risks Technologies*, Princeton, NJ: Princeton University Press.

Reed, C. (2015) 'Dawn of the Plasticene', *New Scientist*, 225: 28–32.

Rich, N. (2019) *Losing Earth: A Recent History*, New York: MCD.

Shie, R.H. and Chan, C.C. (2013) 'Tracking Hazardous Air Pollutants from a Refinery Fire by Applying On-line and Off-line Air Monitoring and Back Trajectory Modeling', *Journal of Hazardous Materials*, 261: 72–82.

Shih, C.-L. and Tu, W.-L. (2017) 'The Scientific Framework and Decision Deadlock in the Environmental Administrative Procedures: Examining the EIA of the Fire Accident in the No. 6 Naphtha Cracking Project', *Journal of Public Administration*, 81: 81–111. (in Chinese)

Stern, R.E. (2013) *Environmental Litigation in China: A Study of Political Ambivalence*, Cambridge: Cambridge University Press.

Temper, L. and Martinez-Alier, J. (2013) 'The God of the Mountain and Godavarman: Net Present Value, Indigenous Territorial Rights and Sacredness in a Bauxite Mining Conflict in India', *Ecological Economics*, 96: 79–87.

Tu, W.-L., Shih, C.-L. and Tsai, W.-J. (2014) 'The Petrochemical Lesson for the Agricultural County: Reviewing Yunlin County's Environmental Supervision on the Sixth Naphtha Cracking Plant', *Journal of Taiwan Land Research*, 17(1): 59–90. (in Chinese)

Tullo, A. (2019) 'C&EN's Global Top 50 Chemical Companies of 2018', *Chemical & Engineering News*, 97(30): 29 July (online).

van Rooij, B. (2010) 'The People vs. Pollution: Understanding Citizen Action against Pollution in China', *Journal of Contemporary China*, 19(63): 55–77.

van Rooij, B., Wainwright, A.L., Wu, Y. and Zhang, Y. (2012) 'The Compensation Trap: The Limits of Community-based Pollution Regulation in China', *Pace Environmental Law Review*, 29(3): 701–745.

Yuan, T.-H., Shen, Y.-C., Shie, R.-H., Hung, S.-H., Chen, C.-F. and Chan, C.C. (2018) 'Increased Cancers among Residents Living in the Neighborhood of a Petrochemical Complex: A 12-Year Retrospective Cohort Study', *International Journal of Hygiene and Environmental Health*, 221(2): 308–314.

Zavestoski, S., Mignano, F., Agnello, K., Darroch, F. and Abrams, K. (2002) 'Toxicity and Complicity: Explaining Consensual Community Response to a Chronic Technological Disaster', *The Sociological Quarterly*, 43(3): 385–406.

Zelizer, V. (1994) *The Social Meaning of Money*, New York: Basic Books.

2 Repairing the ir-repairable

'Geo-biological' recovery of environments after a nuclear disaster

Sezin Topçu

Introduction

The nuclear energy sector undoubtedly demonstrates one of the most significant gaps between institutional disaster recovery strategies, which are mostly dictated by a resilience narrative, and public demand for reparation or at least for recognition of the irreparable. This kind of gap is first and foremost a definitional one and concerns the 'disputed what-ness of disasters' (see Introduction), the organizational (Perrow 1984) and structural (Matsumoto 2013) causes of disasters and the 'abstracted' *vs.* lived consequences of disasters (Michael 2014). With regard to this last aspect, temporal and spatial issues play a crucial role because nuclear system failures often result in 'slow' (Fortun *et al.* 2017) or 'ongoing' (Dudden 2012) consequences (radioelements colonize the environment over long duration and attack the human body slowly but continuously) and because even their non-failure or routine functioning engenders 'slow-motion' catastrophes (Brown 2013) or 'disasters-before-disasters' (Jobin 2017).

Drawing on topical debates relating to the radioactive destruction or 'colonization' of land and *milieux*, this chapter aims to highlight the strategies, doctrines and tools that nuclear states and agencies have elaborated over decades to deal with post-accident recovery. Based on official reports, expert scenarios and estimations and plans for preparedness, recovery and resilience, it explores how the problem of contaminated land has been managed historically both at an international level and in regions victimized by the Chernobyl and Fukushima accidents. It analyzes the contexts, policies and discourses that framed the issue in terms of the technical modalities of evacuation and the need to minimize land loss – a dynamic that I take as a vantage point for the current analysis. My aim is to shed light on the process that led to the stabilization and reinforcement of a biopolitic of recovery that, in the contemporary period at least, exploited biological/body matter for environmental/land recovery. I therefore focus on the official strategies that aimed at social engineering or controlling the social psyche, which, as will be explored further, proved decisive in the generalization and public acceptance of the biological 'sacrifice' of victims for the sake of land recovery as the (new) norm. I thus hope to contribute to the currently expanding social science literature on land management and reconstruction after a nuclear failure (see, *e.g.*, Kojima

DOI: 10.4324/9781003184782-4

2020), a question that has been put on the back burner for many years by analysts of nuclear accidents, who have invested their time instead in other important issues such as crisis management (Lagadec 1988), media coverage and political impacts (Liberatore 1999), environmental and health fallouts (Kuchinskaya 2014), construction of the public memory of catastrophes (Ardt 2012; Kasperski 2020) and compensation mechanisms and the long-term management of victimship (Petryna 2002; Namioka 2012; Brown 2019; Jobin 2020).

On the controversial features of victimization and reparation in nuclear disasters

Regarding damage to health and the biomedical issues resulting from nuclear system failures, the immediacy of victimization, such as the sudden deaths of liquidators and clean-up workers, and the possibility of localizing them easily was what rendered these accidents real, or *what made them exist*, as far as the official bodies were concerned. For their detractors, however, the illnesses that slowly impacted the victims' bodies (thyroid cancers, leukaemias, etc.) were equally important. The fact that these forms of victimization were diffused in time and space was not a legitimate reason for denying them. Their epidemiological character meant they *should* be considered real. The ongoing controversy over the number of victims of the Chernobyl nuclear accident (26 April 1986) is an important example of this kind of definitional gap that separates expert and lay understandings of victimization and reparation. For a decade and a half, the most prominent nuclear and health agencies (WHO, IAEA, NEA-OECD) insisted on the minimal range of '31 to 55 victims', while ecologist, antinuclear and human rights organizations maintained that the Soviet accident had resulted in several hundred thousand victims (Brown 2019). This unprecedented – and mostly 'artificial' (Latour 2004) – polarization was perpetuated by the fact the nuclearists[1] put forward claims of uncertainty, non-knowledge ('we know that we don't know') (Bleicher and Gross 2011) and lack of scientific evidence in order to minimize the risks and damages caused by nuclear system failures. In response, the antinuclearists and the victims denounced what they called a 'crime against humanity' and even 'genocide' and 'globocide' (Anders 2006). For the nuclearists, recovery after a nuclear accident was to a certain extent a question of social psychology. The public should acknowledge the fact that nuclear system failures are much less mortal than, for instance, accidents occurring in chemical-industrial facilities (as in Bhopal). From this perspective, priority was given to mitigating public 'radiophobia', a term popularized after the Chernobyl accident to describe the public's 'illegitimate' concerns or fears around radioactivity risks. For the antinuclearists and certain victim groups, the damage caused by a nuclear accident was irreparable. Countless human bodies were contaminated and made ill, and, many more, including generations to come, would be contaminated in the future.

With regard to environmental damage, the gap between the institutional and public framings of disaster recovery operated at a slightly different level. Above all, it revealed major disparities both in what was considered reversible/

irreversible after a nuclear accident and in the possibility/impossibility of a return to normality. The most recent and most widespread institutional understanding of recovery was neither 'idealized' (a 'disaster is reversible') nor 'heroic' (a disaster is more-than-reversible, in other words it is possible to 'build back better') (see Introduction). Rather, recovery was considered by the international nuclear agencies, experts and decision-makers to be an imperfect and crucial process in which the public's collaboration was key. They also argued that the boundary between pre- and post-disaster situations had already been blurred prior to the major accidents and that nature had been made (radio)hybrid immediately after we entered the era of atomic 'spectacles' (Kirsch 2002) (*i.e.* the 2,000 or so atomic bomb tests that caused widespread global contamination in the 1950s). From this perspective, it was thought that a nuclear accident merely accelerated the continuous transformation of the environment by radioactive pollution over a condensed time period. In terms of the public framing of disaster recovery, the detractors criticized the fatalistic vision or philosophy that the nuclear experts conveyed. They underlined the fact that radioactive fallouts from nuclear accidents caused too much damage to the environment to be considered negligible or just 'supplementary' when seen from a long-term perspective. They also denounced the institutional obsession with quick recovery and argued that imposing less optimal living conditions on entire generations was ethically and politically unacceptable.

In such a controversial and disputed context, the question of who was responsible for deciding the success of recovery operations and under what criteria was key. Past nuclear accidents and their long-term management have shown that the institutional metric for determining the success or failure of recovery relied not so much on material or technical measures (although these existed and were crucial) but on whether or not the public authorities managed to repopulate the areas affected. In a sense, the non-evacuation of people or the re-establishment of human presence in contaminated territories emerged as an important parameter in defining *what* a nuclear disaster was and in particular *when* it ended. The advocates of nuclear power claimed that evacuations should be minimized as far as possible and justified their argument on the basis of the trauma caused to the evacuees. This of course was not the only trauma that should have been taken into account. Various forms of post-traumatic stress disorders, psychological distress and anxiety affected different categories of victims, including those who were not able to leave the contaminated zones, as in the Chernobyl case, for instance. Nevertheless, nuclear and health agencies rarely considered these types of trauma, as if post-traumatic stress were synonymous with evacuation. The antinuclearists' retort was that the decision-makers stigmatized evacuations in order to minimize costs and banalize radioactive harm in the 'reenchanted world of resilience' (Ribault 2019). In a sense, those who governed were accused of trying to *re-cover* what a nuclear accident *dis-covers* – that is, the continuous harm and vulnerability to which nuclearized nations are exposed. Overall, as will be discussed in the next section, zoning policies occupied a central role in these disputes.

On zones, bodies, social engineering and knowledge gaps

In the international nuclear energy arena, post-disaster management (management of territories and victimized populations) has been based on a series of technical, juridical, economic and insurance tools that were first introduced in the United States in the 1950s. Even prior to the launch of the nuclear industries, there was an expert consensus that in the event of a nuclear accident, vast territories would be highly contaminated. By the late 1940s, it had also become universally acknowledged that a significant number of people would need to be evacuated. This constraint depended to a great extent on the choice of plant construction sites and the corresponding urban policies. In 1950, an expert committee from the US Atomic Energy Commission (AEC) proposed that an exclusion or 'quarantine' zone should be incorporated into nuclear reactor site designs. The size of the exclusion zone would be proportional to the power of the installed reactors. However, industrial firms were reluctant to agree to this proposal, arguing that investment should be targeted instead at strengthening reactor security. In 1956, the AEC opted for this latter approach on the premise that evacuation zones (which would be put into practice in the event of an accident) were preferable to exclusion zones (which were to be instituted *de facto*), which could prompt unnecessary fear and anxiety amongst the public (Foasso 2003). In 1957, a research team from the Brookhaven National Laboratory responded to a request from the AEC to develop scenarios for the evacuation of populations in the event of a nuclear accident. The findings of the report they prepared (the so-called "Wash-740" report) were alarming. They showed that a major accident at a 500 MWe reactor could result in the deaths of 3,400 people and the irradiation of more than 40,000. In addition, a huge area of about 240,000 square kilometres (*i.e.* bigger than Florida) would need to be evacuated, and the cost of this operation plus land and health costs would surpass US$7 billion (AEC 1957).

The political fallout from this report was profound (Foasso 2003). To protect the industry against such incommensurable financial risks, the US government, followed quickly by the principal nuclear states, drastically limited the financial liability of nuclear operators in the event of an accident (Price Anderson Act 1957; Paris Convention 1960; Vienna Convention 1966). In a sense, they responded to these exceptional risks with exceptional juridical and insurance arrangements that came down in favour of the nuclear industries (Topçu 2014). It should be noted here that Japan did not join the international movement of liability conventions launched in the 1960s. Japanese law opted instead for 'illimited liability' for nuclear operators in the event of an accident, although it did set a threshold for insurance costs, thereby tacitly limiting the liability of the operators (Nomura 2014).

The highly symbolic nature of the industrial liability costs – this was the only way to convince industrial firms to invest in the nuclear sector – inevitably created the need not only to categorize harm and prioritize remedies/compensation but also to control the public perception of risk and damage. In the 1960s, a major assumption became consolidated within this context, which was that a full evacuation of territories contaminated by a nuclear accident was impossible in technical, economic and social acceptability terms, in the same way that it was considered impossible to fully compensate for the related damage (an assumption confirmed by the accidents in 1979, 1986 and 2011). In other words, the nuclear experts admitted and even suggested that evacuations and compensations should be optimized. This led to the emergence of zoning as a major accident management tool. The modalities of zone management in the event of a nuclear accident (*i.e.* zones whose level of contamination determined the level of state intervention and types of compensation) had already been considered by the authors of the Wash-740 report. A five-level zoning approach was seen as plausible,[2] a method that greatly inspired the zoning and evacuation criteria established after the Chernobyl and Fukushima accidents. In 1991 (after the collapse of the USSR), another significant innovation appeared in the form of 'optional evacuation zones', a topic I will address further below. Hence, while the isolation, quarantine and even 'sacrifice' of the environment surrounding a nuclear site prevailed in the 1960s and 1970s, there was a gradual shift in emphasis to the optimal recovery of destroyed land after the Chernobyl accident.

Indeed, zoning came to serve multiple political functions in the field. The first function, which related to the emergency period, was that it allowed governments and experts to affirm through the use of a technical/rational tool that the problem was localized or confined and that the threat was therefore under control. The second was that the very existence of zones signified there were different levels of impact from radioactivity, which called for different levels of reparation. In other words, one person's experience of injury was to be considered in relation to other people's experiences, and the state was to decide reparation (*i.e.* compensation payouts) based on relative levels of seriousness. The third performative function of zoning concerned the fact that the very diagnostics of degree of harm (via zone hierarchies) implied that recovery over time was possible, because the status of zones could – and even should – evolve. Such a view proved to be particularly widespread in post-2011 Japan. According to current state discourses and policies related to post-accident management, zones are far from static or permanent and should quickly disappear. Overall then, zones were conceived and remain so, especially in the recent period, as dynamic socio-technical tools for an effective management of populations, land and public health. Zonal boundaries are not rigid, and even the 'strictly forbidden' zone(s) are permeable (Houdart 2020). The zones themselves are also subject to permanent recategorization/redefinition, sometimes as a result of social protests. From the outset, Japan adopted the so-called reconquest (of contaminated territories) strategy, which the IAEA described as 'post-accident recovery', aiming 'to re-establish an acceptable basis for a fully functioning society in the affected areas' (IAEA 2015). In the former USSR, return to the evacuated zones was not initially a priority. Indeed, after 1991, the evacuations were even expanded as a result of an initiative from the Ukrainian and Belarusian governments. However, by the late 1990s, 'returning to' or 'remaining in' (since many who should have been evacuated were never actually evacuated) zones contaminated by the Chernobyl accident had, as in post-2011 Japan, become a priority.

Based on the post-Chernobyl injunction to prevent the long-term devaluation or 'sacrifice' of land, and the different forms of compromise between land and human body contamination that it implied, I propose to call the contemporary post-accident reconstruction policies the *geobiological recovery of environments*. It is possible to distinguish at least three major managerial strategies, which I will develop further, at the heart of such a recovery: (1) geomanagement or zoning, whose ultimate form today appears to be the cancellation of the very idea of 'zone' itself; (2) biological or body management, where *states of exception* increasingly serve as the norm for the recovery of contaminated lands through a better exploitation of victims' bodies and health; (3) social management or engineering, which implies a shift away from a material recovery from disasters (in the short term) to the administration of social psychology over the longer term.

It should also be noted here that different forms of knowledge/ignorance production are central to each of these strategies as well as to the geobiological recovery of contaminated lands overall. Drawing on the dynamic field of agnotology (Proctor and Schiebinger 2008; Gross and McGoey 2015) and moving forward from Kuchinskaya's leading work on the production of invisibility in relation to the health effects of Chernobyl in Belarus (Kuchinskaya 2014), the ignorance I refer to here has less to do with secrecy, which can be defined as the confiscation of information or its conditions of production and which has a specific history with regard to nuclear issues (Topçu 2013a), and more to do with not producing knowledge (Frickel *et al.* 2010) or producing oblivion or forgetfulness on a matter that cannot be entirely ignored or kept secret, either because *nature* speaks for/reveals itself (altered species, ill/dead bodies, saturated hospitals/cemeteries, etc.) or because alternative or activist science and expertise speaks on its behalf, thereby revealing important 'knowledge gaps' (Frickel and Bess Vincent 2011). Ignorance production therefore consists of establishing conditions that force individuals to stop knowing, understanding, hearing, reading, being concerned about or even seeing their contaminated environment. Such dynamics are not confined to the nuclear industry; they can be observed in many other technoindustrial sectors that generate large-scale pollution – such as the pesticide sector (Dedieu and Jouzel 2015) and the asbestos industry (McCulloch and Tweedale 2008) – and in most industrial accidents (Frickel and Bess Vincent 2011; Centemeri 2014).

From Chernobyl to Fukushima: towards biopolitical 'zones'

Based on a definition of *contaminated land* as land with radioactivity levels higher than 1mSv (per year), the Chernobyl reactor no. 4 accident is reported to have contaminated around 200,000 square kilometres of land across Europe but mainly (71 per cent) in Belarus, Ukraine and Russia. The atmospheric release after the chain reactions at the three Fukushima units was estimated at approximately 10 to 20 per cent of the levels released after Chernobyl. Although 80 per cent of this was directed towards the Pacific Ocean, the contaminated land still covered around 13,000 square kilometres when radiation levels of above 1 mSv were applied. However, the Japanese state defined contaminated land as any area where radiation levels exceeded 20 mSv, and took on responsibility for decontamination work only in these areas (*i.e.* around 1,000 square kilometres once the forests and mountains, which accounted for 75 per cent of the region in question, were excluded), delegating the decontamination of zones with levels between 1 and 20 mSv to the municipalities (Kojima 2020).

After both the Chernobyl and the Fukushima accidents, the respective exclusion zones were initially determined somewhat arbitrarily. A circular zone was drawn around the destroyed reactor(s) in each case (20 kilometres for Fukushima; 30 kilometres for Chernobyl), and a rapid evacuation of the area was ordered. These exclusion zones underwent significant revisions as more sophisticated contamination maps were drawn up during the first days, weeks and even months after the accidents had occurred. This revision process lasted nine months in Fukushima and several years in Chernobyl. While the initial exclusion zone affected approximately 70,000 people in Japan and 90,000 people in the former USSR, the number of evacuees ultimately reached 200,000 in Japan and 350,000 in the former USSR (Ukraine, Belarus, Russian Federation).

Revalourization of the abandoned lands

There was no planned resettlement of populations in significant portions of the Chernobyl exclusion zones which were divided into subcategories, such as areas where access was forbidden or authorized only for public interest purposes and areas where people could spend the day but not stay overnight. In Japan, however, state officials announced in early 2012 that it was crucial to proceed to the recovery (reconquest) of the evacuated zones including towns within the 20 kilometre circle as far and as soon as possible. As a result, a large-scale decontamination project was launched involving nearly 15,000 workers on a daily basis, but its effectiveness came in for frequent criticism from non-governmental organizations (CRIIRAD 2017). In the case of Chernobyl, the exclusion zone included one city (Pripyat) and several villages. The Fukushima exclusion zone initially comprised five towns (Namie, Futaba, Okuma, Tomioka, Naraha) as well as parts of the city of Tamura and the village of Kawauchi. In 2015, however, Naraha, Tamura and Kawauchi were re-categorized as habitable, followed in 2016 by Minami-Sôma and Katsurao. By the end of March 2017, the evacuation order was scheduled to be cancelled – with financial compensation to be stopped shortly afterwards – for the whole of the officially evacuated zone except for the very limited 'difficult-to-return zones' (Boilley 2016). This latter category concerned zones where radioactive contamination exceeded 50 mSv (the authorized level was 20 mSv in Japan, 1 mSv elsewhere).

Surprisingly, even these highly contaminated zones were in no way considered by the Japanese government to be dead or definitively sacrificed, unlike in Chernobyl. This is why the initial category label, 'forbidden zone', was replaced with the euphemistic 'difficult-to-return zone' category only two years after Fukushima. In addition, the Japanese government announced a few years after the disaster that the evacuation orders would, by 2022, be lifted for these zones too and even for the 16 square kilometre area around the Fukushima plant, which was to be used as a temporary waste storage site for the huge amount of radioactive residue generated by the decontamination process (*i.e.* around 22 million cubic metres). New legislation providing for the revalourization/reconquest of this waste(ful) zone in less than 30 years was passed accordingly (Boilley 2017).

In Chernobyl, the revalorization of the restricted/abandoned zone was managed by other means than the gradual lifting of restrictions. A large number of valourization projects were undertaken, mainly in response to pressure from international nuclear agencies, in the 'sacrificed' city of Pripyat and its surrounding area, which had become a no-man's-land. A memory tourism – with group visits to the Sarcophagus (the Chernobyl power plant shelter structure) – and a scientific tourism developed around Pripyat. In the 2000s, experts from the IAEA launched a conservationist marketing strategy, claiming that Chernobyl's exclusion zone, referred to as the 'dead zone' for many years, *was in fact not dead at all* but rather a 'unique sanctuary for biodiversity' (IAEA 2006a) – a well-established myth that ignored independent scientific evidence on the degradation of biodiversity in the region (Mousseau and Moller 2011; 2014).

It was not just the exclusion zones that were strategically important for the nuclearists. The so-called optional evacuation zones, in particular, were subject to negotiations, controversies and ever-changing categorizations and regulations. This 'optional evacuation zones' category was elaborated in the early 1990s as part of new legislation adopted in Ukraine, Belarus and the Russian Federation. While these zones were not the most contaminated, the radiation levels could exceed the authorized limits in certain hotspots. In a neoliberal climate, individuals who had been living in these zones prior to the accident were 'free' to abandon their lands, homes and villages if they wished. This implied a transfer of responsibility for risk management from the state to the victims, who were expected to bear the costs either way (*i.e.* financial costs if they chose to leave, biological/health costs if they chose to stay). In the former Soviet Union, PR campaigns were run from the mid-1990s onwards to persuade people, especially the residents/former residents of these zones, either not to leave their homes or to return home. In Japan, most of those who had left, 'voluntarily' or on the state's orders, were subject to similar campaigns of persuasion. The post-Fukushima zoning policies resulted in different categories of victims, such as forced evacuees (*kyosei hinansha*) and voluntary evacuees (*jishu hinansha*), as the Japanese government distinguished between those who lived inside and those who lived outside the evacuation zones. Consequently, many people were excluded from the compensation plan launched by TEPCO and the state (Jobin 2020; Kojima 2020). The campaigns to persuade people to return home appeared to be more hostile towards those who had left on their own initiative. They are estimated at 26,600, according to official records. Sociological surveys have reported that these 'refugees' were frequently stigmatized, either directly or indirectly, by state officials and non-victims, as cowards or troublemakers who were jeopardizing the national effort to reconstruct Fukushima (Hasegawa 2015).

States of exception and body management

It is important to note that after both Chernobyl and Fukushima, exceptional health standards were established in order to limit the number of evacuations. As a result, not all those who needed to be evacuated were evacuated. In France, a similar action plan has been in place since the 2000s in the event of an accident. A study conducted by experts from the Institut de Radioprotection et de Sûreté Nucléaire (IRSN, Institute for Radioprotection and Nuclear Safety) a few years before the Fukushima accidents argued that, given the scale of land contamination caused by a major accident, the official measures undertaken in the event of a nuclear catastrophe in France would inevitably be 'non-optimal' in terms of 'sacrificing' agricultural and habitable land. The number of additional cancer cases engendered by such non-optimal choices were accordingly also incorporated into the accident cost estimations. The study showed that, in concrete terms, a major accident at the Dampierre nuclear plant (the case investigated), which is situated in the Loire region approximately 50 kilometres from the city of Orléans, would theoretically require the evacuation of 2.5 million people. However, the French authorities' plan was to evacuate only one-hundredth of this estimated number, or 25,000 victims. The experts added that such non-optimal evacuation measures would generate 17,500 supplementary cancer cases. The cost of these cancers to France's national health system was carefully calculated and incorporated into the accident 'budget' (IRSN 2007; Topçu 2014).

The Japanese government adopted a similar non-optimal land and health recovery policy immediately after the Fukushima chain accidents by increasing the acceptable low-dose level from 1mSv (the international norm fixed by the ICRP – International Commission for Radiological Protection) to 20 mSv, which is the maximal level set for nuclear workers in most nuclear countries (the authorized exposure level for Fukushima workers was raised to 250 mSv). Ignorance production in this context consisted of forcing people to definitively forget the 'good old days' of radioprotection and the 1 mSv threshold level by redefining as normal the 20 mSv level – and thereby transforming everybody (including children) into nuclear workers. Moreover, from 2011 onwards, the Japanese regulatory bodies maintained that the probability of developing radiation-related cancers below the dose limit of 100 mSv was negligible and that smoking and obesity were more risky than low-dose radioactivity (Jobin 2021). They thus circumvented the international scientific consensus on the linear non-threshold model (Hasegawa 2015). This situation shows that ignorance production was also about refounding national boundaries and bastions of truth. In the Chernobyl case, the radiation exposure level in the post-emergency (*i.e.* recovery) period was raised to 5 mSv under the Soviet regime and then lowered again to 1 mSv after 1991 (Russia, Ukraine, Belarus).[3] In practice, however, many people continued to live in regions where radioactivity levels far exceeded the 1 mSv level because their respective governments failed to resettle them. According to data from the IAEA, 5 million people were still living in contaminated areas 20 years after the Soviet accident. The total number of official victims was approximately 7 million across the three countries (IAEA 2006b).

In addition to exceptional health standards, management plans based on individual guidelines were drawn up for those evacuees strongly encouraged to return to the areas surrounding the Chernobyl and Fukushima sites. Indeed, evacuated land was normalized or cleaned up, not only through the decontamination work and application of the relevant technical criteria – which, in some cases, proved to be inefficient or temporary because of the unavoidable migration of radio-elements from one place to another – but also through people's willingness to obey state orders. Very often, people agreed to resettle in their former localities despite insoluble radioactive contamination. These so-called participatory rehabilitation guidelines played a key performative role in this context. They aimed to train victims on how to minimize their exposure to radionuclides as far as possible by providing advice on their daily food intake, use of water, walks in the forest and so on. The experts' assumption here was as follows: If the inhabitants who resettled in these *renormalized* areas continued to live as they had before (*i.e.* if they *did not* pay attention to the new – radioactive – condition of their environment), their land would gradually lose its normality (*i.e.* it would become 'contaminated' or 'exceptional' again), and these people would probably fall ill one day. If, however, they took some 'simple' steps and acted as responsible, informed citizens, they would not necessarily or immediately fall victim to radiation-related illnesses. As a result, the land on which they chose to (re)settle would preserve its normality and would not be stigmatized.

Similar 'participatory rehabilitation' guidelines were elaborated by a group of French experts called the Ethos team (Topçu 2013b), financed by the European Commission in the late 1990s. The guidelines were tested in the Brest region of Belarus, where one-quarter of the territory was contaminated. The Ethos experts saw taking responsibility for one's own health and managing radioactivity risks at individual level as ways to become 'empowered', to shake off the loser or victim mentality and to valourize oneself and one's land and property. They promoted individual efforts to adopt new – exceptional – life standards or habits as the remedy for sick land, to make it functional, hospitable, fertile and thus economically valuable again. Thanks to the victims' collaboration, land would no longer be 'sacrificed'. However, this 'sacrifice' was to silently shift from the territorial to the biological arena (*i.e.* the victims' bodies).

The EU Ethos project further explored ways to make the land in Brest (Belarus) profitable again and gradually open it up to agricultural exploitation – a resilience strategy that had already been explored by the Soviet nuclear authorities during the Cold War, especially after the Mayak nuclear disaster, which was kept secret for 30 years (Brown 2013; Kasperski and Topçu 2016). In the aftermath of the Chernobyl accident, for example, the IAEA and the FAO launched a large-scale project in the Gomel and Mogilov regions of Belarus, which were more contaminated than Brest, with the aim of developing 'clean' rapeseed oil production (World Bank 2002). Similar strategies and guidelines implemented under the leadership of the Ethos and ICRP experts, amongst others, have been in effect in the Fukushima region since 2011 (Kimura 2017; Ribault 2019).

From biological 'sacrifice' to the social psyche

Beyond the biological 'exploitation' of victims' bodies and health, nuclear states and agencies gradually came to realize that the management of social psychology was crucial to a quick 'recovery' of contaminated zones. In the early 1990s, experts from the WHO, the IAEA, the OECD and the World Bank were highly critical of the official management of the consequences of the Chernobyl accident, not because Ukraine, Belarus or the Russian Federation did not or could not assure all the resettlements they had promised to their people, but because they had overpromised. Indeed, the reports and studies from international agencies were almost univocal in condemning the post-Chernobyl evacuation and compensation policies for being overly cautious, economically unsustainable and politically counter-productive. They claimed that the governments' uncareful examination of the pollution situation had unnecessarily increased the devalourization of land and resources, which in their opinion had generally been unfairly labeled as contaminated. They argued that too many evacuations provoked fear, trauma and even mental illnesses such as anxiety and depression amongst the local populations. The concept of radiophobia was developed based on such assumptions. The international bodies also believed that the Soviet and post-Soviet governments' excessive desire to compensate and assist the victims could create a mentality of permanent victimship and a heavy dependence on the state. For example, a group of international experts commissioned by the United Nations Development Programme suggested in 2002:

> Bringing condemned land back into economic use would be a powerful marker of the process of recovery for potential investors and in terms of the psychology of the communities concerned. The issue needs to be carefully considered by these communities, working with appropriate specialists and local and national government agencies. Wherever possible, the assumption should be that local people should have the choice of where to live and work, provided the interests of vulnerable individuals, including children, can be properly protected.
>
> (UNDP 2002)

The health effects were thus minimized and the psychological issues were maximized. In short, it can safely be argued that the international bodies, including first and foremost the IAEA and the WHO, believed the biggest harm from Chernobyl was psychological (Kuchinskaya 2014). In the case of Fukushima, too, the psychologization of harm and the official strategies to control public fear and concern proved to be central (Ribault 2019). At an international level, the UNSCEAR and the IAEA have argued since 2013 that:

> [t]he most important health effect [from the Fukushima accidents] is on mental and social well-being, related to the enormous impact of the earthquake, tsunami and nuclear accident, and the fear and stigma related to the perceived risk of exposure to ionizing radiation.
>
> (UNSCEAR 2013; IAEA 2015)

At a national level, the nuclear experts in Japan took on the mission from the outset of teaching people 'to fear correctly' by popularizing two distinct categories, *anzen* and *anshin*, meaning 'safety' (*i.e.* objective, officially defined safety) and 'feeling of safety' (*i.e.* subjective, emotional, unofficially defined safety), respectively (Shirabe *et al*. 2015). They put forward the experts' ways of defining and measuring the risks as the only way of evaluating the fallout from the catastrophe – a phenomenon that Hirakawa and Shirabe (2015) described as 'scienceplanation'. In this context, the denial of risk was an important component of the scienceplanation policy adopted by the Japanese government, which waited several weeks before reclassifying the severity of the catastrophe from the initial level, 4, to level 7 on the International Nuclear and Radiological Event Scale, and it took more than two months for TEPCO to announce that the Unit 1 reactor had actually gone into meltdown on the very first day of the accident (Figueroa 2013). Overall, the risk communication discourses of the Japanese authorities and expert bodies were embedded in a very specific conception of the public as either ignorant receivers of exaggerated information or victims of 'pure rumours' (*ibid.*).

Indeed, in the post-Fukushima context, *rumour* (*fūhyō* in Japanese) proved to be a major tool not just of risk governance and compensation management but of social engineering more generally. The Japanese government believed that unofficial and critical evaluations of the situation in Fukushima and bad publicity (renamed as 'rumour') about it did more harm than the becquerels. Because the damage from the accidents was 'so difficult to fully comprehend as it is both colorless and odorless' and because it demonstrated 'aspects of a "compound disaster",ature, including the harmful rumors that have spread domestically and overseas' (Reconstruction Design Council 2011), the government launched a war against rumours as a corollary to its policy to reconquest contaminated lands, which some analysts have described as 'disaster nationalism' (Kimura 2016: 151). While appealing for 'hope', 'harmonious coexistence', 'national consensus', 'community empowerment' and the cultivation of 'linkages' (or bonds, *kizuna*) (Reconstruction Design Council 2011; Dudden 2012), this 'war' also appears to have been a powerful ignorance production tool. It made invisible the complex and mostly irreversible nature of the radioactive contamination that polluted the Fukushima region, its land, resources and food products. It also gave the impression that everything had been or could be brought under control (except for 'external threats', such as rumours) in a context in which, a decade on from the accidents, the damaged reactors were still far from stabilized and uncertainties regarding the permanent movement of caesium, iodine, strontium and the many other dangerous radionuclides that colonized the soil, forests, atmosphere, water and people's bodies were likely to keep growing.

Since 2011, this national war against rumours has been more than just a battle over the best or most legitimate expertise within which 'inexpert' viewpoints are likely to be denigrated. It has involved intensive political efforts, such as the government's successful bid to host the Summer Olympics 2020 in Tokyo, the 'Solidarity with Fukushima' campaigns launched in Tokyo and elsewhere (inviting the public to consume food products from the Fukushima region in order to combat the rumours) and more direct methods like the tightening of state control over media coverage, especially in relation to the evaluation of the consequences of Fukushima.

Another area in which the Japanese government's war against rumours played a key role was compensation payouts. In May 2011, Japan's Dispute Reconciliation Committee for Nuclear Damage Compensation (DRCNDC) created a new category of damage to be taken into account in the compensation of victims, called 'rumour-related damage' (*fūhyō higai*). It is defined as

> concern about the risk of contaminated radioactive material in relation to products or services, due to facts that are widely known through media reports, leading consumers or trading partners to refrain from purchasing the product or service, or stop trading in the product or service, resulting in damage.
>
> (DRCNDC 2012: 110)

According to the DRCNDC, rumour-related damage was closely related to the consumers' or trading partners' 'psychological state of wanting to avoid the product or service' (*ibid.*: 111).

The official texts underline the fact that Japan's recognition of rumour-related damage was embedded in ambiguity, since such a categorization unavoidably influenced the rumour-related damage itself (thereby reinforcing the rumour and thus the damage). This is why rumour-related damage, just like 'mental anguish damage' due to evacuation, was categorized as a temporary damage. More important, however, is the fact that a significant proportion of the compensation budget was allocated to rumour-related damage. Neither extended land contamination nor health consequences were considered important.[4] What people considered to be acceptable and safe was framed as a major problem and prioritized in the political agenda. It is clear, even from some official reports (Fassert and Hasegawa 2019: 98–102), that what people lived in (*i.e.* a degraded environment), experienced and suffered from (irradiation, diseases) in their bodies and within the nuclear Anthropocene was given a secondary place.

Conclusion

Numerous reports, sociological surveys, opinion polls and statistical data now highlight the tensions generated, particularly in Japan, by what I have called geobiological recovery. First and foremost, despite intensive official campaigns in Japan stating that it was safe to return to the (de)contaminated zones, the average rate of return in March 2018 was only 15 per cent, and most of this number were older adults (Fassert and Hasegawa 2019). In addition, disenchanted by the institutional recovery policies, the victims have recently intensified juridical action through a collective mobilization for justice (Jobin 2020). They consider that the deteriorated living conditions and health of the affected communities have been underinvested by the state, which has put the biggest emphasis on the decontamination and normalization of previously inhabited zones. While the many 'ordinary' forms of reparation mobilized by farmers (see Chapter 6), mothers (Kimura 2016), environmental NGOs and citizen scientists continue to expand, juridical reparation is becoming the tool of choice for the (re)politicization of the problems posed by the Fukushima chain accidents.

These dynamics indicate, on the one hand, how ineffective top-down recovery or repair policies can be, regardless of how much money is allocated to them to make them succeed. On the other, they reveal the importance of defining what is affected by a disaster (habitable land? people? ecosystems? everything?). Arguably, the decision-makers' sectorization of different types of potential victims (under the form of physical environment *vs*. human beings and their bodies, for instance) aims above all to make public action effective as cheaply and as quickly as possible in order to restore life to what it was (or almost was) before the accident and thus to restore technoindustrial activity and economic growth. While this kind of sectorization has led to a narrow and technicalized form of repair – which I have proposed to call geobiological recovery – in the cases discussed here, such reductionism also offers the advantage that social scientists as well as actors in the field can better decrypt and reframe the issues at stake. One issue concerns, of course, the many, often interconnected, forms of repair. In contrast to the top-down reductionist visions imposed by decision-makers, these various forms of repair should be discussed, negotiated and activated in the case of a nuclear disaster. Another issue concerns the need to recognize that not everything can or will be targeted for repair in a post-accident context, even though the damage may appear, at least for a time, to be *re-covered*.

Acknowledgement

I would like to thank Laura Centemeri and Paul Jobin for their valuable comments on this work.

Notes

1 The category of 'nuclearists' I mobilize here refers to a range of actors (states, industries, government agencies, scientific and media organizations, trade unions) who promote nuclear energy as a 'system' of government (in terms of production/consumption, profit-making, sociopolitical organization and control, etc.). Those I describe as 'anti- nuclearists' reject the generalization of such a system (see Topçu 2013a).

2 R1: urgent evacuation (within 12 hours); R2: evacuation required, but more time is available to prepare; R3: restrictions on agriculture and temporary evacuation; R4: destruction of crops and restrictions on agriculture; R5: no restrictions, but regular radiologic monitoring is required (see AEC 1957: Appendix D).

3 During the emergency period, the threshold levels temporarily set by the USSR were much higher (*i.e.* 500 mSv per year in the period 12–22 May 1986; 100 mSv per year after 22 May 1986) (Kuchinskaya 2014).

4 According to the DRCNDC (2011), the loss in property value (loss of value due to exposure, etc.) was estimated to be around JPY 570.7 billion, whereas loss due to 'rumour-related

damage' (agriculture, forestry, fisheries, manufacturing, services, etc.) was estimated at JPY 1.3039 trillion (see OECD 2012: 59).

References

AEC (US Atomic Energy Commission). (1957) *Theoretical Possibilities and Consequences of Major Accidents in Large Nuclear Power Plants*, The Unites States Atomic Energy Commission: Wash 740 Report.

Anders, G. (2006) *La menace nucléaire: considérations radicales sur l'âge atomique*, Paris: Serpent à Plumes.

Ardt, M. (ed.) (2012) 'Special Issue: Memories, Commemorations and Representations of Chernobyl', *The Anthropology of East Europe Review*, 30(1): 1–140.

Bleicher, A. and Gross, M. (2011) 'Response and Recovery in the Remediation of Contaminated Land in Eastern Germany', in B.L. Allen and R.A. Dowty (eds) *Dynamics of Disaster: Lessons on Risk, Response and Recovery*, London: Earthscan, 187–202.

Boilley, D. (2016) *Fukushima Five Years Later: Back to Normal?*, Hérouville Saint Clair: ACRO Report for Greenpeace Belgium.

Boilley, D. (2017) 'Fukushima: l'obstination de la reconquête', *L'Acronique de Fukushima*. <http://fukushima.eu.org/fukushima-lobstination-de-la-reconquete/>.

Brown, K. (2013) *Plutopia: Nuclear Families, Atomic Cities and the Great Soviet and American Plutonium Disasters*, New York: Oxford University Press.

Brown, K. (2019) *Manual for Survival: An Environmental History of the Chernobyl Disaster*, New York: W. W. Norton & Company.

Centemeri, L. (2014) 'What Kind of Knowledge is Needed about Toxicant-Related Health Issues? Some Lessons Drawn from the Seveso Dioxin Case', in S. Boudia and N. Jas (eds) *Powerless Science? Science and Politics in a Toxic World*, Oxford and New York: Berghahn Books, 134–151.

CRIIRAD (The French Commission for Independent Research and Information on Radioactivity). (2017) 'Catastrophe de Fukushima Daiichi: un cauchemar sans fin', *Trait d'union*, 73. <www.criirad.org/actualites/dossier2011/japon_bis/Fukushima_6_ans_CRIIRAD.pdf>.

Dedieu, F. and Jouzel, J.-N. (2015) 'Comment ignorer ce que l'on sait? La domestication des savoirs inconfortables sur les intoxications des agriculteurs par les pesticides', *Revue française de sociologie*, 56(1): 105–133.

DRCNDC (The Japanese Dispute Reconciliation Committee for Nuclear Damage Compensation). (2012) 'Secondary Guidelines on Determination of the Scope of Nuclear Damage Resulting from the Accident at the Tokyo Electric Power Company Fukushima Daiichi and Daini Nuclear Power Plants (31 May 2011)', in OECD (ed.) *Japan's Compensation System for Nuclear Damage*, Paris: OECD.

Dudden, A. (2012) 'The Ongoing Disaster', *The Journal of Asian Studies*, 71(2): 345–359.

Fassert, C. and Hasegawa, R. (2019) *Shinrai Research Project: The 3/11 Accident and its Social Consequences. Case Studies from Fukushima Prefecture*, Paris: Report of the French Institute for Radioprotection and Reactor Safety (IRSN/2019/00178).

Figueroa, P.M. (2013) 'Risk Communication Surrounding the Fukushima Nuclear Disaster: An Anthropological Approach', *Asia Europe Journal*, 11(1): 53–64.

Foasso, C. (2003) *Histoire de la sûreté de l'énergie nucléaire en France (1945–2000): technique d'ingénieur, processus d'expertise, questions de société*, PhD thesis in History, Lyon: University of Lyon II.

Fortun, K., Knowles, S.G., Choi, V., Jobin, P., Matsumoto, M., de la Torre III, P., Liboiron, M. and Murillo, L.F.R. (2017) 'Researching Disaster from an STS Perspective', in U. Felt, R. Fouche, C.A. Miller and L. Smith-Doerr (eds) *The Handbook of Science and Technology Studies*, Cambridge, MA: The MIT Press.

Frickel, S. and Bess Vincent, M. (2011) 'Katrina's Contamination: Regulatory Knowledge Gaps in the Making and Unmaking of Environmental Contention', in B.L. Allen and R.A. Dowty (eds) *Dynamics of Disaster: Lessons in Risk, Response, and Recovery*, London: Earthscan, 11–28.

Frickel, S., Gibbon, S., Howard, J., Kempner, J., Ottinger, G. and Hess, D.J. (2010) 'Undone Science: Charting Social Movement and Civil Society Challenges to Research Agenda', *Science, Technology, & Human Values*, 35(4): 444–473.

Gross, M. and McGoey, L. (eds) (2015) *Routledge International Handbook of Ignorance Studies*, London and New York: Routledge.

Hasegawa, R. (2015) 'Returning Home after Fukushima. Displacement from a Nuclear Disaster and International Guidelines for Internally Displaced Persons', *Migration, Environment and Climate Change: Policy Brief Series*, 4(1): 1–8.

Hirakawa, H. and Shirabe, M. (2015) 'Rhetorical Marginalization of Science and Democracy: Politics in Risk Discourse on Radioactive Risks in Japan', in Y. Fujigaki (ed.) *Lessons From Fukushima: Japanese Case Studies on Science, Technology and Society*, Cham, Switzerland: Springer, 57–86.

Houdart, S. (2020) 'En déroute. Enquêter non loin de la centrale de Fukushima Daiichi, Japon', *SociologieS* (online). <http://journals.openedition.org/sociologies/14049>.

IAEA (International Atomic Energy Agency). (2006a) *Chernobyl's Legacy: Health, Environmental and Socio-Economic Impacts and Recommendations to the Governments of Belarus, the Russian Federation and Ukraine: The Chernobyl Forum 2003–2005*, Second Revised Version, Vienna: IAEA.

IAEA (International Atomic Energy Agency). (2006b) *Environmental Consequences of the Chernobyl Accident and their Remediation: Twenty Years of Experience: Report of the Chernobyl Expert Forum 'Environment'*, Vienna: IAEA.

IAEA (International Atomic Energy Agency). (2015) *The Fukushima Daiichi Accident: Report by the Director General*, Vienna: IAEA.

IRSN (The French Institute for Radioprotection and Nuclear Safety). (2007) *Examen de la méthode d'analyse coût – bénéfice pour la sûreté*, Paris: IRSN (Report N° DSR 157).

Jobin, P. (2017) '"Nuclear Gypsies" in Fukushima Before and After 3/11', in L.S. Macdowell (ed.) *Nuclear Portraits: Communities, The Environment, and Public Policy*, Toronto: University of Toronto Press, 274–311.

Jobin, P. (2020) 'The Fukushima Nuclear Disaster and Civil Actions as a Social Movement', *The Asia Pacific Journal*, 18(9): 1–27.

Jobin, P. (2021) 'Nuclear Labor, Its Invisibility, and the Dispute over Low-Dose Radiation' in K. Cleveland, S.G. Knowles and R. Shineha (eds) *Legacies of Fukushima: 3.11*, Philadelphia: University of Pennsylvania Press.

Kasperski, T. (2020) *Les politiques de la radioactivité. Tchernobyl et la mémoire nationale en Biélorussie contemporaine*, Paris: Petra.

Kasperski, T. and Topçu, S. (2016) 'De Maïak à Tchernobyl, la "guerre" radioactive: Une liquidatrice témoigne', *Mouvements*, 87. <mouvements.info/de-maiak-a-tchernobyl/>.

Kimura, A.H. (2016) *Radiation Brain Moms and Citizen Scientists: The Gender Politics of Food Contamination after Fukushima*, Durham, NC: Duke University Press.

Kimura, A.H. (2017) 'Fukushima ETHOS: Post-Disaster Risk Communication, Affect, and Shifting Risks', *Science as Culture*, 27(2): 1–20.

Kirsch, S. (2002) 'Watching the Bombs Go Off: Photography, Nuclear Landscapes, and Spectator Democracy', *Antipode*, 29: 3. <https://doi.org/10.1111/1467-8330.00045>.

Kojima, R. (2020) *Reconstruire dans l'après – Fukushima: responsabiliser et vulnérabiliser par le risque*, PhD thesis in Sociology, Paris: Université Paris-Est Marne-la-Vallée.

Kuchinskaya, O. (2014) *Politics of Invisibility: Public Knowledge About Radiation Health Effects After Chernobyl*, Cambridge, MA: MIT Press.

Lagadec, P. (1988) *États d'urgence. Défaillances technologiques et déstabilisation sociale*, Paris: Seuil.

Latour, B. (2004) 'Why has Critique Run Out of Steam? From Matters of Fact to Matters of Concern', *Critical Inquiry*, 30(2): 225–248.

Liberatore, A. (1999) *Management of Uncertainty: Learning from Chernobyl*, London: Routledge.

Matsumoto, M. (2013) '"Structural Disaster" Long before Fukushima: A Hidden Accident', *Development & Society*, 42(2): 165–190.

McCulloch, J. and Tweedale, G. (2008) *Defending the Indefensible: The Global Asbestos Industry and Its Fight for Survival*, Oxford: Oxford University Press.

Michael, M. (2014) 'Afterward: On the Topologies and Temporalities of Disaster', *The Sociological Review*, 62(S1): 236–245.

Mousseau, T.A. and Moller, A.P. (2011) 'Conservation Consequences of Chernobyl and Other Nuclear Accidents', *Biological Conservation*, 144: 2787–2798.

Mousseau, T.A. and Moller, A.P. (2014) 'Genetic and Ecological Studies of Animals in Chernobyl and Fukushima', *Journal of Heredity*, 105(5): 704–709.

Namioka, S. (2012) 'Politiques de dédommagement pour les agriculteurs de Fukushima? Le cas de la Nōminren', *Ebisu. Études Japonaises*, 47: 151–163.

Nomura, T. (2014) 'Le droit japonais de la responsabilité des dommages nucléaires et son évolution après l'accident de Fukushima', *Lavoisier. Revue Juridique de l'Environnement*, 39: 629–639.

OECD. (2012) *Japan's Compensation System for Nuclear Damage*, Paris: OECD.

Perrow, C. (1984) *Normal Accidents: Living with High-Risk Technologies*, New York: Basic Books.

Petryna, A. (2002) *Life Exposed: Biological Citizenship after Chernobyl*, Princeton, NJ: Princeton University Press.

Proctor, N.R. and Schiebinger, L. (eds) (2008) *Agnotology: The Making and Unmaking of Ignorance*, Redwood City, CA: Stanford University Press.

Reconstruction Design Council. (2011) *Towards Reconstruction: 'Hope beyond the Disaster'*, Report to the Prime Minister of Japan (25 June 2011). <www.mofa.go.jp/announce/jfpu/2011/7/pdfs/0712.pdf>.

Ribault, T. (2019) 'Resilience in Fukushima: Contribution to a Political Economy of Consent', *Alternatives: Global, Local, Political*, 44(2–4): 94–118.

Shirabe, M., Fassert, C. and Hasegawa, R. (2015) 'From Risk Communication to Participatory Radiation Risk Assessment', *Fukushima Global Communication Program Working Paper Series*, 21: 1–8.

Topçu, S. (2013a) *La France nucléaire. L'art de gouverner une technologie contestée*, Paris: Seuil.

Topçu, S. (2013b) 'Chernobyl Empowerment? Exporting Participatory Governance to Contaminated Territories', in S. Boudia and N. Jas (eds) *Toxicants, Health and Regulation since 1945*, Studies for the Society for the Social History of Medicine Series 6, London: Routledge, 135–158.

Topçu, S. (2014) 'Organiser l'irresponsabilité? La gestion (inter)nationale des dégâts d'un accident nucléaire comme régime discursif', *Écologie & Politique*, 49: 95–114.

UNDP (Unites Nations Development Programme). (2002) *The Human Consequences of the Chernobyl Nuclear Accident. A Strategy for Recovery.* A Report Commissioned by UNDP and UNICEF with the support of UN-OCHA and WHO. <www.by.undp.org/content/belarus/en/home/library/democratic_governance/publication_3.html>.

UNSCEAR (Unites Nations Scientific Committee on the Effects of Atomic Radiation). (2013) *Sources, Effects and Risks of Ionizing Radiation. UNSCEAR 2013 Report. Vol. 1. Scientific Annex A. Levels and Effects of Radiation Exposure Due to the Nuclear Accident after the 2011 Great East-Japan Earthquake and Tsunami*, New York: UN.

World Bank. (2002) *Belarus Chernobyl Review*, World Bank: Report n° 23883-BY. <http://documents.worldbank.org/curated/en/674871468767985013/pdf/multi0page.pdf>.

3 After the (Green) Revolution comes (ecological) restoration

Scientists and peasants in Pontal do Paranapanema, Brazil

Daniel Delatin Rodrigues

Introduction

The purpose of this chapter is to analyze, from a repairing perspective, the ecological restoration of degraded ecosystems exposed to the dynamics of 'slow violence' (Nixon 2011: 2), a term whose meaning is intended as 'violence that occurs gradually and out of sight, a violence of delayed destruction that is dispersed across time and space, an attritional violence that is typically not viewed as violence at all'. In particular, we are interested in discussing how ecological restoration is conceived in the Brazilian context and how it has been enacted in a specific case: that of the Pontal do Paranapanema, a region situated in the west of São Paulo state.

In this region, the need for repairing environments is not so much the result of an extreme event but rather of a historical continuum of violence against humans and non-humans, where precariousness and the threat of socio-ecological disruption are a condition of daily existence. More precisely, our focus will be on analyzing the perspectives and practices of restoration supported (or contested) by scientists and *assentados*[1] engaged in one specific project: the *macaúba* project.

The purpose of the *macaúba* project, launched in 2010, was never to go back to the supposedly pristine nature, nor to ignore the demands of non-humans in the name of decoupling socio-economic activities from ecological constraints.[2] By reinforcing the potentialities of new forms of ecological association offered by the *macaúba* plant (*Acrocomia aculeata*), the project's goal has been to increase local biodiversity and, at the same time, to promote forms of local economic organization orientated towards improving the living conditions of *assentados*. However, to achieve these goals it was necessary to create a shared capacity amongst different agents (humans and non-humans) that could guarantee the reproduction of this new multi-species assemblage over time.

As will be discussed further, the Pontal region is a territory marked by struggles for access to land, land being mostly occupied by landowners illegally, with the complicity of judges and politicians (very often, in turn, the owners of large estates). Since the 1980s, conflict around land access has become part of local socio-political dynamics, mostly by the initiative of social movements, in particular the Landless Workers' Movement (MST).[3]

DOI: 10.4324/9781003184782-5

We contend that, in this case, ecological restoration can be fruitfully studied through the framework of *dispositifs* and practices of repairing socio-ecological relations. As discussed in this book's introduction, the notion of repairing should be considered from a relational perspective, one that can show how repairing practices involve socio-technical, environmental and cultural aspects. Repairing in this perspective means to intervene in degraded ecosystems to redesign interactions between humans and non-humans, organics and minerals, with the aim of creating conditions for more just and sustainable socio-ecological becoming. As defined by Biehl and Locke (2010: 317) the category of becoming, borrowed from the work of Deleuze and Guattari (1987), can highlight the 'human efforts to exceed and escape forms of knowledge and power and to express desires that might be world altering'. The different intervention methods in degraded ecosystems are related to how this redesign takes place. In other words, it is important to question what kind of repairing practices are considered 'good' restoration, and why. In our case study, this will mean questioning how actors give form to interspecies relationships, justify their decisions, and what forms of co-involvement are thus produced.

In our understanding, *dispositifs* and practices of ecological restoration produce *agencements* (see Deleuze and Guattari 1987) of humans and non-humans in situated and experimental conditions. According to this *agencement* perspective, ecological restoration is always more than simply the sustainable management of natural resources, and it always partially deviates from preconceived expectations in terms of repairing. As suggested by Tsing (2015: 22–23), *agencements* can be defined as 'open-ended gatherings' which generate an openness to unexpected becoming when repairing meets ecological restoration. This implies paying attention both to human actors' 'normative expectations' (Dodier and Barbot 2016) and to how human and non-human actors are enrolled in a dynamic that creates new pathways for a multiplicity of life-forms.

As we discuss in the first section of this chapter, the idea that ecological restoration means a return to the 'original nature' of the past does not have any serious scientific grounds. The impossibility of restoring the past raises the problem of the legitimacy of imposing or favouring certain associations, whereby ecological restoration defines a space in terms of where and how plants and animals can live. Reading ecological restoration through the notion of repairing is a way to make visible and to investigate the power to define the possibilities of existing in an ecosystem. Thus the framework of repairing opens a potential avenue for the expression of critique. In fact, the power to define what to restore and how is usually a matter for experts, but a repairing perspective allows the inclusion of other agents, such as environmental activists and farmers. Through the example of the *macaúba* project, we want to show how restoration can be a way to create a possibility for multi-species coexistence that can actively reject/resist the exclusively extractivist-productivist focus that industrial agriculture still tends to impose in restoration projects in Brazil through the frame of 'natural services'. In our case study, the extreme social vulnerability of *assentados* is not ignored by scientists and technicians, who are sensitive to their difficulties beyond being concerned with biodiversity issues. However, the *assentados* are also faced with a variety of 'modes of ordering' (Law 1994) which are at play at the local level and are largely beyond their control, as they are enacted through public policies (that regulate fluxes, circulation and ownership), political struggles (including the violence of landlords and armed militias) and dominant economic models, especially multinational companies in the agribusiness sector that work with GMO seeds, agrochemicals and technical assistance – what in Brazil has been defined as the agricultural modernization package.

Understanding ecological restoration as a socio-ecological experimental practice

Ecological restoration transforms the ecological destruction generated by the impacts of modernization trajectories (Scott 1998) in a field of research and intervention. Historically, the field took shape around two journals: *Ecological Restoration* (born in 1981) and *Restoration Ecology* (born in 1993). The latter became the official journal of the Society for Ecological Restoration (SER), which was founded in 1988.

Two different approaches progressively took shape in this field: a mainstream ecological restoration approach, focused on ecosystem productivity, and an alternative one, focused on the idea of multi-species assemblages. Following Isabelle Stengers (2000), one can say that the mainstream approach exemplifies the kind of 'royal science' that imposes a model to be reproduced everywhere, despite differences, while the alternative approach is an example of a 'nomadic science' that, in contrast, uses singularities as an opportunity for experimentation. As a nomadic science, ecological restoration should be based on experimenting with alternative forms of co-existence without reducing ecosystems to providers of 'natural services' (Castree 2008).

Ecological restoration was born nomadic. In fact, unlike conservation biology and the conservation devices that accompanied it (Soulé 2014), ecological restoration originated from the rejection of a strict separation between nature and culture while promoting an experimental practice of socio-ecological assemblages.

As explained by Court (2012), these 'experiments' were based on the hybridization of agents (human and non-human) and temporality (old and new 'natural' fragments). Ecological restorers, by induction, created ecological systems that 'worked'. The purpose was not to recreate an ideal ecosystem but instead to assemble varied components in a new ecosystem, not completely known in advance, which would result from these assemblages (Clewell 1993).

Rejection of the ideal of recovering an 'authentic nature' has allowed the development of ecological restoration practices in two directions. On the one hand, traditional ecosystems can serve as a reference system for a socio-biodiverse composition when historical data and ecological conditions are reunited (*i.e.* the existence of species that allow a return to something similar that existed in the past) (Higgs 2003). On the other hand, restoration practices can be oriented to the creation of neo-ecosystems (Hobbs *et al.* 2006). In this latter case, the practice is that of following the existing connexions in the field to optimize resources.

According to Pickett and Parker (1994), it is the understanding of nature in flux (rather than in equilibrium) that brought ecological restoration practitioners to pay attention to ecosystems as open systems that are regulated by processes that take place outside their borders: this implies that ecological restoration should take into account human populations and communities, beyond the notion of ecosystems as simply natural spaces. Two consequences follow (Pickett and Parker 1994: 75–76): the first is that ecological restoration is seen as a process, marked by change and openness, incorporating movements and interactions between organisms, material and energy flows, succession paths and changes in patchiness. The second is the importance of the ecological context, which redefines the inputs and outputs of a system – that is, its connexions. This notion of context reminds ecologists that the system is embedded in heterogeneous and dynamic landscapes. In this experimentation, multiple agents can be considered bioengineers, or builders of nature (see Handel 2013).

According to Gross (2002: 24), 'restoration does not follow a set action masterplan; it is pieced together and built up, thought about and tried out, formulated and reformulated, always in negotiation with other people and nature'. Ecological restoration practitioners should embrace 'ignorance and surprise', because it is through dealing with these issues that the process of ecological and social learning takes place. Restorers should then regard uncertainties as a constitutive feature of their practice that reveals its experimental condition (Gross 2010).

Approaching ecological restoration as social-material experimentations also brings to the foreground the socio-cultural dimensions involved in ecological restoration. That is, while it is important to study how scientists act to modify the composition of ecosystems, one should be equally attentive to the socio-cultural forms that are generated in this process. Limiting the perspective to just the interactions between non-human agencies is often combined with the uncritical adoption of objectives that the anthropologist Eric Higgs (2003) denounces as close to the idea of 'commodification of nature'. Engineers, scientists and technicians involved in ecological restoration thus become managers, whose function is to guarantee the increase of natural systems' productivity. This commodification is related to the purified distinction between nature and culture that makes ecological restoration practices vulnerable to being 'captured' (Pignarre and Stengers 2005) by agro-industrial logics.

Against a productivist understanding of ecological restoration, Higgs (2003: 127–128) highlights that 'good ecological restoration' should always include consideration of economic, social, cultural, political, aesthetic and moral aspects, through combining ethical and technical issues.

However, for Higgs, as for Gross, ecological restoration should include social aspects in its practice, as if the social needs to be added in order to prevent ecological restoration from becoming an exclusively technological practice. Conversely, as I am going to show in discussing the *macaúba* project, the social aspect of the restoration cannot be added afterwards because it is produced simultaneously with the ecological system design. But before presenting the case study, it is important, in order to better grasp its specificities, to explain how ecological restoration has been practiced in the Brazilian context, with a focus on the Pontal do Paranapanema region.

Restoration, exploitation and ecological transformations in Pontal do Paranapanema

In the Brazilian context, the beginning of ecological restoration in the 1980s was theoretically and practically associated with the science of forestry (Hatje 2016). Following James Scott (1998), we can say that the science of forestry cannot be dissociated from state-promoted large-scale projects of territorial planning and economic development. Regulated by central authorities to manage timber reserves and stocks, the science of forestry aims at creating forests that can be managed rationally so as to optimize the production of the forest as a resource. Instead of managing species with several growth phases, as is the case in wild forests, scientific management of forests requires the creation of a homogeneous space-time frame. This is the mechanism used to force the multiplicities of life trajectories into the logic of promoting nature's productivity. Since their appearance in the late eighteenth century, these 'social engineering' initiatives were meant to design a manageable environment for economic purposes. In this sense, the new forest science 'was called cameral science, an effort to reduce the fiscal management of a kingdom to scientific principles that would allow systematic planning' (Scott 1998: 14).

The need to create a manageable forest required the selection of suitable species for the production of the desired benefits. This, in turn, produced a parallel movement of identifying species defined as wild or considered as pests and therefore useless or even dangerous. Moreover, to recreate the forest as a manageable system, scientists must engage in research and experimentation with associations of species. They should be able to stabilize a heterogeneous set of elements in a system capable of perpetuating itself over time and in a given space.

The association between the forest and the productivity of natural services has been a reference for the way practitioners of ecological restoration in Brazil have traditionally planned their practice and analyzed its potential, its risks and the limits of restoration interventions. By focusing predominantly on the arboreal aspects of ecosystems (Durigan and Melo 2011), restorers adapted their scientific model to a paradigm that prioritized, according to Reis *et al.* (2006: 5), a 'climax situation of formed forest'. If, in the beginning, the practice of ecological restoration was linked with the goals of a protective forest, mostly to control soil erosion and water quality, recently the language adopted by some practitioners has justified the intervention of restoration to increase the ecosystem and agriculture productivity (Rodrigues *et al.* 2009). Reis *et al.* (2006) showed that these methodologies were based primarily on planting a certain number of species of tree to attain the climax situation more quickly. These techniques worked by introducing species and excluding components that could deregulate the system: 'in this context, the ecosystem is seen as a factory of productivity and with a collection of selected and isolated species in a defined space' (Reis *et al.* 2006: 5). These critics show that restoration practitioners depend on this ideal model of fixed and immutable nature – nature that is separated from social dynamics and can be engineered to optimize its ecological functions (Boyd *et al*. 2001).

Before 1980, the decision on whether or not to carry out restoration was left to the Brazilian state. It was mainly as a result of the implementation of hydroelectric projects that reforestation actions were found to be necessary to mitigate environmental impacts. As observed by Durigan and Melo (2011: 329):

> The huge riparian forest recovery around Itaipu dam reservoir on the Brazil-Paraguay border, one of the largest restoration projects in the world, was started in 1979, before the legal imposition, and reforested more than 60,000 hectares with native and exotic species.

According to Rodrigues *et al*. (2009: 1246), 'Laws regulating the use of native forests have existed in Brazil since 1965 but have rarely been respected.[4] Only in the 1980s did increasing social concern for the Atlantic Forest pressure governments to enforce these laws more rigorously'.

Gradually, the restored forest acquired new functions beyond that of being a *dispositif* to protect endangered species, land and water (Rodrigues *et al*. 2009; Oliveira 2011), and new actors were involved in the maintenance of biodiversity and restoration actions. From a context dominated by debates between governmental agencies and NGOs in the 1960s and 1970s (Viola 1987), farmers were gradually transformed into agents responsible for safeguarding the existing forest remnants. The 1980s saw the strengthening of movements for democratization and the end of military dictatorship (Dean 1996; Bacha 2004), at the same time as a reformulation of the ecological perspective in a socio-ecological key, as demonstrated by the struggle of *seringueiros* in the north of the country led by Chico Mendes (1944–1988).

The framework of sustainable development (as defined in the Brundtland report of 1987) brought a new perspective on the relationship between agriculture and biodiversity conservation, as exemplified by the National Programme for Strengthening Family Agriculture (PRONAF), launched in 1996 by the federal government. Once they became part of the *dispositifs* of conservation and restoration, small farmers were forced by environmental legislation to expand forest areas by managing them in such a way that agriculture and biodiversity could be articulated. (They were punished if they refused.) Rural areas were transformed into priority areas for experimentation with the sustainable management of natural resources (Viana and Amador 1998). However, planting a 'natural' forest required an infrastructure for providing the variety of species considered suitable for 'good' restoration through forest nurseries; it also required an extensive workforce to maintain a 'natural' forest, something that proved to be extremely expensive.

Instead of focusing on reproduction of the past, the practice of restoration became progressively more open to experimentation and attentive to the interaction between agents. The objective was that of 'restoring the basic ecological processes of the forest by the stimulation and acceleration of natural succession, aiming to recover the forest's ability to maintain itself' (Rodrigues *et al*. 2009: 1244). The idea was that scientists should consider dynamic processes of inter-action without seeking a predefined climax situation. Restorers began to take into account the relationships that were created through pollination, between the dispersing agents (birds, mammals), the microorganisms and insects that pro-duce diversity, as well as the importance of soil composition (Reis *et al*. 2006). The role of the farmers can no longer be that of guardians of biodiversity, but rather one in which they are enrolled in inter- and intraspecies interaction as dynamic processes of *agencement* composition.

The practice of ecological restoration we have observed during our research in Pontal do Paranapanema needs to be situated in this evolution of restoration practices, at the point in which the stability of agents is no longer a given: scien-tists are no longer simply engineers of nature, farmers are no longer guardians of biodiversity, and non-humans are not mere fragments of an original nature to be recreated. Moreover, the intense political conflicts in the region have turned the collaborations between the various actors into a challenging (and fragile) process of association.

Because restoration is not orientated towards the return to a specific nature that existed in the past, nor is it a way to create an ecosystem entirely dependent on human designs and objectives, the operative mechanism to recreate and repair socio-ecosystems is based on the negotiation of socio-ecological perspectives and trajectories. To 'negotiate' here refers to the practical activity of experimenting with encounters and dealing with what emerges from such encounters. This exper-imentation involves selection of the area, the composition of the different species (according to the growth phases and dimensions of the trees), the techniques used for planting trees (such as direct planting, sowing or spontaneous growth) and the distance between the trees. Spacing is a central issue, since it has an impact on the possibility of using machinery, such as tractors, instead of human labour. All these aspects contribute to the design of the ecosystem and determine the way in which life processes can develop and what kinds of attachment the *assentados* will form in everyday life, both to work and to leisure activities.

This kind of experimentation also implies the production of social practices that can attach a durable human/non-human relationship – for example, through the identification of a non-human agent (in our case, the *macaúba* plant) that can sup-port the actions of human agents (*assentados*) and a specific agricultural approach (agro-ecology). Moreover, the *macaúba* project is a politically engaged project, in that it attempts to enable a different form of socio-ecological arrangement that can resist the productivity logic of the commodification of nature and at the same time create different paths to both biodiversity and *assentamentos*.

The *macaúba* project was developed by the Luiz de Queiroz Agrarian Studies Foundation (FEALQ), of the Luiz de Queiroz School of Agriculture at the Univer-sity of São Paulo (ESALQ-USP), with funding from the then Ministry of Agrarian Development (MDA) through the Secretariat of Family Agriculture (SAF) as part of the National Programme for the Production and Use of Biodiesel (PNPB).

The first phase of the *macaúba* project (2010–2012), according to Sergio Ribeiro (of the MST),[5] had limited scope, 'with only 15 families participating'. The low take-up, he said, was partly due to the farmers' unfamiliarity with the proposal. They were sceptical about the purpose of 'planting thorns', given that the *macaúba* is full of thorns. It was not made clear by the ESALQ/USP team how this intervention could benefit the local socio-ecological context – whether by the connexion with the development plans of the State of São Paulo or the national energy plan for biofuels. In Sergio's opinion, in a project such as this, with many actors and issues, 'the concreteness was lost' in the practical relationships with the community. The second phase of the project (the object of our fieldwork), developed from 2013 to 2015, was aimed at promoting agroforestry systems in the region of Pontal do Paranapanema, operating in four municipalities (Caiuá, Mirante do Paranapanema, Presidente Epitácio and Teodoro Sampaio), with the participation of 55 *assentados* (family members included).

The Pontal do Paranapanema region has been marked by radical socio-ecological transformations. Instituted by decree in 1943, the Great Reserve of Pontal do Paranapanema originally covered 247,000 hectares. The designation of an entire region as a reserve was an attempt to regulate and put an end to the fierce disputes between state authorities, rural workers and landlords over land tenure related to the mostly illegal occupation (by landlords) of the existing land (Dean 1996).

Over a period of almost 100 years (1850–1930), the land occupation of the region was marked by major discontinuities and oscillations. The first settlement was established by Emperor Dom Pedro II: its purpose was the creation of an advanced border detachment as protection against Paraguayan incursions that threatened to compromise the territorial integrity of Brazil (Leite 1998). Occupation was also related to economic factors (Dean 1996), since the region was supplying raw materials (woods) for energy production to industries in São Paulo (Monbeig 1984). According to Leonidio (2009: 37), the initial occupation of the region between 1850 and 1930 'was characterized by a combined relationship of three extremely violent processes: land grabbing, the extermination of indigenous populations [Kaigang and Caiuas] and destruction of the natural environment'.

According to Leite (1998), the fires many farmers in the region used as a strategy to consolidate their ownership made state efforts for conservation of the area as an ecological reserve ineffective. In fact, the decades between 1940 and 1960 were marked by acceleration of the region's deforestation (Dean 1996), with the formation of pastures and the creation of plantations, mainly of coffee, cotton and mint, and the implementation of the first agro-industry for the processing of cotton. A crisis in the cotton and coffee trade between 1960 and 1980 led to vast areas being turned over to livestock, a rural exodus and land concentration (Santos 2012).

The situation of land concentration and the social inequalities resulting from the very process of occupation of Pontal do Paranapanema are the main causes of conflicts in the region. The struggles undertaken in Pontal and in other regions of the country, mostly on the initiative of the MST, and the expropriations that took place provoked a reaction amongst the many *latifundiarios* (large landowners). The Ruralist Democratic Union (UDR) was founded in 1985 in Presidente Prudente (the most important city, economically and politically, in the region) to defend the landowners' interests and resist what was seen as an attempt to violate their private property. The actions promoted by the group included the creation of an armed militia, justified as a form of legal self-defence, to prevent occupations and expel, with extreme violence, the occupiers.

After the occupation of the region, the semideciduous seasonal forest that had previously prevailed was replaced by pasture and agriculture, leaving only approximately 5 per cent of the area covered by the Great Reserve (Ditt 2002: 28); according to Santos (2012: 169), the percentage could be as low as 2 per cent. This type of occupation induced a series of radical reconfigurations of the territory as a result of the removal of vegetation, which led to soil erosion and the silting up of rivers. Changes in recent decades have altered the landscape of Pontal in which the areas used for agriculture and cattle-rearing began to predominate over the remaining forest fragments.

It is in this context that ecologists from local NGOs, biologists and agronomists from universities, and public agencies have tried to develop a new model of ecological restoration through the launch of the *macaúba* project. Three different types of specialist were thus involved in the project: academic researchers working in the field of agrarian and ecology science, technicians in public agencies, and members of the MST with scientific-technical training in the agrarian field. In this last case, scientific knowledge was seen as a tool in the peasant struggles and in the development of more autonomous and ecologically responsible agricultural practices. Implementation of the project, however, has meant dealing with political conflicts, the constraints of economic viability, and public policies (such as food security and bioenergy). All these issues have constrained the way technical and ecological knowledge has been applied in the project and, more generally, its transformative potential.

The precariousness of repairing *agencements* in the *macaúba* project

The *macaúba* project was coordinated by Paulo Kageyama (1945–2016), a researcher born in the region, who tried to address two interconnected issues: promote the conservation and restoration of biodiversity with agro-ecology and agroforestry techniques that could change the industrial agriculture production. By working directly with local MST members, the project was an attempt to give a socio-technical solution to an ecologically degraded landscape while fulfilling the need for local food security. Food security has been a priority of the Ministry of Agrarian Development and the object of one of the most important programmes developed in the first term of the presidency of Luiz Inácio Lula da Silva (2003–2006).

It is important to highlight that the *macaúba* project was linked to previous projects in the region, but it aimed at redefining the way ecological restoration was presented to the public in terms of the kinds of obligation and demand it imposed on *assentados*. Extended over time and space, it relied on the implementation of diverse types of *dispositif*: a federal food procurement programme for schools, a biodiversity conservation plan for the region, a national programme for biofuel production, and a national human rights and food security policy. In the region, several initiatives developed by NGOs and by the Land Institute of São Paulo State (ITESP) already existed that aimed to help the *assentados* to solve the environmental problems that confronted the settlements.

Vast areas for grazing cattle and sugar cane production dominate the region's landscape. The practice of burning, which has only recently diminished, continues to cast fine, toxic soot into the air. The prospect of transforming the landscape, productive systems and settlers' range of activities was part of the political strategy of the MST, which sought to create an alternative parallel dynamic to the agribusiness model.

To give an idea of the context in which the project has been carried out, let us consider the Dona Carmen settlement in the municipality of Teodoro Sampaio (SP), where our case study was conducted.[6] It was literally surrounded by animal pasturelands (mainly for cattle, which have particular impacts on the soil) and sugar cane plantations. Planes frequently flew over the area spraying agrochemicals. Settlers were concerned and fearful of the consequences for the inhabitants, both humans and non-humans. As Dona Cida,[7] a local leader of the MST, observed: 'The poison falls from the sky and then goes into the body of everything.' The creation of *matinhas* (small areas with trees) in the settlement was discussed by the *assentados* as a way of building barriers that would prevent, or at least diminish, exposure to agrochemicals. It was a defensive strategy that sought to guarantee a safe space for experimentation with alternative models of agriculture. My first conversation with Dona Cida was dominated by her fear of agrochemical poisons, attack by ants and the lack of water. The *assentados* were, in her view, literally under attack.

The *macaúba* project was presented to the Dona Carmen settlers as a project of social promotion and ecological regeneration. With a mixture of surprise and hope, farmers wondered how one more project could help them stabilize and improve their living conditions. In a public discussion I attended in 2014, some *assentados* were happy with the idea of their land becoming an attractor to animals, mostly with the return of birds they knew in their childhood. But this was an unusual restoration project, as stressed by João Dagoberto dos Santos,[8] an agrarian engineer-researcher of ESALQ and member of the project. He told me that, in his opinion, 'This was not a restoration project in the strictest sense of the word.' In fact, projects that mix social and ecological dimensions in their objectives, that are experimental in their methodology and based on a practice of situated composition, are usually considered a deviation from what should be the standard strategy of intervention (Bradshaw 1993; 1994). This shows how the mainstream practice of ecological restoration is far from the original 'nomadic' spirit of the discipline.

Still, according to project technician and MST leader Luis dos Santos,[9] the Agroforestry Systems (SAF) project developed by ESALQ-USP researchers was a continuation of several actions in the region dating back at least as far as the 1990s. Before the arrival of the university, the Ecological Research Institute (IPÊ) was already developing projects where forest remnants were associated with new forms of agriculture. These were mostly isolated interventions in the *assentamentos* of the 'coffee with forest' kind – that is, the interspersed planting of coffee species and tree species native to the region. Moreover, in 2010, another group of *assentados* linked to the Cooperative of Trade and Services of the Agrarian Reform Settlers of Pontal do Paranapanema (COCAMP) managed to implement a project called Café Sombreado (Shady Coffee), which again interspersed coffee plants with native species. These previous experiences made it possible for a project like *macaúba* to be developed with some 'naturalness, but not without difficulties', according to Luis.

Sergio Ribeiro, an MST technician from the settlement of São Bento, explained that when the ESALQ team started working in the region between 1998 and 1999, the initial aim was to research native species around the Morro do Diabo State Park, well known for having the largest population of black lion tamarin (*Leontopithecus chrysopygus*), one of the rarest and most endangered primate species in the world. This was the first time researchers had tried to involve the *assentados*. A second occasion was after 1999, because of the connexion with COCAMP: in this case, it was already aimed at the development of SAFs.

Luis dos Santos described the agroforestry proposal as a 'novelty for people who found it strange to plant food between trees'. The installation of a new predation dynamic can be seen as an alternative form of regulation and control of the local assemblage of living beings, instead of the use of massive chemical inputs for the control of pests. When approaching settlers for the *macaúba* project, researchers started by presenting a series of successful cases to provide practical examples of the new associations, that 'an animal eating another animal' could bring 'soil improvement [. . .] for better production' (interview with Luis). In parallel, they supported the promotion of *semente creolas* (native species of seeds), in which more than 100 families took part. This project required work on soil preparation, the delivery of limestone (to correct soil acidity) and the training of *assentados*.

During the second phase of the macaúba project (2013–2015), there were misunderstandings over technical restoration procedures in the relationship between technicians (from both MST and ESALQ/USP) and *assentados*. According to Luis (MST), 'You make mistakes, we make mistakes about what will be good. The researcher may be wrong in thinking that something will be good that perhaps is not good for the *assentados*.' In his view, the perspective of *assentados* and researchers depended on the 'culture' of each person, but also on the time that is needed to understand these positions, the time necessary 'to know what the other person is thinking'. Culture, in this sense, became a criterion to decide who to involve in the project. It was necessary 'to trace the profile [. . .] where he came from, what types of activity he developed during his life, what trajectory he followed': it was a way to identify those more likely to participate with a certain expertise or flexibility in adapting and promoting new ways of socio-productive organization.

The choice of *macaúba* as the catalyst for this process came about through the intersection of a demand for the cultivation of species for the production of biodiesel (encouraged by a consumption demand within the federal government's energy plan) and researchers' concern to promote the exploitation of native species in family agriculture. The leading actors did not ignore the risk of transforming land for food production into land for energy production. The macaúba had the advantage that it was a native species of the region and could be found in great quantity in the *assentamentos*. Moreover, macaúba can be used in the production of biofuel, but also for human and animal consumption. According to Carlos (technician from ITESP),[10] it was estimated that more than 5,000 kilogrammes of oil would be produced per hectare. *Macaúba* was considered to be low cost and highly adaptable to different types of soil and environmental conditions. This would enable the creation of income even for small areas, one of the most pressing problems for *assentados* who struggled to guarantee a minimal income.

The researchers sought 'the creation of a network of regional actors that promotes the sustainability of the production chain in the medium and long term' (interview with Carlos) through agroforestry systems and agro-ecology in the rural settlements. But one complication the project had to face was that there was no minimum-price policy in the region for the harvesting, processing and selling of the product for the trade through the National Supply Company (CONAB). Two forest inventories were carried out in 2013 and 2014 to evaluate the potential of the *macaúba* extractivism. Covering an area of 140 hectares, they showed a potential production of 233,000 kilogrammes and 798,000 kilogrammes of *macaúba* fruits, respectively, as presented by the ESALQ/USP team.[11] During one of the presentations made by the team in Presidente Epitacio, they pointed out that the commercialization of Pontal fruits seemed more research-oriented than productive; despite this, the 12 families involved in the collection of fruits were motivated to continue this action, which was, in principle, more profitable than dairy farming, the main productive chain in the region.

Plantations were designed as composition of variable scales and maturations: a regional pool of species was given to each farmer, but the model allowed flexibility in the choices they made. The most common combinations were a mixture of *macaúba*, cassava, okra, pumpkins, string beans, banana, corn and papaya, but these associations were often blended with existing species such as lemon and passion fruit. The average size of each *lote* (plot) was around 15 hectares. For each of the project participants, an area of about 1 hectare on their property was selected for the creation of an agroforestry system. Success in this experimentation in coexistence, and acceptance of the project, depended on the *assentados'* capacity to maintain this new assemblage (of agents and time) in the daily modes of organizing socio-ecological reproduction. At the same time, in order to be successful, the experiment required a continuous connexion between the ecological knowledge of the ESALQ/USP team and the situated experiences of *assentados* on the ground. The expertise acquired in a situated way was of crucial importance to this process for both *assentados* and the ESALQ/USP team. According to Luis dos Santos (MST), the *assentados* could 'benefit from discussing our concrete situations from a perspective of quality of life improvement' (interview with Luis). For the ESALQ/USP team, this experience provided the opportunity to engage in a more creative perspective of doing applied research, as put by Ana Carrilli,[12] a postgraduate student.

But there was another major critical aspect. Although motivated by efforts to change power relations and agricultural models in Brazilian rural areas, the project could not counter the pressure to produce for the market or reduce the risks related to contamination by pesticides. According to Antonio (MST),[13] the strong alliance between elected representatives and economic actors was a key factor in maintaining pressure on small-scale agriculture: 'politicians, judges and landowners all worked together to maintain this toxic model'. Because of this pressure, farmers were forced to engage in some productive activities, such as rearing cattle or planting sugar cane, for 'immediate financial return'. In some cases, farmers had no choice other than to stop cultivating their land and try to find a job in the nearest urban centre. As interspecific agents (Tsing 2012), *assentados* had to build relationships with many non-human agents, but the stabilization of these relationships required continuous management work. In some cases, the *assentados'* intention to repair socio-ecological relations led, in fact, to the loss of their source of subsistence. Analyzing this and other projects in Pontal do Paranapanema, Ferrarini and Marquez (2019) suggest the same conclusions: the short-term nature of these projects, despite all the efforts and the interest that the research interventions raise, is not enough to provide a long-term solution to a situation of ecological degradation, political pressure and economic and social precarity. Like other projects supported by universities and public agencies, they are funded by limited resources and cannot afford the time for active participation on the part of the interested public.

Amongst the sources of precariousness, ants also played an important role. Although ants are an important agent in the organic composition of the soil, they can become 'dangerous and destructive' (interview with Luis) in ecological restoration areas. In our case, the settlements were established in areas with little forest cover and depleted and compartmentalized soil. The *lotes*[14] were dominated by large amounts of green panic grass (*Panicum maximum*) and signal grass (*Brachiaria*), which required, and still require, intense preparation to make planting in the area viable. These exotic species were introduced during the modernization of agriculture from 1960 onwards and became invasive in the 1970s (Durigan and Melo 2011). In sandy soil, dominated by colonial grass, ants proliferated. With the soil compacted by the weight of herds of cattle and without a tree or shrub that could cover the ground and provide food, ants sought a source of food in *assentados'* plantations. According to Dona Cida, 'if we don't use poison here, the ants put an end to it all.'

The farmers we interviewed told us of several attempts to control ants without resorting to chemical products. However, even when effective, these solutions were short-lived. Project technicians advised the farmers not to use insecticides. They suggested that multiplying the organic matter could control ants, arguing that ants would naturally stop attacking *assentados'* corn and cassava plantations if new sources of food were provided. For this purpose, it was necessary to modify the local management practices, including management of the workforce. Although some farmers were successful, others failed and had to use insecticides. One of the techniques used by farmers to 'fool' the ants was the use of PET bottles, cut in half and placed over the planted seedlings to keep the ants away. In a region where temperatures can reach more than 40 °C in the summer, the plastic covers created an unsustainable environment for the seedlings.

For the ESALQ/USP team, the ants were an important natural agent that contributed to the improvement and regeneration of the soil. However, ants brought problems, not only to the reforestation project, but, more broadly, to the whole socio-ecological arrangement guaranteeing the subsistence of the *assentados*, the stability of which depended on food production both for family consumption and for sale. The timescale for successful biological control was not the timescale of the *assentados*, concerned primarily with finding a quick response to ensure that what was planted did not become food for ants. The solution proposed by scientists and technicians could not provide modalities of coexistence between species while preserving the sources of *assentados*' subsistence. The *assentados* described the ants as 'insatiable' and 'all-destructive' and said they required constant efforts to control them. Ants were also the topic of conversation during private visits or at public meetings to present and discuss the project.

These disagreements show us not only the limitations of these experiments but also that ecological restoration is a negotiation in which effective local repairing often requires intervention in the larger multi-species assemblages. As an initiative led by a university research centre, the *macaúba* project was developed with a limited time horizon. Its end did not mean the end of the relationship between researchers and settlers. However, a transition project like the one developed in the *macaúba* project requires continuity, whether for the development of applied research to guarantee the construction of alternatives and better living conditions for the *assentados* or to assure them that the transition risks will not be faced alone. Borrowing the notion of 'response-ability' from Haraway (2016), we can say that in our case study, repair practices, acting on precarious and vulnerable situations, need to create 'sustain-abilities': instead of returning to a previous situation, ecosystem repair practices must build for humans and non-humans the capacity for durable co-involvement – that is, practical and technical skills that can guarantee long-term conditions for new multi-species assemblages to resist and expand in adverse contexts.

Final remarks

Scientists carrying out restoration projects have to assess a negotiable limit, since the restoration action will raise the issue of management not only of the new non-human agents introduced but also of those human and non-human agents that are already in place and which will have their habits and routines redefined. In particular, in our case, restoration implied a change in the working routine between the field and the forest. The practice of ecological restoration can thus generate new relationships and communities, but also new risks and uncertainties. One of the most feared aspects reported by the settlers was precisely the time – and security – required to shift from a production system of monoculture based on the techniques of industrial agriculture to one that required continuous adjustment of multi-species assemblages: in this coexistence, the *assentados* should enter into a permanent negotiation with non-human actors, following their connexions and reactions without relying on the unilateral power of agrochemical agents.

Isolated between areas of monoculture, the experimental units of the *macaúba* project were meant to be centres supporting the development of repairing *agencements*, in ecological and social terms. The community meetings were opportunities for *assentados* to express their doubts and perspectives in a shared effort to create an alternative local economy. Although they comprised a small percentage of the total number of farmers in the settlements, their faith in the possibility of building new paths of local development was a crucial dimension of the project.

However, as observed for other projects in the same region (Ferrarini and Marquez 2019), the critical aspect of this type of project lies precisely in its experimental character: by transforming the *assentamentos* into laboratories for applying knowledge produced at universities, these projects end up generating dynamics that, due to the lack of material resources and institutional support, limit the continuity of socio-ecological changes over time. The political changes that have taken place in Brazil since 2016 (with the impeachment of the president of the Republic, Dilma Rousseff of the Workers' Party) have not only dramatically affected the technical and financial assistance available to the *assentamentos* but also caused a huge cut in resources meant for university research and extension work, which in Brazil are defined as a way of applying knowledge to projects of public interest. The election to the presidency of the far-right candidate Jair Bolsonaro in 2018 put these experiences in a difficult situation insofar as researchers and *assentados* could count neither on credit lines to finance projects nor on political support. As Bolsonaro was elected with a platform that identified the MST as a terrorist/criminal organization and defined the *assentamentos* as an example of inefficiency and a waste of public resources, little space was left for the construction of a rural development policy that could be multiple in its forms and objectives. As in the 1940s, fires continue spreading in 2020 without any intervention from the federal government, and as in Pontal colonization, they have been used as a technique to destroy multi-species assemblages for monocultures, mostly soy, and cattle grazing.

Agents committed to the ecological restoration of Brazilian ecosystems must deal with this hostile reality. But this does not mean halting all efforts: in 2020, the MST launched a plan to plant 100 million trees in all Brazilian regions, with the aim of recovering degraded areas through the implementation of agroforestry systems.[15] This shows us, perhaps, a new road for restoration actions, one that is promoted and articulated not by agents outside the communities, such as technicians and scientists from public agencies and universities, but precisely by those agents who, due to the problematic situations that affect them, must constitute themselves as an interested public and therefore engage in the construction of collective, experimental and contextual responses (Stengers 2015).

Notes

1 The *assentamento* is a unit of agricultural production, introduced by governmental policies and aimed at reordering land use – hence the appearance of a new social category in the rural space, the *assentado* (settler).
2 The official name of the project is the Macaúba Project: Consolidating the Biodiesel Chain with Family Agriculture in Pontal do Paranapanema, Promoting Income Generation, Food Security and the Use and Conservation of Local Biodiversity. It was carried out by the Luiz de Queiros School of Agriculture of the University of São Paulo (ESALQ/USP) and by the São Paulo Agribusiness Technology Agency (APTA) in partnership with EMBRAPA Environment, National Institute of Colonization and Agrarian Reform (INCRA), Land Institute of the State of São Paulo (ITESP), Energy Company of the State of São Paulo (CESP) and associations of small producers based in the region of Pontal do Paranapanema.
3 Created in 1984 in Cascavel, Paraná (southern region), to mobilize the population in the face of the implementation of agrarian reform. The occupation of unproductive lands has become one of the movement's main fighting tactics (Stédile 1997).
4 This law was modified in 2012 after years of pressure from agribusiness sectors, with great parliamentary representation, demanding a reduction in the dimensions that should be restored.
5 At the time of this research, Sergio was one of the many settlers who worked in Pontal. At the same time, he was being trained to become an agrarian engineer in a programme set up by the MST and several universities in São Paulo state. Interviewed on 2 February 2015.
6 This study is the result of 14 months of intermittent field research in the region (2014–2016). The methodology was based on field data collected through participant observation (meetings, visits to *assentados*) and interviews (with *assentados*, technicians from the State of São Paulo ITESP, leaders of the MST and ESALQ/USP team). The research was developed within the PhD programme of Social Sciences in Development, Agriculture and Society of the Federal Rural University of Rio de Janeiro (CPDA/UFRRJ) with financial support from the CNPQ, and supervised by Maria José Teixeira Carneiro.
7 Dona Cida (70 years old in 2015) was not directly involved in the coordination of the project but figured as a participant. Interviewed on 25 November 2014.
8 Interviewed on 12 February 2015.
9 Interviewed on 25 April 2015.
10 Interviewed on 10 April 2015.
11 https://core.ac.uk/download/pdf/76491776.pdf, viewed 12 September 2020.
12 Interviewed on 19 May 2015.
13 Antonio, 61 years old, was a settler in Dona Carmen and had no previous agriculture experience before meeting the MST in the middle of the 1990s. He joined the movement and decided to become a settler to 'live the land'. He was one of the most engaged participants in the *macaúba* project. Interviewed on April 8, 2016.
14 A *lote* is defined as a portion of land to which the farmer is entitled in the settlement process.
15 https://mst.org.br/2020/02/07/100-milhoes-de-arvores-conheca-o-plano-nacional-de-plantio-do-mst/, viewed September 17, 2020.

References

Bacha, J.C.C. (2004) 'O uso dos recursos florestais e as políticas econômicas brasileiras: Uma visão histórica e parcial de um processo de desenvolvimento', *Revista Estudos Econômicos*, 34(2): 393–426.

Biehl, J. and Locke, P. (2010) 'Deleuze and the Anthropology of Becoming', *Current Anthropology*, 51(3): 317–351.

Boyd, W., Prudham, W.S. and Schurman, R.A. (2001) 'Industrial Dynamics and the Problem of Nature', *Society and Natural Resources*, 14(7): 555–570.

Bradshaw, A.D. (1993) 'Restoration Ecology as a Science', *Restoration Ecology*, 1(2): 71–77.

Bradshaw, A.D. (1994) 'The Need for Good Science – Beware of Straw Men: Some Answers to Comments by Eric Higgs', *Restoration Ecology*, 2(3): 147–148.

Castree, N. (2008) 'Neoliberalising Nature: The Logics of Deregulation and Reregulation', *Environment and Planning A: Economy and Space*, 40: 131–152.

Clewell, A.F. (1993) 'Ecology, Restoration Ecology and Ecological Restoration', *Restoration Ecology*, 1(3): 141.

Court, F.E. (2012) *Pioneers of Ecological Restoration: The People and Legacy of the University of Wisconsin Arboretum*, Madison: University of Wisconsin Press.

Dean, W. (1996) *A ferro e fogo: A história e a devastação da Mata Atlântica brasileira*, São Paulo: Companhia das Letras.

Deleuze, G. and Guattari, F. (1987) *A Thousand Plateaus: Capitalism and Schizophrenia*, Minneapolis: University of Minnesota Press.

Ditt, E.H. (2002) *Fragmentos florestais no Pontal do Paranapanema*, São Paulo: Annablume/IPÊ/IIEB.

Dodier, N. and Barbot, J. (2016) 'The Force of Dispositifs', *Annales. Histoire, Sciences Sociales*, 2016(2): 421–450.

Durigan, G. and Melo, A.C.G. (2011) 'Panorama das políticas públicas e pesquisas em restauração ecológica no estado de São Paulo, Brazil', in E. Figueroa (ed.) *Conservación de la biodiversidad en las américas: lecciones y recomendaciones de política*, Santiago: Universidad de Chile, 355–387.

Ferrarini, O.G. and Marquez, P.E.M. (2019) 'Projetos agroecológicos no Pontal do Paranapanema: A visão de agricultores assentados e o papel das políticas públicas', *Retratos de Assentamento, Araraquara*, 21(2): 92–115.

Gross, M. (2002) 'New Natures and Old Science: Hands-on Practice and Academic Research in Ecological Restoration', *Science Studies*, 15(2): 17–35.

Gross, M. (2010) *Ignorance and Surprise: Science, Society, and Ecological Design*, Cambridge, MA: MIT Press.

Handel, S. (2013) 'Giant Clam Shells, the Intermediate Disturbance Hypothesis, and a Big Box of Markers', *Ecological Restoration*, 31(3): 235–236.

Haraway, D. (2016) *Staying with the Problem: Making Kin in the Chthulucene*, Durham, NC and London: Duke University Press.

Hatje, R.B.H. (2016) *A restauração ecológica e a ditadura da floresta*, Tese (Ambiente e Sociedade): UNICAMP/Campinas.

Higgs, E. (2003) *Nature by Design: People, Natural Process and Ecological Restoration*, Cambridge, MA: MIT Press.

Hobbs, R. *et al.* (2006) 'Novel Ecosystems: Theoretical and Management Aspects of the New Ecological World Order', *Global Ecology and Biogeography*, 15: 1–7.

Law, J. (1994) *Organizing Modernity*, Oxford, UK and Cambridge, MA: Blackwell.

Leite, J.F. (1998) *A ocupação do Pontal do Paranapanema*, São Paulo: Hucitec/Unesp.

Leonidio, A. (2009) 'Violências fundadoras: O Pontal do Paranapanema entre 1850 e 1930', *Ambiente e Sociedade*, 12(1): 37–47.

Monbeig, P. (1984) *Pioneiros e fazendeiros de São Paulo*, São Paulo: Hucitec.

Nixon, R. (2011) *Slow Violence and the Environmentalism of the Poor*, Cambridge, MA: Harvard University Press.

Oliveira, R.E. (2011) *O estado da arte da ecologia da restauração e sua relação com a restauração de ecossistemas florestais no bioma Mata Atlântica*, Thesis in Science Forestry, UNESP/Botucatu.

Pickett, S.T. and Parker, V.T. (1994) 'Avoiding the Old Pitfalls: Opportunities in a New Discipline', *Restoration Ecology*, 2(2): 75–79.

Pignarre, P. and Stengers, I. (2005) *La sorcellerie capitaliste: pratiques de désenvoûtement*, Paris: La Découverte.

Reis, A., Tres, D.R. and Bechara, F.C. (2006) 'A Nucleação como novo paradigma na restauração ecológica: "espaço para o imprevisível"', in *Simpósio Sobre Recuperação de Áreas Degradadas com Ênfase em Matas Ciliares*, São Paulo: Instituto de Botânica.

Rodrigues, R.R., Lima, R.A.F., Gandolfi, S. and Nave, A.G. (2009) 'On the Restoration of High Diversity Forests: 30 Years Experiences in the Brazilian Atlantic Forest', *Biological Conservation*, 142: 1242–1251.

Santos, J.D. (2012) *Desenvolvimento rural, biodiversidade e políticas públicas: desafios e antagonismos no Pontal do Paranapanema*, São Paulo: ESALQ/Piracicaba/Tese (Recursos Florestais).

Scott, J. (1998) *Seeing Like a State: How Certain Schemes to Improve the Human Condition Have Failed*, New Haven, CT: Yale University Press.

Soulé, M. (2014) *Collected Papers of Michael E. Soulé: Early Years in Modern Conservation Biology*, Washington, DC: Island Press.

Stédile, J.P. (1997) *A reforma agrária e a luta do MST*, Petrópolis: Editora Vozes.

Stengers, I. (2000) *The Invention of Modern Science*, Minneapolis, MN: University of Minnesota Press.

Stengers, I. (2015) *In Catastrophic Times: Resisting the Coming Barbarism*, London: Open University Press.

Tsing, A. (2012) 'Unruly Edges: Mushrooms as Companion Species', *Environmental Humanities*, 1: 141–154.

Tsing, A. (2015) *The Mushrooms at the End of the World: On the Possibility of Life in Capitalist Ruins*, Princeton, NJ: Princeton University Press.

Viana, V. and Amador, D. (1998) 'Sistemas agroflorestais para a recuperação de fragmentos florestais', *Série Técnica IPEF*, 12(32): 105–110.

Viola, E. (1987) 'O movimento ecológico no Brasil (1974–1986): Do ambientalismo à ecopolítica', *Revista Brasileira de Ciências Sociais*, 1(3): 1–23.

Part II

Everyday life, justice and memories in recovery after disasters

4 Repairing as struggle for narrative justice

The dam failure of Vega de Tera, Spain (1959–2019)

Santiago Gorostiza and Marco Armiero

Introduction

As they do every year, on 9 January 2019, the survivors of the disaster of Ribadelago joined with local inhabitants to celebrate a mass in memory of the victims of the Vega de Tera dam failure. The year 2019 marked the 60th anniversary of the 1959 disaster, which destroyed the town of Ribadelago (Zamora, Spain), killing 144 people amongst the nearly 500 inhabitants. Despite the occasion, and in stark contrast to the well-attended 50th anniversary, celebrated 10 years earlier, no regional or state political authorities were invited to the commemorations. 'They don't deserve it', declared the local mayor (Saavedra 2019).

This bitter statement was prompted by the unfulfilled promises made by regional and state politicians back in 2009. The wishes of local authorities and neighbours to establish a 'Museum of the Memory of Ribadelago' had been well received, but when the economic crisis started in 2008, plans were abandoned, leading to a feeling of resentment amongst locals. For them, this was yet another proof of the authorities' loss of interest in the Vega de Tera dam disaster, although it remains to this day the worst dam-related disaster in the past two centuries of Spanish history. Indeed, 60 years later, in the very town that was wiped away by the waters, only a few memorials bear witness to the disaster that destroyed it.

When telling the story of the collapse of the Vega de Tera dam and the flood that wiped away Ribadelago during the first hours of 9 January 1959, one could say that the events unfolded in a matter of minutes. The dam broke approximately around midnight, and in less than an hour the resulting flood flowed down the Tera valley and destroyed the town, dragging dozens of neighbours to the depths of Sanabria Lake. This one-day narrative, however, tends to portray disasters as tragic 'accidents'. Instead, we argue that when the sun came up over Sanabria Lake on 9 January 1959, the disaster was far from over. In fact, it had just begun, and as shown by the bitter remark of the town mayor in 2019, its consequences still live on. In other words, in this chapter we aim at expanding the time frame in the analysis of the Vega de Tera dam failure to highlight the long aftermath (see the introduction by Centemeri, Topçu and Burgess in this volume; Fortun *et al.* 2017). In this chapter we use the word 'narrative' as an overarching concept which includes all the strategies employed to systematize, transmit and make sense of

DOI: 10.4324/9781003184782-7

events. According to the literary scholar David Herman, narrative is 'a basic human strategy for coming to terms with time, process and change – a strategy that contrasts with, but is in no way inferior to, 'scientific' modes of explanation that characterize phenomena as instances of general covering laws' (Herman 2007: 3).

While we acknowledge that examining the time before and after the dam failure is equally important to challenge the notion of disasters as temporally delimitated phenomena, we focus on the aftermath of the dam failure to test the heuristic potential of an approach to recovery in terms of reparation. We combine a repairing perspective with a political environmental history approach (Barca 2016) that pays attention to how economic compensations were put in place and how the trial failed to accommodate the claims of the survivors. By focusing our attention on the aftermath of the disaster, when Ribadelago vanished from national and international attention, we aim to show how the disaster continued unfolding in time, from ruins to courts and from laboratories to regulations. It inhabited survivors, their land, homes, and memoirs; and yet to this day, it remains barely a footnote in Spanish narratives about hydropower modernization (Swyngedouw 2015).

The case of Ribadelago shows how, in the aftermath of the disaster, the Francoist dictatorship prioritized anticipating and averting similar disasters, rather than identifying those responsible or repairing the victims. The failure of the Vega de Tera dam sparked a full revision of the legislation about dam security in Spain, including the creation of the Dam Surveillance Service. In other words, the functional understanding of repairing (Dodier 1995) as the improvement of dam-building standards and control obscured survivors' quest for repair as justice and recognition for the victims. In this context, memory emerges as a strategic tool for reclaiming the individual and collective agency of the survivors, as part of a wider process to achieve social repair (Aijazi 2015). By analyzing the long aftermath of the disaster, in this chapter we argue that the survivors fought to achieve both a judicial and a narrative reparation.

As disasters create breaches in the material and social infrastructures, they also provoke fractures in the collective memories. Often in the aftermath of the disaster an official memory is imposed, one which naturalizes injustices and erases socio-ecological conflicts. Building upon Radstone and Hodgkin, we can call it a regime of memories, thereby stressing how deeply the production of memories is a function of power relationships (Radstone and Hodgkin 2006). We argue that the regime of memories imposed upon communities affected by environmental injustices produces what environmental historian Stefania Barca calls narrative injustice – that is, an organization of the public discourse which normalizes injustices, rendering them invisible (Barca 2014: 539). For survivors of disasters, as well as for communities affected by environmental injustices, the struggle also involves the repair of collective narratives aiming to make visible what was invisibilized, make audible what was silenced, make conflictual what was pacified.[1]

Finally, from a historical perspective, the failure of the Vega de Tera dam must be interpreted in the context of the Francoist project of Spanish modernization, where hydropower played a central role. By contributing to construct and solidify the very dictatorship through public works, civil engineers had become very relevant actors within the Francoist regime (Camprubí 2014; Swyngedouw 2015; Camprubí 2017). If dams are 'hallmarks of technological progress and national pride' and assume 'the status of modern shrines' (Kaika 2006: 295), then it follows that their unexpected collapse may reveal metaphorical cracks in the political regime that erected them. Therefore, the crux of the matter for the Francoist regime was that the hydropower industry lay at the heart of the investigation that followed the disaster. In fact, 60 per cent of Hidroeléctrica de Moncabril, the company that built the Vega de Tera dam and several others in the region, was owned by the public National Institute of Industry (Instituto Nacional de Industria, INI).[2] Such a technological disaster necessarily put the role of engineers in the spotlight – both company engineers who had designed and supervised the dam construction and state engineers whose duty was to control its quality standards and construction process. This helps to explain how the story of the worst dam disaster of the past two centuries of Spanish history remains an uncomfortable event in the national narrative of modernization.

Our research is based on original archival research and oral primary sources. On the one hand, we combine media and historical press sources with the proceedings of the trial, consulted at the Archivo Histórico Provincial de Zamora. We also consulted the collection of interviews with local inhabitants and survivors compiled in 2009 by the Museo Etnográfico de Castilla y León (Zamora). As with other cases of near-forgotten disasters (Armiero 2011), it was the work of local researchers, not academics, which was key to access the relevant archival sources and provide the first critical historical accounts of the events. In the case of Ribadelago, we interviewed the author of the first book devoted to the disaster, and follow it in our narrative (García Díez 2001). We also interviewed other journalists involved in the observation of the 50th anniversary of the disaster in 2009, as well as María Jesús Otero, survivor and member of the Children of Ribadelago association.

The chapter is organized in four sections. The section 'Reports and ruin' focuses on the impact of the disaster in Ribadelago and the surrounding region, discussing the press coverage of these events. Next, we analyze the investigation of Hidroeléctrica de Moncabril, examining how power asymmetries between the victims and the hydropower company manifested during the trial. Following this, we discuss the importance of the Vega de Tera dam failure in the development of Spanish dam safety regulations. (This importance, however, did not bring about an explicit acknowledgement of the victims nor of the destroyed town.) Finally, we examine the processes of mourning and remembering, but also of forgetting. In the conclusion, we underline how the slow emergence of memory about the traumatic events of Ribadelago in 1959 has gradually broken the prevailing silence amongst the survivors.

Reports and ruin

The year 1959 was a highly symbolic year for the Francoist regime. It marked the 20th anniversary of General Francisco Franco's victory in the Spanish Civil War (1936–1939), commemorated in April with the opening of a vast memorial and mausoleum, the so-called Valley of the Fallen (Valle de los Caídos). Later, in December, Dwight D. Eisenhower became the first US president ever to visit Spain, touring the streets of Madrid together with the Spanish dictator, and certifying the rehabilitation of Spain as a US ally. Finally, 1959 saw the approval of the National Plan of Economic Stabilization, which marked a milestone in the liberalization of the Spanish economy and is still referred to by many historians as the moment that divided the dictatorship into two periods.

However, before all these events took place, a remote small town in the province of Zamora hit the international headlines when the year had barely started. On 9 January 1959, news started spreading, through Spain and abroad, that the town of Ribadelago had been wiped away by the waters of a broken dam. The buttress dam of Vega de Tera, built in the early 1950s by the company Hidroeléctrica de Moncabril, had collapsed during the night. The waters released – approximately 8 million cubic metres – flowed down the Tera valley and destroyed the town of Ribadelago, near the shore of Sanabria Lake.

When the first members of the police were able to reach the town, they found the survivors in the middle of ruins, water and mud. The human and material losses were, at first sight, incalculable. The disaster had occurred around midnight, while most of the local inhabitants were sleeping. No alarm had been received before the water level started increasing. Most of the survivors found shelter in high points such as the town church or the near hills, where they stayed throughout the cold night. Nearly one-third of the approximately 500 inhabitants of Ribadelago – mostly workers at the hydropower projects in the region and peasants – were killed, and only 25 of the 150 houses were left standing (Museo Etnográfico de Castilla y León 2008: 26). The lands cultivated by locals were ruined and most of the cattle were gone. During the following days, the efforts to find the missing people managed to locate only 28 corpses, but the total recount of the missing went as high as 116. Together with debris, animals, trees and houses, they had been dragged to Sanabria Lake, the largest glacial lake in Spain. It had absorbed the flood, and no other towns were affected. All efforts to find the bodies of the missing victims under the waters of the lake were unsuccessful. In contrast to the ruin of Ribadelago, the power station and the small town constructed by Hidroeléctrica de Moncabril to house its engineers were barely touched by the flood, which came from the Tera River valley (García Díez 2001: 125–161; Museo Etnográfico de Castilla y León 2008: 20–22; Remesal 2009: 15–37).

While supporting the relief work for the survivors, the police also reported social unrest in Ribadelago and the region. These secret reports bear witness to the anger of locals against Hidroeléctrica de Moncabril, the hydropower company responsible for the Vega de Tera dam. According to the Information Service of the Civil Guard (Servicio de Información de la Guardia Civil), local inhabitants had long feared a dam failure in Vega de Tera. Many had worked at construction on the dam and were well acquainted with its flaws, including significant water leaks, and they blamed the company for the disaster. Most of all, they underlined the lack of technical direction, the construction flaws and the poor quality of the building materials used. According to the Civil Guard, the whole region, outraged, held responsible the senior officers of the company (García Díez 2001: 191–199).

Ribadelago made the front page of the Spanish newspapers, but the national press reflected none of these critiques. Francoist press authorities ordered newspapers to adopt a 'suitable' tone to report on the disaster (García Díez 2001: 203–204). Reports emphasized the immense tragedy that fell upon the town as bad destiny, praised the Christian resignation of the survivors and underlined the public efforts to bring relief to the town (Museo Etnográfico de Castilla y León 2008: 24). The newspapers paid great attention to the charity events organized all over Spain in solidarity with Ribadelago, from small festivals in far provinces to a football match in Madrid between Fortuna Dusseldorf and a team combining players of Real Madrid and Atlético de Madrid, presided over by Franco's wife, Carmen Polo. All the international messages of condolence to Spain were also published in the press as signs of support to the regime, with special attention to the one sent by the Pope (Remesal 2009: 109–117).

While informing their readers about the commissions set up by the dictatorship to investigate the dam failure, the press also reproduced narratives that naturalized the disaster. The 'intense rains' of the days prior to the dam failure were mentioned in almost all reports, and would enjoy a long life as an explanation for the dam failure.[3] Some reports talked of 'overflowing' (not breaking) of the dam (Remesal 2009: 111). One of them went as far as cynically stating that many of the neighbours of Ribadelago died because they could not swim.[4] Finally, several newspapers reported an alleged earthquake detected in Portugal, hinting at a possible relation with the dam failure, even if later reports ruled it out (García Díez 2001: 199–200; Remesal 2009: 68–69).

As weeks passed, the media attention slowly vanished from Ribadelago. Brief references to the charity events continued to be published, along with the dramatic and futile attempts to find those disappeared in the lake. Following the paternalistic culture of the regime to the letter, the dictatorship issued a decree announcing the 'adoption' of Ribadelago by General Francisco Franco and putting the reconstruction of the town in the hands of the Ministry of Housing (Ministerio de la Vivienda 1959). The progress of the construction of 'Ribadelago de Franco', as the new town would be baptized, received the most attention from the press. Little information, however, was published about the legal proceedings related to the dam failure.

Courts and laboratories

With more than 100 victims to be found and identified, massive material losses to be accounted for and the challenge of determining the causes of the dam failure, the legal proceedings related to the Vega de Tera dam failure were the most complex ever faced at the Zamora Province Court (Audiencia Provincial de Zamora). One of the major challenges confronted by the Court was determining what caused the dam break in the first place and who could be held responsible for it. To make things worse, the remote location of the dam, hardly accessible during the winter months, slowed down all investigations. The Zamora Province Court started by establishing a commission of experts to investigate the causes of the failure. By July 1959, they submitted a first report, underlining the remarkable water leaks suffered by the dam prior to the disaster and pointing at construction flaws.[5] Such an assessment caused an outcry at the offices of Hidroeléctrica de Moncabril, whose lawyers challenged this hypothesis and insistently demanded a second report (García Díez 2001: 326).

In the meantime, however, the investigation moved forward. In October 1959, the Zamora Province Court announced the names of those to be legally prosecuted. Amongst these were the persons responsible for designing and building the Vega de Tera dam, including the engineers and manager of Hidroeléctrica de Moncabril and several on-site work supervisors. There was, however, a significant absence in the list: no state official was included in it, despite the fact that the state – through the Confederación Hidrográfica del Duero – was ultimately responsible for the quality control in the dam construction (García Díez 2001: 287–288, 339). The trial put Hidroeléctrica de Moncabril face to face with the Zamora Province Court and the survivors, while any potential responsibility of the state was left aside.

The Zamora Province Court interviewed the survivors and accounted for the loss of human and animal lives, as well as material losses. Soon after, still amidst the ruins, representatives of the company started visiting the neighbours of Ribadelago who might be entitled to some form of compensation. They reminded them that the legal process could take years and reparations, if any, might come only after a long wait. Instead, they offered to settle any claims by immediately paying a part of the losses. Badly in need of resources to resume their lives, and fearing that compensation, if any, could take years, many accepted, legally renouncing any further reparations from the company (García Díez 2001: 253–283; Remesal 2009: 97–102).

However, some of the local inhabitants of Ribadelago who had worked at the dam-building projects in the region reached out to Santiago Moreno, a young lawyer in Zamora who they knew well. A labour attorney and a socialist sympathizer who had supported several workers in other legal cases, Moreno accepted the case and soon he started conducting his own assessment of the losses of Ribadelago's neighbours. He was closely followed by the Civil Guard, and he received anonymous phone calls and 'suggestions' that he drop the case. Despite these warnings, Moreno remained committed. As his son later said, 'It was not simply about confronting a powerful company, but the regime that protected it' (Remesal 2009: 93). Moreno particularly struggled to find engineers who would prepare and sign expert reports about dam construction and maintenance for the case.[6] The only one willing to do so was a former director of public hydraulic works during the Spanish Second Republic (1931–1939) – the democratic political regime against which General Franco had risen in arms. However, as a result of his public responsibilities during the 1930s, this engineer had been purged and could not legally act as an expert (García Díez 2001: 292; Remesal 2009: 93–98; Otero Puente 2019).

In contrast to the difficulties experienced by Moreno, the lawyers of Hidroeléctrica de Moncabril succeeded in their demands to have a second report from the commission of experts in charge of the investigation about the dam failure.

This was finally granted by the Zamora Province Court in September 1960, and following the suggestion of the company, the structural engineer Eduardo Torroja (1889–1961) joined the committee. Torroja was a world-renowned authority in structures and building materials, and the director of the Technical Institute for Construction and Concrete (Instituto Técnico de la Construcción y el Cemento, ITCC). The ITCC, originally an independent institute, had become associated with the state in the post-war years (Camprubí 2014: 20). The analysis carried out for the second experts' report took place at ITCC, and started amidst a controversy on the origin of the materials examined, as the representatives of the victims complained that these had been collected under the supervision of an employee of Hidroeléctrica de Moncabril (García Díez 2001: 326).

Eduardo Torroja passed away in June 1961 and his son took his place on the commission. Before his death, however, he had managed to make a discovery that would change the whole trial (García Díez 2001: 326–333; Remesal 2009: 69–71). According to the laboratory experiments and simulations carried out – and contradictory to the previous scientific literature – he found that the differences between the moduli of elasticity of the masonry and the concrete were much greater than previously known. In other words, the concrete slab, extremely stiff, rested upon highly deformable masonry buttresses. As a result, as water filled the reservoir, tensile stresses created cracks in the concrete slab. Horizontal forces then started acting upon the base of the buttresses and, as soon as the first failed, the pressure of water pouring through the breach did the rest (see Figure 4.1).[7]

Figure 4.1 Missing part of the Vega de Tera dam after the failure, around 1959

From this perspective, according to Torroja (and the co-authors of the report), the collapse of the Vega de Tera dam was 'unavoidable'. Ironically, this was good news for Hidroeléctrica de Moncabril. If a previously unknown miscalculation on this typology of dam explained its collapse, the disaster could not have been predicted and the engineers could not be blamed for it. Other factors, such as construction flaws, the poor condition of the materials used, or the abundant water leaks, shifted to the background.

Under these circumstances, the lawyers of Hidroeléctrica de Moncabril redoubled their efforts to settle any claims for losses from the victims. In a telling letter to the Zamora province governor, dated in November 1961, the president of the hydropower company notified of good progress in the payment of compensation to survivors. However, he emphasized that a group of people, all of them 'under the professional direction of a sole lawyer from Zamora', had so far failed to reach an agreement. The president of the company asked the governor to let these people know that the intention of the company was to reach a friendly agreement. But if this was not possible, he warned, the company would eventually appeal any legal decision establishing any kind of compensation (García Díez 2001: 292–293). The Zamora lawyer was obviously Santiago Moreno, who, together with his clients, was the object of renewed pressures. Many of the remaining survivors needed money and feared a long legal process leading nowhere. After Hidroeléctrica de Moncabril promised to pay the difference between the compensation offered and that granted by the court, should the latter be higher, they all ended up accepting the compensation offered (García Díez 2001: 296–298; Remesal 2009: 97–102; Otero Puente 2019).

The trial finally took place at the Zamora Provincial Court between 11 and 15 March 1963. In contrast to the focus on the disaster four years earlier, this time the national press devoted only brief references to the case. Many of the witnesses who were called chose not to attend the trial at all. The experts stated that the Vega de Tera dam was well built, and that it collapsed due to a fundamental and previously unknown design flaw in this type of dam, as Torroja had put in his report (García Díez 2001: 298–306). One of the experts went as far as stating that Hidroeléctrica de Moncabril had in fact been very generous with the resources invested in constructing the dam.[8]

The verdict was announced on 20 March 1963.[9] The tribunal accepted that the reason for the dam collapse was a flaw in its design, thus saving the accused from much harder penalties. However, it also underlined that the significant leaks and other problems in the construction of Vega de Tera were known to the managers and engineers, which should have stopped them from filling the reservoir to its maximum capacity. The tribunal condemned five of the 11 accused to one year of prison for an offence of reckless endangerment, while the remaining six were acquitted. Amongst the condemned was Gabriel Barceló, the director of Hidroeléctrica de Moncabril. He and the rest of the accused immediately appealed to the Spanish Supreme Tribunal (García Díez 2001: 302–306).

The sentence also established the economic reparations to be paid to the survivors and the victims' families on the basis of human and material losses suffered. According to the sentence, the following compensation was assigned for the deceased people: 100,000 pesetas for each adult; 75,000 for each person between 16 and 21 years of age; and 50,000 for each person younger than 16 years.[10] Many of the victims who had accepted the lower amounts offered by Hidroeléctrica de Moncabril reclaimed the difference, which in several cases was significant. After a few years, their claims were rejected in March 1967, on the basis that when they accepted reparations from the company they had given up their right to any further compensation. With many of the surviving families scattered or emigrating, the payment of the remaining reparations became long and complex (García Díez 2001: 306–309, 361–374).

The four convicted engineers were luckier. On April 1965, two of them were acquitted by the Supreme Tribunal, which nonetheless confirmed the sentences imposed on Gabriel Barceló and Eduardo Nicanor Díaz.[11] However, after only a couple of weeks, both were pardoned by Franco himself (García Díez 2001: 306). A few years later, in 1968, Gabriel Barceló was decorated with the Great Cross of the Order of Civil Merit (*Ministerio de Asuntos Exteriores* 1968). The following year, Hidroeléctrica de Moncabril was absorbed by Unión Eléctrica Madrileña (Anes *et al.* 2001: 48). In summary, the Francoist regime played a deceptive game in the reparation process, initially setting the prosecution against the company and the judicial reparation mechanisms, but eventually pardoning the offenders by making use of its extrajudicial power.

Rules and regulations

As previously explained, according to the second experts' report, the flaws in the project design of the Vega de Tera dam made its collapse inevitable and unpredictable. There were, however, two similar dams in Spain, one already operating and the other under construction. The first was the Puente Porto dam, completed in 1953. It was considered Vega de Tera's twin dam, and was located upstream from Ribadelago, only eight kilometres away from Vega de Tera. In the aftermath of the disaster, it represented a source of concern for the survivors of Ribadelago and the state authorities. After inspecting it and attesting to significant water leaks, state engineers ordered that the structure be reinforced and reduced the water level to half the capacity of the dam. Puente Porto remained in this situation until the 1990s, when it was repaired and improved (García Díez 2008; Alonso Pérez *et al.* 2011). The other dam similar to Vega de Tera was Vado de las Cabras (Segovia), which was being built at the time. In August 1959, the state administration reformulated the project, which did not reach the height originally planned, but it started operating in 1960 (González Fernández 2003).

The wrecked Vega de Tera dam was abandoned and became a ruin (see Figure 4.2). However, its failure marked a milestone for the regulation of dam

Figure 4.2 The broken dam: the Vega de Tera dam after its collapse, 1959
Source: Archivo General de la Administración, reference F/1572 (used with permission)

construction and management in Spain. In 1959, the Francoist administration established the Dam Surveillance Service (Servicio de Vigilancia de Presas) and set up the Commission of Rules for Large Dams (Comisión de Normas para Grandes Presas) with the task of elaborating a set of regulations for dam construction and management (Ministerio de Obras Públicas 1959). These regulations were provisionally approved in 1962, including an article stating that masonry could not be used in buttress dams (see article 79, Ministerio de Obras Públicas 1962). Five years later, in 1967, an updated version of these regulations came into effect, and remains valid to this day (Ministerio de Obras Públicas 1967).[12]

In other words, a 'functional' understanding of repairing – one that identified and anticipated dysfunctions in managing the risk of dam failure – was instrumental to the hydro-political projects of Francoist Spain, in which dam building took off between 1955 and 1970, with the construction of 276 dams that increased the total reservoir capacity from 8,000 to 37,000 cubic metres (see Introduction; Dodier 1995; Swyngedouw 2015). As argued in 1961 in an article about dam surveillance published in the *Revista de Obras Públicas* (the journal of the Professional Association of Spanish Civil Engineers), dams were the 'supporting columns' of a nation. However, they could turn into a major threat, for a disaster in these public works would have not only a direct economic impact on the nation but also a psychological one (Fernández Casado 1961). Remarkably, this article made no mention of Ribadelago, showing how the dam failure of Vega de Tera was uncomfortable for the national narrative of modernization. After all, it took the disaster of Ribadelago to spark the full revision and modernization of dam building and management regulations in Spain.

From this perspective, the dam regulations of the 1960s in Spain were a direct result of the Vega de Tera dam failure in the same way that the creation of the Spanish School of Engineers in the early nineteenth century was related to the Puentes dam failure (Rubín de Célix Caballero 2003). By improving on the previous technical standards, the experience of each disaster reaffirmed faith in technology and engineering. As put by José Antonio Torroja Cabanillas, son of Eduardo Torroja and contributor to the second experts' report, 'Unfortunately, technology also advances on the basis of catastrophes' (García Díez 2001: 349). Disasters are thus portrayed as an 'unfortunate' opportunity for collective learning, which leaves victims as a poignant 'price for progress' to be paid.

Emphasizing this 'epistemic' contribution of disasters goes hand in hand with portraying these episodes as sanitized from the social responsibility or malpractice of specific actors. When in 2018 the *Revista de Obras Públicas* published a brief article that contained the first reference to the destruction of Ribadelago ever published in the journal, the failure of Vega de Tera dam was presented as a tragic event caused by a technical error of design that was unknown at the time (Becerril Bustamante 2018).

Despite the importance of the disaster of Ribadelago for the regulation of dam construction and management, a veil of silence fell immediately upon the events. The functional understanding of repairing eclipsed the quest of repairing as a search for justice and recognition of the victims. The dictatorship succeeded in avoiding the emergence of a critical political discourse – a struggle which also manifested in the graveyards and memorials built in Ribadelago.

Graveyards and memorials

Most of those who died as a result of the Vega de Tera dam failure have no graves. Only 28 bodies were ever found; the remaining 116 were presumably dragged to the depths of Sanabria Lake. For the survivors and many of the region's inhabitants, the largest glacial lake of the Iberian Peninsula became a lacustrine cemetery, last resting place of more than 100 victims of the disaster.

Beyond the strong symbolism of Sanabria Lake as a living, natural memorial, there are also human-made memorials in the old and new towns of Ribadelago. The new town of Ribadelago de Franco – named after the dictator – serves as a telling reminder of the recovery path that was followed after the dam failure, against the wishes of the survivors. Built from scratch after the disaster, the new town is in a location that remains in the shade for most of the year, far from the lands that local inhabitants cultivated. Moreover, its avant-garde architectural style is ill suited for the cold climate of the region (see Figure 4.3). This

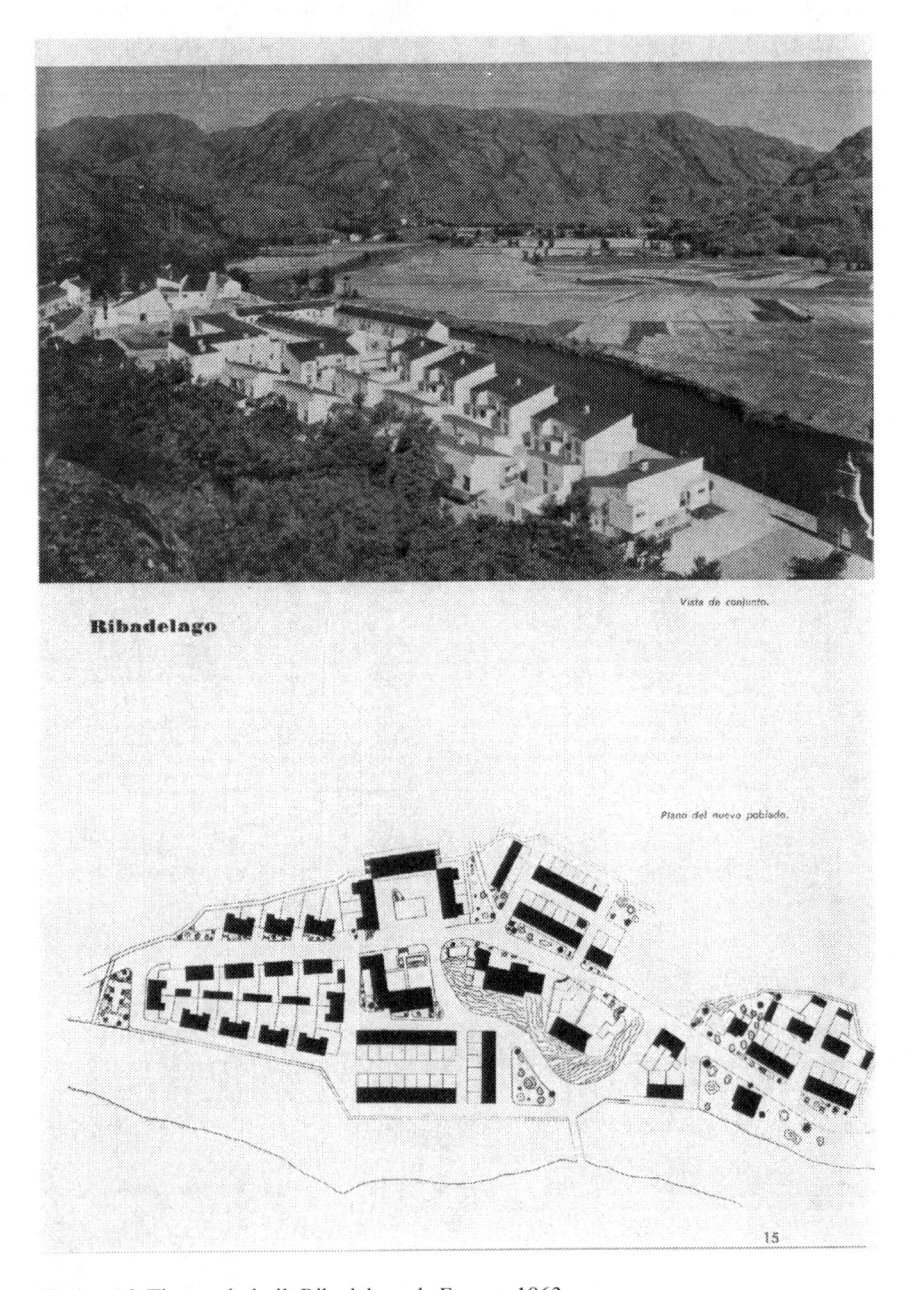

Figure 4.3 The newly built Ribadelago de Franco, 1963

Source: *Arquitectura*, 54, June 1963, 15 (used with permission)

marginalization of local inhabitants from the reconstruction efforts, carried out with ideas of improving their environment but without taking local conditions into account, has been a usual path of recovery after disasters (see Introduction). This was what occurred, for instance, after the destruction of the town of Longarone, in Italy, caused by the 1963 Vajont dam disaster (Armiero 2011), and in L'Aquila after the 2009 earthquake and the forced relocation of the inhabitants to newly built communities (the so-called new towns) outside the city (Lindblom *no date*; Emidio di Treviri 2018: 113–116).

The building works of Ribadelago de Franco advanced fast and, when completed, the houses were sold at cost price – not handed over – to those survivors that could afford it. In 1961, when the town was inaugurated, less than 20 per cent of the families of Ribadelago moved to the new town (García Díez 2001: 272–273; Museo Etnográfico de Castilla y León 2008: 23–24).

In Ribadelago de Franco, the Ministry of Housing also commissioned a monument to honour the victims. The sculptor José Luis Sánchez prepared an innovative monument with a structure of iron, which included two crosses and two sculpture sets: a Calvary (sculpture of the Crucifixion) and a bronze-made Pietà (sculpture of Virgin Mary cradling the dead body of her son). But when the sculptor presented his work, the Francoist Minister of Housing, José Luis Arrese, bluntly refused the Pietà. Arrese considered that its gesture – looking towards the sky, open-mouthed, screaming – signified protest and outrage, and he ordered the head to be remade with a more pious and resigned gesture (see Figures 4.4 and 4.5). The revised version that was finally delivered by the sculptor and accepted by the Ministry of Housing looked down to the ground – or to the lake – and had its mouth shut (Ruiz Trilleros 2012: 100–102; Otero Puente 2016). Nonetheless, in the end the memorial promoted by the Ministry of Housing did not find a place in Ribadelago de Franco. The inhabitants rejected the location determined by the ministry in the central square of the town, which they considered a space of leisure and celebration unfitting for such a memorial. The ministry then placed the monument next to the lake, but it was later dismantled. Some parts of the sculpture were moved to the altarpiece and other locations around the new church of Ribadelago de Franco (Otero Puente 2016; Saavedra 2018).

Amid the ruins of the old town of Ribadelago, however, humble memorials sprouted soon after the disaster (see Figure 4.6). It was not the public authorities but the very survivors who erected several stone steles, each of them bearing the name of a person or a family who disappeared on the night of the disaster (Museo Etnográfico de Castilla y León 2008: 47). As years passed, the old town started growing again. Some of the survivors and their descendants rebuilt their former houses, sometimes including a discreet plaque that mentioned the 1959 events. These public displays of memory of the disaster can be interpreted as part of a slow, wider process of 'social repair' led by the survivors, towards the recovery of individual and collective agency (see Aijazi 2015).

However, it took two decades after the death of Franco for the first formal memorials to be built in Ribadelago. In 1995, a monument in memory of all the vanished persons was unveiled (Esteban 2009). And on the way to the 50th

Figure 4.4 The different designs of José Luis Sánchez for the Ribadelago monument: *Cabeza de piedad*

Source: Archivo fotográfico de Mónica Ruiz Trilleros and Archivo fotográfico de José Luis Sánchez (used with permission)

anniversary of the disaster, several key events took place. The survivors formally established an association called Children of Ribadelago (Hijos de Ribadelago), while the ethnographic museum of Castilla y León carried out several interviews with survivors and published a book (Museo Etnográfico de Castilla y León 2008). Finally, more than 1,000 people attended the 50th anniversary of the disaster on

Figure 4.5 The different designs of José Luis Sánchez for the Ribadelago monument: *Modelado de la piedad*

Source: Archivo fotográfico de Mónica Ruiz Trilleros and Archivo fotográfico de José Luis Sánchez (used with permission)

9 January 2009, when a two-metre-tall statue of a woman protecting her child, representing the survivors of the disaster, was unveiled at the old town of Ribadelago next to a plaque bearing the names of the 144 deceased (see Figure 4.7) (Esteban 2009). Later that year, a documentary about the dam failure aired on Spanish TV and rated as amongst the most watched throughout the country (López 2009).

In the last years, the project of creating a permanent Museum of the Memory of Ribadelago has advanced slowly and remains uncertain. But the remaking of symbols goes on. In 2018, more than 40 years after the death of the dictator, the town council of Ribadelago de Franco approved renaming the town as 'Ribadelago Nuevo' (Agencia EFE 2018; Pérez 2019; Saavedra 2019).

Figure 4.6 Memorial to a disappeared couple in the old town of Ribadelago, erected by
their children

Source: Photo by Araceli Saavedra (used with permission)

Figure 4.7 Memorial to the victims of the Ribadelago disaster, unveiled in 2009
Source: Photo by Araceli Saavedra (used with permission)

Conclusion

By exploring the case of Vega de Tera dam disaster, we have challenged 'one-day narratives' that tend to portray disasters as accidents. Instead, we expanded our time frame and focussed on the various processes of repairing during the disaster's aftermath. From the perspective of the functional understanding of repair, following the dam failure, the dictatorship launched a legal effort to develop regulations for dam safety and management. The regulations were approved in 1967 and are still valid today. Such reparation was instrumental to the political project of Francoism, where hydropower played a fundamental role. While expanding dam construction and developing new regulations for dam safety, the Francoist regime disclaimed public responsibility in the Vega de Tera dam failure. In the end, the dictator himself pardoned those convicted, absolving them of even the insignificant punishments imposed.

While the state administration modernized dam regulations, the hydropower company responsible for the Vega de Tera dam failure pressed survivors to accept extrajudicial compensations, with the cooperation of local and regional Francoist authorities. Hidroeléctrica de Moncabril and the Francoist regime succeeded in suppressing the emergence of a critical political discourse after the dam failure. Legal censorship ensured that only 'suitable' accounts of the disaster were published, focusing on the public efforts to bring reconstruction and repair to the inhabitants of Ribadelago, while portraying them as a resigned, ignorant and docile rural population. It was not until after the end of the dictatorship that repairing as a quest of justice and recognition for the victims started to take shape. During the 2000s, the survivors established an association and the first critical books on the events were published. The 50th anniversary of the dam failure involved an exhibition, a new monument and a documentary aired on the Spanish public TV. During the last 10 years, several socio-environmental groups in Spain have referred to the case of Ribadelago to warn about the dangers of dam building and expansion (Stop Yesa por seguridad – YESA NO 2009; Europa Press 2019).

By expanding the time frame of the disaster of Ribadelago, we have illustrated how memory and narrative injustices are relevant to understanding the recovery after disaster (Barca 2014). In particular, the case of Ribadelago shows the strategic importance of memory in relation to social repair (Aijazi 2015). Following Stefania Barca, the silence imposed upon the survivors of Ribadelago can be interpreted as a narrative injustice or a toxic narrative (Barca 2014; Armiero *et al.* 2019); that is, as an ensemble of strategies aiming to normalize or silence environmental injustice while delegitimizing any alternative storytelling. Narrative injustice goes beyond corporate actors' usual attempts to cover the evidence of their crimes. It has the wider scope of erasing even the possibility of telling the stories of injustices, to preserve their memories. It polices collective and even personal memoirs through the imposition of 'correct' meanings and feelings which organize what should be remembered and how. In this sense, narrative violence is never only a silencing tool but always implies the imposition of a hegemonic toxic narrative, which remains embedded into the places, stories and lives of communities affected by environmental injustice.

In cases like dam failures, narrative violence means erasing from the lexicon and even the syntax any possible reference to a human factor that might lead to disaster. It can be said, for instance, that people have died but not that they have been killed. Likewise, a dam failure is often called an accident because the names we give to phenomena dictate how we see those very phenomena. In Ribadelago, narrative violence is well embodied in the beheading of the screaming Pietà that should have been placed in the rebuilt town. The imposition of a resigned, pious figure with the mouth shut and the glance lost in the depths of Sanabria Lake is an almost perfect expression of that narrative violence in the sense that it aims to impose an official narration of the disaster and a correct exercise of memory and mourning. Either the submitted mother of the sculpture or the complete amnesia of the official (hi)storytelling – this is what narrative violence looks like in Ribadelago.

A struggle for social repair in the form of 'narrative justice' is common to different associations, survivors and descendants who fight to uncover their stories, countering decades of oblivion and silencing. In many of the cases, museums that memorialize the story silenced for decades are a vital step in these processes of narrative reparation. Dam disasters are not an exception. The Vega de Tera dam failure is just one episode of a major story that started in the late nineteenth century: that of the hundreds of dam failures that have taken place before and after 1959 (McCully 2001: 118–119). These examples show that dam disasters, despite the official discourses often portraying them as impossible, happen time and again; and that knowledge and power asymmetries are central in silencing stories of dam failures and its aftermaths. In mobilizing the past and unearthing the stories of historical disasters and social resistance, it is crucial to connect these stories in space and time (Huber *et al.* 2016). Memory, in other words, becomes a key strategy for social repair and for the recovery of individual and collective agency of the survivors (Aijazi 2015).

There are several examples where the memory of dam failures has been nationalized in the form of museums or memorials. In Los Angeles, California, local activists fought for years to obtain the status of 'national monument' for the abandoned ruins of the Saint Francis dam, which collapsed in 1928. It was finally approved in March 2019.[13] Saint Francis is thus to become the second national monument devoted to a dam failure in the US, after the Johnstown Flood National Memorial (Pennsylvania), which commemorates the more than 2,000 deaths caused by the failure of the South Fork Dam, in 1889.[14] Nationalizing the memory of these events, however, comes sometimes with new problems. It is the case of Vajont (Italy), where 2,000 were killed in October 1963 as a result of a massive landslide that fell into a reservoir – as had been predicted by several locals and journalists, against the opinion of engineers. On the 40th anniversary of the disaster (2003), the cemetery of Fortogna was transformed into a national memorial, following a decree by the president of the Italian Republic. Redesigned without the participation of the survivors, the old cemetery and its personal memorials were razed. A sterile, renovated memorial was built instead. The imposition of this 'antiseptic' remembrance, anesthetizing suffering and rage, was felt by some of the survivors as another act of violence (Armiero 2011: 193–194).

For these reasons, the participation of survivors and local inhabitants appears as key for memory to develop a sense of narrative reparation, as part of a strategy for social repair. A Museum of the Memory of Ribadelago, if finally achieved, will need to display the story of the disaster with the participation of those who experienced it, and beyond the dramatic days of January 1959. It cannot compensate for the injustice suffered by the local inhabitants, but at least it will provide an opportunity to tell a different story than that of the resigned and pious victims, sacrificed for scientific and technical progress. It is a story that matters in the small town of Ribadelago and across the globe.

Acknowledgements

Research for this book chapter benefited from European Commission funding under the Marie Curie Actions Initial Training Networks, Call identifier FP7-PEOPLE-2011-ITN, Contract no. 289374, 'ENTITLE'. Santiago Gorostiza acknowledges financial support from the Spanish Ministry of Science and Innovation, through the "María de Maeztu" programme for Units of Excellence (CEX2019-000940-M). Part of this research was carried out thanks to a Trent R. Dames Fellowship at the Huntington Library (California), between 16 April and 16 June 2018. Santiago Gorostiza thanks José Antonio García Díez, María Jesús Otero, Araceli Saavedra, Mónica Ruiz Trilleros and Agustín Remesal for their kind attention and patience in replying to his questions. The authors are grateful to the editors of this book and to Ekaterina Chertkovskaya and Alejandro Pérez-Olivares for their comments on earlier versions of the manuscript. Any errors that remain are our own.

Notes

1 We see the struggle for narrative justice as related to that for recognition because it implies that justice is mainly concerned with 'what kind of standing [an individual deserves] vis-à-vis other persons' (Iser 2019). However, we believe that the struggles for narrative justice have a stronger collective nature and a clear antagonist agenda.

2 See the advertisement of Hidroeléctrica de Moncabril, featuring the recently inaugurated Vega de Tera dam, in *ABC*, 16 March 1957, 8.

3 As late as June 1963 an article in the magazine *Arquitectura* celebrated the newly built town of Ribadelago de Franco, explaining that the dam broke as a result of heavy rains. Dirección General de Arquitectura (1963) 'Ribadelago', *Arquitectura* 54, no. June 1963: 15–18.

4 *Informaciones*, 10 January 1959, 1.

5 In the verdict of the trial, the tribunal underlines the importance of the water leaks suffered by the dam prior to its collapse, and points out that this was one of the main points stressed in the first experts' report. AHPZ archive, 18/59 (Ribadelago), box 2.

6 The same occurred in Italy with the Vajont dam disaster. The public prosecutor could find only one Italian academic willing to testify against the powerful hydropower corporation under trial for the death of 2,000 people. He was Floriano Calvino, the brother of the famous Italian writer Italo Calvino and an adjunct professor. He then lost his job (Armiero 2011: 190).

7 For a summary in English of the causes of the Vega de Tera dam failure, see De Wrachien and Mambretti 2009: 282–283. The complete report, with Eduardo Torroja as lead author, can be found at AHPZ archive, 18/59 (Ribadelago). For a recent PhD thesis modelling the Vega de Tera dam failure, see Prieto Calderón (2014).

8 *ABC*, 15 March 1963, 51.

9 See the full verdict at AHPZ archive, 18/59 (Ribadelago), box 2.

10 AHPZ archive, 18/59 (Ribadelago), box 2.

11 *ABC*, 22 April 1965, pp. 61–62.

12 In this case, the reference to the use of masonry in buttress dams comes in article 47, and unlike five years earlier, includes an additional sentence stating that masonry will not be allowed 'unless specially justified' (Ministerio de Obras Públicas 1967). For the current legislation regarding dam safety in Spain, see Ministerio para la Transición Ecológica (1967).

13 See 'America's newest national monument honors the lesser-known history of the St. Francis Dam disaster'. <https://roadtrippers.com/magazine/st-francis-dam-disaster-monument/>. (last accessed 8 October 2019).

14 See Johnstown Flood National Memorial, Pennsylvania <www.nps.gov/jofl/index.htm> (last accessed 8 October 2019).

References

Agencia EFE. (2018) 'Ribadelago de Franco (Zamora) cambia su nombre por Ribadelago Nuevo', *Cadena COPE*, 1 September. <www.cope.es/actualidad/noticias/ribadelago-franco-zamora-cambia-nombre-por-ribadelago-nuevo-20180901_254050>.

Aijazi, O. (2015) 'Theorizing a Social Repair Orientation to Disaster Recovery: Developing Insights for Disaster Recovery Policy and Programming', *Global Social Welfare*, (2): 15–28. <https://doi.org/10.1007/s40609-014-0013-x>.

Alonso Pérez, J. *et al.* (2011) 'Acondicionamiento de la presa de Puente Porto (Zamora)', in R. Romeo García *et al.* (eds) *Dam Maintenance and Rehabilitation II*, London: Taylor & Francis, 967–973.

Anes, G., Fernández, S. and Temboury, J. (2001) *Endesa en su historia (1944–2000)*, Madrid: Fundación Endesa.

Armiero, M. (2011) *A Rugged Nation: Mountains and the Making of Modern Italy*, Cambridge: The White Horse Press.

Armiero, M. *et al.* (2019) 'Toxic Bios: Toxic Autobiographies: A Public Environmental Humanities Project', *Environmental Justice*, 12(1): 7–11. <https://doi.org/10.1089/env.2018.0019>.

Barca, S. (2014) 'Telling the Right Story: Environmental Violence and Liberation Narratives', *Environment and History*, 20(4): 535–546. <https://doi.org/10.3197/0967340 14X14091313617325>.

Barca, S. (2016) 'On "The Political" in Environmental History', *Journal for Ecological History*, 1.<https://seeingthewoods.org/2017/04/05/uses-of-environmental-history-stefania-barca/>.

Becerril Bustamante, J.A. (2018) 'Ribadelago', *Revista de Obras Públicas*, 3599: 58–59.

Camprubí, L. (2014) *Engineers and the Making of the Francoist Regime*, Cambridge, MA: The MIT Press.

Camprubí, L. (2017) *Los Ingenieros de Franco: ciencia, catolicismo y Guerra Fría en el estado franquista*, Barcelona: Crítica.

De Wrachien, D. and Mambretti, S. (eds) (2009) *Dam-break Problems, Solutions and Case Studies*, Southampton, UK: WIT Press.

Dodier, N. (1995) *Les hommes et les machines. La conscience collective dans les sociétés technicisées*, Paris: Métailié.

Emidio di Treviri (2018) *Sul fronte del sisma. Un'inchiesta militante sul post-terremoto dell'Appennino centrale (2016–2017)*, Roma: DeriveApprodi.

Esteban, V. (2009) 'Más de un millar de personas homenajea a los supervivientes de Ribadelago', *ABC*, 10 January. <www.abc.es/espana/castilla-leon/abci-mas-millar-personas-homenajea-supervivientes-ribadelago-200901100300-912355566234_noticia.html>.

Europa Press. (2019) 'CHA cree un 'atropello' que el Gobierno central en funciones otorgue el visto bueno medioambiental a mina Muga', <www.20minutos.es/noticia/3664056/0/cha-cree-atropello-que-gobierno-central-funciones-otorgue-visto-bueno-medioambiental-mina-muga/> (accessed 30 June 2020).

Fernández Casado, J.L. (1961) 'Vigilancia de presas', *Revista de Obras Públicas*, (2954): 368–370.

Fortun, K. *et al.* (2017) 'Researching Disaster from an STS Perspective', in U. Felt *et al.* (eds) *The Handbook of Science and Technology Studies*, Cambridge, MA: The MIT Press.

García Díez, J.A. (2001) *Ribadelago – Tragedia de Vega de Tera*, 2nd edition, Salamanca: A. Saavedra.

García Díez, J.A. (2008) 'Endesa refuerza la presa de Puente Porto, que lleva 50 años a media explotación', *La Opinión de Zamora*, 17 October.

González Fernández, J.M. (2003) 'Reparación de la presa de El Tejo', in J.A Llanos *et al.* (eds) *Dam Maintenance and Rehabilitation*, London & New York: Taylor & Francis, 719–726.

Herman, D. (2007) 'Introduction', in D. Herman (ed.) *The Cambridge Companion to Narrative*, Cambridge and New York: Cambridge University Press, 3–21.

Huber, A. *et al.* (2016) 'Beyond "socially Constructed" Disasters: Re-politicizing the Debate on Large Dams through a Political Ecology of Risk', *Capitalism Nature Socialism*, 5752, September, 1–21. <https://doi.org/10.1080/10455752.2016.1225222>.

Iser, M. (2019) 'Recognition', in *The Stanford Encyclopedia of Philosophy*. <https://plato. stanford.edu/archives/sum2019/entries/recognition/> (accessed 1 July 2020).

Kaika, M. (2006) 'Dams as Symbols of Modernization: The Urbanization of Nature between Geographical Imagination and Materiality', *Annals of the Association of American Geographers*, 96(2): 276–301. <https://doi.org/10.1111/j.1467–8306.2006.00478.x>.

Lindblom, J. (no date) *L'Aquila Disaster Response: Migration, Loss and Resettlement*, Italy, Clisel Geoarchive. <https://geoarchive.clisel.eu/geoarchive/laquiladisasterrespon-semigrationlossandresettlementitaly> (accessed 30 June 2020).

López, M. (2009) '1,3 millones de espectadores vieron "Tragedia en Ribadelago"', *La Opinión de Zamora*, 15 January. <www.laopiniondezamora.es/zamora/2009/01/15/13-millones-espectadores-vieron-tragedia-ribadelago/327487.html>.

McCully, P. (2001) *Silenced Rivers: The Ecology and Politics of Large Dams*, 2nd edition, London: Zed Books.

Ministerio de Asuntos Exteriores. (1968) 'DECRETO 1943/1968, de 18 de julio, por el que se concede la Gran Cruz de la Orden del Mérito Civil a Gabriel Barceló Matutano', *Boletín Oficial del Estado*, 195: 12068.

Ministerio de la Vivienda. (1959) 'DECRETO 121/159, de 15 de enero, por el que se declara adoptado por el Caudillo el pueblo de Ribadelago (Zamora) y se encomienda su reconstrucción al Ministerio de la Vivienda', *Boletín Oficial del Estado*, 18: 1234.

Ministerio de Obras Públicas. (1959) 'DECRETO 1740/1959, de 8 de octubre, restableciendo las Jefaturas o Comisarías de Aguas', *Boletín Oficial del Estado*, 244: 13129–13131.

Ministerio de Obras Públicas. (1962) 'ORDEN de 21 de agosto de 1962 por la que se aprueba la "Instrucción para proyecto, construcción y explotación de grandes presas"', *Boletín Oficial del Estado*, 218: 12879–12896.

Ministerio de Obras Públicas. (1967) 'ORDEN de 31 de marzo de 1967 por la que se aprueba la "Instrucción para proyecto, construcción y explotación de grandes presas"', *Boletín Oficial del Estado*, 257: 14716–14738.

Ministerio para la Transición Ecológica. (1967) 'Legislación aplicable en materia de seguridad de presas', <www.miteco.gob.es/es/agua/temas/seguridad-de-presas-y-embalses/marco-legislativo/legislacion.aspx> (accessed 15 September 2019).

Museo Etnográfico de Castilla y León. (2008) *Ribadelago: 9 ene 1959 00h24: en el cincuenta aniversario de la rotura de la presa de Vega de Tera y el desastre de Ribadelago de 9 de enero de 1959*, Zamora: Museo Etnográfico de Castilla y León.

Otero Puente, M.J. (2016) 'José Luis Sánchez y Ribadelago', *La Opinión de Zamora*, 7 July. <www.laopiniondezamora.es/opinion/2016/07/07/jose-luis-sanchez-ribadelago/937619.html>.

Otero Puente, M.J. (2019) 'El dolor de aquella desoladora injusticia', *La Opinión de Zamora*, 18 February. <www.laopiniondezamora.es/opinion/2019/02/19/dolor-desoladora-injusticia/1144975.html>.

Pérez, A. (2019) 'Una subvención de la Junta rescata del olvido el Museo de la Memoria de Ribadelago', *El Norte de Castilla*, 29 July. <www.elnortedecastilla.es/zamora/subvencion-junta-rescata-20190729085102-nt.html>.

Prieto Calderón, J.L. (2014) *Reconstrucción histórica, estructural, hidrológica, hidráulica y socioeconómica de la catástrofe de Ribadelago (Rotura de la presa de Vega de Tera)*, Universidad de Vigo, Escuela Técnica Superior de Ingenieros de Minas. <www.investigo.biblioteca.uvigo.es/xmlui/handle/11093/368>.

Radstone, S. and Hodgkin, K. (2006) 'Regimes of Memory: An Introduction', in S. Radstone and K. Hodgkin (eds) *Memory Cultures: Memory, Subjectivity, and Recognition*, New Brunswick, NJ: Transaction Publishers, 1–22.

Remesal, A. (2009) *Sanabria en la Memoria. 1959–2009. Tragedia en Ribadelago*, Salamanca: La Raya Quebrada.

Rubín de Célix Caballero, M. (2003) 'Seguridad de presas: Pasado, presente y futuro', *Ingeniería y Territorio*, 62: 12–21.

Ruiz Trilleros, M. (2012) *La escultura construida de José Luis Sánchez*, Universidad Complutense de Madrid. <http://eprints.ucm.es/16497/1/T33882.pdf>.

Saavedra, A. (2018) 'La Piedad de Ribadelago, censurada', *La Opinión de Zamora*, 24 August. <www.laopiniondezamora.es/comarcas/2018/08/25/piedad-ribadelago-censurada/1105740.html>.

Saavedra, A. (2019) 'El Museo de la Memoria, en el olvido', *La Opinión de Zamora*, 9 January. <www.laopiniondezamora.es/comarcas/2019/01/09/museo-memoria-olvido/1136185.html.

Stop Yesa por seguridad – YESA NO. (2009) 'Ribadelago, 50 años de la tragedia que arrasó 144 vidas', <https://rioaragon.wordpress.com/2009/01/14/ribadelago-50-anos-de-la-tragedia-que-arraso-144-vidas/ (accessed 30 June 2020).

Swyngedouw, E. (2015) *Liquid Power: Contested Hydro-modernities in Twentieth-century Spain*, Cambridge: MIT Press.

5 Preparing for future pandemics and repairing vulnerable environments

Consequences of the 1997 bird flu outbreak in Hong Kong

Frédéric Keck

In this chapter, I want to reflect on the relations between two apparently opposite frameworks of disaster management: repair and prepare. While repairing is a means to recover from past disasters, preparing is a technique to anticipate future disasters. There is a connexion between these two notions if repairing, rather than turning toward the past through accusation, is orientated toward the future through anticipation. However, following the suggestions of this book, I want to depart from an instrumental or functionalist view of these techniques and move to a more ontological description of 'prepare' and 'repair'. Taking the case of pandemic preparedness, which is one of the global priorities of disaster management, my analysis focuses on vulnerable environments where humans are at risk of being infected by a flu virus coming from birds. Rather than taking vulnerability and risk as quantitative frames, which is often the case in the literature on disaster management, I describe them as relations between humans and non-humans whose perception varies based on ecological histories and religious practices.

As I have argued elsewhere (Keck 2020), pandemic preparedness drives humans to take the perspectives of non-humans (birds, bats, pigs, cows, etc.) through the early warning signals they send of emerging infectious diseases. On their side, Centemeri *et al.* (see Introduction) argue that a repairing perspective requires us to take into account 'disaster recovery through a consideration of the variety of material ecologies that become visible as a result of their misfunctioning and the efforts to repair them'. Joining these two perspectives in this contribution, I want to question how the experience of the disaster can lead us to reframe the frontiers between species. Taking the contemporary figure of the 'sentinel post' as an ethnographic site, where early warning signals of pandemics are captured in *dispositifs* such as the introduction of unvaccinated chickens in a poultry farm, I study how techniques of preparedness have reorganized relations between humans and birds in Hong Kong. Being more sensitive than other living beings to infectious threats, sentinels play a central role in the reorganization of multi-species ecologies at the time of pandemics.

The articulation of the perspectives of 'repair' and 'prepare' brings new light, I hope, to the literature on pandemics published in the past 20 years. Two kinds

DOI: 10.4324/9781003184782-8

of narratives can be distinguished in this growing field, which will continue to expand with the current pandemic of Covid-19. On the one hand, a historical perspective looks at how the influenza pandemic of 1918–1919, which killed probably 50 million people, has affected human societies and served as a reference to think about other epidemics and pandemics, such as pneumonic plague in 1910, HIV/AIDS beginning in the early 1980s and continuing to date, or SARS in 2003 (Kolata 1999; Abraham 2007; Kleinman and Watson 2006; Lynteris 2016). Paradoxically, the influenza pandemic has been described as a forgotten disaster. It occurred at the end of the First World War, and it was not experienced as a collective disaster but rather as an event that struck individuals, redoubling the losses of the war (Crosby 2003; Honigsbaum 2019). Only after epidemiological surveys were conducted did the influenza pandemic appear as a scourge more damaging than the war itself, which killed roughly 20 million people. The interwar years then appeared as a period of reparation not only of the first global war, with the debate on economic reparations (Mallard 2011), but also of the flu pandemic, with the debate on the reorganization of the scientific field and the public health system (Rasmussen 2007).

The second range of literature on pandemics shows how the emergence of new infectious diseases such as Ebola, or HIV/AIDS in the 1980s, led global authorities to prepare for future pandemics. This literature, most often published by anthropologists, looks at the scenarios of anticipation of the future built around the pandemic as an event with low probability but catastrophic consequences, and the techniques implemented to mitigate these consequences, such as sentinels, simulation and stockpiling (Adams *et al.* 2009). It has showed that these techniques of pandemic preparedness did not begin in the 1980s with emerging infectious diseases, but were built during the Second World War, when the United States feared an influenza outbreak linked to its involvement in the war, as a kind of repetition of the trauma of 1918, and at the beginning of the Cold War, when civil defense invented scenarios to prepare for a nuclear attack (Bresalier 2011; Caduff 2015; Lakoff 2017). In that literature, the focus is less on reparation and more on anticipation, less on equity in the distribution of environmental risks and more on trust in the perception of early warning signals. These two ranges of literature should not be opposed too strictly, since anthropological works also refer to historical archives, but it is striking, in this work, to learn that pandemic preparedness relied less on the memory of previous pandemics and more on the imagination of other generic threats.

The narrative I propose in this chapter takes place between these two contrasted views, retrospective and prospective, of pandemics. Focusing on pandemic preparedness in Hong Kong, I will show that, after 1997, an influenza pandemic was an event for which the population was getting prepared but also was a disaster that had already happened, in the massive killing of birds to eradicate the reservoir of the disease. In this disjunction between a disaster actually affecting birds' lives and a disaster that could potentially affect human life, the massive death of birds was perceived by Hong Kong citizens as a signal of human extinction (Lynteris 2019). The prospective and the retrospective are thus trapped in narratives of situations where human lives and bird lives are entangled with emerging viruses, leading to a multi-species approach of disaster recovery (Haraway 2007; Kirksey and Helmreich 2010; see also Chapter 3). Following this approach, I will ask how the decision to kill or cure bird lives has been understood as signal of what could happen to human lives, on which grounds it has been justified and how the fabric of memory and heritage has absorbed this traumatic event (Kirschenblatt-Gimblett 1998).

This chapter relies on the ethnographic research I conducted in Hong Kong between 2007 and 2013, based on interviews with virologists, ornithologists, poultry farmers, retailers and consumers as well as scientific and administrative literature on avian influenza. After describing the measures implemented in Hong Kong to prepare for an influenza pandemic coming from birds, I will focus on a specific location, Kadoorie Farm and Botanical Gardens, which recapitulates all the tensions experienced by the Hong Kong population in trying to repair the massive loss of bird life at the time of the handover of the British colony to the Chinese People's Republic. I returned to Kadoorie Farm every time I went to Hong Kong, as I always felt that it was a site of intense historical reflexivity and ecological sensitivity. I consider it as a good sentinel post in its attempt to conserve its bird population rather than destroy it under the threat of bird flu.

Hong Kong's new identity as a sentinel post for avian influenza

Bird flu outbreaks have punctuated the history of Hong Kong, in its transition from a garrison entrepôt and financial centre for the British Empire to a sentinel post in the global economy under threat of a pandemic coming from China, as a never-ending disaster. This history of pandemic preparedness begins in 1972 when Kennedy Shortridge created an influenza unit at the Department of Microbiology of the University of Hong Kong – even if mythical narratives draw the genealogy of this department to 1894, when Alexandre Yersin, trained in Paris by Louis Pasteur, built a hut to study the transmission of plague in Pokfulam, the area of Hong Kong where the Department of Microbiology was later created (Peckham 2013). Shortridge had been trained in microbiology at the school of medical sciences launched in Australia after the Second World War by Frank Macfarlane Burnet, who built the first hypotheses on the mutations of influenza viruses, which led global health organizations to adapt vaccination (Anderson 2004). While his colleague Robert Webster had observed that these mutations occurred amongst wild birds, considered as the animal reservoir of influenza viruses, and were then transmitted to humans via pigs (Webster and Campbell 1972), Shortridge observed that the last flu pandemics, in 1957 and 1968, started in the south of China. Since China was not a member of the World Health Organization at that time, the emergence of flu viruses was not detected early. Shortridge built networks of personal relations (*guanxi*) with veterinarians in Guangdong, and collected samples of flu viruses from ducks and pigs in the area. He had observed that rice paddies of south China used wild ducks as pesticides, a system known as *daotian yangya* (Zhang *et al.*

2009; Fearnley 2018) – thus bringing them in close proximity to humans and pigs. He concluded that this traditional ecology was an 'influenza epicenter' for the rest of the world. 'The densely populated intensively farmed area of Southern China adjacent to Hong Kong', he wrote with the renowned British influenza expert Charles Stuart-Harris, 'is an ideal place for events such as interchange of viruses between host species' (Shortridge and Stuart-Harris 1982: 812).

In the preface to a reference book on avian influenza, Shortridge mentioned the memory of the 1918 flu pandemic in Australia:

> My mother's compelling stories about the devastating reaches of the pandemic have stayed with me since my earliest years. What started out as a spark of interest has led me to search the hows and whys of influenza pandemics through birds and mammals.
>
> (Greger 2006: XI)

Surprisingly, the 1968 flu pandemic, called 'Hong Kong flu', left few traces in the memory of the Hong Kong population, probably because the Hong Kong government was then much more concerned with the social troubles caused by the arrival of refugees from the Cultural Revolution and the threat of social uprisings caused by 'Chinese spies' (Caroll 2007: 150). But it affected strongly the health of the population: 500,000 persons were infected, or 15 per cent of the population, while the pandemic killed 1 million persons worldwide, with a lethality rate of 0.5 per cent but severe symptoms (Knott 2018). The colonial government of Edward Youde launched a massive policy of welfare state in the 1970s to cope with the social and sanitation needs of refugees (Caroll 2007: 168).

Consequently, Shortridge's work in collecting flu samples from south China aimed both at repairing and anticipating pandemics: because flu viruses are severe when they jump from animals to humans, the best way to repair the trauma of the past pandemics was to prepare for the next pandemic by monitoring animal reservoirs.

Shortridge's strategy proved successful in 1997, 25 years after he implemented it. The British colony was about to return to Chinese sovereignty, after a treaty was signed by Margaret Thatcher and Deng Xiaoping claiming that Hong Kong and China would be 'one country, two systems' (Caroll 2007: 179). Cases of a new influenza virus, called H5N1 by the experts of the World Health Organization, were detected in February 1997 amongst 12 humans, eight of whom died, and killed 5,000 chickens. Shortridge went to markets and raised the alarm. There were 1,000 live poultry markets in Hong Kong at that time, and in some of them 36 per cent of chickens tested positive for H5N1. He recalled,

> One moment birds happily picked their grains, the next they fell sideways in slow motion, grasping for breath with blood slowly oozing from their guts. I had never seen anything like it. I thought, "My God. What if this virus were to get out of this market and spread elsewhere?"
>
> (Greger 2006: 35)

Because the flu vaccine was made on chicken eggs, it was impossible to vaccinate chickens and humans against this new virus, which was lethal to both. In November 1997, Shortridge consequently recommended the Hong Kong government make a difficult decision that had been already used in the United States for similar outbreaks of influenza in poultry farms: kill all the live poultry in the territory to eradicate the animal reservoir of the virus. A team of civil servants from the Agriculture Department was assigned to this difficult task, which was repeated every time an influenza virus was detected in poultry farms or markets. 'Most of them had never seen live poultry before. They had to learn. Now some of them have become experts in poultry culling', the head of the Agriculture Department later declared (Kolata 1999: 240). The term 'culling' is used euphemistically to describe the killing of infected animals to clean the flock, but Shortridge said to me in an interview, 'We didn't cull, we conducted a slaughter!'[1] Shortridge justified this massive killing as a preemptive measure to lower the probability of a flu pandemic starting from Hong Kong.

> Poultry were killed market-by-market as signs became evident, leading to the pre-emptive slaughter of all poultry to prevent human infection. Early detection and reaction was the order again in 2002 and 2003. Thus, there now lay the prospect for influenza-pandemic preparedness not only at the human level but, better still, at the baseline avian level with the ideal that if a virus could be stamped out before it infected humans, an influenza incident or pandemic will not result. In 1997, the world was probably one or two mutational events away from a pandemic, while in 2002, with earlier detection, it was probably three or four events away.
>
> (Shortridge 2005: 10)

This massive killing was a shock for the Hong Kong population, since most of them came from rural provinces of mainland China and shared a similar approach to farming based on a small household with chickens and pigs.[2] It was not uncommon before 1997 to see backyard poultry in Hong Kong, but this practice was forbidden by the government after 1997. Poultry farms were allowed under strict conditions: ducks, who carried the virus without symptoms, could not be raised, and chickens were to be sent to a central market for inspection.

The violent eradication of established practices in agriculture, which in actual fact led to the disappearance or strict control exerted on animal species, echoed the fears that Hong Kong citizens had about returning under Chinese control. In a way, Hong Kong citizens identified with the slaughtered chickens, geese, ducks and quails. There were many fears before 1997 that the Hong Kong population would be crushed by the Chinese People's Liberation Army just as it had crushed students in the Tiananmen square in 1989 – an event mourned annually on 4 June in the parks of Hong Kong. A Chinese saying goes: 'Kill chickens to warn monkeys' (*sha ji jing hou*) – meaning, in this context, that the massive killing of chickens symbolized China's restored sovereignty over Hong Kong. The killing of more than 1 million poultry may also have recalled Mao Zedong's 1958 mobilization of the Chinese population against sparrows, which were considered pests

(Shapiro 2001: 88). It was a major trauma in the relations between the Hong Kong population, their government and their natural environment.

The idea that the early detection of viruses in their animal reservoirs and rapid intervention led to prevent a pandemic was confirmed in 2003 with the SARS (severe acute respiratory syndrome) crisis caused by a coronavirus that circulated amongst bats and transmitted to humans through the civet cats consumed in Chinese traditional medicine. The virus returned to its animal reservoir when civet cats were killed and their sale forbidden. Shortridge then wrote an article with his two colleagues at the Hong Kong University Department of Microbiology, Guan Yi and Malik Peiris, who had identified the SARS virus in animals and humans, in which he concluded:

> The studies on the ecology of influenza [carried out] in Hong Kong in the 1970s, in which Hong Kong acted as a sentinel post for influenza, indicated that it was possible, for the first time, to do preparedness for flu on the avian level.
>
> (Shortridge, Peiris and Guan 2003)

Shortridge and his colleagues' article was infused with the idea that live poultry markets, a tradition in Hong Kong, needed to be modernized and regulated, just like Chinese traditional medicine in mainland China or 'wet markets' in Singapore – a term connoting the daily cleaning of markets where animals are sold and killed in front of the consumers. Hong Kong microbiology experts recommended these strong biosecurity measures after 2003 to control the risk of infection between humans and birds in live poultry markets, which added up to the measures of inspection implemented in 1997 (Woo *et al.* 2006).

Biosecurity meant not only the extraordinary *mise-en-scène* of killing poultry in the central market of Hong Kong, or organizing simulations of bird flu outbreaks in markets and hospitals, but also the more ordinary work of surveillance and control in farms and markets (Lakoff and Collier 2008). As the H5N1 avian influenza virus emerged in Hong Kong in 1997 and spread to the rest of the world after 2005, the measures imposed in Hong Kong were used as a model for those recommended by international administrations to countries facing the risk of transmission from birds to humans. Margaret Chan, who had managed the outbreaks of H5N1 and SARS in Hong Kong between 1997 and 2003, was elected head of the World Health Organization in 2006, and she promoted the International Health Regulation, which made pandemic preparedness a priority. Being a sentinel post of influenza meant that Hong Kong was at the vanguard of measures to control zoonotic diseases with pandemic potential, and functioned as a kind of experimental site for measures that should be imposed on the whole Asian continent.

Changing relationship between humans and bird life in Hong Kong

The measures imposed by the Hong Kong government to regulate the live poultry industry were so strong that they clearly aimed at reducing or even suppressing this traditional activity. Retailers had to kill all the live poultry at the end of the day and wash their shop every night, and the market was closed for one day every week to clean it from potential infections. Because of the liberal tradition of the Hong Kong government due to its position as a hub in the global trade between East and West (Grantham 1965), it was impossible to forbid selling live poultry on the territory, as the Beijing authorities had done after the first cases of avian influenza in the capital city. But it was clearly a paradox to see live poultry sold in the markets of a modern city highly aware of the risks of zoonotic transmission. Hong Kong citizens were attached to the tradition of eating a 'fresh' chicken, which was supposed to be more tasty and safer than 'chilled' poultry imported from mainland China. While the government encouraged the purchase of 'chilled' poultry in supermarkets, the purchase of live poultry declined only gradually.[3] A fresh chicken was compared by Hong Kong consumers to a fresh fish that could be chosen in a pond before being eaten in a restaurant or at home. Looking at the live poultry was part of the pleasure of eating its meat, by contrast with pork or beef, whose meat was sold in pieces. Consequently, poultry farming in Hong Kong remained a strong economy, with 30 farms raising around 50,000 chickens each. They were organized in a trade union to cope with the risks of avian influenza, as all the chickens on the farm had to be killed if there was a single case of infection. Biosecurity measures on the farms, such as nets to protect the poultry from wild birds or ponds to clean the boots of workers and the wheels of trucks entering the farm, were perceived as obstacles by poultry farmers and often not respected (Liu 2008).

One biosecurity measure in particular is relevant to the argument I wish to make, as it is very eloquent with respect to the relations between humans and birds in Hong Kong. While vaccination was compulsory against influenza, some chickens were left unvaccinated at the entrance of cage rows, with a ratio of 60 sentinels for 4,000 chickens. They were found dead in quantity when an influenza virus entered the farm, which allowed the farmer to raise an alert. The use of sentinel birds is common for a range of infectious diseases, such as the West Nile virus, transmitted to humans by mosquitoes, and for which chickens are put into cages to check if they seroconvert to the disease that is lethal in humans but not in birds (Doherty 2012). The Chinese word for sentinel birds is *shaobingji*, which literally means 'chickens whistling like soldiers'. This implies that chickens are allies of humans in their fight against a virus that circulates asymptomatically amongst wild birds: they die first of a virus that could ravage the human species if turned into a pandemic.

As I was thinking of Hong Kong's new identity in a changing ecology, the analogy between the position of sentinel chickens in a poultry farm and the position of Hong Kong as a sentinel post between China and the global economy struck me in two ways. On one side, it could be argued that sentinels are sacrificed when the farm or the territory is exposed to infectious threats: in dying, they raise the alarm so that the farm or the territory can be cleaned. This interpretation is common in what anthropologists define as 'pastoral societies' which rely on the sacrifice of some living beings to save the rest of the flock. But sentinel chickens do not always die, and their conservation in a space of exposure allows humans to know more about the presence of microbes in the environment. Sentinel chickens are used in a liminal space between humans and birds because they display their common vulnerability. Their function is not only to repair by ridding the territory of its cursed parts but also to prepare by displaying sites of exposure. This view of sentinels as mediators of communication is commonly shared by hunting societies. It is striking to know that the domestication of the red junglefowl (*Gallus gallus*) occurred in south China between 10,000 and 7,000 years ago, before this species became globalized as a major source of the industrialization of meat production, and that archaeologists assume, based on bone remains, that it was domesticated for the purpose of divination (Simmons 1991: 298). Preparing for pandemics through the use of sentinel birds might thus be linked to an old technique of anticipation in the transition from hunting to pastoral societies. In this perspective, repair and prepare can be contrasted as the classical anthropological operations of sacrifice and divination, which are often entangled in human societies but must be distinguished as different techniques to manage the life and death of non-human animals.

The emergence of the H5N1 virus in 1997 can be characterized as a disaster in two senses. Literally, it destroyed all the live poultry in the territory, to which Hong Kong citizens were attached, as backyard chickens or duck farms were forbidden by the government and live poultry farms and markets were strictly regulated. Metaphorically, it destroyed a sense of identity of Hong Kong citizens under British rule as strong producers of a global industry, and shaped a new sense of identity under their new government by Chinese sovereignty. Preparing for future pandemics was a way to repair this lost identity, by converting a trading post into a sentinel post. Hong Kong became a sentinel post for the global spread of avian influenza like sentinel chickens at the entrance of poultry farms to raise alert about the spread of the virus. Several movies produced by Hong Kong filmmakers reflected this vulnerability of Hong Kong under Chinese rule, configured by the doctrine 'one country, two systems', such as Johnny To's *Sparrow* (2008) which depicts a woman as a bird trapped in a cage. To understand how art can become a way to express this new relation between humans and bird, I will look at the politics of cultural heritage and natural conservation in the case of a specific site: the Kadoorie Farm.

The Kadoorie Farm: a centre for bird conservation and historical heritage

The politics of heritage in Hong Kong has been described as a mix of weak initiatives from the government and strong mobilizations from citizens (Veg 2007). As real estate pressure leads to the destruction of historical buildings, and because Hong Kong is not famous as a cultural tourism destination, the heritage of the British colony has rarely been preserved, by contrast with the Portuguese colony of Macao, which was inscribed on the UNESCO World Heritage List in 2005. However, 10 years after the handover of the British colony, non-governmental organizations to preserve the heritage have developed, promoting cultural trails on which one may view traditional Hakka houses or defending historically valuable colonial buildings against destruction. The Hong Kong Heritage Museum opened in 2000 in Sha Tin, east of the New Territories, with beautiful displays about Cantonese opera and fishermen's techniques. The Tai Kwun Centre for Heritage and Arts opened in 2018 in Soho, in the busy streets of Hong Kong, located in the former Central Police Station. But none of these places deals with traditional relations between humans and birds in Hong Kong. To learn about them, you can go to one of the four aviaries opened to the public in Hong Kong parks or to the Bird Market in Mong Kok, where exotic birds are displayed or sold. However, there is only one place that keeps local birds as cultural heritage and testimony of a disastrous history, and this is the Kadoorie Farm.

The Kadoorie Farm and Botanic Garden is located along the road between Nam Cheong and Tai Po, right in the middle of the New Territories. It is a series of small metal buildings, streams, terraces and forest trees along the slopes of Tai Mo Shan, the highest mountain in Hong Kong, reaching 1,800 metres above sea level. Kadoorie Farm was created in 1956 by two bankers, the brothers Horace and Lawrence Kadoorie, who owned Hong Kong's most prestigious hotel, The Peninsula, and the main power company in China. In 1951, with the arrival of refugees from mainland China, the brothers set up an association to teach them agricultural techniques that would allow them to become independent. Their motto was: 'Helping people to help themselves'. This motto had already earned success and prestige for the Kadoorie brothers when they financially supported European immigrants in Shanghai in the 1930s (Kaufman 2020). The Kadoorie Farm was designed as a site of demonstration where agriculture techniques were displayed with pigs and chickens. Local farmers were taught how to build cages, select breeds, hatch eggs, ventilate (as backyard poultry-keepingwas replaced by enclosed barns) and vaccinate (particularly against Newcastle disease, which killed chickens massively without being transmissible to humans). Refugees who learnt how to raise animals were given pigs and chickens if they built a farm in the valley. This philanthropic endeavor was also a way to meet the demands of the market. Because of the boycott of Chinese products by the United States, poultry raised in Hong Kong was exported and sold to the Chinese diaspora in North America. In 1949, there were 145 farms breeding about 1,000 chickens in Hong Kong, but in a few years there were more than 1,000 farms raising around 100,000 chickens each (Yeung 1956).

This model of livestock development gradually declined and was transformed into a model of biodiversity conservation, as the US market turned to chickens from mainland China and as the bird flu outbreak damaged the poultry industry in Hong Kong. In 1995, the Legislative Council passed an ordinance that established the Kadoorie Farm and Botanic Garden Corporation (KFBGC) with a mission to educate the public about nature conservation. The Kadoorie family was still on the board of the company and heavily funded it. Horace Kadoorie had introduced parrots and flamingoes on the farm who outlived him after he passed away in 1995. A statue of him smiling and sitting on a bench welcomes visitors entering the park. In 1994, just before his death, he supported the creation of a raptor sanctuary to provisionally host vulnerable wild birds. It had been proposed by his friend Jim Ades, a British officer and passionate birdwatcher who collected birds in the wild and rescued those he found sick or which had been illegally passed through the border with China. Horace Kadoorie hired Jim Ades' son, Gary, as the head of the Fauna Conservation department. Under Gary Ades' management, this rescue activity became a major attraction, with more than 1,000 birds rescued every year. Visitors come to see the flamingoes and parrots, often not knowing that they are as old as the farm itself, but also the eagles and owls who have just been rescued. The centre provides biographies for the birds, detailing when they were brought, what injuries they suffered and when they might be released. Raptors are released every Sunday on the summit of the mountain from the Kadoorie Brothers Memorial Pavilion, two small Chinese temples overpassing the valley. A memorial race is organized there every year. This pavilion is believed to be inhabited by the souls of the birds who were rescued and released there.

One of the agents working at the rescue centre of KFBGC at the time of my research, named Captain Wong, was very active in the protection of birds. He was appalled by the birds found dead in natural parks where Buddhist practitioners released birds – a tradition called *fangsheng*, 'let live'. These birds were trapped in the wild and sold in the Bird Market of Mong Kok to be released in improper environments, and the stress of being caged often led them to die. With the support of birdwatchers' associations in Hong Kong and Taiwan, Captain Wong organized a conference in Taipei in 2007 to document this practice. He negotiated with the Hong Kong government and the Hong Kong Buddhist Association to replace the release of birds with the release of reptiles and amphibians – turtles, fish, frogs and the like. Captain Wong was proud to invite Buddhist practitioners to the bird release ceremony at the Kadoorie Brothers Memorial Pavilion on Sundays. It was a kind of secular ritual, where the souls of birds were traced through a GPS antenna that allowed birdwatchers to follow their movements in the wild. Books were distributed to Buddhist practitioners indicating where to properly release wild birds. Called 'scientific release handbooks' (*kexue fangsheng shoushu*), they were modeled after the handbooks of Buddhist prayers that accompany animal release.

Another memorial site in the Kadoorie Farm was closed to the public: a cage containing chickens, which bore a warning to the visitors: 'The Chicken Display House will be closed until further notice to ensure the chickens at the Kadoorie Farm and Botanic Gardens are protected from any possible outside contamination while bird flu concerns still exist in Hong Kong.' Farm authorities saw it as a centre for the conservation of local breeds, particularly the Wai Chow, the White Wai Chow and the Guangzhou chicken, which disappeared from mainland China during the Cultural Revolution. Shing Tam-Yip was the head of the breeding team, taking care of the 2,500 chickens and nine pigs (the pigs were the 'mascots' of the farm). A passionate birdwatcher and plant scientist trained at Hong Kong University, Shing Tam-Yip detailed to me the measures of protection of these chickens against avian influenza.[4] If the virus entered the farm, he said, it would be the end of these local breeds. The Kadoorie Farm had its own system of alert, more severe than that imposed by the government, with three levels: vigilant, serious and urgent. Indeed, in case of an outbreak of bird flu in the surroundings of the farm, the cost of culling the birds would measure, not the value of the meat, but the genetic knowledge preserved by decades of selection. All but 60 chickens were vaccinated. The unvaccinated chickens acted as sentinels, scattered all over the aviaries. These chicken farms had to be closed to the public in 1997 with the emergence of the H5N1 flu virus. Shing Tam-Yip told me that before 1997, the selection of the purest breed was a public ceremony, but it became private after 1997 for safety reasons. Selection consisted in sexing the males from the females, ringing the females, preserving the males who had the highest value and destroying the rest of the males. Shing contrasted the killing of one-day-old chicks for selection to the massive killing of poultry as a preventive measure against bird flu:

> We use CO_2. This is not torture. For 10 seconds they shake a lot, but after 20 seconds it is silent. When they killed poultry at the central market of Cheung Sha Wan, the quantity of gas was not enough. Poultry died after a very long time. It was really torture. People watching on television felt distress.

By many accounts, the Kadoorie Farm counters the biosecurity measures adopted against avian influenza by the Hong Kong government, and pursues a science of conservation that remedies the politics of destruction of birds. While the Hong Kong government culls all chickens when some of them are found infected with the influenza viruses, hoping to gradually cancel the live poultry activity itself, Buddhist associations pray for the souls of the birds and release them in natural parks, duplicating the economy of chickens as commodities by an economy of souls. Birdwatchers are breaking with this economy of pastoral care by what can be analyzed as techniques of hunting societies (Keck 2020). Coming from a colonial history of hunters (Fan 2004; MacKenzie 1988; Moss 2004; Peckham 2014), they have built a conservatory in the middle of the territory where 'pastoral' techniques of power are reversed into 'cynegetic' techniques of power. Raptors are released with GPS antennas to follow their movements, and chickens are selected scientifically to reduce their suffering. Birdwatchers, following techniques of hunters, empathize with birds at their death and share the vulnerability of birds in a world threatened by disasters (Viveiros de Castro 1992). Sentinel chickens in effect communicate with humans about the threats that affect them in common by bearing the signs of zoonotic viruses, while the Hong Kong government relies on politics of sacrifice when it kills live poultry to eradicate the avian reservoir of these viruses.

The Kadoorie Farm can be analyzed as a 'ruin' of the Hong Kong colonial past, in the sense developed by Anna Tsing (2015). With its memorials, metal buildings and old flamingoes as reminders of the founding brothers, it resists the standardization of the poultry industry. Paradoxically, while the Kadoorie brothers taught Chinese immigrants in Hong Kong how to raise chickens in an intensive and industrial manner, these chicken breeds are now conserved because they cannot be scaled up to the globalized chicken industry (Tsing 2005) – also called the 'chickenization' of the global farms (Silbergeld 2016). They are also conserved as challenges to the 'livestock revolution', displaying the strengths of biodiversity against the exposure of standardized poultry to emerging viruses (Fearnley 2018). After being a model of the global industry during the era of 'made in Hong Kong' commodities, the Hong Kong territory has become a model for the 'endangerment sensibility' (Choy 2011; Dias and Vidal 2016). In the environmental movement emerging in China (Hathaway 2013; Weller 2006), Hong Kong citizens are cognizant of the threats to their environment and careful to conserve the habitats and animals with which they live. This engagement in the reparation of an environment threatened by industrialization and its correlated diseases consists in a sense of shared vulnerability with all the living beings inhabiting the same territory (Pelluchon 2020). Here, repair is not opposed to prepare, as in the contrast between sacrifice and divination that we have seen before, but the conservation of a diversity of poultry breeds is considered as a means to mitigate the emergence of flu viruses from birds.

Final remarks

In the introduction of this chapter, I suggested a distinction between repair as a functionalist distribution of blame in a space measured by risk and repair as an ontological engagement in a damaged environment. I have suggested that preparedness as a technique to imagine future disasters could rely on this ontological sense of repair. To do that, I focused on Hong Kong as a sentinel post for pandemic preparedness and, in its very centre, the Kadoorie Farm as a site of cultural heritage and natural conservation. Because viruses transmitted from birds to humans have unpredictable behaviors, measuring risks of transmission on poultry farms or markets within biosecurity constraints is less interesting than comparing different perceptions of relations between humans and birds. Indeed, preparedness is a technique to imagine disasters through early warning signals, for instance in the *dispositif* of sentinel chickens amongst ordinary poultry farms in Hong Kong. Kadoorie Farm can be conceived as an extraordinary sentinel technology to conserve what would be lost in case of a bird flu outbreak: the diversity of bird species. While precautionary measures against infectious diseases coming from animals have often used pastoral measures of sacrifice, techniques of preparedness such as sentinels are closer to divination in hunting societies. In that sense, I have contrasted modes of repairing environments relying on sacrifice when the risk of transmission is too high and others relying on divination when infectious outbreaks escape measures of probabilities.

In the first part of this chapter, I showed how poultry farmers have integrated pandemic preparedness in their daily practices through the use of sentinel birds. Rather than contesting biosecurity measures imposed by the government, they have defended the value of the Hong Kong breed by contrast with the Chinese breed. The diversity of bird species has become a way to repair a territory damaged by the sacrifice of infected birds and to prepare for future outbreaks. In the second part of the chapter, I studied the confrontation between ornithologists and Buddhist practitioners at Kadoorie Farm as potentially conflicting ontological engagements. The latter see birds as carrying signs of future goods in an economy of souls, while ornithologists see them as carrying signs of threats in a vulnerable ecology. Ornithologists have found a compromise between these two opposite views by releasing wild birds equipped with tracking technologies. While religious practitioners in this case repair the damages of infectious outbreaks by praying for the souls of animals, conservationists have found a way to prepare for species extinction by following bird movements. This tension between conservation and compassion in managing risks of transmission at the frontiers between species is instructive in a continent where humans and non-humans share a common vulnerability. While the management of pandemic risks is often conceived as a sacrifice of animal species considered as reservoirs of infectious diseases, the description of techniques of repair and prepare in Hong Kong reveals other ways to valorize and mitigate the diversity of human and non-human animals.

Notes

1 Kennedy Shortridge, interview with author, Hong Kong, 2 February 2009.
2 In an interview I did in January 2009 with farmer Wang Yichuan, who was also the head of the Hong Kong Poultry Farmers Association, he recalled that this trade union was founded in 1949 with 145 farms breeding around 1,000 chickens. Sixty years later, the number of poultry farmers had been reduced to 30. He considered himself as an heir of ordinary Chinese immigrants who came to Hong Kong with poultry as a source of wealth.
3 Between 2002 and 2008, the number of live chickens purchased in Hong Kong per year declined from 30 million to 5 million, while the number of chilled chickens purchased in Hong Kong per year increased from 1 million to 35 million (Agriculture, Fisheries and Conservation Department of the Hong Kong government).
4 Shing Tam-Yip, interview with author, 15 February 2009.

References

Abraham, T. (2007) *Twenty-First-Century Plague: The Story of SARS, with a New Preface on Avian Flu*, Hong Kong: Hong Kong University Press.

Adams, V., Murphy, M. and Clarke, A. (2009) 'Anticipation: Technoscience, Life, Affect, Temporality', *Subjectivity*, 28(1): 248–265. <https://doi.org/10.1057/sub.2009.18>.

Anderson, W. (2004) 'Natural Histories of Infectious Diseases: Ecological Vision in Twentieth-Century Biomedical Sciences', 19: 39–61. <www.jstor.org/stable/3655231>.

Bresalier, M. (2011) 'Uses of a Pandemic: Forging the Identities of Influenza and Virus Research in Interwar Britain', Social History of Medicine, 25(2): 400–424. <https://doi.org/10.1093/shm/hkr162>.

Caduff, C. (2015) *The Pandemic Perhaps: Dramatic Events in a Public Culture of Danger*, Oakland: University of California Press.

Caroll, J.M. (2007) *A Concise History of Hong Kong*, Hong Kong: Hong Kong University Press.

Choy, T. (2011) *Ecologies of Comparison: An Ethnography of Endangerment in Hong Kong*, Durham, NC: Duke University Press.

Crosby, A.W. (2003) *America's Forgotten Pandemic: The Influenza of 1918*, Cambridge, MA: Cambridge University Press.

Dias, N. and Vidal, F. (eds) (2016) *Endangerment, Biodiversity and Culture*, London: Routledge.

Doherty, P. (2012) *Sentinel Chickens: What Birds Tell Us about Our Health and the World*, Melbourne: Melbourne University Press.

Fan, F.-T. (2004) *British Naturalists in Qing China: Science, Empire, and Cultural Encounter*, Cambridge, MA: Harvard University Press.

Fearnley, L. (2018) 'After the Livestock Revolution: Free-grazing Ducks and Influenza Uncertainties in South China', *Medicine Anthropology Theory*, 73: 33–57.

Grantham, A. (1965) *Via Ports: From Hong Kong to Hong Kong*, Hong Kong: Hong Kong University Press.

Greger, M. (2006) *Bird Flu: A Virus of Our Own Hatching*, New York: Lantern Books.

Haraway, D. (2007) *When Species Meet*, Minneapolis: University of Minnesota Press.

Hathaway, M. (2013) *Environmental Winds: Making the Global in Southwest China*, Berkeley: University of California Press.

Honigsbaum, M. (2019) *The Pandemic Century: One Hundred Years of Panic, Hysteria and Hubris*, London: Hurst.

Kaufman, J. (2020) *The Last Kings of Shanghai: The Rival Jewish Dynasties That Helped Create Modern China*, New York: Viking.

Keck, F. (2020) *Avian Reservoirs: Virus Hunters and Birdwatchers in Chinese Sentinel Posts*, Durham: Duke University Press.

Kirksey, E. and Helmreich, S. (2010) 'The Emergence of Multispecies Ethnography', *Cultural Anthropology*, 25(4): 545–576.

Kirschenblatt-Gimblett, B. (1998) *Destination Culture: Tourism, Museums, and Heritage*, Berkeley: University of California Press.

Kleinmann, A., and Watson, J. (eds) (2006) *SARS in China: Prelude to Pandemics*, Stanford: Stanford University Press.

Knott, K. (2018) 'How Hong Kong Flu Struck without Warning 50 Years Ago, and Claimed over a Million Lives Worldwide', *South China Morning Post*, 13 July.

Kolata, G. (1999) *Flu: The Story of the Great Influenza Pandemic and the Search for the Virus That Caused It*, New York: Simon & Schuster.

Lakoff, A. (2017) *Unprepared: Global Health in a Time of Emergency*, Oakland: University of California Press.

Lakoff, A. and Collier, S.J. (2008) *Biosecurity Interventions: Global Health and Security in Question*, New York: SSRC-University of Columbia Press.

Liu, T.-S. (2008) 'Custom, Taste and Science. Raising Chickens in the Pearl River Delta, South China', *Anthropology & Medicine*, 15(1): 7–18.

Lynteris, C. (2016) *The Ethnographic Plague: Configuring Disease on the Chinese-Russian Frontier*, London: Palgrave Macmillan.

Lynteris, C. (2019) *Human Extinction and the Pandemic Imaginary*, London: Routledge.

MacKenzie, J. (1988) *The Empire of Nature: Hunting, Conservation and British Imperialism*, Manchester and New York: Manchester University Press.

Mallard, G. (2011) 'The Gift Revisited: Marcel Mauss on War, Debt, and the Politics of Reparations', *Sociological Theory*, 29(4): 4–34.

Moss, S. (2004) *A Bird in the Bush: A Social History of Birdwatching*, London: Aurum Press.

Peckham, R. (2013) 'Matshed Laboratory: Colonies, Cultures, and Bacteriology', in R. Peckham (ed.) *Imperial Contagions: Medicine, Hygiene, and Cultures of Planning in Asia*, Hong Kong: Hong Kong University Press, 123–147.

Peckham, R. (2014) 'Game of Empires: Hunting in Treaty-Port China', in J. Beattie, E. Melillo and E. O'Gorman (eds) *Eco-Cultural Networks and the British Empire*, New York and London: Bloomsbury, 202–232.

Pelluchon, C. (2020) *Réparons le monde. Humains, animaux, nature*, Paris: Rivages.

Rasmussen, A. (2007) 'Réparer, réconcilier, oublier: Enjeux et mythes de la démobilisation scientifique, 1918–1925', *Histoire@Politique*, 3(3): 8–8.

Shapiro, J. (2001) *Mao's War against Nature. Politics and the Environment in Revolutionary China*, Cambridge: Cambridge University Press.

Shortridge, K.F. (2005) 'Avian Influenza Viruses in Hong Kong: Zoonotic Considerations', *Wageningen UR Frontis Series*, 8: 9–18.

Shortridge, K.F., Peiris, J.M.S. and Guan, Y. (2003) 'The Next Influenza Pandemic: Lessons from Hong Kong', *Journal of Applied Microbiology*, 94: 70–79.

Shortridge, K.F. and Stuart-Harris, C.H. (1982) 'An Influenza Epicentre?', *Lancet*, ii: 812–813.

Silbergeld, E.K. (2016) *Chickenizing Farms and Food: How Industrial Meat Production Endangers Workers, Animals and Consumers*, Baltimore: Johns Hopkins University Press.

Simmons, F.J. (1991) *Food in China: A Cultural and Historical Inquiry*, Boston: CRC Press.

Tsing, A.L. (2005) *Friction: An Ethnography of Global Connection*, Princeton: Princeton University Press.

Tsing, A.L. (2015) *The Mushroom at the End of the World: On the Possibility of Life in Capitalist Ruins*, Princeton: Princeton University Press.

Veg, S. (2007) 'Cultural Heritage in Hong Kong, the Rise of Activism and the Contradictions of Identity', *China Perspectives*. <http://journals.openedition.org/chinaperspectives/1663>.

Viveiros de Castro, E. (1992) *From the Enemy's Point of View, Humanity and Divinity in an Amazonian Society*, Chicago: The University of Chicago Press.

Webster, R.G. and Campbell, C.H. (1972) 'The in Vivo Production of "new" Influenza A Viruses', *Virology*, 48(2): 528–536.

Weller, R. (2006) *Discovering Nature: Globalization and Environmental Culture in China and Taiwan*, Cambridge: Cambridge University Press.

Woo, P.C.Y., Lau, S.K.P. and Yuen, K.Y. (2006) 'Infectious Diseases Emerging from Chinese Wetmarkets: Zoonotic Origins of Severe Respiratory Viral Infections', *Current Opinion in Infectious Diseases*, 19(5): 401–407.

Yeung, E. (1956) *Poultry Farming in Hong Kong*, Unpublished Undergraduate Essay, Department of Geography and Geology, University of Hong Kong.

Zhang, J.-E., Rongbao, X., Xin, C. and Guoming, Q. (2009) 'Effects of Duck Activities on a Weed Community under a Transplanted Rice-Duck Farming System in Southern China', *Weed Biology and Management*, 9(3): 250–257.

6 Broken techno-ecological systems and art as reparative gestures

Line Marie Thorsen

Introduction: art after disaster

I first moved to Japan in 2012–2013 as an art historian and aspiring anthropologist, seeking to understand the role of art and artists in the wake of the 11 March 2011 disaster. On that day, a massive 9.0 magnitude earthquake struck off the coast of north-eastern Japan, adjacent to the Tōhoku region. The resulting catastrophe has since been named 'the triple disaster' or simply 3/11. The latter refers to the date, while the former refers to the simultaneity of three disastrous events: first, the earthquake itself and the destruction it caused; second, the series of large tsunami triggered by the earthquake; third, the damage caused by the tsunami to the Fukushima Daiichi nuclear power plant, located on the coast. The impact caused a meltdown and explosions at the power plant, resulting in extensive radioactive contamination. This date became a catalyst for reflection and action at many levels, amongst activists and artists as well as throughout civil society at large.

The earthquake itself leveled buildings and cracked pavements but caused relatively minor damage, due in large part to the extent of quake-proof engineering in Japan. The tsunami set off by the earthquake, however, was devastating. Tidal waves inundated villages and cities along the coast of Tōhoku. Entire fishing ports and towns were washed away and more than 15,000 people lost their lives (Hindmarsh 2013: 3). These first two events were nonetheless relatively limited in duration and scale. However, the damage from the nuclear meltdown, the third disaster of 3/11, has been and continues to be much more extensive and unmanageable. In addition to human and non-human casualties, evacuations, destroyed houses and livelihoods, the geographic reach of pollution from nuclear fallout was and continues to be widespread and unpredictable; some isotopes have a radioactive half-life of up to 24,000 years (NRC 2019). All things considered, 3/11 was and is a disaster with a dizzying array of repercussions, calling for equally diverse modes of action.

As I learned during my first year of field research, one mode of action which was fairly visible in the public sphere and the immediately affected areas came from artists collaborating with various groups of volunteers. At the time, many people from the Japanese 'cultural scene' (see, *e.g.*, 3331 Arts Chiyoda 2011), quickly transformed their artistic practices into what I have referred to as 'acute art

DOI: 10.4324/9781003184782-9

practices' (Thorsen 2014). These practices can be understood as artistic activities that emerged in the disaster's immediate aftermath and which were fundamentally shaped by the urgency of the situation and especially the destruction caused by the earthquake and tsunami. Artists, much like other concerned volunteers, traveled to tsunami-struck areas, joined relief efforts, and engaged in a variety of reconstruction actions, sometimes within, but oftentimes outside, traditional art spaces.

The third disaster of 3/11, the nuclear meltdown, elicited similar immediate and acute artistic responses. Yet, alongside these responses, other long-term and deliberately crafted art forms gradually emerged with a critical goal. Following the nuclear disaster, many affected groups began to reckon with the processes of Japanese modernization (industrialization, urbanization, growing energy and commodity consumption, etc.) throughout the 20th century, with many viewing its ideals as responsible for events like the Fukushima Daiichi meltdown. In short, the Fukushima disaster became increasingly tied to a wide range of ecological and environmental issues and impacts of modernization and industrialization. Thus, the power plant meltdown triggered or strengthened an approach to radically rethinking artmaking and ways of life. Though sometimes slow, the process has far-reaching commitments to restorative practices centred on environmental health. In particular, as I put forth in this chapter, some artists and cultural practitioners became organic and 'natural farmers' (Fukuoka 1993) in an effort to both extricate themselves from the energy infrastructures that caused such destruction and create imaginative spaces to define how life can and should exist in the ruins of industrial modernity.[1]

In this chapter I will consider both forms of artistic practices – the acute and the gradual or long-term – as entwined, yet distinct types of reparative acts that overlap within relatively 'marginal art' forms (鶴見 (Tsurumi) 1967) – that is, as practices and aesthetic principles at the frontier between art and everyday activities. In analyzing artistic responses to 3/11, I suggest that such endeavours should be approached from within local cultural theories of art in order to understand how these art practices create meaning and value in a given material, historical and sociopolitical setting. Specifically, following cultural theorist Tsurumi Shunsuke, I understand 'marginal art' as art that is meant for and produced from places and circumstances that are foremost concerned with experiences of daily life (*ibid.*). The nuances of Tsurumi's theory will be developed later in the chapter, including the way he viewed marginal art as fundamentally connected to both civic movements and moments of discontent. I will demonstrate that marginal art may also comprise reparative gestures, aimed at refashioning and reimagining broken objects, as well as broken techno-ecological systems – both energy systems and ecosystems.

When I refer to these art practices as 'reparative', I intend the notion of repair to hold a double connotation. First, I use 'repair' to describe the literal process of artists fixing things that were or are, in one form or another, broken. Second, however, I draw on specific theoretical traditions to conceive of repair and reparative gestures as critical practices within complex socio-technical and techno-ecological systems (Strebel *et al.* 2018), undertaken by those who live and work at the margins. According to Steven J. Jackson (2014: 223), repair is above all what occurs in 'the aftermath':

> [Repair is] growing at the margins, breakpoints and interstices of complex socio-technical systems as they creak, flex and bend their way through time. It fills in the moment of hope and fear in which bridges from old worlds to new worlds are built, and the continuity of order, value, and meaning gets woven, one tenuous thread at the time.

In the aftermath of the triple 3/11 disaster, marginal art, I aim to show, became a site of reparative gestures, weaving old and new worlds together.

Marginal art: art as farming and art as aid

In the summer of 2015, I attended the Echigo Tsumari Art Triennale in Niigata, Japan, seeking to examine the way in which artists attend to environmental and ecological issues. Every three summers, the triennale takes place in the rural and mountainous area of Niigata prefecture, also known as Echigo Tsumari. It is a massive festival, both in scale and scope, with hundreds of works displayed and curated in nearly 200 villages, across an area of 760 square kilometres ('About Triennale – Echigo-Tsumari Art Field', no date). Festival participants must travel from village to village to visit the various art installation sites. Along the way, they traverse mountains, farmlands and forests and encounter local populations, flora and fauna. The process is slow and often difficult, which is indeed the intention. Participating artists as well as visitors are encouraged to observe and engage with the local environment in line with one of the festival's key aims, namely, to remind the public, via artistic mediation, that 'humans are a part of nature' (Kitagawa 2015).

A few months prior to this Niigata visit, I had become aware of a growing phenomenon in East Asia of artists turning to farming. This trajectory reveals a desire to engage questions related to local ecological destruction and global climate change by situating the climate crisis and other large-scale environmental issues within a local framework and by practicing environmental stewardship via sustainable forms of farming and the production of healthy foods. Later, during the Echigo Tsumari Art Triennale, amongst the terraced mountainside rice fields in the town of Matsudai, I noticed that several fields contrasted with the conventional monocrop model. Some fields had multiple crops organized in the easily recognizable permaculture design: mixed vegetables grown in circles and spirals, planted in mounds of compost soil, covered with hay (*e.g.* Mollison and Holmgren 1978). Other fields seemed less tidy compared to the conventional ones, with weeds, insects, slugs and other living things scattered amongst the rice and soy plants. When I revisited the art festival during the fall, other features caught my attention. Whereas conventional rice farming in Japan is today primarily performed by machines, the edges of these 'alternative' fields were lined with sickles and sleigh-like boats, which are dragged along the watery terraces and serve as a dry place for storing sheaves of rice after they are cut with a sickle.

Some fields were marked by yellow signs indicating that they were also part of the art festival and thus were to be considered works of art. And as I learned, these fields belonged to groups of artists who had been transforming themselves into sustainable farmers, searching for new ways of living in the wake of the 3/11 nuclear disaster. These are some of the creative practitioners in Japan who turned to farming as a steady, long-term commitment to addressing and rethinking the practices that gave way to the vulnerable and complex systems of modernization, ecological collapse and disasters like the Fukushima Daiichi meltdown. Within festival spaces interspersed across the Japanese countryside, art and farming as long-term practices of environmental repair and critiques of modernity collided with 3/11 as a catalyst for new modes of artmaking.

As mentioned, 3/11 set a broad range of artistic activities into motion, including acute as well as steady, long-term art forms. While art as farming belongs to the latter, the former, art as emergency aid, will be detailed later in the chapter.[2] These two categories reveal both important similarities and differences. The artist-farmers, including those in Matsudai, did not drastically shift their art practices or modes of living immediately after 3/11. They largely continued their work as usual, while also slowly preparing for and gradually transforming their art and lifestyles in often major ways. Such transformations might translate into leaving the city with their families, adopting an entirely new line of work (like farming) or implementing radical and lasting changes to their existing art practices. In contrast, artists who produced immediate responses to 3/11 took action as both artists and concerned citizens, offering their various skills to people in tsunami-affected areas, clearing debris, cooking for the displaced, or repairing damaged belongings. Later on, many transformed this kind of aid work back into art within an institutional setting, by exhibiting elements of their aid practices or documenting the process, thus opening additional space for reflection around 3/11 (see *e.g.* Takehisa 2012). However, this mostly took the form of limited projects tied directly to 3/11 (the first two events, in particular), after which people generally resumed their pre-3/11 art practices.

Before analyzing the two forms of reparative artmaking in further detail, it is prudent to unpack these creative forms and phenomena. At their core, these art forms represent highly situated ways of practicing art that addresses everyday experiences and ordinary life. The potential reactions of art institutions and audiences had little bearing on the way in which art practices unfolded in either of the two response forms. On the contrary, a common thread seems to be the desire to practice art in a way that is meaningful for disaster victims, villagers or farmers – in other words, for ordinary citizens.

Farming and other fairly ordinary activities, like repairing a shattered vase, have most likely always existed as artistic forms, if one moves beyond elitist, Eurocentric notions of 'art'. However, in the shadow of disasters that are ongoing (*e.g.* climate change) and immediate (*e.g.* 3/11), the artistic and aesthetic potential in both acute and long-term 'ordinary' engagements is even more pronounced. Art in this sense is what Tsurumi Shunsuke refers to as 'marginal art' – marginal because it belongs to long-standing traditions connected to aesthetic practices that emerge when everyday life intersects with environmental issues and socio-political action. In the next section, I dissect the category of 'marginal art' and explain how it connects to both short- and long-term disaster response, as well as to the everyday aesthetic sensibilities emerging from art's engagement with ordinary experiences of extraordinary events.

The legacies of marginal art in Japan and beyond

The concept of marginal art is formulated by Tsurumi Shunsuke[3] in his book *Genkai Geijutsuron* (1967), usually translated into English as *On Marginal Arts* (Sugimoto 2007). In Japan and East Asia more broadly, Tsurumi is widely regarded as an important public intellectual and cultural critic of post-war Japan. More recently, he has been at the heart of East Asian scholarly conversations on contemporary art, in part due to the centrality of environmental questions raised by various forms of marginal art that he helped theorize (福住 (Fukuzumi) 2008). Such broad-based recognition notably stems from Tsurumi's analytical work in *Genkai Gejutsuron*, where he divides 'art' (singular) into three distinct art forms: pure art, popular art and marginal art. It is important to note that this trichotomy is not a normative or prescriptive ideal, but rather an analytical model responding to the processes by which art had *already* been grouped into categories with the introduction of Western-centred notions of 'art' in Japan and elsewhere. These three categories are thus descriptive of art practices Tsurumi saw as pre-existing phenomena in post-war Japan.

Tsurumi argues that what is commonly referred to simply as 'art' describes in reality only *one* kind of art, namely the professionalized form displayed in galleries and museums. Canonized in art history books, this form of art is seen as stemming from the 'West' and its analytical frameworks (鶴見 (Tsurumi) 1967: 14). Such pure art (*junsui geijutsu*) is professional art which simultaneously caters to and requires the appreciation and appraisal of other art professionals (鶴見 (Tsurumi) 1967: 14). While non-professionals may be able to relate to or appreciate this type of art, its value or worth as 'pure art' can be validated only by professionalized standards. Interestingly, Tsurumi himself does not elaborate on the actual pieces of art which belong to this category. However, in my analysis, this form corresponds quite closely to the art that is consecrated in institutional cultural settings, or what is sometimes referred to as the 'art world' (Danto 1964; Thorsen 2019: 238–248).

Popular art, on the other hand, is art made by professional artists for non-professional masses, which is not to be confused with 'pop art' in the style of Andy Warhol or Murakami Takeshi – both of whom, in Tsurumi's terms, belong in the pure art category. The translation 'popular art' was proposed by Tsurumi himself (鶴見 (Tsurumi) 1967: 14); however, the Japanese term *taishuu geijutsu* strongly connotes 'masses' or 'general public', which is reflected in the fact that for Tsurumi, popular art principally takes the form of commercial and design products. Popular art reveals, perhaps more clearly than pure art, that Tsurumi's categories imply a somewhat provocative shift in how the 'art world' identifies who an artist is and what art is in the first place. To Tsurumi, designers and public relations professionals *are* artists-turned-entrepreneurs, whose art is directed at marketing and sales on the mass market, rather than gallery spaces and art-world approval (鶴見 (Tsurumi) 1967: 14–15).

Finally, marginal art (*genkai geijutsu*) sits at the seemingly opposite end of the spectrum from pure art and designates art made *by* non-professionals *for* non-professionals. This category covers a wide range of rather ordinary expressive activities that are integral to everyday life, yet distinguish themselves, according to Tsurumi, by their cultivation of aesthetic experiences amidst a slew of unremarkable day-to-day doings (鶴見 (Tsurumi) 1967: 15). Tsurumi offers many examples, including the organizing and display of family photo albums, home decorations, the curation of Japanese-style cultural/religious festivals, flower arrangements, manicured farmland and agricultural tools, as well as work songs heard in the fields. Broadly speaking, the artistic marginality of these practices contrasts with their cultural significance. Marginal arts are, according to Tsurumi, perhaps the most significant artistic and cultural form, as they carry the most experiential and public weight.

Although Tsurumi's writing dates back to the 1950s, today in Japan and other East Asian countries, many of these activities are still considered ordinary in a sense. At the same time, amongst daily, monthly and yearly traditional practices, these activities stand out as remarkable moments or events, often designed to prompt such moments in the future. Nowadays, activities like farming are being revived as marginal arts, often in spaces like the Echigo Tsumari Art Triennale. In doing so, they challenge their own 'marginality', understood here as the implicit distancing and devaluing of marginal arts, *as* art – a process that began during the period of modernization in Japan, with the emergence of 'pure art' and the critical reception of certain art world institutions. In this context, it is worth noting that the Japanese term *genkai* denotes 'limit' or 'border'. It is Tsurumi himself who translated this term into 'marginal art', but the original meaning is significant for the way it directly makes reference to art that lies at the frontier of other art forms as well as ordinary life. This arguably underscores its transitory qualities and points to spaces of negotiation at and around the borders between art forms themselves – where they *are* drawn and where they *should* or *could* be (re)drawn. This, I suggest, is precisely the feature of marginal art which makes it relevant to understanding reparative art practices in the face of disastrous events as well as in long-term environmental engagements.

Marginal art, then, is by no means a new phenomenon, nor can it be equated with contemporary art theories of 'socially engaged art' or 'relational aesthetics' (Bourriaud 2009; Bishop 2012), seen as recent 'turns' in ('Western') art. According to Tsurumi, it may well represent one of the oldest art forms. He credits the original definition of marginal arts to the poet and children's-book author Miyazawa Kenji, who lived between 1896 and 1933. Miyazawa dedicated his life to 'peasant culture' and embraced art as a broad, all-encompassing category, which could and should include various expressions of creativity practiced in peasant life (Kikuchi 2004: 36; Miyazawa 2007).

Marginal arts today: the case of the Seppuku Pistols

Today, this entire intellectual branch – and Tsurumi's work in particular – has received new interest for the possibility it offers to grapple with artistic practices that emerge in response to socio-political and environmental issues and public concerns. Art critic Fukuzumi Ren was arguably the first contemporary scholar to revisit Tsurumi's marginal art concept through a number of essays that eventually resulted in the book *Kyō no Genkaigeijutsu* (*Marginal Art Today*) (福住 (Fukuzumi) 2008). The starting point for Fukuzumi's argument centres on the way boundaries between pure art, popular art and marginal art are seemingly eroding, or at least shifting, within contemporary art and art criticism spheres. How institutions define and validate what is to be considered art, he suggests, matters less than it used to. For this reason, Tsurumi's theory is key in understanding art more broadly today.

Exploring these shifts, Fukuzumi curated the exhibition *100 Marginal Arts of Today* at the Matsudai Nohbutai Snow-Land Agrarian Culture centre, in Matsudai, as part of the 2015 Echigo Tsumari Art Triennale. This exhibition presented a vast array of marginal art practices – amongst them some of the artists-turned-farmers in the wake of 3/11, but also the band and performance group the Seppuku Pistols. In fact, in addition to farming as a means of exploring lifestyles independent from risky energy systems like nuclear power, a few artist-farmers are also part of the Seppuku Pistols. The band, composed of quite a few musicians, describes its sound as acoustic, anti-modern punk rock. They play only acoustic instruments, yet draw heavily on the electric instrumental rawness, do-it-yourself, and anti-establishment attitude of punk rock (as evidenced by their name, an allusion to the 1970s British punk band the Sex Pistols). Tellingly, they date their origins to 11 March 2011, although they have existed as a more 'conventional' band since 1999. Much like artists turning to farming, the Seppuku Pistols experienced 3/11 as a confrontation with the inadequacies of modern technologies. As they bluntly stated in a recent interview with *The Wire*: 'These events made us feel lame that we can't do shit without electricity. So we changed [. . .] our style' (Kopf 2020).

The Seppuku Pistols participated in Fukuzumi's 2015 exhibition. As an event and performance, they walked the 30 kilometres from the triennale centre in the city of Tokamachi to the Matsudai Nohbutai cultural centre, playing traditional Japanese instruments like *taiko* (large drums), *yokobue* (traverse bamboo flute) and *shime-daiko* (small drums), all in the style of punk rock. Crowds of local residents and festival guests followed the procession along the route.

Seppuku references the samurai term for ritual disembowelment via the cutting open of one's own stomach. The name places the group squarely within a cultural history dating back to pre-modern Japan. At the same time, it also carries a critique of aspects of Japanese culture seen as rooted in the expectation of violent and public self-sacrifice in service of the 'greater good' (from samurai to kamikaze pilots) (Calichman 2008: vii–xvi). As some have argued, 'traditions' surrounding civic self-sacrifice had disastrous human and environmental consequences in the twentieth century, as a similar sense of sacrifice was expected from people and other organisms living next to polluting factories, or even nuclear power plants (Walker 2011).

Through their events and performances, the Seppuku Pistols draw attention to this cultural history and its present-day implications, urging their audiences to think back to a time before modernization and to imagine a future that excavates past knowledge and practices, placing them at the forefront of human and eco-logical sustainability while abandoning activities that sacrifice too much. As such, their work and actions do not simply romanticize the 'good old days' vis-à-vis the complexities of modernity. They represent, in fact, a much more nuanced invita-tion to reflect upon the practices we wish to keep and cultivate as well as those we must shed, on what is needed and what is not.

In the vein of Tsurumi, they have placed themselves in the genre of marginal art based on civic attachments and cultural histories of disastrous encounters with modernization. Also, by creating marginal art in the aftermath of 3/11, they are highlighting and exploiting the cracks in 'the system', in all its techno-ecological and political-repressive meanings. Here, the reparative gesture is not aimed at the power plant or the ideologies that created it, but rather at a past that can be recu-perated and translated into other future imaginaries.

As the Seppuku Pistols illustrate, the notion of marginal art often contains a direct or indirect connexion to socio-political mobilization against modernization and industrial destruction. In *A Cultural History of Postwar Japan* (1987), Tsurumi even describes many of the practices he identifies as marginal art in *Genkai Geijutsuron* as practices that have since been directly mobilized against industrial pollution. One such example is the transformation of pre-modern *renga* practices (a form of collaborative or linked poetry) into community 'circles': 'In general, a circle is a small, voluntary and temporary community, meeting at regular intervals in pursuit of a common interest, such as flower arrangement, *haiku*, movies or reading.' Yet because of its collective composition, Tsurumi (1987: 108–109) adds:

> [A] circle may form around a specific political problem which has affected people badly [. . .]. It tenaciously pursues a specific issue and may achieve partial victories solely through its independence of political parties, since it thus has greater appeal for the public at large and can solicit support from a wider sphere.

The gatherings the Seppuku Pistols create around their music and then expand into discussions of socio-political and material issues could well be said to exemplify a contemporary community circle.

Tsurumi is also explicitly inspired by the work of John Dewey, as his depic-tion of circles resembles, in the Deweyan sense, (mini-) publics, *i.e.*, collectives built from shared experiences and concerns (Dewey 1991). Circles, Tsurumi argues, have played a central role in powerful activist practices: against the methyl mercury poisoning of Minamata (Jobin 2005); against oceanic pollu-tion; and against the development of atomic and hydrogen bombs in the 1950s (Tsurumi 1987: 108–109). Thus, marginal art has for a long time also constituted a form of political activism and disaster response. Whereas the Seppuku Pistols and artist-farmers figure here as examples of long-term artistic commitments to change after 3/11, I will now turn to the *acute* responses of artists in the wake of 3/11, through gestures resembling those described by Tsurumi above. I hereby aim to show the variety of reparative gestures in artistic practices as well as their creative significance *as* marginal art.

Acute art practices

In 2011, artists responded immediately to fashion themselves, their practices and skills into disaster aid which took a variety of forms, addressing primarily the earthquake and tsunami aspects of the triple disaster. Incarnating what I call 'acute art practices' (Thorsen 2014), these artists went straight to the epicentres of destruction and, alongside many other civilians, converted their skills into disaster relief. For instance, installation artist Katō Tsubasa had for a long time created temporary house-like structures, which he would install on a public city square and ask passers-by to help him *Pull and Rise* – as the events are called – by pulling at ropes attached to the structures. In the process, large groups of people would eventually gather around the common effort to raise the large structure, and that cooperation was in fact at the heart of the artistic intervention. The structures themselves would be demolished, but the gathering spurred connexions that stretched well beyond the events themselves. Immediately after 3/11, Katō transformed his construction skills from the pull-and-rise events to help tear down damaged buildings and rebuild new ones. His activities created gathering points and common spaces around the demolition and reconstruction of tsunami-damaged buildings, in communities that had been torn apart following 3/11 (Takehisa 2012: 134–135).

Another such example is the effort of Murakami Takashi[4] to transform tsunami ruins into disaster memorials and to organize the planting of *sakura* trees[5] by schoolchildren to mark the tsunami's landfall (3331 Arts Chiyoda 2011: A-054). Both were disaster-related projects which Murakami initiated as part of his own coping process, since his own studio and home had been destroyed on 3/11. Murakami had long been active in socially engaged art forms, so when the tsunami washed away lives and homes, his quest to engage local populations in the creation of tsunami memorials worked as a rather direct extension of his artistic practice. As with Katō, a key component of Murakami's work was the gathering of people around the common issues forced upon them by the disaster. Significantly, Murakami's gatherings also concerned future generations: the memorials are first and foremost meant to remind people of the destructive potential of tsunami and how far inland they can reach.

A third example is the work of Nishiko. In the wake of the disaster, she set up a number of workshops to repair broken items, like lamps and vases, that people would bring to her. During the repairs, there would be conversations about life, loss and grief (Nishiko (ニシコ) 2012). Much like Katō and Murakami, Nishiko's own transformation of artistic skills into disaster relief served as a platform for the collective processing of trauma.

Through their practices, artists like Katō, Murakami and Nishiko provided immediate aid and helped people process the events of 3/11 by creating space for conversations about what had happened and what life had become. They were joined by hundreds of other creative and aesthetic practitioners, who turned their skills into disaster aid, relief, and repair (*e.g.* 3331 Arts Chiyoda 2011; Takehisa 2012; Chim↑Pom and 椹木 野衣 2015; 岩瀬 2015). I call these 'acute' art practices (Thorsen 2014) to underline the fact that they represent a form of artistic practice that emerges and takes shape as a reaction to certain extreme events. In other words, as the disaster unfolded and its repercussions continue to be felt, it has demanded that artists and many others (re)adjust their response to align with the urgency and fragility interlaced with such massive and, indeed, acute destruction. This experience of being called to action around shared issues, while also actively cultivating gathering places and communality, resembles the practices of marginal art. I will expand upon this in more detail via the Repairing Earthquake Project (地震を直すプロジェクト),[6] created by Nishiko. Its first phase was launched between September and November 2011.

Repairing earthquake: art amidst the debris

Like many other artists, Nishiko directly developed her acute art practice of restoration through encountering and anticipating the needs of some of the local populations most affected by the earthquake and tsunami (Nishiko (ニシコ) 2012: 176). As I detail in previously published work (Thorsen 2013: 9–10), Nishiko's immediate reaction to 3/11 was not really *as* an artist at all. At first, she simply went to the tsunami-struck areas offering her help to local NGOs, eager to aid in whatever way possible. It was not until a few months later that her Repairing Earthquake Project materialized as an art project of repairing broken items.

Nishiko set up workshops in NGO headquarters, community centres and, later on, in gallery spaces and museums, where people could bring her their broken items (lamps, vases, plates and such) so that she could mend them. Having never performed this type of repair before, Nishiko was cautious about making promises regarding the results. What she did offer, however, was a commitment to listen to and engage with the stories people brought along with their broken things. During a conversation in 2012, she spoke to me about one of many formative events leading her to launch her unique reparative project, which took place in the summer of 2011, shortly after she arrived in Tōhoku to help:

> I went to an area in Higashi-Matsushima and started to walk around in the debris from the tsunami. I met a man there who was just walking around. He didn't know what to do. He told me he didn't have anything to do anymore. He lost everything. He lost his wife, his home, and his mother was still missing. He told me that right after the disaster he was so busy, and it was better when he was busy, but now he didn't know what to do.
>
> (Author's conversation with Nishiko, 4 December 2012)

When Nishiko first caught sight of this man, he was walking around in the area where his house used to be – looking, it turned out, for some personal documents in the debris. The rummaging for papers in the ruins of a shattered town seemed to her more like an attempt to keep busy than an act laced with any expectation of finding them. Nonetheless, she decided to help him look for the documents and while doing so she learned, amongst other things, why he was there 'keeping busy' (Author's conversation with Nishiko, 4 December 2012; Thorsen 2013: 10). From this encounter, the Repairing Earthquake Project slowly took shape in her mind.

Through this and many other interactions in the first months following the 3/11 disaster – when Nishiko explored the devastated areas, listened, helped and was herself helped in turn – she gradually developed the method of repairing the objects she found in the ruins. The workshops slowly emerged, and people began bringing her their broken objects for repair (Nishiko (ニシコ) 2012; Thorsen 2014: 58). Later still, her material practice would be temporarily relocated inside a few locally recognized art museums (*e.g.* Takehisa 2012), as part of collective exhibitions dedicated precisely to the various expressions of art after 3/11.

In addition to representing an immediate and acute artistic response to the disaster, Nishiko's practices also serve as an example of the fluidity between marginal art and pure art, as well as between acute and long-term aesthetic reparative practices. Nishiko's art project quite emblematically illustrates the kind of aesthetic practices which emerged in the period immediately following the 3/11 disaster and their often 'marginal' and reparative orientations, which indeed become quite literal and material in Nishiko's case. These practices encompass multiple reparative qualities at once – in tangible/material, communal and indeed existential senses – largely because they emerge as marginal art engagements, almost in the style of the 'circles' described by Tsurumi. As with the Seppuku Pistols, Katō Tsubasa and Murakami Takashi, the primary aim was the facilitation of spaces within which the public affected by the disaster could discuss the issues (trauma, destruction, loss, uncertainty) they were individually and collectively facing in the aftermath of 3/11.

Conversely, because Nishiko did not initially have a 'pure art' agenda, her work began as a 'marginal art' gesture, affording her a position from which to observe the things around her that needed both material and metaphorical repairing. Whether or not the ensuing practice could be validated institutionally *as* art was not of importance. Rather, the shift into 'pure art' territory, with exhibitions in acclaimed art institutions (like Mito Art Tower in late 2012, see Takehisa 2012), only came much later, as she transitioned into a more hybrid 'pure-marginal' art practice.

As an acute art practice, Nishiko's Repairing Earthquake Project was especially attentive to the immediate material environments affected by the disaster. However, in the first phase described here, she did not necessarily reckon with larger or more systemic aspects of 3/11, nor with what we would usually consider environmental and 'ecological' concerns in a broader sense. I return now to farming as art, to consider how the practical-as-artistic characteristics of acute art gradually evolved and gave birth to other marginal art forms, as the disaster called for a deeper and more long-term reckoning with environmental devastation.

Reparative art practices: slow, yet long-ranging

For the group of artists who began transforming and merging their art with farming, the nuclear contamination event of the 3/11 disaster became a particularly powerful catalyst for rethinking ways of creating art and modes of living more broadly. As I have shown in this chapter, the immediate impact and destruction caused by the earthquake and tsunami called for a certain form of acute response that was circumscribed in terms of space and time (forming quickly and concentrated around Tōhoku). However, the nuclear disaster conjures a more extensive and complicated spatiotemporal horizon for artistic intervention.

The impact of the tsunami on the coastal Fukushima Daiichi nuclear plant had direct consequences in the area immediately surrounding the plant. However, radioactive matter spreads uncontrollably, and a combination of under- and mis-information meant that, from the outset, people did not know where they could safely evacuate (Morita *et al.* 2013). Making hard and sometimes tragic decisions during a life-and-death situation was thus part of the collective experience.

From the moment the nuclear reactors spewed out the first clouds of smoke, radioactive contamination began moving unevenly beyond the boundaries of the evacuation zone. And while clearing the destruction caused by the earthquake and tsunami was already an immense task, nuclear contamination proved to be almost impossible to remove (Blowers 2013). Thus, in addition to its geographic reach, the time frame of the disaster stretched far into the future.

In line with this experience, the artistic response has arguably come to demand of itself an equally wide range of imaginative capabilities, along with alternative ways of practicing art altogether. Artist-farmers described to me how they began to question themselves and their communities about a number of issues: which social/material structures and patterns provide the basis for a nuclear disaster; how this basis ties into other undesirable and destructive practices; and how to move away from and mend ways of living that prompt such events and other forms of environmental disaster. To the artist-farmers, the answer was in part found in moving away from cities and experimenting with energy-independent farming practices.

This is where the Fukushima Daiichi nuclear meltdown intersects with larger socio-political issues, not least of which are environmental destruction and ecological crises. To some, farming became a sort of first step into experimentally separating themselves from the very conditions that make a nuclear power plant necessary in the first place. Nonaka Katsuya, who is a musician and performer with the Seppuku Pistols, a graphic designer, skateboarder, documentarist and (now) rice farmer, serves as a prime example of this experiential trajectory. I first met Nonaka in 2017 while attending the Echigo Tsumari Art Triennale in the town of Matsudai. Yet, without knowing it, I had already seen his rice fields two years earlier, when they stood out amongst the other terraced fields of rice for their somewhat untidy appearance.

Like the Seppuku Pistols as a group, Nonaka began his transition to full-time farming after the Fukushima Daiichi disaster, when he could not see himself continuing a lifestyle of unhindered energy consumption which implicated him in the catastrophe and its extensive environmental consequences. Nonaka has thus been farming for a relatively short period of time, and as a monocrop rice farmer, he finds inspiration in organic principles and the 'local' (Japan-based) teachings of farmer and farming philosopher Fukuoka Masanobu (Fukuoka 1993; Char and Yeung 2018: 178). Fukuoka has written extensively on his practices of 'natural' or 'do-nothing-farming', which advocates farming with as little human and 'industrial' intervention as possible, encouraging a delicate multi-species co-habitation (Fukuoka 1993; 2010).

In his book *Sowing Seeds in the Desert* (2013), Fukuoka argues that particular attention must be paid to symbiotic relations if we are to survive or even halt the various forms of desertification our planet is experiencing. To Fukuoka, as well as Nonaka, there is a strong link between conventional farming and environmental degradation on a local and global scale.

However, Fukuoka's work also offers reflections on Japan's extensive nuclear history, as linked to a broader and key critique of Japan's process of modernization. As Fukuoka argues in several of his books, the rapid modernization of Japan, from the Meiji period (1868–1912) onwards, instilled a cultural belief in technological progress that has proven detrimental to people's relationship with the environment. In *The One-Straw Revolution* (2010), Fukuoka articulates a problematic connection between the need for chemical fertilizers and nuclear power. Both are based on the belief that difficult problems demand complicated, technology-based solutions. Typical examples are the problems caused by soil desertification and pollution from power plants, which are addressed through technological measures that in turn produce even more pollution and difficult-to-manage side effects. Fukuoka suggests that such problems should instead be solved using more modest solutions (Fukuoka 2010: 83–84).

Much like Fukuoka, artist-farmers like Nonaka have attached a kind of symbiotic sensibility to the utter lack of concern industrial farming and nuclear power have for the environment. This is why he turned to farming outside of large cities and away from Tōhoku. Still, with 3/11 as a trigger point, his lifestyle changes and practices – though formally and temporally distinct – are grounded in a similar sentiment to that which made Nishiko open workshops to repair broken things. One might argue that Nonaka, alongside his farming friends and colleagues, is also in the process of repairing. His work represents an attempt to gradually resolve the ever-looming problems associated with 'modernization' by slowly learning how to restore soils, while simultaneously creating spaces of opportunity to imagine and practice modest solutions to still more complex techno-ecological problems. For artists, the tradition of marginal art – like housekeeping, farming or community circles – produces well-curated spaces and knowledge bound in long-standing customs that do not force such artists to be reductive about art, farming or disaster aid.

Nonaka has several rice fields where he cultivates organic seedlings of the flavorful Japanese short-grain rice variety *koshihikari*. This variety is quite popular, and many of the conventional farmers in the area cultivate the same crop. But unlike Nonaka's, theirs are not organic; they are not planted, tended to, or cut by hand. Theirs do not share water with other organisms, or at the very least, are expected not to. In contrast, the water surrounding Nonaka's rice is filled with other species like birds, small fish, leeches, frogs, bugs, slugs and snails. Each year, he has plenty of rice to harvest – not despite the diversity of life-forms in his rice fields, but more likely because of it.

As a result of this way of farming, some of the desertification effects that Fukuoka saw and criticized on conventional farmland is less prevalent on Nonaka's lands. The overwhelming majority of Japanese farmers, including in the Niigata area, farm 'conventionally', and Japan is still one of the countries using the highest quantity and most severe forms of pesticides in the world, resulting in an immense loss of biodiversity (Katayama *et al.* 2015). Artist-farmers like Nonaka work slowly but surely against this statistical pattern in their everyday practices, by experimenting with alternative farming methods. This is arguably the reason farming is vital in learning other, less destructive ways of living symbiotically with the environments we inhabit. In these efforts, the Japanese marginal art–based practices I have analyzed here converge, in their distinct ways, with related modes of 'everyday environmentalism' (Schlosberg and Coles 2016) that have emerged in other cultural contexts, as a practice of redesigning material flows based on ecological care (Puig de la Bellacasa 2017). Ecological care, seen through practices such as agro-ecological farming, can be considered as 'an opportunity to regenerate socio-ecological dynamics through *learning anew how to inhabit* an environment' struck by a catastrophe (Centemeri 2019: 97, original italics).

Ecological care means questioning what matters in everyday life with the goal of cultivating new habits and activities. It implies developing a form of self-reflection on how one assigns value to beings, things and places. These processes of ordinary valuation shape ecologies (Centemeri 2018) in that everyday practices are central to our efforts to repair and relearn how to inhabit environments in less destructive ways. This kind of reflection on everyday life is, in turn, tied to the realization that ecological catastrophe is ultimately not driven by 'exceptional' and 'external' events like the earthquake and tsunami on 3/11. Nuclear power plants and their meltdowns, with the ensuing uncontainable contamination and pollution for decades to come, ecological crises and their links to climate change, loss of biodiversity, soil erosion and acidification, ocean acidification, deforestation and much more, are *also* and primarily interconnected with ordinary and everyday activities. It is the comprehension of such connexions that led artists to turn to farming, and explains why art as farming matters as marginal art.

Conclusion: reparative gestures in marginal arts

In this chapter, I have shown how the triple 3/11 disaster in Japan was a catalyst for the critical reassessment of techno-ecological systems and forms of life across broad segments of the cultural and artistic sector, with numerous and diverse repercussions. In the immediate responses of what I call acute art practices, embodied in Nishiko's Repairing Earthquake Project, the aim is not necessarily long-term change in everyday activities. Rather, by reworking the discourse surrounding disaster relief, artists begin to accommodate, reflect and aid those subjected to violent transformations, offering reparative gestures that are both tangible and metaphorical. I have also argued that a certain reflectiveness on the way everyday activities feed into current and approaching disastrous events – whether technical or ecological – is at the root of how some Japanese artists transform their practices for marginal arts in long-term, gradual and deliberate ways. What makes these practices gradual arguably stems from the desire to transform ordinary practices so fundamentally that they may become test sites for exploring other ways of living, perhaps even inspiring others to do the same.

In the end, there is no strict separation between these two kinds of art-based practices of repair. Nishiko eventually returned to the interests she had prior to the 3/11 disaster. Many farming artists up-rooted and re-rooted their lives and practices completely, adopting a wider set of ecological values and ways of addressing the environmental devastation of industrial modernities.

Central to my argument here is the insistence that both modes make sense when understood as marginal arts. In the terms of cultural theorist Tsurumi Shunsuke, these are and have always been art forms rooted in everyday practices, which are at times directly mobilized as aid and tools to be used in the fight against environmental ruin. In other words, within the scope of marginal art, artists are not accountable to 'pure art' institutions. What matters is how they make sense of the situated struggles in which they are invested, and the kinds of reparative gestures they perform and produce within their given ecologies.

Notes

1 Here I paraphrase the argument and title of Anna Tsing's *The Mushroom at the End of the World – On the Possibility of Life in Capitalist Ruins* (Tsing 2015).
2 It is important to clarify that the two categories I present here are in no way representative of the myriad of artistic responses to the disaster, but are rather two forms amongst many which have stood out in my research.
3 All Japanese names presented here conform to local standards, with the family name preceding the given name.
4 Not to be confused with the well-known pop artist of the same name, Murakami is a socially engaged artist from Tōhoku and founder of the 3/11 community art association MMIX Lab (Murakami 2011).
5 *Sakura* are the famous cherry blossom trees, which hold deep cultural significance in Japan and are cherished as messengers of spring.
6 The Japanese title is closely related to the English one, meaning 'repairing' or 'mending' the earthquake. However, the word 直す (*naosu*) is only one of many possible words in

Japanese referencing repair. *Naosu* in particular connotes repairing as healing, correcting and converting back to a former state.

References

3331 Arts Chiyoda (ed.) (2011) ３．１１つくることが生きること *(Creating to Live)*, *Kokumin Taiiku Taikai*, Yamaguchi-shi: Yamaguchi-ken.

About Triennale – Echigo-Tsumari Art Field (no date) www.echigo-tsumari.jp/eng/about/overview/ (accessed 15 September 2016).

Bishop, C. (2012) *Artificial Hells: Participatory Art and the Politics of Spectatorship*, London and New York: Verso Books.

Blowers, A. (2013) 'The Future Is Not Nuclear: Ethical Choices for Energy after Fukushima', in R.A. Hindmarsh (ed.) *Nuclear Disaster at Fukushima Daiichi: Social, Political and Environmental Issues*, 1st edition, Routledge Studies in Science, Technology and Society, v. 21, New York: Routledge, 175–193.

Bourriaud, N. (2009) *Relational Aesthetics*. Nachdr. Dijon: Presses du réel.

Calichman, R. (ed.) (2008) *Overcoming Modernity: Cultural Identity in Wartime Japan*, New York: Columbia University Press.

Centemeri, L. (2018) 'Commons and the New Environmentalism of Everyday Life. Alternative Value Practices and Multispecies Commoning in the Permaculture Movement', *Rassegna Italiana di Sociologia*, L. Pellizzoni (ed.), 64(2): 289–313.

Centemeri, L. (2019) 'Rethinking Environmentalism in a "Ruined" World. Lessons from the Permaculture Movement', in J. Hoff, Q. Gausset and S. Lex (eds) *The Role of Non-state Actors in the Green Transition: Building a Sustainable Future*, London and New York: Routledge, 95–113.

Char, E. and Yeung, G. (2018) *Farmers' Horizon: Urban x Rural, Japan x Hong Kong Connect: Echigo Tsumari Art Triennale*, 1st edition, G. Chiu (ed.), trans. J. Lam, Hong Kong: Elite Production.

Chim↑Pom and 椹木 野衣 (2015) *Don't Follow the Wind*: 展覧会公式カタログ. 東京: 河出書房新社.

Danto, A. (1964) 'The Artworld', *The Journal of Philosophy, American Philosophical Association Eastern Division Sixty-First Annual Meeting*, 61(19): 571–584.

Dewey, J. (1991) *The Public and Its Problems*, Athens: Swallow Press.

Fukuoka, M. (1993) *The Natural Way of Farming: The Theory and Practice of Green Philosophy*, trans. F.P. Metreaud, Madras: Bookventure.

Fukuoka, M. (2010) *The One-straw Revolution: An Introduction to Natural Farming*, New York: New York Review Books.

Fukuoka, M. (2013) *Sowing Seeds in the Desert: Natural .Farming, Global Restoration, and Ultimate Food Security*, Vermont: Chelsea Green White River Publishing.

Hindmarsh, R.A. (ed.) (2013) *Nuclear Disaster at Fukushima Daiichi: Social, Political and Environmental Issues*, 1st edition, New York: Routledge studies in science, technology and society, v. 21.

Jackson, S.J. (2014) 'Rethinking Repair', in T. Gillespie, P.J. Boczkowski and K.A. Foot (eds) *Media Technologies: Essays on Communication, Materiality, and Society*, Cambridge, MA: The MIT Press, 221–239.

Jobin, P. (2005) 'The Tragedy of Minamata. Sit-In and Face-to-Face Discussion', in B. Latour and P. Weibel (eds) *Making things Public: Atmospheres of Democracy*, Cambridge, MA; Karlsruhe, Germany: MIT Press; ZKM/Center for Art and Media in Karlsruhe, 988–993.

Katayama, N. *et al.* (2015) 'A Review of Post-War Changes in Rice Farming and Biodiversity in Japan', *Agricultural Systems*, 132: 73–84. <https://doi.org/10.1016/j.agsy.2014.09.001>.

Kikuchi, Y. (2004) *Japanese Modernisation and Mingei Theory: Cultural Nationalism and Oriental Orientalism*, London and New York: Routledge Curzon.

Kitagawa, F. (2015) *Art Place Japan: The Echigo-Tsumari Triennale and the Vision to Reconnect Art and Nature*, English edition, New York: Princeton Architectural Press.

Kopf, B. (2020) 'Never Mind the Banzais, Here's the Seppuku Pistols', *The Wire Magazine – Adventures in Modern Music*. <www.thewire.co.uk/in-writing/essays/never-mind-the-banzais-here-s-the-seppuku-pistols> (accessed 23 November 2020).

Miyazawa, K. (2007) *Miyazawa Kenji: Selections*, H. Sato (ed.), Berkeley: University of California Press (Poets for the millennium, 5).

Mollison, B. and Holmgren, D. (1978) *Permaculture One: A Perennial Agricultural System for Human Settlements*, Melbourne: Transworld Publishers.

Morita, A., Blok, A. and Kimura, S. (2013) 'Environmental Infrastructures of Emergency: The Formation of a Civic Radiation Monitoring Map during the Fukushima Disaster', in R.A. Hindmarsh (ed.) *Nuclear Disaster at Fukushima Daiichi: Social, Political and Environmental Issues*, 1st edition, Routledge Studies in Science, Technology and Society, v. 21, New York: Routledge, 78–96.

Murakami, T. (2011) *MMIX LAB*. <https://mmix.org/what.htm> (accessed 5 May 2020).

Nishiko (ニシコ). (2012) *Repairing Earthquake Project・First Phase (*地震を直すプロジェクト・第一段階地震を直すプロジェクト・第一段階*)*, 1st edition, Nishiko. <www.nishiko55.com/eq>.

NRC (Backgrounder on Radioactive Waste). (2019) <www.nrc.gov/reading-rm/doc-collections/fact-sheets/radwaste.html> (accessed 27 November 2020).

Puig de la Bellacasa, M. (2017) *Matters of Care: Speculative Ethics in More than Human Worlds*, Minneapolis: University of Minnesota Press (Posthumanities, 41).

Schlosberg, D. and Coles, R. (2016) 'The New Environmentalism of Everyday Life: Sustainability, Material Flows and Movements', *Contemporary Political Theory*, 15(2): 160–181. <https://doi.org/10.1057/cpt.2015.34>.

Strebel, I., Bovet, A. and Sormani, P. (2018) *Repair Work Ethnographies*, New York: Palgrave Macmillan.

Sugimoto, Y. (2007) 'Marginal Art', in G. Ritzer (ed.) *The Blackwell Encyclopedia of Sociology*, Oxford, UK: John Wiley & Sons, Ltd. <https://doi.org/10.1002/9781405165518.wbeosm024>.

Takehisa, Y. (ed.) (2012) *Artists and the Disaster: Documentation in Progress*. Contemporary Art Center Art Tower Mito.

Thorsen, L.M. (2013) 'Aesthetics of Concern: Art in the Wake of the Triple Disaster of North-Eastern Japan and Hurricane Katrina', *COPAS*, 14(2): Spec. COPAS issue on sentiment.

Thorsen, L.M. (2014) *Acute Art Practices: The Mobilisation of Contemporary Art Practices for the Articulation of Public Concerns in the Wake of the Great North-eastern Japan Earthquake*, University of Copenhagen.

Thorsen, L.M. (2019) *On the Margins of Eco-Art: Aesthetics, Plants and Environmental Imaginations in East Asia*, PhD thesis, University of Aarhus.

Tsing, A.L. (2015) *The Mushroom at the End of the World: On the Possibility of Life in Capitalist Ruins*, Princeton: Princeton University Press.

Tsurumi, S. (1987) *A Cultural History of Postwar Japan, 1945–1980*, London and New York: New York: KPI; Distributed by Methuen (Japanese studies).

Walker, B.L. (2011) *The Toxic Archipelago: A History of Industrial Disease in Japan*, Seattle, WA; Chesham: University of Washington Press.

岩瀬 (Iwase) 昭典 (Akinori) (ed.) (2015) 表現者たちの「3・11」: 震災後の芸術を語る *(Creative Practitioners on 3.11: Talking about Art after the Earthquake)*, 河北新報社編集局.

福住 (Fukuzumi), 廉 (Ren). (2008) 今日の限界芸術. 横浜: BankART 1929.

鶴見 (Tsurumi), 俊輔 (Shunsuke). (1967) 限界芸術論 *(Genkai Geijutsuron)*. 東京: 筑摩書房.

7 Plurality of temporalities, complexity and contingency in repairing after dam failures in Minas Gerais

Francis Chateauraynaud and Josquin Debaz

Introduction

Through the screens of our globalized world, the accelerated interconnectedness of disparate phenomena makes disasters seem increasingly devastating, which in turn casts further uncertainty on the state of the world.

In social sciences, disasters have been traditionally defined as events of rupture, which unleash violence and confusion upon routine, ordinary and ordered practices, at both the individual and collective level. The study of disasters merits such academic attention because these situations make visible both dramaturgical (human, non-human and even inhuman) modalities of action, power and knowledge relations, and capacities for reconstruction and reparation. They prompt stakeholders to renegotiate the normative orders that enable them to 'make society', as Janine Barbot and Nicolas Dodier show, in relation to the normative repertoires used by victims of public health disasters (see Barbot and Dodier 2015; and their chapter in this volume).

Social scientists can study disasters before they happen, observing actors who warn of impending emergencies. Alternatively, they can analyze disasters from the vantage point of the crisis situations they engender, often contributing through applied research to their management. They may also take interest in the aftermath – the long, often very long, restoration and rebuilding processes that follow catastrophic events. In all these cases, the phenomena of rupture or disruption seriously challenge the analytical grids of social science research (Moreau 2017). Catastrophic events force one to consider the unthinkable and to leave the epistemic comfort zone of social science models and theories. The pragmatist tradition, recently revived in sociology, cannot eschew this need to reconsider conceptual frameworks when analyzing disasters.

To this end, we will discuss here the ways in which disaster research is informed by the 'pragmatic sociology of transformations' approach that we have been developing since the 1990s. This sociological approach has been developed to analyze the social dynamics of risk issues, with an initial focus on the European context later expanded to the international context, with a specific attention to the US and global institutions (Chateauraynaud and Debaz 2017). It deals with controversies over environmental and health risks, and opens new perspectives

DOI: 10.4324/9781003184782-10

in the study of what we define as 'long-term critical processes'. These dynamics comprise a complex series of events and 'tests' that simultaneously modify *dispositifs* and environments, evaluative norms and practical experiences. This approach breaks away from not only binary visions that reduce social phenomena to various oppositions (such as agency versus structure) but also from ones simplifying social processes to their cartography or to the evolution of narrative or rhetorical frames.

Disasters fuel the dynamics of controversy. In fact, long-term critical processes are built on ruptures, emergencies, upsurges, bifurcations and turning points. In particular, one of the most obvious effects of a turning point is to transform the projected space of futures, or in other words, to alter the possible trajectories at play in the future. A disaster always disrupts the linear view of what is expected to happen next, forcing individuals, collectives, and institutions to reflect on the reconstruction of the future.

In this regard, the study of long-term critical processes reveals that it is necessary to investigate, through multi-scale ethnography, these dynamics through both the analysis of public discourses and the direct observation of interactions in the ecosystems and social worlds affected by hazards and disasters. It is through ethnographic fieldwork that the existence of a multiplicity of local solutions, new configurations and alternatives, and even new forms of experimental interactions between human devices and non-human environments can be grasped (Tsing 2015). The elaboration of this perspective draws on the work of anthropologist Anna Tsing, who explores the concrete possibilities of a life without the promise of what she depicts as the peculiar modern compromise between stability and progress. Her aim is to draw – and bring awareness to – a world composed of a diversity of assemblages operating across scales.

In order to demonstrate the interest of this approach in improving our understanding of recovery after disaster, this chapter proposes to confront the complexity of what we define as 'interacting milieus' (Chateauraynaud and Debaz 2017) through the study of two major disastrous events: the failures of two Brazilian mining dams, at Bento Rodrigues in November 2015, and at Brumadinho in January 2019. The opportunity to conduct research in Minas Gerais around dams and the Brazilian extractive industry proved to be a real epistemic experiment to test the descriptive and analytical tools we have been developing while working in European contexts. Equally significant, this experience underscored the importance of collaborating with local researchers.

Our goal in this chapter is twofold. On the one hand, and on a more theoretical level, we seek to clarify how, within the pragmatic sociology of transformation, we combine pragmatism and complex systems theories – showing that this approach is attentive to both the systemic dimensions of disasters and the indeterminacy experienced on the ground concerning the possible courses of action. On the other hand, and beginning with our ongoing research in Brazil, we want to present the different pathways by which a variety of individual and collective actors, in post-disaster situations, look for ways to 'reconstruct' their ways of life. This can occur through new projects and by reorganizing their sensory ties to the surrounding world, while keeping away from formal procedures of reparation. We adopt the term 'reconstruction' to designate the transformative meaning of reparation that the editors of this book define in the introduction. In our research, in fact, the notion of repair has been widely appropriated by the actors responsible for the disaster. Our choice to name these processes 'reconstruction' aims to differentiate them from the technical procedures of fixing what has been damaged or the judicial procedures seeking compensation. In fact, the reconstruction of ways of life does not require a predefined goal, and success is completely unforeseeable.

Catastrophe, disaster and collapse: meanings in transformation

As mentioned in the introduction of this book, there is a consensus in disaster research to consider disaster as 'a fundamental disruption in the social system (of whatever size) that renders ineffective whatever patterns of social intercourse prevail' (Introduction: p. 21). What is specific to a pragmatic investigation of disasters is an openness to the wide range of interpretations used by actors to deal with past, present or future 'disruptions', understood as a loss of control over the world (*i.e.* no longer having the capacity to act and react) (Revet and Langumier 2015).

In practice, actors can rely on different meanings of disruption or rupture, according to the experiential contexts. In one sense, the concept of disruption can refer to an unexpected event taking populations by surprise and denoting a complete lack of anticipation or preparedness, as was the case with the 9/11 terror attacks in the United States.

A second sense of disruption emerges when an event was expected but occurs in an abnormal or chaotic way. This was what happened in March 2011, when Japan was shaken by an earthquake which was followed by a tsunami and then by the unprecedented nuclear accident that destroyed several reactors at the Fukushima nuclear power plant (see Chapter 6). The account of the incident by the plant manager, Yoshida Masao, dramatically illustrates how first-hand experience can be incommensurable with remote representations of a disaster (Guarnieri and Travadel 2018). Moreover, the focus placed on the nuclear accident has relegated to the background many other consequences of the tsunami (Takezawa 2016). This kind of disruption is related to a loss of collective vigilance, a decrease in control and a lack of maintenance. Typically, following an accident, investigators discover that early warning signs were not heeded and that security protocols were overlooked or transferred to agents with little knowledge of a site's technological history and thus its vulnerabilities. Contemporary casuistry provides countless examples within this framework, from the Bhopal gas tragedy (India, 1984), to the explosion of the AZF fertilizer factory in Toulouse (France, 2001), to the Deep Water Horizon oil spill (Gulf of Mexico, 2010) to the collapse of the Genoa Bridge (Italy, 2018).

A third type of disruption must be also considered: the chronic, imminent disasters which are increasingly approaching yet imperceptible. Their interpretation, assessment and management feed into the production of scenarios and causality models, the allocation of responsibility and the search for diverse solutions. The pragmatic sociology of transformations has mainly been mobilized to study this kind of silent, pervasive or gradual destructive process. These 'slow disasters' include, amongst others, endocrine disrupters, air pollution health impacts and the sixth mass extinction. In each one of their reports, the Intergovernmental Panel on Climate Change (IPCC) and the Intergovernmental Science-Policy Platform on Biodiversity and Ecosystem Services (IPBES) confirm and formalize the ever-increasing scale of climate change and biodiversity loss and their dreadful consequences for living conditions on Earth. In this scenario, disaster is more of a gradual drift towards a nightmarish world than a punctual event. For instance, when an actor declares that GMOs which are colonizing crops 'will lead to a catastrophe', the semantic network carried by the term 'catastrophe' is very different from the following one: 'one of these days, a nuclear power plant will fail, and it will be a catastrophe'. In fact, each body of objects and actions defines its own space of possible disasters.

This form of persistent, ongoing Catastrophe (with a capital *C*) provides the basis for apocalyptic scenarios which announce major collapse on a global scale, with incalculable consequences at the local level. This vision of global and systemic collapse pushes us into a borderland, stretching between epistemic dimensions (data production, model building, scenario proposals) entwined with axiological considerations (desirable or undesirable futures, ethics of responsibility toward the fate of the planet and future generations). Such collapse narratives are in line with the concept of the Anthropocene, referring to an irreversible alteration of the biosphere induced by human activities which greatly accelerated after the Second World War.

How disasters in their multiplicity resonate with the Catastrophe, in its global understanding, varies from one environment to another. For example, it is worth noting that the global concept of the Anthropocene is translated differently at the regional level, as in the case of Brazil (see Issberner and Léna 2016).

In the context of the looming Catastrophe, two dividing lines have been called into question in recent decades: the distinction between natural and man-made disasters, and between intentional disasters (war, genocide, technological crime) and unintentional disasters (domino effect or an unlikely conjunction of circumstances). There is increasing awareness that disasters are socially produced, meaning they are directly related to political and economic decisions that have an impact on the vulnerability of populations. This is the case even for extreme events stemming from 'natural' causes, such as Hurricane Katrina in 2005 in the United States, the storm Xynthia in 2010 in France (see Chapter 9), or more recently, the large wildfires in the Amazon in 2019.

Still, not all is doomed. Disasters can also reveal alternative paths forward and possibilities of still livable worlds that are generally flattened and reduced by the formula 'back to business as usual'. Before, during or in the wake of a disaster, there is a permanent and tragic tension between expectations (Koselleck 2004) and new avenues for the future (Duval 1990), the return of the normal state of affairs and the creation of fresh blueprints (Chateauraynaud and Debaz 2017).

At the heart of the re-staging of possible worlds, there is a constant tension between destiny and possibility. One approach to these issues that Ulrich Beck introduced to sociology, which is also present – albeit with important nuances – in the works of such critical thinkers as Ellul, Anders, Jonas, Illich and more recently, Dupuy (2002), is to understand the possibility of disaster(s) as the battleground for the determination, or indeterminacy, of the future. With this in mind, Dupuy's thesis of 'enlightened catastrophism' is undoubtedly ambiguous, at least from an analytical point of view. Indeed, this interpretive framework states that it is by considering the disaster as theoretically inevitable that it will be avoided in practice. However, this standpoint is pragmatically unrealistic: if nuclear engineers, surgeons, airline pilots, train drivers or dam designers adopted such a catastrophic regime, they would hardly be able to carry out their work calmly and intervene adequately in the *dispositifs* in order to prevent an extreme event from occurring. It is by addressing early warning signs, weak signals and micro-phenomena that actors succeed in preventing risk and danger from concretizing.

Directly present in and grappling with environments, actors deploy temporal and spatial mediations in everyday activities. Even though actors may lose their grasp on real processes at any moment, when directly grappling with environments, they deploy temporal and spatial mediations in everyday activities (Bessy and Chateauraynaud 2014). By no means do we endorse a hubris of some sort that would endow techno-scientific thought with an infinite capacity for problem-solving through new technological solutions – what French philosopher Tibon-Cornillot, drawing largely on Jacques Ellul, called the 'surge of techniques' (*déferlement des techniques*; see Tibon-Cornillot 2003). A middle ground must be found between technological catastrophism – a trend that does not facilitate the comprehension of the vulnerability of socio-technical systems (Roe 2013) – and the pragmatic recognition of actors' capacities. According to Dewey's understanding of social inquiry (Dewey 1927), social actors are able to identify, discuss and organize the solutions to problems.

The contribution of a pragmatic approach to complexity: catastrophe and contingency

A pragmatic approach to disasters does not merely involve the serious consideration of actors' problem-solving capacities and the specificity of the situations in which the 'what-ness' of the event is defined (see Centemeri *et al.* in this volume). A pragmatic perspective also implies an examination of the link between disruption and what we refer to as a 'triple contingency'.

In his *Introduction to System Theory*, Niklas Luhmann (2013) revisits the concept of 'double contingency', originally formulated in sociology by Talcott Parsons. On the one hand, one can say that 'X is contingent on Y' pointing to the dependence of X on a particular context Y. On the other hand, contingency means that 'nothing is impossible and nothing is necessary'. This formula originates from monotheistic theology; in order to be almighty, God must be able to conceive a totally different world.

Accordingly, Luhmann's systems theory acknowledges the possibility of a major disruptive event that forces a system and its subsystems to shut down, making it impossible to restart in normal conditions. In this framework, however, genuine causes of disasters are essentially external. This very point led to an interesting controversy pitting Luhmann against Ulrich Beck, who theorized that modern systems contain the seeds of disaster (Lantz *et al.* 2002).

In addition to the two aforementioned forms of contingency highlighted by Luhmann – that is to say, a dependence on context and an openness to possibilities that never exclude the impossible – a third form of contingency may be considered: the encounter, overlap or convergence of heterogeneous series of events that were not necessarily meant to collide. Within classical logics, it may be possible to reduce this latter form to the first two (*i.e.* contextuality and possibility). Yet this third approach to contingency grasps things *in the making*, in the very process of transformation – hence the special interest in non-linearity within the pragmatics of transformations.

This also explains why, in the study of disasters as part of long-term critical processes, the analysis of the systemic level must be complemented with the direct observation of exchanges in fields of action. From a pragmatics of transformations perspective, a systemic approach – where the idea of a system, more or less integrated, is built to control or determine everything (as in, for example, neoliberal capitalism) – is always strengthened by observation of the many milieus, scenes and theaters of operation where 'friction' and dispute may arise. From this tension, many forms of what we define as 'reconstruction' may emerge around the experience of disasters.[1]

Obviously, the systemic approach implies an attention to the operations of socio-technical engineering that structure and maintain relationships of equivalence, reductions and translations of events and experiences in a common computational space. As this mode of reasoning is hegemonic, when communities yearn for autonomy, independence or difference, they must challenge the version of the desirable future that is computed within the system. This is the reason why 'rebellion of milieus' and critical movements always rely heavily on the two logics of incommensurability and irreducibility (see Centemeri 2015).

The challenge for a pragmatic description of disasters is to maintain shocks, frictions, shifts, silent processes and forms of regulation and reconstruction in the same framework. Any disaster, whatever its forms, forces actors to rethink the things on which their social world relies. In so doing, they may engage in *a contrario* reasoning, reversing the classic question within social sciences. The real question, in fact, becomes how order is possible, rather than how to explain deviance from the norm. Nevertheless, recognizing alternative and incommensurable trajectories raises the question of how to define the common criteria of successful reconstruction.

The pragmatic perspective shows that the stability of norms and representations, including computations, depends on how knowledge and experience are grounded. Given that every controversy surrounding a risk or disaster is associated with the confrontation between evidence logic and visions of the future, it is necessary to trace the collective production of evidence concerning causality and damages. Concurrently, the manufacturing of possible or probable futures, as well as their transformations over time, must be seriously studied. This requires an examination of the futures in the making, through the different regimes of articulation (Latour 2003) that tend to fix them. This leads actors to formalize or clarify various modes of criticality. In order to stabilize a vision of the future, they have to articulate an internal critique of pre-existing *dispositifs*, with global political configurations and roots in local practices – or 'attachments' – which generate counter-evaluations (Centemeri 2019; see also Chapter 6).

Combining pragmatism and theories of complex systems thus requires a trans-disciplinary analysis. While pragmatism barely seeks to study system effects, complexity theorists remain unconvincing when they deal with individual or collective actions. An articulation of concepts and tools from both fields may be logical, in order to properly address the constant change of scale in which the actors evolve as well as the plurality of interpretations they elaborate. It is also a question of overcoming the weakness of models based on monotonous causality, especially as far as disasters are concerned.

The re-articulation of critical analysis and empirical inquiry that we advance in order to study multi-scale controversies involves a shift in methodological and theoretical boundaries. On the one hand, it implies a renewal of phenomenology based on the idea of 'interacting *milieus*': the place-based dimension of social phenomena is combined with the interest in exploring how actors themselves take into account the variations of scale, both spatially and temporally. The 'sensory world' is the place of frictions, confrontations, interactions and sometimes of direct juxtapositions or superimpositions, between heterogeneous milieus. Most critical situations arise at the junctions between these milieus, whose interactions and exchanges create an infinite number of possible combinations which, under certain contingent conditions, can produce disrupting events. By resorting to the idea of interactions between milieus, we try to escape the nature/culture or human/non-human dichotomies. On the other hand, this implies the possibility of integrating several formal properties associated with complex systems into a pragmatic approach to transformations.

Within dynamic systems, a large number of agents interact, and these inter-actions have repercussions on multiple levels. Such interactions lead to minor changes, chaotic stretches, sudden accelerations or disruptions. In addition, the study of dynamic systems avoids the trap concerning the determination of linear causality, with feedback and bifurcation mechanisms generating undetermined outcomes. Finally, if stability can be temporarily observed on a particular scale, it conceals or ignores instability or metastability on another scale. Under such conditions, the production of knowledge and expertise cannot be reduced to a mass of definitively fixed statements distributed in concentric circles around hard cores; it must also be approached by means of critical review processes. In these cases, exceptions or outliers are as relevant as regularities. Quite often for the prominent stakeholders, 'repairing' means reinstating routines and regularity, in order to restore the computing space that solidifies their domination. Conversely, some try to take advantage of any destabilization in order to advance new agendas, as in the idea of 'disaster capitalism'. This restrictive use of the repair framework obscures repair when understood as the open-ended and experiential process of 'reconstructing' a livable world.

A focus on reconstruction processes enables us to recognize that, along with controversy or conflict, disasters are major levers that stakeholders use to amend their own representations and beliefs, even if large structures do not show any abrupt inflection.[2] Most often, intense and collective revision work aims to prevent the return of the material and social conditions that put these forces into motion ('No more war!' people shouted after the First World War). This work of critical revision (Livet 2016) is confronted with the equally intense work of relativization ('Nothing can be done about it', 'The show must go on!'), whereby the problematic *dispositifs* are paradoxically reinforced. Nevertheless, there is a risk of perspectivism in reducing the description of critical processes to the study of confrontations between actors and arguments around causes and causalities. A perspectivist approach considers that actors individually produce their own narrative and interpretation of an event, and that the role of social sciences is to expose and render all these versions intelligible.

By relying on the theoretical frame we have detailed thus far, our previous and current research shows that three major phenomena become particularly salient following catastrophes. First, disasters make visible and contribute to the creation of asymmetries and fractures within what we have defined as 'interacting *milieus*'. Second, reconstruction following a disaster imposes both cognitive and political tasks on those affected, who are forced to find a pathway between four logics of reversibilization: reparation (in a technical and legal sense), compensation, adaptation and resilience. Finally, disasters lead to the revision of actors' visions of the future, through the use of scenarios, forecasts and even fiction. These phenomena are key to the understanding of the social and ecological consequences of the Mariana Dam collapse, especially in light of the repairing practices designed by corporations, state jurisdictions and the federal government. The following section will discuss how the pragmatics of complexity may aid in grasping the non-linear and negotiated nature of the reconstruction process.

Lessons from Mariana and Brumadinho

On 5 November 2015, a tailings dam suddenly broke above the village of Bento Rodrigues in the Mariana district (Minas Gerais), unleashing a staggering amount of toxic mud (600 million cubic metres of mud loaded with iron and heavy metals). After devastating the village and killing 19 people, the mud swept along the 650 kilometres of the Rio Doce for 17 days, reaching the Atlantic Ocean at the mouth of the river, in the Linares district (Espirito Santo). Due to its long-term impact on river and coastal zone ecosystems, and because it deprived many cities and communities of drinking water, this disaster is considered the most serious environmental catastrophe in Brazilian history.

There is a noticeable gap between the scale of the Mariana disaster and the limited attention it received in the European public debate. Although the disaster received international media coverage in the direct aftermath and on its first and second anniversaries, the event did not lead to international mobilizations.

The Mariana disaster is part of a long series of dam collapses – such as the Mount Polley dam collapse in Canada (2014) and the catastrophe of Ajka in Hungary (2010) – which have gained much notoriety. However, as far as French-speaking media is concerned, the Mariana case resulted in only a few reports and newspaper articles, without translating into substantial concern on a national scale. In contrast, in Brazil the event has been considered a major breaking point – ecologically, economically, socially and culturally – as witnessed by the number of published studies (Milanez and Losekann 2016; Caldas 2017; Serra 2018; Losekann and Mayorga 2018; Magalhães Pinheiro *et al.* 2019).

Our contribution to the existing literature relies on fieldwork undertaken between 2016 and 2019, from Bento Rodrigues (where the dam collapsed) to Regência (where the river ends), as part of an interdisciplinary Franco-Brazilian academic program of exchange and collaboration. Our research combined in-depth interviews and multi-site ethnography targeting 'interacting milieus', located around mining sites and along the river. The project aimed to examine the consequences of the dam failure in the context of the political changes in Brazil over the past decade, by looking at how diverse logics and rationalities guiding the response to the disaster are at odds when observed from different actors' perspectives. In particular, we focus on two conflicting logics in dealing with recovery: reparation/compensation and adaptation/resilience. These logics point to different collective ways to 'grasp' the situation that actors mobilized to make sense of the disaster. From this perspective, those involved appear to be unequally endowed with capacities for action and reaction – and therefore unequally protected against the destructive effects of the disaster.

But before entering into the details of our fieldwork, it is important to note that since the collapse of the Mariana Dam in November 2016, two major political changes have occurred in Brazil. There has been a marked shift in the government with the election of Jair Messias Bolsonaro to the presidency, with the support of an alliance of conservative political parties, armed forces and evangelicals. The new government has been criticized for promoting a federal policy incompatible with environmental concerns. What's more, the collapse of the Brumadinho Dam in January 2019 further evidenced the vulnerability of tailings dams. The previous governments, led by the Partido dos Trabalhadores (PT), never really stepped away from 'extractivist' policy, as amply demonstrated by the cases of Belo Monte Dam in the Amazon, the struggles to ban asbestos or the subsidies provided to oil companies despite the Rio+20 commitments (Jaichand and Sampaio 2013). With the Mariana and the Brumadinho accidents, however, the political pressure regarding environmental issues has become more pronounced.[3] As Brazilian political scientist Giuseppe Cocco noted in a paper comparing Mariana with Chernobyl (with the latter seen as the 'forerunner of the Soviet Union collapse'), the dam failure and the pollution of Rio Doce were interpreted by many observers as 'the symbol of a Brazilian triple crisis: economic, political, and environmental' (Cocco 2016). Many actors we met in the field in 2016 reported that the growth of the Brazilian mining industry has been increasing the vulnerability of a series of dams considered obsolete, poorly maintained or subject to repeated shocks. The large number of deaths caused by the failure of the second dam in Brumadinho dramatically confirmed scenarios previously dismissed as baseless conjectures or doomsayer views.

A self-styled innovative legal reparation process serving the status quo

As argued by Barbot and Dodier (Chapter 10), exploring the 'ecology of repara- tion *dispositifs*' offers the opportunity to investigate the processes involved in the assessment of the damage caused by a disaster, their characterization and the assigning of responsibility, as well as the possibilities of obtaining fair deci- sions in civil and criminal cases, at local and international levels. Regarding the Mariana disaster, the magnitude of the environmental and social consequences of the dam collapse were considered unprecedented. Using this exceptionality as an argument, the corporations involved in the disaster, namely Samarco-Vale-BHP, promoted a self-styled innovative legal reparation process, based on a 'Transac- tion and Adjustment of Conduct Term' (*Termo de Transação e Ajustamento de Conduta*, TTAC). Signed by the Brazilian federal and state governments, as well as the mining companies, this text was meant to guide recovery operations and compensation procedures. The creation of the Renova Foundation by the TTAC, in March 2016, reflects the legal injunction to respond to the gravity and com- plexity of the situation by setting up a governance system to manage recovery processes involving the largest number of stakeholders. The founding of Renova was also meant to facilitate the allocation of responsibility within Samarco, a com- pany owned by two mining multinationals: Brazilian Vale and Anglo-Australian BHP Billiton. The strategy requires mediation as the proper solution to prevent a coalition of complaints filed against the corporations (on mediation, see Chap- ter 8). Many observers have considered the foundation as a public relations device dedicated mainly to restoring the reputation of the firms at the local, national and international levels (Leonardo *et al.* 2017).

The March 2016 agreement, signed under the Roussef presidency, provisioned that Samarco-Vale-BHP would inject around $6.1 billion into the foundation over 15 years, without excluding the possibility of further financial obligations. How- ever, a new agreement was signed in October 2018 lowering the compensation for victims, while also allowing for the possibility of resuming mining operations.

The extrajudicial agreement did not prevent actions based on judicial *dispositifs* of reparation. The class action lawsuit filed in the High Court in Liverpool (one of BPH's headquarters) created a new opening in the judicial process, exposing the company to one of the largest environmental lawsuits in Europe.[4] The choice to act outside Brazilian courts can be understood in light of the difficulties encountered by victims and their relationship with the national judicial system. With regard to criminal liability, on 20 October 2016, the Federal Public Prosecutor's Office of Minas Gerais indicted some 21 executives of Samarco, Vale, BHP Billiton and VogBR for environmental crime and homicide. The Brazilian courts suspended the proceedings in August 2017. The breach of the Brumadinho Dam in January 2019 added fuel to the fire, due to the high number of fatalities.

As a further illustration of the complex and intricate repair process in the judicial sphere, it is important to remember that in September 2017, the Minister of Mines, Fernando Coelho Filho, avoided responsibility for the collapse of the dam and labeled it an 'accident' caused by 'destiny'.[5] In November of the same year, the river itself attempted to take legal action against the Brazilian state, via the Latin American association Pachamama.[6]

In addition to activating legal mechanisms concerning reparations/compensation, the Mariana Dam disaster paved the way for specific institutional resilience/adaptation strategies which are to a certain extent interconnected with the ways reparations and compensation have been organized.

Institutionally, the political management of pollution usually unfolds along an 'avoid-mitigate-compensate sequence', at least ideally (Bigard 2018). For standardized regulation aimed at tackling urgent and global risks, the European Environmental Agency (EEA) advocates a slightly different framework that should articulate four concepts: avoid, adapt, restore and mitigate (EEA 2015: part. 3).

Many critics have pinpointed the systemic flaws exposed by the Mariana disaster, elaborating on the 'avoid' guideline. In this context, the dam collapse and its consequences document the absence of serious water governance in Brazil where, instead of setting up integrated river basin management, multiple ministries carry out a *'pulverização de ações'*, literally a 'sprinkling' of measures (Motta Pinto-Coelho 2015). Hence, this situation highlights 'the need to strengthen the state's role of exerting control over activities potentially causing great damage, not only environmental ones' (Sérgio Mendes César and Ricardo Carneiro 2017).

At a more general level, some scholars consider Mariana as an exemplification of the paradox famously coined by Karl Polanyi:

> [A] paradox, where the force of the state is necessary in order to impose the market logic and to control the associated risk of social disruption caused by increasing social tensions [. . .] While Samarco is responsible for repairing the damage caused, the State remains the primary duty bearer to uphold human rights of affected communities.
>
> (Morgan *et al.* 2016: 375)

However, since the management of repercussions from the Mariana disaster has been delegated to the Renova foundation, the process is quite different from the classical divide or opposition between the state and market. The 'restoring' occurs through the funding of environmental projects, but if we consider the social impacts, the process focuses on the issue of 'mitigation', in particular through subsidies for fishermen (Viana 2016).

This seems to more closely resemble an indirect process of compensation, given that the mining industry seeks to maintain its activities without an actual, thorough overhaul of its risk policy. At the same time,

> [g]overnment agencies still lack the capacity to enforce increasingly-complex environmental legislation. The result is that the industry engages in self-monitoring. [. . .] In spite of the headlines and outrage, people whose livelihoods are affected by a mining disaster may never be fully compensated.
>
> (Labonne 2016)

This tragic realization reveals structural conditions of vulnerability, pointing to long-term processes that contributed to the Rio Doce catastrophe and that seem to go beyond the scope of reparations processes.

Public mobilizations and reconstruction initiatives

Following a very common pattern observed in many cases of disaster, one can identify the opposition between, on the one hand, a reductionist objectification of damage and, on the other hand, a process of 'subjectivization' grounded in the demands of affected persons or victims who aim to be in control of 'their own destiny' (Zhouri *et al.* 2017).

Immediately after the Mariana Dam collapsed, a constellation of grassroots citizens' movements emerged thanks to the mobilization of scientists and local communities. Stakeholders from different backgrounds came together to produce a counter-expertise incorporating multiple experiences and knowledge based on the model of civic epistemologies. This concept refers to the specific ways in which the public investigates and expects the state's expertise, knowledge and reasoning to be produced, tested and implemented in decision making (Fischer 2000; Jasanoff 2004).

Their mobilization was primarily centered on the need for an immediate emergency response, to address the huge mudslide that was affecting the river. This response – which saw the occasional participation of Samarco's technicians – was oriented toward establishing a 'zero level' of environmental measurements to assess the evolution of the pollution; without a proper knowledge of the ecosystem before a disaster, the evaluation of its impact is always incomplete (Souza Miranda and Marques 2016). In the early stages of this process, a citizen-science group called GIAIA (*Grupo Independente de Avaliação do Impacto Ambiental*) was formed to conduct independent research, free from 'political and financial interests', and to make the environmental data and analytical product widely accessible.

In October 2017, at the mouth of the Rio Doce in Regência, we encountered another form of collaborative experience, set up by a group of agents working with the Instituto Chico Mendes (ICMBio), the Brazilian Institute of the Environment and Renewable Natural Resources (IBAMA), TAMAR (an organization for the protection of sea turtles from extinction), the Institute for Energy and

Environment (IEMA) and various universities. These experts were engaged in a process of measuring, monitoring and conserving the estuarine ecosystem, particularly that of a species of protected marine turtles. They also attempted to follow the 'Samarco mud', by means of satellite tracking and sampling, down to the Abrolhos archipelago, 250 kilometres farther offshore.[7]

All these collectives can be said to be actively involved in the construction of the disaster's factuality. They try to maintain their distance from industrial rebuilding actions, in order to establish sufficient independence, and thus safeguard their freedom of speech and action. While some of them believe that it is more effective to act in tandem with the official process, or even to receive funding from the Renova foundation, others – such as the Participa program, launched by Federal University of Minas Gerais (UFMG) to help affected populations and monitor environmental damage – reject any form of collaboration.

Acting at another level of evaluation and action, the International Union for Conservation of Nature (IUCN) founded the Rio Doce Panel. Yolanda Kakabadse, the Ecuadorian environmentalist who has been named chair of the Rio Doce Panel, defines one of its tasks: 'Contribute guidance to the efforts to rehabilitate the watershed, and ensure a good quality of life for the affected communities' (Kakabadse 2018; see also IUCN Rio Doce Panel 2018). She insists on the panel's role as an international epistemic authority, providing an 'independent eye on restoration with a landscape perspective' (Kakabadse 2018). This science-based approach aims to identify environmental stressors in order to 'help local people rebuild their environment and livelihoods' (*ibid.*). Unlike the previous programs, however, this panel is not openly criticizing the Brazilian government and industrial sector.

More recently, a new wave of mobilization has emerged: that of memory, as part of the construction of the disaster's factuality (see Chapter 4). Its traces are scattered across several fields (scientific, administrative, judicial, community-based, religious) and circulate in different dimensions (spatial, temporal and organizational). The issue of memory is of utmost importance because, in order to move on, stakeholders and institutions must deal with the tension that exists between remembering and forgiving (Bosk 1979). Thus, the following phase of our field investigation consisted of identifying the actors and sites involved in determining which knowledge about the disaster was to be remembered. One of the more implicated actors in this effort is the Movimento dos Atingidos por Barragens (Movement of People Affected by Dams, or MAB). Created in 1991 as a national platform bringing together Catholic organizations and unions, it gathered families who opposed hydroelectric dams (Bednik 2019: 195–197), and has been very active in some areas of Brazil, especially in the Amazon basin. The MAB is active in denouncing the invisibilization of victims of the Mariana disaster and the injustices they suffer in the Renova-led process of repair.

Other initiatives were also launched to keep alive the memory of the disaster and of the largely irreparable damage caused by the mudslide. Such initiatives included the creation of the newspaper *A Sirene* (subtitled *Para Não Esquecer*,

'Lest We Forget'), artistic performances, and at a more local level, citizens' marches or even religious rites meant to 'heal' the river.

However, despite these forms of collective action, for both the Mariana and the Brumadinho disasters, most of the local population remains trapped in the complexity of various procedures at different institutional levels. Everything appears to be on standby in several spheres of activity: the sphere of compensation; the sphere of eco-toxicological monitoring of the river and of the coastal zone; the sphere of dramaturgical action giving rise to a multiplicity of artistic performances or achievements; and the sphere of technological expertise on dams. This raises the question of how to interpret the discrepancy, or rather the widening chasm, between the normative expectations of social science researchers, who assume the existence of active and reactive citizens, and the local populations that are often passive or not actually interested in engaging in any kind of mobilization. It is therefore urgent to reflect on how we, as social scientists, can create a fair and balanced research-based picture that does not over-estimate either generalized apathy or citizen mobilization.

Critical tensions revolving around expected behaviors and forms of anticipation expose several conceptions of resilience and vulnerability (Revet and Langumier 2015). We believe, like the geographer Terry Cannon,[8] that it is important not to use resilience as a substitute for the notion of vulnerability, since it downplays the importance of power relations. According to Cannon and Müller-Mahn (2010), through its analogy with physical and ecological systems, the term 'resilience' introduces the idea of a rational balance, potentially achieved at the expense of the people themselves.

These kinds of imbalances have been denounced by the environmental justice movement in the United States. This movement has contributed to a redefinition of risk assessment policies by making tangible the cumulative processes and interactions between social and environmental forms of injustice (London *et al.* 2007; see also Lockie 2016). Along the same lines, a marked discrepancy between public policies and local experiences has been evidenced in numerous social science studies, which emphasizes the need to take into greater consideration questions of scale, scope and duration (Fischer 2003).

In the case of Mariana and Brumadinho, the region's dependence upon industries (mining, paper, coffee plantations and oil), and the fact that a large part of the inhabitants are employees of these industries, give the very notion of 'adaptation' a more technocratic than ecological significance, in the sense that these adaptations will concern only technical design and security procedures. This calls for a re-politicization of dam safety issues, in terms of 'capital-driven destructions' (Huber *et al.* 2016).

To quote American anthropologist Eben Kirksey (2015: 219): 'Capitalist enterprises [. . .] may well be unstoppable'. If realizing this imbalance of power can lead to 'feelings of futility', it is nevertheless true (and our case confirms it) that '[a]longside legions of cynical critics, as well as communities of experts and working professionals promoting corporate and government interests, a multitude of tinkerers and thinkers are transforming feelings of futility into concrete action, cynicism into happiness and hope' (*ibid.*). In this sense, resilience can possibly be understood as another generic formula for describing the art of doing, undoing and redoing which underpins daily activities.

Conclusion

The study of dam collapses in Brazil broadens the body of critical processes analyzed by the pragmatic sociology of transformations. The Mariana and Brumadinho cases belong to the general class of disasters that reshape the field of possibilities and visions of the future based on forecast models. At the same time, they alter connexions between actors and arguments. They therefore test the theory of turning points and of the non-linearity of public issues.

After the Mariana and Brumadinho dam collapses, a challenging question remains unanswered: Under which circumstances can a series of disasters loosen the grip of the extractive industry on the 'land of mines' (Minas Gerais)? The very notion of 'extractivism' – referring to the process of extracting natural resources from the earth – is highly utilized by ecological criticism and critical social sciences. It can reference any exploitation of natural resources because, more generally, it refers to the fundamental asymmetry that benefits the industrial and financial sectors at the expense of the increasingly vulnerable environment and working class. It establishes a system heading for the Global Disaster: exploiting resources beyond the capacity for renewal; reinforcing mechanisms of inequality and extreme dependencies (especially North *vs.* South, but centered around hegemonic megacities); and pursuing a development and consumption regime that is clearly unsustainable.

The mining sector is not an outdated issue within social science and disaster research. The promise of a dematerialized life expanding in a digital world, allegedly relying on the limited consumption of resources, is challenged by the quest for rare earths, at the heart of geopolitical dynamics (Pitron 2018). Finally, the intersection between this critical approach and the mining economy reveals a historical stability in the technical and political management of accidents, the impact on ecosystems and forms of life, and modes of reparation/reconstruction. Nevertheless, the inertia of the dominant economic system may one day find itself shattered by an exceptional series of disasters.

Studying the management of repairing strategies in the long term does not really produce any startling conclusions. Solutions developed in response to the Mariana disaster show how actors assessed the notions of reparation, compensation, adaptation or resilience by making various arrangements to overcome the tensions between economic, social and environmental issues. In fact, concerning environmental damage, actors uphold opposing views of notions such as biodiversity, ecosystems, life forms, equilibrium, social impact or even balancing mechanisms. If carried out in close proximity to local actors and groups, fieldwork shows that the computation spaces and the chains of equivalence involved in ecological assessments are not commensurate with sensitive and direct experiences. Therefore, the establishment of a reparation process rarely results in any unanimous agreement, even more so in our case where the river itself is the host of a plurality of modes of existence.

Our investigations give substance to the pragmatist argument that, beyond being the *loci* of events and public controversies, interacting milieus are also the cradles of real transformations and reconstructions. This potential for transformation is eclipsed by an analysis focused exclusively on the dynamics of complex systems that can always be modeled by treating human environments as sets of quantifiable variables (demography, housing, energy, transport, economic activities, environmental indicators, etc.). Thus social sciences must position experience at the centre of collective post-disaster reparative processes.

Acknowledgements

The authors wish to express their gratitude to their Brazilian colleagues, especially Mauricio Serva and Teresa da Silva Rosa. They also wish to thank Sébastien Le Pipec for the English editing. Any remaining errors are ours.

Notes

1 One way to combine these two perspectives is to consider the so-called system as a nest of subsystems evolving at their own pace and scale but whose inputs and outputs can be grasped.
2 The performativity of precedents and turning points has been emphasized by both narrative studies (Abbott 2001) and controversy studies (Chateauraynaud 2016).
3 'Jair Bolsonaro could be a disaster for the environment, scientific research. Scientists fear risks to academic freedom, biodiversity, and Brazil's role in the global struggle against climate change', in *Brasil de Fato*, 21 October 2018. <www.brasildefato.com.br/2018/10/27/jair-bolsonaro-could-be-a-disaster-for-the-environment-scientific-research> (last accessed 10 February 2021).
4 'BHP Billiton facing £5bn lawsuit from Brazilian victims of dam disaster', *The Guardian*, 6 November 2018.
5 'Ministro de Minas e Energia chama catástrofe de Mariana de "fatalidade"', *O Globo*, 20 September 2017.
6 'Em ação inédita no país, Rio Doce entra na Justiça contra desastre', *Gazeta Online*, 09 November 2017.
7 'Ibama e ICMBio apuram se lama da Samarco atingiu Abrolhos', *Legado Brasil*, 7 January 2016.
8 Terry Cannon is the co-author of the report 'Resilience to Extreme Weather' of the Royal Society in which we find one of the broadest definitions of resilience as 'an umbrella term linking established concepts of risk and sustainability in a dynamic way, as it relates to the capacity of a system to deal with change. It encompasses but is broader than disaster risk reduction' (Royal Society Science Policy Centre 2014: 18).

References

Abbott, A. (2001) *Time Matters: On Theory and Method*, Chicago: University of Chicago Press.
Barbot, J. and Dodier, N. (2015) 'Victims' Normative Repertoire of Financial Compensation: The Tainted hGH Case', *Human Studies*, 38: 81–96.

Bednik, A. (2019) *Extractivisme*, Lyon: Le Passager clandestin.

Bessy, C. and Chateauraynaud, F. (2014) 'L'attention aux choses', Postface to *Experts et Faussaires. Pour une sociologie de la perception*, Paris: Pétra. An English version is available online: 'Being Attentive to Things: Pragmatic Approaches to Authenticity' (2015).

Bigard, C. (2018) *Éviter-Réduire-Compenser: d'un idéal conceptuel aux défis de mise en œuvre. Une analyse pluridisciplinaire et multi-échelle*, PhD thesis, Université de Montpellier.

Bosk, C.L. (1979) *Forgive and Remember: Managing Medical Failure*, Chicago: University of Chicago Press.

Caldas, G. (ed.) (2017) *Vozes e Silenciamentos em Mariana: crime ou desastre ambiental?*, Campinas, SP: BCCL/UNICAMP.

Cannon, T. and Müller-Mahn, D. (2010) 'Vulnerability, Resilience and Development Discourses in Context of Climate Change', *Natural Hazards*, 55(3), December: 621–635.

Centemeri, L. (2015) 'Reframing Problems of Incommensurability in Environmental Conflicts Through Pragmatic Sociology. From Value Pluralism to the Plurality of Modes of Engagement with the Environment', *Environmental Values*, 24(3), June: 299–320.

Centemeri, L. (2019) *La permaculture ou l'art de réhabiter*, Versailles: Éditions Quae.

Chateauraynaud, F. (2016) 'Towards a new Matrix of Risks: Learning from Multi-Scale Controversies', in European Environment Agency (ed), *Report of the EEA Scientific Committee Seminar on Emerging Systemic Risks*, Copenhagen: European Environment Agency.

Chateauraynaud, F. and Debaz, J. (2017) *Aux bords de l'irréversible. Sociologie pragmatique des transformations*, Paris: Pétra.

Cocco, G. (2016) 'La catastrophe du Rio Doce, le Tchernobyl brésilien', *Multitudes*, 1(62): 5–13.

Dewey, J. (1927) *The Public and Its Problems*, New York: Holt.

Dupuy, J.-P. (2002) *Pour un catastrophisme éclairé. Quand l'impossible est certain*, Paris: Seuil.

Duval, R. (1990) *Temps et vigilance*, Paris: Vrin.

EEA. (2015) *The European Environment: State and Outlook*, Copenhagen.

Fischer, F. (2000) *Citizens, Experts, and the Environment: The Politics of Local Knowledge*, Durham: Duke University Press.

Fischer, H. (2003) 'The Sociology of Disaster: Definitions, Research Questions, and Measurements. Continuation of the Discussion in a post-September 11 Environment', *International Journal of Mass Emergencies and Disasters*, 21(1): 91–107.

Guarnieri, F. and Travadel, S. (2018) *Un récit de Fukushima – Le directeur parle*, Paris: PUF.

Huber, A., Gorostiza, S., Kotsila, P., Beltrán, M.J. and Armiero, M. (2016) 'Beyond "Socially Constructed" Disasters: Re-politicizing the Debate on Large Dams through a Political Ecology of Risk', *Capitalism Nature Socialism*, 28(3): 48–68.

Issberner, L.-R. and Léna, P. (eds) (2016) *Brazil in the Anthropocene: Conflicts between Predatory Development and Environmental Policies*, London: Routledge.

IUCN Rio Doce Panel. (2018) *Impacts of the Fundão Dam Failure: A Pathway to Sustainable and Resilient Mitigation*, Gland: IUCN.

Jaichand, V. and Sampaio, A. (2013) 'Dam and Be Damned: The Adverse Impacts of Belo Monte on Indigenous Peoples in Brazil', *SSRN*, 30 December.

Jasanoff, S. (ed.) (2004) *States of Knowledge: The Co-production of Science and Social Order*, London: Routledge.

Kakabadse, Y. (2018) 'Changing Tide for the Rio Doce: Bringing a River Back to Life', *IUCN Crossroads blog*, 19 March. <www.iucn.org/crossroads-blog/201803/changing-tide-rio-doce-bringing-a-river-back-life> (accessed 10 February 2021).

Kirksey, E. (2015) *Emergent Ecologies*, Durham, NC: Duke University Press.

Koselleck, R. (2004) *Futures Past: On the Semantics of Historical Time. Series: Studies in Contemporary German Social Thought*, New York: Columbia University Press.

Labonne, B. (2016) 'Mining Dam Failure: Business as Usual?', *The Extractive Industries and Society*, 3: 651–652.

Lantz, P., Murard, N., Bonneuil, C., Chauvel, L. and Ramaux, C. (2002) 'À plusieurs voix sur La société du risque', *Mouvements*, 3(21–22): 162–177.

Latour, B. (2003) 'What if we Talked Politics a Little?', *Contemporary Political Theory*, 2: 143–164.

Leonardo, F., Izoton, J., Valim, H., Creado, E., Trigueiro, A., Silva, B., Duarte, L., and Santana, N. (2017) *Rompimento da barragem de Fundão (SAMARCO/VALE/BHP BIL-LITON) e os efeitos do desastre na foz do Rio Doce, distritos de Regência e Povoação, Linhares (ES)*, Relatório de pesquisa, GEPPEDES.

Livet, P. (2016) 'Emotions, Beliefs, and Revisions', *Emotion Review*, 8(3): 240–249.

Lockie, S. (2016) 'Beyond Resilience and Systems Theory: Reclaiming Justice in Sustainability Discourse', *Environmental Sociology*, 2(2): 115–117.

London, J.K., Sze, J. and Lievanos, R.S. (2007) 'Problems, Promise, Progress, and Perils: Critical Reflections on Environmental Justice Policy Implementation in California', *UCLA Journal of Environmental Policy*, 26(2): 255–289.

Losekann, C. and Mayorga, C. (eds) (2018) *Desastre na bacia do Rio Doce. Desafios para a universidade e para instituições estatais*, Rio de Janeiro: Fólio Digital.

Luhmann, N. (2013) *Introduction to Systems Theory*, Cambridge: Polity Press.

Mendes César, P.S. and Carneiro, R. (2017) 'A gestão ambiental em Minas Gerais: Uma análise do sistema de gestão ambiental e do rompimento da barragem de rejeitos em Mariana', *Revista Livre de Sustentabilidade e Empreendedorismo*, 2(2): 192–217.

Milanez, B. and Losekann, C. (eds) (2016) *Desastre no vale do Rio Doce. Antecedentes, impactos e ações sobre a destruição*, Rio de Janeiro: Fólio Digital.

Moreau, Y. (2017) *Vivre avec les catastrophes*, Paris: PUF.

Morgan, G., Peinado Gomes, M.V. and Perez-Aleman, P. (2016) 'Transnational Governance Regimes in the Global South: Multinationals, States and Ngos as Political Actors', *Revista de Administração de Empresas*, 56(4): 374–379.

Pinheiro, T.M., Polignano, M.V., Goulart, E.M.A. and de Castro Procópio, J. (eds) (2019) *Mar de lama da Samarco na bacia do rio Doce: em busca de respostas*, Belo Horizonte: Instituto Guaicuy.

Pinto-Coelho, R.M. (2015) 'Existe governança das águas no Brasil? Estudo de caso: O rompimento da Barragem de Fundão, Mariana (MG)', *Arquivos do Museu de História Natural e Jardim Botânico*, 24(1/2).

Pitron, G. (2018) *La guerre des métaux rares: La face cachée de la transition énergétique et numérique*, Paris: Les Liens Qui Libèrent.

Revet, S. and Langumier, J. (2015) *Governing Disasters: Beyond Risk Culture*, New York: Palgrave Macmillan.

Roe, E. (2013) *Making the Most of Mess: Reliability and Policy in Today's Management Challenges*, Durham and London: Duke University Press.

Royal Society Science Policy Centre (2014) *Resilience to Extreme Weather, Report, 2.* <https://royalsociety.org/-/media/policy/projects/resilience-climate-change/resilience-full-report.pdf> (accessed 10 February 2021).

Serra, C. (2018) *Tragedia em Mariana. A historia do maior desastre ambiental do Brasil*, Rio de Janeiro: Record.

Souza Miranda, L. and Marques, A.C. (2016) 'Hidden Impacts of the Samarco Mining Waste Dam Collapse to Brazilian Marine Fauna – An Example from the Staurozoans (Cnidaria)', *Biota Neotropica*, 16(2): e20160169.

Takezawa, S. (2016) *The Aftermath of the 2011 East Japan Earthquake and Tsunami: Living among the Rubble*, Lanham: Lexington Books.

Tibon-Cornillot, M. (2003) 'En route vers la planète radieuse – déferlement des techniques, insolence philosophique', *Rue Descartes*, 3(41): 52–63.

Tsing, A. (2015) *The Mushroom at the End of the World: On the Possibility of Life in Capitalist Ruins*, Princeton, NJ: Princeton University Press.

Viana, J.P. (2016) *Os pescadores da bacia do Rio Doce: subsídios para a mitigação dos impactos socioambientais do desastre da Samarco em Mariana, Minas Gerais*, IPEA, Nota Técnica, 11 May.

Zhouri, A., Oliveira, R., Zucarelli, M. and Vasconcelos, M. (2017) 'The Rio Doce Mining Disaster in Brazil: Between Policies of Reparation and the Politics of Affectations', *Vibrant*, 14(2): e142081.

Part III

The role of law in repairing environments

8 A green criminological approach to environmental victimization and reparation

A case for environmental restorative justice

Lorenzo Natali and Matthew Hall

Introduction

Over the past 25 years, 'green criminology' has become known internationally as a theoretical perspective oriented towards opening criminological paradigms to issues of environmental harms and crimes. It allows for diverse theoretical orientations to dialogue with the aim of connecting and analyzing crimes, harms and injustice related to the environment – including animals, vegetal forms of life, ecosystems, the planet and biosphere (Lynch and Stretesky 2003; Natali 2013; South 1998; 2014; South *et al.* 2013: 28; White 2011). It represents a 'conceptual umbrella' under which researchers and scholars examine and rethink the bio-physical and socio-economic consequences of environmental harm – such as pollution, the deterioration of natural resources, the loss of biodiversity and climate change (see South *et al.* 2013: 28–29) – and the possible responses. According to a definition elaborated by Pierce Beirne and Nigel South (2007: XIII), green criminology studies those harms to human beings, environment and non-human animals perpetrated by institutional actors endowed with powers – governments and corporations – but also by people in their ordinary life.

Some classic examples of crimes against the environment include the Minamata disaster (Japan), the Love Canal disaster (USA), the Bhopal disaster (India), the Exxon Valdez oil spill (Alaska), the Deepwater Horizon oil spill (Louisiana) the use of Agent Orange and of other deforestation chemicals (see South 1998). These events define a 'shared geography of prototypical disasters' (Centemeri 2006: 59) which are like stages in a sort of global collective memory that has led to the progressive acknowledgement of the global reach of industrial, technological and environmental risk. It is along these paths that criminologists have started to become aware of the importance of including environmental issues in their field, seen as the result of human activities. The complexity of environmental crimes and harms challenges the traditional socio-criminological categories and, more generally, compels a profound re-thinking of the idea of modernity itself (South 1998; Pellizzoni and Osti 2008: 270; Latour 1995: 166–167). Green criminology tries to overcome the inability of mainstream criminological knowledge to ask

DOI: 10.4324/9781003184782-12

the decisive question of how the social sphere and the natural sphere are interwoven, transcending some dichotomies of modern thought – such as those between persons and things, between technology and society, between culture and nature and, last but not least, between retribution and reparation (Halsey 2006). In this regard, green criminology suggests that we need not only new conceptual tools but also different ways to respond to the disastrous consequences of the human-environment relationship.

In this chapter, first we discuss theoretical frameworks that can help to advance the interdisciplinary debate on environmental harms and that are connected with the idea of repairing from a green criminological perspective. Second, we highlight the importance of theoretical and empirical research on environmental human and non-human victims. Third, we make the case for wider utilization of restorative justice and mediation-based approaches as means to provide alternative or parallel justice mechanisms in case of environmental crimes and harms and as paths to 'repair' the human-environment relationship disrupted by fast and slow disasters. We show how environmental restorative justice approaches can help to overcome a purely 'accusatory' vision of repairing, through taking into account other dimensions of repairing that, in our opinion, are equally if not more relevant to recovery after disaster. As the editors of this book argue in the introduction, 'repairing', understood as *asking for reparation*, points to the righting of a wrong. In this sense, the juridical term 'reparation' performs an 'accusatory' function, invoking a kind of repair that entails identifying the actor who caused the damage in question, denouncing the formal injustice of damages suffered, and determining corresponding faults, crimes, victims and perpetrators. However, as we will show by exploring the idea of environmental restorative justice, legal systems are not well adapted to meet the objectives implied in resolving the juridical and moral questions posed by the complex consequences of environmental disasters, thus causing feelings of injustice to persist in those who are most affected.

In this sense, with this contribution we try to say something 'to' criminology as well as 'about' the contribution that criminology makes to the broader debates currently taking place in environmental humanities, especially to the debate on recovery after environmental disaster.

Green criminology and its multifold approach

Since its inception, green criminology has been marked by a constitutive analytical openness that allows it to extend beyond the boundaries of a specific criminological tradition, becoming an interdisciplinary laboratory for thinking about environmental issues in the richest and broadest sense. Various denominations have been proposed for this theoretical and methodological orientation and each of them involves a different approach, namely: (1) 'eco-global criminology' (White 2011) which focuses on the transnational dimension of environmental harm and on the notion of ecological justice; (2) 'conservation criminology' (Gibbs *et al.* 2010), with a specific interest in (i) the conservation and management of natural resources and (ii) the integration of criminology with the sciences that study natural resources; and (3) 'green cultural criminology' (with a constructivist orientation) that studies the processes of construction of the notions of crime and harm from the social, cultural and political perspectives (see Brisman and South 2014). In particular, the expression 'environmental criminology', favouring a legal definition of environmental crime, has been partly discarded because it was already used to indicate a well-established criminological tradition that studies the spatial distribution of crime and enhances the role of so-called situational crime prevention in the reduction of crime (see also South and White 2013).

Even more clearly than in the case of sociology (Pellizzoni and Osti 2008), the criminological discipline is *overdue* in facing the challenges raised by the ecological crisis. The introduction of a 'green' perspective in criminology has, at least until very recently, been considered a 'novelty' with respect to mainstream approaches (Goyes and South 2017). At the same time, it is also important to acknowledge the existence of a whole literature of sociology of deviance, of criminology and of political economy that, beginning in the 1970s, has taken into account environmental issues before the birth of an explicit *green* criminological orientation. The topics of this literature include the role of organized crime in the control and management of toxic waste, the illegal trafficking of protected species and the analysis of environmental injustice. However, these relevant studies, only recently rediscovered, have never represented a coherent and compact narrative in the history of criminology (Goyes and South 2017: 166). This is why a green criminological perspective substantially enriches a socio-criminological horizon (see also South 1998).

Furthermore, the fact that many of these previous works come from different disciplines and sometimes do not belong to the academic circles of the North American tradition has contributed to the rise of an 'epistemological blindness' about them (Santos 2014). This reflection points to an important facet that concerns the context of origin, and of expansion, of green criminology. Initially, the study of green criminological issues was largely restricted to the prevalently English-speaking areas of North America, Europe and Australia. Soon, however, the field was extended to embrace the experiences of the Global South. Today, therefore, green criminology goes well beyond the cultural and geographical confines that generated it. In this sense, instead of being seen as a limiting 'label', green criminology can be more correctly seen as a 'symbol' which guides and inspires the empirical research and the theoretical development in this field (Goyes and South 2017: 167).

What is considered a crime from a criminological perspective is not necessarily something defined as a crime by law. What falls within the limits of criminal law (and what does not) is the result of a continuous social process, intimately political, as it incorporates the basic principles and visions of the kind of society in which one desires to live (see White 2011: 5). Moreover, the assessment of a specific event as 'deviant', 'harmful' or 'criminal' varies according to the historical period, the socio-cultural worlds and the geographical background in which this assessment is made. Therefore, many different definitions of the same event can coexist, often conflicting with one another in an attempt to allow a certain judgement of (social and environmental) value to prevail (Natali 2017; see also Centemeri 2015). The process according to which an event may become and be defined as an 'environmental crime' is socially constructed and is linked to the changed environmental sensitivity that characterizes our times. According to some criminological approaches to the environment, the *harm* is defined on the basis of social and ecological criteria and cannot be described only by the legal/illegal character of the activities that produced it. This position is certainly problematic from a strictly juridical point of view (White 2018), but represents a socio-criminological *insight* that is essential in valourizing a reading of environmental crimes capable of intercepting past, present and future dimensions of injustice.

To get directly to the heart of the criminological questions introduced by green criminological contributions, it seems useful to clarify the criteria concerning which behaviours *could or should* be included within the expression 'environmental/green crime'. The central issue here is the definition of crime, analyzed in the complex intertwining between justice and power which characterizes it. In this regard, some scholars have adopted a predominantly *legal-procedural approach* to environmental issues, focusing the attention on violations of regulations imposed by law (of penal, civil or administrative relevance); others have taken a *socio-legal approach*, which also includes the observational and evaluating field actions not proscribed by law (South *et al.* 2013: 35). This distinction is modulated in various versions by single scholars. In any case, an exclusively legal definition of environmental crime is mostly insufficient, firstly because one of the major perpetrators of environmental crimes is the late modern State itself (Halsey 2004: 836; White 2008; 2011: 6). Moreover, it is because environmental crimes are placed along the legal-illegal continuum (including both criminal and lawful actions) that criminological analysis should not stop at behaviours forbidden by the law, as Edwin Sutherland reminded us in the 1940s (Ruggiero and South 2013). An example of definition of environmental crime in this field may help in illuminating these aspects. Michael Lynch, one of the founding fathers of green criminology, highlights the point that any criminological perspective that intends to confront an environmental issue adequately must also carry a vision of political economy. Moving from an approach to environmental crimes sensitive to the question of power within society, Lynch, with Stretesky (2003), traces in the meaning of the term 'green' the coexistence of two matrices: on the one hand, the one that comes from the corporate actors and on the other hand, the one that is the result of the activism of the movements for 'environmental justice' – movements oriented towards the fight against inequalities and discrimination of gender, ethnicity and social class. It is from this *environmental justice perspective* that Lynch and Stretesky (2003: 222) derive their definition of green crime. More concretely, the definition of *green crime* proposed by the authors is the following: 'a green crime is an act that (1) may or may not violate existing rules and environmental regulations; (2) has identifiable environmental damage outcomes; and (3) originated in human action' (Lynch and Stretesky 2003: 227). Accepting this definition means not assuming the juridical picture as 'given' but rather contributing to its interpretation, evaluation and construction, starting from the social reality that it is intended to regulate. From a criminal policy perspective, it also means pointing out those behaviours that *should* be considered criminal because of the harms they cause (Lynch and Stretesky 2003: 228–229).

The dynamics related to power and its manifestations in the defining processes inevitably raise the question of which notion of justice to adopt. Concerning this level, it is necessary to underline that the different definitions of justice provide different theoretical foundations to what we think as 'harmful' and/or 'criminal' from the environmental point of view and parallel to it, they allow the articulation of concepts relating to *who* can be considered a 'victim' (Walters *et al*. 2013: 3–4). This in turn allows us to reflect more specifically on what 'repairing' such harm might look like.

In this regard, Rob White suggests three key areas of socio-criminological research that have precise repercussions on the actual definition of environmental crime: (1) *environmental justice*, which has as its privileged object of analysis the well-being of human beings with regard to the environment; (2) *ecological justice*, directly interested in the environment and encapsulated in the concept of 'ecological citizenship'; and (3) *justice amongst species*, which is interested in the well-being and the rights of non-human animals (White 2011). Also with regard to the notion of justice, we confront a broad definition of green/environmental crime that can include those dimensions of harm and (in)justice which are rarely recognized by the legal system and by the criminal justice system (White 2008: 11).

Finally, the notion of environmental crime is controversial in a way not too dissimilar from the notion of crime in general. This depends first of all on *who* defines the harm and on the criteria used to evaluate something as an harm – for example, legal criteria or ecological criteria, references to criminal justice or to environmental justice (White 2011: 3). If the basic premise of green criminology is that we must 'take environmental crime seriously', to do this we need notions of crime and reparation that go beyond the traditional ones (White 2011: 18) to encompass new emerging dimensions of justice. And we need also to explore what is specific to processes of environmental victimization.

Environmental victimization and the need for different responses to socio-environmental harm

While green criminology has devoted much attention to study environmental crimes and harms, the processes of environmental victimization have received little empirical attention (Bisschop and Vande Walle 2013: 34–35; Hall 2013: 218). In this regard, Michael Lynch (2013: 45–48) shows the high number of victims missed by traditional criminological approaches. These latter are still marginally concerned with environmental crimes and their serious consequences (Lynch *et al*. 2013: 998). Rather like the victims of white-collar crimes, environmental victims often remain hidden in the shadows (White 2011: 109; Davies *et al*. 2014).

More generally, environmental victimization poses a series of new questions that criminal justice systems are unprepared to face (Hall 2013: 219–220). First, the harms can be suffered by an extended group or even community of victims, sometimes representing rival interests. Second, the perpetrators are often corporations or states (White 2011: 103–104; 2013). This latter case shows the importance of developing a notion of 'crime' that encompasses 'lawful, but awful' acts and omissions (Hillyard *et al.* 2004; Passas 2005). Finally, the causality nexus is extremely complex to reconstruct, sometimes leading to environmentally harmful acts being considered as 'crimes without victims' (see Bisschop and Vande Walle 2013: 40; Centemeri 2006).

The relevant scientific literature shows how the difficulties encountered in establishing a causal relationship between the polluting activities and the contaminating effects may offer perpetrators an easy escape route (Williams 1996). For example, the various strategies of neutralization of responsibility on the part of corporations or the state include: denying the problem (Cohen 2001); putting into perspective what is now seen as damaging but that could be interpreted differently in the future; and reproaching, blaming, dividing and confusing the victims (Williams 1996). For all these reasons, it is important to explore the nature of environmental victimization as an active social process, which implies relationships of power, control and resistance (White 2011: 106).

According to Hillyard and Tombs (2004), focusing on 'harm' rather than crime has several advantages, a number of which seem to particularly resonate with the impacts of environmental pollution and climate change. Hillyard and Tombs (2004) argued that 'social harms' – that is, harms that detrimentally affect people's lives but are not officially proscribed by criminal law – should become the main focus of criminological inquiry. They point to the somewhat stalled progress of critical criminology compared to its heyday in the 1960s and 1970s, giving way more recently to an empiricist 'applied science' orientation driven largely by whatever 'crime problem' or alleged problem appears to attract the most political attention. On this basis, they advocate a return to a criminology based on social harms. This is significant for our argument because it suggests criminology should concern itself with resolving and repairing harms which are not necessarily formally recognized as criminal actions, as it is the case with much environmental degradation related to human activities.

As 'crime' arguably has no ontological reality given that the activities so labelled vary dramatically over time and between societies (Hulsman 1986), 'the criminal law fails to capture the more damaging and pervasive forms of harm' (Hillyard and Tombs 2004: 12). It is thus clear that focusing on harm could potentially include the often legally ambiguous activities that foster environmental damage, including air pollution, waste dumping and discharging chemicals into waterways under licence and within regulatory limits, as well as those already covered by civil and administrative systems. Indeed, even when such activities are criminal in the strict legal sense, focusing on harm allows us to account for such activities in cases where whatever mechanisms of justice that are available at the national, transnational, and international levels fail to adequately prosecute such transgressions.

Another salient point made by Hillyard and Tombs (2004) is that the social harms approach allows the consideration of 'mass harms' covering large areas and large numbers of victims. This also resonates with the problems inherent to environmental degradation, where the effects may spiral out to include great swathes of animal, vegetal and human life. Traditional criminology, by contrast, has struggled to fully embrace the concept of mass victimization (especially in relation to non-humans) and, except for limited inroads into the fields of state crime and corporate crime, has largely remained focused on the individual. For similar reasons, Hillyard and Tombs argue that the social harms approach challenges the still-individualistic conceptions of crime.

Rob White (2008: 92), one of the leading theorists in the green criminology literature, reflects on the concept of harm, introducing the notion of 'consideration of environmental harms', intended as the process to *identify* the victims of such harms. Criticizing more mainstream criminological notions, White makes the important point that victims of environmental harm should include also the biosphere and non-human animals. This implies that a too limited definition of 'harm' would defeat the purpose of the critical exercise: to be inclusive, rather than exclusive. As such, White (2008) stresses the importance of moving from *defining* harm to *debating* harm, because only the latter can lead to real-life, operational developments: 'Defining harm is ultimately about philosophical frameworks as informed by scientific evidence and traditional knowledges; debating harm is about processes of deliberation in the "real world" and of conflicts over rights and the making of difficult decisions.' (White 2008: 24)

Such a conceptual move is in line with assuming a fundamental radical uncertainty concerning the 'what-ness' of situations of environmental harm and the necessity of a process of 'inquiry' – in the Deweyan sense – in order to cognitively and normatively qualify the situation, through attributing causes and responsibilities, identifying damages and victims (see Introduction).

Of course, such a view presents real difficulties for those seeking to develop *legal* systems for addressing environmental harms, which must ultimately be based on concrete and predictable definitions (Williams 1996). While attributing a precise definition to environmental harm is problematic (certainly with regard to legal systems) and perhaps undesirable, there is increasing evidence that whether or not such harms are criminalized, they are a pervasive and significant contemporary public problem.

Even within the critical school of victimology, which seeks to focus attention on more hidden forms of victimization traditionally ignored or unrecognized by criminal law, victims of environmental harms have been overlooked, despite the first call made by Williams in 1996 to develop what was then termed 'environmental victimology'. Williams begins by addressing environmental victimization and notes the 'obvious need for social justices to parallel formal legal processes' (Williams 1996: 200). Williams advocates moving away from prevailing concepts of 'environmental justice', which he criticizes as too subjective (arguing that concepts of 'harm' are subjective as opposed to 'crime') and overly swayed by activism. For Williams, 'environmental victims' are: 'those of past, present, or future generations who are injured as a consequence of change to the chemical, physical, microbiological, or psychosocial environment, brought about by deliberate or reckless, individual or collective, human act or omission' (Williams 1996: 35).

This definition embodies intergenerational justice (Hiskes 2008) and, importantly for Williams, is grounded in the notion of 'injury', considered as more objective and measurable than 'harm'. Williams (1996) argues that this is a useful starting point if the goal is to develop functioning legal systems around environmental victimization, especially in criminal justice. However, Williams' definition, beyond restricting victimization to legally proscribed activities, does not include non-human victims.

The anthropocentric bias of the notion of victim is visible also in the seminal contribution of Nils Christie (1986). He famously argues that the victims' movement, and particularly policy-makers' attention to victims of crime, was limited in focus to those victims displaying 'ideal' characteristics: being weak, being a stranger to a 'big and bad offender', carrying out an innocent activity, and cooperating with the authorities. Christie does not problematize the basic assumption that a victim is assumed to be an individual human.

Further development of this branch of victimological study has been slow to progress from this point, even as green criminology as a whole has gathered pace. Skinnider (2011) emphasizes the need for such specific research, given the difficulties of applying broad-brush victim reforms to environmental harm: 'The characteristic of the collective nature of this kind of victimisation needs to be understood, particularly with its implications for victims to seek assistance, support and redress which have predominately developed for traditional crimes involving individual victims.' (Skinnider 2011: 26)

Notwithstanding such arguments, there are isolated exceptions to the general proposition that something 'more', or at least 'different', is needed for environmental victims over and above that which is already being provided for victims of crime.

The most significant example is the application of the US Crime Victims' Rights Act (CVRA) of 2004 to victims of environmental crime (see Hall 2013). Heralded as a major breakthrough by proponents of a more judiciable form of victims' rights, the CVRA introduced the concept of victims' rights into the US penal code for the first time. The act contains provision for 'service rights' for victims, including the provision of information to them by the justice system, protection and compensation, as well as procedural rights for victims of crime 'to be reasonably heard at any public proceeding in a district court involving release, plea, sentencing, or any parole proceeding'.[1] The most significant feature of the legislation, however, is the enforcement mechanisms it creates. Here, individuals or the federal government may assert victims' rights at the district court level. If the victim or the government are still not satisfied with the enforcement of these rights they may file a petition with the Court of Appeals to order their enforcement. A court's decision to deny any of these rights may also be asserted as an error by the prosecution in the case. Even more significantly, in limited circumstances victims may move for a new trial on the basis of the denial of their rights.[2] The CVRA does not apply to the states, as it is not an amendment to the Bill of Rights or to the US Constitution. Nevertheless, the act was incorporated into the Federal Rules of Criminal Procedure, which is followed by all judges in federal criminal cases, in April 2008. The act does not give victims the right to sue the federal government for breach of their rights, but remains one of the most robust systems of rights enforcement for victims seen in any jurisdiction.

The first application of the CVRA to victims of *environmental* crime followed the explosion of a BP oil refinery in Texas in 2005. In this case the US Fifth Circuit court ruled that the government had violated victims' rights under the CVRA by failing to consult with those locals affected by the explosion (mostly in the form of personal injury and property damage) in the agreement of a plea bargain with BP. This was despite the fact that the number of victims stretched into the hundreds and the CVRA neither includes nor, on a standard reading, conceives harm caused by environmental damage. More recently, in the case of *W.R. Grace & Co.*, the named company was prosecuted under environmental legislation for 'knowingly endangering' the residents of Libby, Montana, by exposing them to asbestos through mining activities. The federal judge in the case had ruled that 34 prospective victims of these activities (local residents) did not fall under the definition of victim within the CVRA[3] and as such excluded them from the trial proceedings. At appeal, in *Re Parker; U.S. v U.S. District Court* and *W.R. Grace & Co.*[4] the United States Ninth Circuit Court of Appeals reversed this decision, thus confirming that prospective victims of environmental harm are indeed included within the ambit of rights provided under the 2004 act. The case is interesting not only for the specific result, but as a demonstration of the extent of the term 'victim'. It gives weight to the contention that it includes (or should include) environmental crimes even where there is no specific mention of this category of harms within the rights-enabling legal instrument.

However, given the still limited research on the impacts of environmental harm on humans and other living organisms, it is impossible to paint a full picture of these impacts. Particularly concerning is the lack of research asking (human) environmental victims *themselves* about their experiences and support needs. We still lack detailed data on the lives of people living in polluted areas, describing *from their perspective* what they know of, think about and feel towards the reality in which they live (Natali 2016). Such an orientation raises the following question regarding how people live and make sense of their experiences in polluted places. Empirical research on the inhabitants of highly polluted places has revealed the multiple interpretations guiding their decision to act individually or collectively (or to abstain from acting) in response to their environmental victimization (Auyero and Swistun 2009: 159; Allen 2018).[5] Moreover, social and cultural perspectives on environmental victimization processes have proved extremely important in showing that experiences of environmental suffering are not simply individual: they are collectively created in the wider social macrocosmos where the residents situate themselves. Concerning this, the rich tradition of science and technology studies (STS) (Fortun *et al.* 2017) can profitably meet these new criminological frontiers – and in some cases it has already happened (Gibbs *et al.* 2010) – in order to strengthen even more the interdisciplinary and transdisciplinary effort needed to face the phenomena under consideration (see also Popa and Guillermin 2017). In particular, these studies orient the criminological agenda towards the analysis of the consequences of the constitutive uncertainty of toxicity – as highlighted by the difficulty of defining the nexus of cause-effect for the purpose of legal proof of toxic damage (Goldstein 2017; Jasanoff 1995; Auyero and Swistun 2009).

What is clear from the literature is that the impacts of environmental victimization are extremely varied and wide-ranging, which is a key reason for states' difficulty in implementing proscribed or firm procedures of regulation and restitution. The health impacts on *humans*, at least, of various legal and illegal environmentally destructive practices are certainly becoming more understood. The regularity with which alarming new statistics reveal the impact on human health of environmental pollution reflects the significance of the challenges faced by the world's legal and administrative systems, and by green criminologists hoping to understand these patterns of social change. The World Health Organization (WHO) estimates that, in 2016, worldwide, ambient air pollution contributed to 7.6 per cent of all deaths globally (WHO 2018). Of course, mortality rates represent only a very small proportion of all human health impacts from air pollution. Indeed the WHO's 2000 working group on the Quantification of the Health Effects of Exposure to Air Pollution identified premature deaths as the least numerically significant of a whole continuum of health effects. These included such diverse impacts as cardiovascular hospital admissions, chronic change in physiologic function and lower birth rates (WHO 2008). Beyond air pollution, Patz *et al.* (2000) report that the long-term consequences of climate change will have adverse impacts on public health via a diverse range of consequences including heat-related illnesses and deaths, extreme weather events, water and food-borne disease and vector and rodent-borne diseases. Ruggiero and South (2010) cite numerous cases of death and illness in areas exposed to hazardous waste materials, including the so-called cancer villages of China, where residents' increased susceptibility to several classifications of tumours has been directly attributed to their exposure to cadmium and mercury released through e-waste recycling. In Italy, Martuzzi *et al.* (2009) have identified a statistically significant increase in cancer mortality and congenital anomalies in Campania, Italy – a region subject to intense environmental pressure due to uncontrolled and illegal practices of industrial waste dumping (see also Armiero and Fava 2016).

The above examples do not incorporate the whole set of impacts on humans and non-human animals, and vegetal forms of life, of environmental 'disaster events' like the Deepwater Horizon oil spill. The human health implications of this event – including both physical and mental health implications – are now the subject of a rapidly escalating scientific literature (Lee and Blanchard 2010; Yun *et al.* 2010). Another prominent example is the 1984 gas leak in Bhopal (India), whose negative long-term health impacts include respiratory and neurological disorders (Cullinan *et al.* 1996), as well as significant harms to animal and vegetal life in the region. While such disasters have received extensive media attention and notoriety, the crucial point is that publicly recognized victims are inevitably a tiny minority of all those suffering health complaints due to environmental harms; and certainly when considering effects beyond the human population (Agnew 2013).

An environmental restorative justice approach to environmental disasters?

To address environmentally destructive activities by giving voice to environmental victims and respecting the complexity of environmental harm, criminologists are increasingly turning to justice mechanisms. Restorative justice has been variously defined, but basically it seeks to repair both crime-induced physical and psychological damage and put all parties back to the position they were in prior to the disaster event (Marshall 1999) in order to deal with the aftermath of the offense and its implications for the future. Restorative justice – whose best known tool is victim-offender mediation – is a model of justice characterized by taking care of the negative consequences caused by a crime, promoting the regeneration of social bonds starting from the wounds originated by the crime and favouring an active role for the victims, the offenders and the communities in the search for possible solutions to repair the damage and to heal the fracture caused by the deviant act. It is, therefore, a paradigm that tries to go beyond the logic of punishment, moving from a relational reading of the criminal phenomena, seen primarily as a conflict which causes a break in symbolically shared social expectations. The crime should no longer be considered only an offence against society or a behaviour that damages the established order – and that requires a punishment to be expiated – but as a conduct intrinsically dangerous and offensive which can cause deprivation, suffering, hurt and even death to the victim and which mainly requires, on the part of the offender, the activation of forms of reparation of the harm caused (Ceretti *et al.* 2001: 307).

The environmental issue and the management of environmental conflicts have arrived with a certain delay in the scope of restorative justice in criminal matters. Restorative justice has mainly been used in other contexts: crimes against humanity (*e.g.* the Truth and Reconciliation Commission in South Africa), violent crimes and juvenile delinquency (juvenile justice system). If one of the most important points for those who deal with restorative justice is the question regarding its transformative capacity for victims, offenders, community and systems of justice, in the environmental scenario this aspect will have to take into account the peculiarities of the contexts and of the actors involved. Also, in the specific field of green criminology, restorative justice is recognized by many authors as a useful way for a complex management of our relationship with nature where there are harms to be repaired in ways that cannot be reduced to the punishment of the perpetrator (White 2011).

Although information on the application of restorative processes to cases of environmental harm is scant and mainly anecdotal, there is a small but growing literature on what has been variously termed 'environmental mediation' and environmental 'alternative dispute resolution' (ADR). Interestingly, much of the available literature on such processes comes from attempts to galvanize support for such schemes in the early 1980s. As in the context of restorative justice, the term 'mediation' is variously defined, although one concise definition is provided by Douglas J. Amy: 'Put most simply, environmental mediation is a process in which representatives of environmental groups, business groups and government agencies sit down together with a neutral mediator to negotiate a binding solution to a particular environmental dispute' (Amy 1983: 1).

From the green criminological perspective, this understanding immediately raises questions concerning how 'the environment' could be represented in any mediation. Even in more anthropocentric terms, the extent to which 'environmentalists' or 'environmental groups' represent the *real* victims of environmental harm (whether human or animal) is a moot point. Furthermore, one of the few studies to examine environmental ADR empirically suggests that when environmental (human) victims engage representation, or collectively group together to increase bargaining power, the process becomes overly complex and cumbersome: 'Far from the conventional expectation that representation hastens the resolution of environmental disputes, our empirical results suggest ADR becomes less effective when many agents are involved.' (Matsumoto 2011: 665)

Generally, the key advantages of mediation or ADR in environmental cases are claimed to be considerably lower costs (to public and private interests) compared to criminal or civil justice resolutions, as well as shorter timescales (see Mernitz 1980). However, empirical testing of these claims has been very limited. One exception is Sipe's (2007) demonstration, via quantitative analysis, that environmental mediation produces a statistically significant increase in settlement rates compared to civil law actions, but no difference in compliance rates compared to administrative sanctions.

Much of the literature concerning environmental mediation is US-based, which inhibits drawing more generalized conclusions applicable in different cultures, especially to the Global South. Nevertheless, in one of the first test cases, Gerald Cormick and Jane McCarthy of the University of Washington's Environmental Mediation Project were appointed by the governor of Washington State to serve as mediators in a dispute amongst environmentalists, farmers, developers and public officials over the damming of the Snoqualmie River, as an alternative to criminal prosecutions or administrative and civil sanctions. According to Shmueli and Kaufman (2006: 17), the resulting agreement illustrated one of mediation's main assets – its capacity to generate such creative solutions (in the sense that they avoid litigation or other formal legal process) that satisfy the interests of all parties involved. Certainly, the adaptability of mediation and other restorative options is a significant benefit because, as Shmueli and Kaufman (2006) note:

> Each environmental conflict has a unique cast of characters, a history unlike any other except in broad strokes, a singular pattern of resources, interrelationships among parties, a special set of issues and a unique set of moves that defies simple classification and comparison.
>
> (Shmueli and Kaufman 2006: 20)

In particular, the above example demonstrates how mediation can combine public and private disputes in a way that is both efficient and provides an outcome accounting for both sides (see also Ferrari *et al.* 2019). Regarding the 'private' side, Matsumoto (2011: 660) notes that mediation is a fitting solution for a situation in which, as in many pollution disputes, 'the polluter and its victims are located near each other and will remain in place and maintain an on-going relationship after their dispute is resolved'. Elsewhere, however, the divide has never been so strict. For instance, Merryman (1968: 4) notes that, in the US, 'law students are not taught about a division of law into those fields; they do not find the vision employed in statutes, decisions or doctrines'. In fact, this issue raises a far larger question for green criminology, as this area may represent, like restorative justice before it, a longer-term trend towards coexisting public and private systems for delivering criminal justice.

Positive features notwithstanding, environmental mediation also brings difficulties, a quite relevant one being that 'those who have the time and resources to participate in a mediation process are not necessarily representative of the interest groups affected by the decisions issuing from this process' (Shmueli and Kaufman 2006: 21). This might be especially true given the economic and social standing of many human victims of environmental harm and thus, the concern may be that the harm experienced directly by actual victims is not being repaired by such processes.

Amy (1983) further discusses the opinion expressed in some quarters of environmentalism that mediation of any kind benefits big industry (*i.e.* the polluters). Amy contends that most environmental mediation takes place in a context of palpable political bias, power imbalance and the illusion of voluntariness. For example, Dryzek and Hunter (1987) suggested that in the aftermath of the 1984 Bhopal disaster, in which highly toxic methyl isocyanate gas was released from a gas plant owned by the Texas-based Union Carbide Corporation, the culpable company was very keen to engage in attempts by Environmental Mediation International to establish a good compensation scheme, rather than pursuing more legalistic (criminal or civil) routes. While Amy (1983) is generally more optimistic about the overall benefit of mediation in these cases than the worst of these concerns suggests, he still injects a note of caution into his conclusion: 'There is no simple answer. As a rule, it would benefit environmentalists to have a healthy suspicion of mediation, especially when the offer to mediate comes from their opponents' (Amy 1983: 19).

Of course, this is a rather pessimistic interpretation of the motives of corporations wishing to engage in environmental mediation. An alternative perspective is that mediation and ADR are usual routes for corporations to resolve conflicts with one another, so it may simply be the approach with which they are most familiar.

Overall, the cause of environmental mediation is severely inhibited by the lack of quite basic empirical data on the nature of settlements (including information about agreed compensation), the processes used, and the effectiveness/enforcement of these agreements. Without such information, it is very difficult to test the more alarmist claims of (*inter alia*) power imbalances. It is also problematic that most available information comes only from developed countries that do not bear the higher brunt of environmental harms.

A further complication is that the literature on environmental mediation has not yet addressed the problem of *competing interests*, not just between polluter and public bodies but also between public bodies, environmental groups, and human and non-human animal victims ostensibly on the 'same side' (Hall 2013).

Conclusion

In this chapter we explored the intersection of green criminology, environmental harm and restorative justice in order to explore the implications of repairing the massive damage, loss and destruction of environment.[6] Much more than a set of techniques for doing justice for the environment, restorative justice responses to environmental harm have profound philosophical consequences: 'It is about repairing the harm of the Anthropocene. [. . .]. It is about tempering human power over earth systems and dominations of the powerful over the less powerful.' (Braithwaite *et al*. 2019: 9) In doing so, restorative justice would create a better chance to heal disrupted relationships and 'repair' the harm done to the environment – the ecological harm.

Questions regarding environmental harm and victimization present complex practical challenges as they concern intrinsically multidisciplinary fields, both highly politicized and global in their reach (White 2011: 122). Including in criminological discourses the most advanced theorizing on these issues is not merely an academic endeavour. On the contrary, such action should help to progressively raise awareness amongst decision-makers about the necessity of changing some background visions informing actual policy options for (not only criminal) law relating to the environment. Many authors have noted how the prevailing representations of nature seriously limit the conception of juridical constructions and criminal policies to effectively meet environmental victims' needs and repair harms.

The fundamental questions, therefore, are no longer (or no longer only) 'who deserves to be punished' and 'with which sanctions' but 'what can be done to repair the harm'; where to repair does not mean to counterbalance reductively the harm caused in economic terms. Being achievable through positive action, in fact, reparation has a profound value and, above all, an ethical depth that makes it much more complex than mere compensation (Ceretti and Brunelli 2018). An essential feature of restorative justice is that it aims to redirect or at least complement society's retributive response to crime. A retributive system of justice is punitive in nature, with the key focus on using punishment as a means to deter future crime and to provide a punishment proportionate to any harm committed. Rather than focusing on retribution, restorative justice focuses on harms and consequent needs; addresses obligations resulting from those harms; uses inclusive, collaborative processes; involves those with a stake in the situation (victims, offenders, community members; society at large); and seeks to put right the wrongs. This approach presupposes the intrinsic irreparability of any act of injustice and at the same time re-launches the possibility of planning a responsible behaviour for the future.

In restorative justice imagination, 'changing the lenses' – as Howard Zehr (1990) wrote 30 years ago – means first of all to enhance the 'active' participation of all the persons involved in the criminal case (offender, victim and community) no longer dispossessed of the conflict generated by the offense, but directly involved in the management of its destructive effects. Changing the lenses also means to give back a place to the victims. The symbolic structure of this justice upholds, in fact, the recognition of the victim and the reparation of the offence in its global dimension, also considering the emotional dimension of the offence and the deriving social feelings – social feelings that, very often, orientate the victims towards the loss of trust towards men, women and institutions, to then give birth to an experience of insecurity, capable of even modifying one's way of life.

Although environmental questions tend to be left for the 'experts', citizens' active participation is vital for the processes of reparation for harm. In this respect, it is necessary to widen the basis of knowledge and understanding of environmental issues (Natali 2010). Science is often the principal tool in deliberations concerning the interventions to repair the impact of humans on the environment. This suggests a 'functional understanding of repairing' that implies recurring to specific devices meant to deal with technical issues (see Introduction). However, science offers only one kind of knowledge (White 2008: 78). It is, therefore, necessary to introduce all relevant knowledge produced by the scientific community and by citizens, including that gathered from the inhabitants' experiences of a territory and its symbolic dimensions, their social memory and their imagination of future possible scenarios. This route begins by attempting to 'give voice' to those social actors who often lack the necessary power to significantly influence their own environment. Giving value to the reflexive and narrative dimensions of knowledge, including the voices of victims in contexts also open to other actors (institutions, experts, civil society), is an important step towards creating the conditions for knowledge, recognition and possible reparation of the effects of each environmental crime considered. Here a dimension of 'repairing as taking care' clearly emerges (see Introduction). To achieve this goal, social and cultural perspectives are crucial to problematize what constitutes environmental victimization (Hall 2013; 2017) and what constitutes repairing. For those dealing with restorative justice, one of the most important issues is its transformative capacity towards the victims, culprits, community and justice systems; in the environmental scenario, this aspect must account for the peculiarities of the contexts and the actors involved. Through dialogic and emotive confrontation with the victim, the culprits have the opportunity to understand the full extent and the real consequences of their actions from the perspective of those who have directly suffered the harmful consequences. If we refer these statements to the multinationals that have committed environmental crimes, the scenario become more complex. The juridical persona of the multinational immunizes and de-sensitizes the social actors who guide the corporation – directors and managers – against personally feeling negative emotions such as remorse or shame for the harms caused. Meeting the victims and learning of their needs and suffering might contribute, in this sense, to overcoming the protective corporate veil. Finally, through the routes of restorative justice, the victims and community might be able to regain some control over resolving the conflict and repairing the damage – coherent with the principles of democratic participation in decision-making processes in the environmental field. However, as White (2017) suggests, repairing harm should not be conflated with restorative justice *per se*.

Although it is unrealistic to expect restorative justice to be effective in all, or even many, cases of environmental crimes, the proposed collaborative model can, nonetheless, contribute to repair the resulting harms of environmental victimization. Therefore, in the environmental field, it will be necessary to 'change the lenses' through which we view the laws, norms and justice systems. It is necessary to imagine a different system of justice: this does not mean cultivating an utopia but, rather, imaginatively orienting towards possible futures, applying languages and models of justice other than the traditional ones. Restorative justice – founded on the idea of spontaneous participation and aimed at constructing, together and actively, a work of reparation on an act's destructive effects – represents a possible horizon far from any all-encompassing ambition.

Following this course, a desirable social and environmental policy should focus on alleviating situations characterized by harms and socio-environmental injustice (at both the individual and collective levels), and on favouring the well-being of the most exposed and vulnerable groups of society. Amongst its objectives will be social and environmental justice (distributive equity), social and environmental security (protection against serious environmental risks), peaceful management of socio-environmental conflicts and the strengthening of public participation in environmental policy-making. This is exactly the decisive task that green criminology, and its large and variegated community of scholars, has been undertaking for some years. Including these phenomena within the criminological and victimological horizon – and thereby inaugurating new frontiers of social research – means providing criminology with sensitive tools of sufficient complexity to know, recognize, and answer the global challenges of what has been defined as the Anthropocene: the historical and geological era when mankind becomes a real telluric force, capable of transforming and destroying, with often irreparable consequences, the environment and its inhabitants.

Notes

1 18 USC § 3771(a)(4).
2 18 USC § 3771(d)(4).
3 18 USC § 2241–2233.
4 Nos. 09-70529, 09-70533 (9th Cir.).
5 Barbara Allen's innovative type of epidemiological inquiry is interesting in this respect (see Allen 2018).
6 The late Scottish barrister Polly Higgins defines 'ecocide' as the extensive damage to, destruction of or loss of ecosystem(s) to such an extent that peaceful enjoyment by the inhabitants of that territory is severely diminished (see also Higgins *et al.* 2013).

References

Agnew, R. (2013) 'The Ordinary Acts that Contribute to Ecocide: A Criminological Analysis', in N. South and A. Brisman (eds) *The Routledge International Handbook of Green Criminology*, Abingdon: Routledge, 58–72.

Allen, B.L. (2018) 'Strongly Participatory Science and Knowledge Justice in an Environmentally Contested Region', *Science, Technology & Human Values*, 43(6): 947–971.

Amy, D. (1983) 'The Politics of Environmental Mediation', *Ecology Law Quarterly*, 11(1): 1–19.

Armiero, M. and Fava, A. (2016) 'Of Humans, Sheep, and Dioxin: A History of Contamination and Transformation in Acerra, Italy', *Capitalism Nature Socialism*, 27(2): 67–82.

Auyero, J. and Swistun, D.A. (2009) *Flammable: Environmental Suffering in an Argentine Shantytown*, Oxford: Oxford University Press.

Beirne, P. and South, N. (2007) 'Introduction: Approaching Green Criminology', in P. Beirne and N. South (eds) *Issues in Green Criminology: Confronting Harms Against Environments, Humanity and Other Animals*, Collumpton: Willan.

Bisschop, L., and Vande Walle, G. (2013) 'Environmental Victimisation and Conflict Resolution: A Case Study of E-Waste', in R. Walters, D. Westerhuis, and T. Wyatt (eds) *Emerging Issues in Green Criminology: Exploring Power, Justice and Harm*, Basingstoke: Palgrave Macmillan, 34–56.

Braithwaite, J., Forsyth, M. and Cleland, D. (2019) 'Restorative Environmental Justice: An Introduction', in E. Biffi and B. Pali (eds) *Environmental Justice Restoring the Future. Towards a Restorative Environmental Justice Praxis*. <https://earthrestorativejustice.org/article/36455/booklet-environmental-justice-restoring-the-future> (accessed 25 May 2020).

Brisman, A. and South, N. (2014) *Green Cultural Criminology: Constructions of Environmental Harm, Consumerism and Resistance to Ecocide*, London: Routledge.

Centemeri, L. (2006) *Ritorno a Seveso. Il danno ambientale, il suo riconoscimento, la sua riparazione*, Milan: Mondadori.

Centemeri, L. (2015) 'Reframing Problems of Incommensurability in Environmental Conflicts through Pragmatic Sociology. From Value Pluralism to the Plurality of Modes of Engagement with the Environment', in *Environmental Values*, 24(3): 299–320.

Ceretti, A., Brunelli, F. (2018) 'Giustizia riparativa e mediazione reo-vittima', in F. Danovi and F. Ferraris (eds) *ADR. Una giustizia complementare*, Milano: Giuffré, 275–296.

Ceretti, A., Di Ciò, F. and Mannozzi, G. (2001) 'Giustizia riparativa e mediazione penale: esperienze e pratiche a confronto', in F. Scaparro (ed.) *Il coraggio di mediare. Contesti, teorie e pratiche di risoluzioni alternative delle controversie*, Milan: Guerini & Associati, 307–356.

Christie, N. (1986) 'The Ideal Victim', in E. Fattah (ed.) *From Crime Policy to Victim Policy*, Basingstoke: Macmillan, 17–30.

Cohen, S. (2001) *States of Denial: Knowing About Atrocities and Suffering*, Cambridge: Polity Press.

Cullinan, P., Acquilla, S. and Dhara, V. (1996) 'Long Term Morbidity in Survivors of the 1984 Bhopal Gas Leak', *National Medical Journal of India*, 9(1): 5–10.

Davies, P., Francis, P. and Wyatt, T. (eds) (2014) *Invisible Crimes and Social Harms*, Basingstoke: Palgrave Macmillan.

Dryzek, J. and Hunter, S. (1987) 'Environmental Mediation for International Problems', *International Studies Quarterly*, 31(1): 87–102.

Ferrari, C., Mancini, F.M., Damiani, G., Dini, V., Figliomeni, M., Avellis, L., Marcheggiani, S. and Mancini, L. (2019) 'Environmental Damage and Environmental Mediation: Italian Guidelines', *Microchemical Journal*, 149: 1–6.

Fortun, K., Knowles, S.G., Choi, V., Jobin, P., Matsumoto, M., de la Torre III, P., Liboiron, M. and Murillo, L.F.R. (2017) 'Researching Disaster from an STS Perspective', in U. Felt, R. Fouché, C.A. Miller and L. Smith-Doer (eds) *The Handbook of Science and Technology Studies*, Cambridge, MA: The MIT Press.

Gibbs, C., Gore, M.L., McGarrel, E.F. and Rivers III, L. (2010) 'Introducing Conservation Criminology. Towards Interdisciplinary Scholarship on Environmental Crimes and Risks', *British Journal of Criminology*, 50(1): 124–144.

Goldstein, D.N. (2017) 'Invisible Harm: Science, Subjectivity and the Things We Cannot See', in *Culture, Theory and Critique*, 58(4): 321–328.

Goyes, D. and South, N. (2017) 'Green Criminology Before "Green Criminology": Amnesia and Absences', *Critical Criminology*, 25: 165–181.

Hall, M. (2013) *Victims of Environmental Harm: Rights, Recognition and Redress under National and International Law*, Abingdon: Routledge.

Hall, M. (2017) 'Exploring the Cultural Dimensions of Environmental Victimization', *Palgrave Communication*, 3.

Halsey, M. (2004) 'Against "Green" Criminology', *British Journal of Criminology*, 44(6): 833–853.

Halsey, M. (2006) *Deleuze and Environmental Damage: Violence of the Text*, Aldershot and Burlington: Ashgate.

Higgins, P., Short, D. and South, N. (2013) 'Protecting the Planet: A Proposal for a Law of Ecocide', *Crime, Law and Social Change*, 59: 251–266.

Hillyard, P., Pantazis, C., Tombs, S. and Gordon, D. (eds) (2004) *Beyond Criminology: Taking Harm Seriously*, London: Pluto Press.

Hillyard, P. and Tombs, D. (2004) 'Introduction', in P. Hillyard, D. Tombs and C. Pantazis (eds) *Beyond Criminology: Taking Harm Seriously*, London: Pluto Press, 1–9.

Hiskes, R. (2008) *The Human Right to a Green Future: Environmental Rights and Intergenerational Justice*, Cambridge: Cambridge University Press.

Hulsman, L. (1986) 'Critical Criminology and the Concept of Crime', in H. Bianchi and R. van Swaaningen (eds) *Abolitionism: Towards a Non-Repressive Approach to Crime*, Amsterdam: Free University Press, 35–59.

Jasanoff, S. (1995) *Science at the Bar: Law, Science, and Technology in America*, Cambridge, MA: Harvard University Press.

Latour, B. (1995; 1st edition 1991) *Non siamo mai stati moderni. Saggio di antropologia simmetrica*, Milano: Elèuthera.

Lee, M. and Blanchard, T. (2010) *Health Impacts of Deepwater Horizon Oil Disaster on Coastal Louisiana Residents*, Baton Rouge: Louisiana State University Press.

Lynch, M. (2013) 'Reflections on Green Criminology and Its Boundaries: Comparing Environmental and Criminal Victimization and Considering Crime from an Eco-city Perspective', in N. South and A. Brisman (eds) *Routledge International Handbook of Green Criminology*, London: Routledge.

Lynch, M., Long, M., Barrett, K. and Stretesky, P. (2013) 'Why Green Criminology and Political Economy Matter in the Analysis of Global Ecological Harms', *British Journal of Criminology*, 53: 997–1016.

Lynch, M. and Stretesky, P. (2003) 'The Meaning of Green: Contrasting Criminological Perspectives', *Theoretical Criminology*, 7(2): 217–238.

Marshall, T. (1999) *Restorative Justice: An Overview*, London: Home Office Research Statistics Directorate.

Martuzzi, F., Mitis, F., Bianchi, F., Minichilli, F., Comba, P. and Fazzo, L. (2009) 'Cancer Mortality and Congenital Anomalies in a Region of Italy with Intense Environmental Pressure Due to Waste', *Occupational Environmental Medicine*, 66: 725–732.

Matsumoto, S. (2011) 'A Duration Analysis of Environmental Alternative Dispute Resolution in Japan', *Ecological Economics*, 70: 659–666.

Mernitz, S. (1980) *Mediation of Environmental Disputes*, New York: Praeger.

Merryman, J. (1968) 'The Public Law-Private Law Distinction in European and American Law', *Journal of Public Law*, 17: 3–19.

Natali, L. (2010) 'The Big Grey Elephants in the Backyard of Huelva, Spain', in R. White (ed.) *Global Environmental Harm: Criminological Perspectives*, Cullompton and Devon: Willan Publishing.

Natali, L. (2013) 'The Contemporary Horizon of Green Criminology', in A. Brisman and N. South (eds) *Routledge International Handbook of Green Criminology*, London and New York: Routledge.

Natali, L. (2016) *A Visual Approach for Green Criminology: Exploring the Social Perception of Environmental Harm*, London: Palgrave MacMillan.

Natali, L. (2017) 'The Contribution of Green Criminology to the Analysis of "Historical Pollution"', in F. Centonze and S. Manacorda (eds) *Historical Pollution: Comparative Legal Responses to Environmental Crimes*, Cham: Springer, 21–55.

Passas, N. (2005) 'Lawful but Awful: "Legal Corporate Crimes"', *The Journal of Socio-Economics*, 34(6): 771–786.

Patz, J., McGeehin, M., Bernard, S., Ebi, K., Epstein, P., Grambsch, A., Gubler, D., Reiter, P., Romieu, I., Rose, J., Samet, J. and Trtanf, J. (2000) 'The Potential Health Impacts of Climate Variability and Change for the United States: Executive Summary of the Report of the Health Sector of the U.S. National Assessment', *Environmental Health Perspectives*, 108(4): 367–376.

Pellizzoni, L. and Osti, G. (2008) *Sociologia dell'ambiente*, Bologna: Il Mulino.

Popa, F. and Guillermin, M. (2017) 'Reflexive Methodological Pluralism: The Case of Environmental Valuation', *Journal of Mixed Methods Research*, 11(1): 19–35.

Ruggiero, V. and South, N. (2010) 'Critical Criminology and Crimes against the Environment', *Critical Criminology*, 18: 245–250.

Ruggiero, V. and South, N. (2013) 'Green Criminology and Crimes of the Economy: Theory, Research and Praxis', *Critical Criminology*, 21(3): 359–373.

Santos, B. de S. (2014) *Epistemologies of the South: Justice against Epistemicide*, Boulder: Paradigm Publishers.

Shmueli, D. and Kaufman, S. (2006) *Environmental Mediation*, The Center for Environmental Policy Studies Series no. 24, Jerusalem: Center for Environmental Studies.

Sipe, N. (2007) 'An Empirical Analysis of Environmental Mediation', *Journal of the American Planning Association*, 64(2): 275–285.

Skinnider, E. (2011) *Victims of Environmental Crime: Mapping the Issues*, Vancouver: The International Centre for Criminal Law Reform and Criminal Justice Policy.

South, N. (1998) 'A Green Field for Criminology? A Proposal for a Perspective', *Theoretical Criminology*, 2(2): 211–234.

South, N. (2014) 'Green Criminology: Reflections, Connections, Horizons', *International Journal for Crime, Justice and Social Democracy*, 3(2): 5–20.

South, N., Brisman, A. and Beirne, P. (2013) 'A Guide to a Green Criminology', in N. South and A. Brisman (eds) *Routledge International Handbook of Green Criminology*, London: Routledge, 27–42.

South, N. and White, R. (2013) 'The Antecedents and Emergence of a "Green" Criminology', in R. Agnew (ed.), *Annual Meeting Presidential Papers? Selected Papers from the*

Presidential Panels: Expanding the Core: Neglected Crimes, Groups, Causes and Policy Approaches, American Society of Criminology.

Walters, R., Westerhuis, D.S. and Wyatt, T. (2013) 'Introduction', in R. Walters, D.S. Westerhuis and T. Wyatt (eds) *Emerging Issues in Green Criminology: Exploring Power, Justice and Harm*, London: Palgrave Macmillan.

White, R. (2008) *Crimes Against Nature: Environmental Criminology and Ecological Justice*, Cullompton: Willan Publishing.

White, R. (2011) *Transnational Environmental Crime: Towards an Eco-global Criminology*, Abingdon: Routledge Publishing.

White, R. (2013) 'Resource Extraction Leaves Something Behind: Environmental Justice and Mining', *International Journal for Crime and Justice*, 2(1): 50–64.

White, R. (2017) 'Reparative Justice, Environmental Crime and Penalties for the Powerful', *Crime, Law and Social Change. An Interdisciplinary Journal*, 67(2): 117–132.

White, R. (2018) 'Ecocentrism and Criminal Justice', *Theoretical Criminology*, 22(3): 342–362.

Williams, C. (1996) 'An environmental victimology', *Social Science*, 23(1): 16–40; reprinted in R. White (ed.) (2009) *Environmental Crime: A Reader*, 200–222, Cullompton: Willan Publishing.

World Health Organization. (2008) *Quantification of the Health Effects of Exposure to Air Pollution Report of a WHO Working Group*, Bilthoven: WHO Regional Office for Europe.

World Health Organization. (2018) *World Health Statistics 2018*, Bilthoven: WHO Regional Office for Europe.

Yun, K., Lurie, M. and Hyde, P. (2010) 'Moving Mental Health into the Disaster-Preparedness Spotlight', *The New England Journal of Medicine*, 263: 1193–1195.

Zehr, H. (1990) *Changing Lenses: A New Focus for Crime and Justice*, Scottsdale, PA: Herald Press.

9 Reenact, commemorate and make amends after storm Xynthia through a judicial *dispositif*

Sandrine Revet

Introduction

When a disaster strikes, human societies act in order to respond to the change and destruction brought about by the event. Based on a linear or circular vision of what a disaster is (with an assumed sequence such as event, response, recovery, reconstruction, mitigation, preparation for the next disaster), much of the literature in social sciences research on disasters has focused on the various actions people and groups carry out in order to 'respond to', 'recover from', 'build back better', 'mitigate' and 'prepare for' the next disaster.[1] The notion of 'recovery' has been at the centre of many studies because it helps to examine the way societies face the crisis or cope with it (Oliver-Smith 1986; Davis and Alexander 2015). In this literature, the notion of recovery refers to a variety of dimensions, from cleaning up the debris left by the disaster to the influence of social capital in collective recovery. With the development and dissemination of an approach framing recovery in terms of 'resilience' (Quenault 2015; Revet 2020), new research has emerged focusing on how societies go back to their 'normal' or 'previous' state (Aldrich 2012; Chamlee-Wright and Storr 2011).

Anthropology has engaged in these discussions for a long time (Faas and Barrios 2015) and has also contributed to elaborating a critical reading on the recovery-resilience paradigm. Discussions have focused on the 'neoliberal perspective' underlying this concept (Barrios 2017) and on 'locating' recovery in order to situate it as interwoven with everyday practices rather than within a framework of exceptionalism (Hastrup 2011).

A growing number of anthropological studies focus on how victims of a disaster make use of the justice system and of a judicial *dispositif* (Fortun 2001; Zenobi 2014; Benadusi and Revet 2016; Falconieri 2016). In particular, they examine the increasing number of cases in which victims file a suit in criminal court following a disaster (Binder 2016). The uses of such a *dispositif* encompass a variety of situations. Trials can be used by victims in order to publicize a situation, to voice a claim, to ask for compensation or to claim 'reparation' in the many material, monetary, symbolic and moral dimensions of this term. Considering these various uses, this chapter aims to examine the multiple ways in which a judicial *dispositif* can be operationalized in order to seek to 'repair' after a disaster.

DOI: 10.4324/9781003184782-13

In order to explore the possibilities and limitations of using a judicial *dispositif* to try to repair after a disaster, I analyze a particular event in the criminal trials that followed the extensive destruction and 29 deaths that occurred in the French municipality of La Faute-sur-Mer caused by storm Xynthia, in 2010. During the first trial, the court transported the proceedings to the scene of the disaster and organized a march through the very site destroyed by the flood. This march was attended by the members of the court, defendants, plaintiffs and their lawyers. It was covered by the media and surrounded by the police. The route passed by landmarks representing the destroyed houses, the level that had been reached by floodwater and many other physical and human elements of the disaster. Based on an ethnographic observation of the entire trial, in this chapter I focus specifically on the march. I analyze the march as a part of the judicial *dispositif*[2] (Dodier and Barbot 2016) destined to qualify the facts and modes of action of people who engaged in the trial. Beyond the qualification process, specific to the judicial *dispositif*, I suggest that the walk along the dike can be understood as a judicial tool of reenactment, as a way to commemorate the disaster and as a ritual of making amends.

As discussed in the introduction of this volume:

> The juridical term 'reparation' performs an 'accusatory function, invoking a kind of repair that entails identifying the actor who caused the damage in question, denouncing the formal injustice of damages suffered and determining corresponding faults, crimes, victims and perpetrators' (Dodier 1995, translated from French). In this case, the disaster is framed as a moral or juridical crisis requiring reparation through remuneration or other assistance to the party that has been wronged. This implies resorting to the legal or moral code and to the *dispositif* of the trial (Dodier and Barbot 2016).
>
> (Introduction: pp. 30–31)

I suggest that the notion of reparation in a criminal trial can also encompass other dimensions of the attempt to recover following a disaster, depending on the way participants make use of the judicial *dispositif*.

This research is based on eight weeks of ethnographic fieldwork during the two trials (five for the first trial and three for the second). I also attended the rendering of the two judgements and conducted 16 interviews, in Les Sables-d'Olonne, Poitiers and Paris, with the main actors in the proceedings before, during and after the trials.[3] I conducted observations outside the two courtrooms as well, since I resided each time in the places where the trials were held, observing side events, dinners, the way people took over certain spaces during the trials, the alliances that were forged outside the courtroom and the work of journalists. Finally, thanks to the help of colleagues in my research centre, I monitored the media coverage of the first trial and how it was presented on various websites. This enabled me to collect 490 documents related to this first trial, from the press (national and local), Internet pages (websites, blog posts) and reports on the storm.[4]

In the following section I begin with a brief account of the events linked to storm Xynthia, which hit France and other parts of western Europe in 2010. I focus on the small coastal municipality of La Faute-sur-Mer and examine the storm's context and its consequences, as well as the trials that took place four years (for the first trial) and five years (for the appeal trial) after the disaster. I then analyze the march organized by the court in September 2014 during the first trial, through the judge's point of view and through my observation of the uses the plaintiffs and the defendants made of it. This analysis leads me to three conclusions. First, the walk was conceptualized by the court as a sensory experience that would allow for some of the elements of the written legal case to become obvious and discernible to all participants. In this sense it can be considered as a 'reenactment' of the disaster, repairing the fractured timeline of the events to present a more whole version of what happened. But the walk was also used by the plaintiffs as a memorial ceremony. In this sense, the walk served as a mechanism for repairing the victims by allowing them to journey through and build a collective memory of the disaster, strengthened by the memorial, a located and mate-rialized site established in 2014, four years after the disaster. Finally, the sequence of the walk was used by the ex-mayor – one of the defendants – as a way of making amends and publicly asking for pardon. Here, the walk was used to try to repair a moral fault. However, although the trials and the march may have played some role in repairing La Faute-sur-Mer, I conclude by showing that the judicial *dispositif* cannot easily solve the moral crisis caused by the disaster, despite the different appropria-tions and uses people who were engaged in the trial made of it.

Brief chronology of storm Xynthia and the trials that followed

In February 2010, storm Xynthia hit several European countries. Combined with a high sea level caused by spring tides, the storm caused significant floods and ruptures of dikes. A total of 59 deaths related to the storm were reported in Europe, including 53 in France, of which 29 occurred in the small seaside municipality of La Faute-sur-Mer (situated in the department of Vendée), where a majority of elderly people died, sometimes with the grandchildren who were visiting them during the winter vacation.[5] Initiated by the French state, the judicial process that followed the storm led to the indictment of five people on the charge of 'involun-tary manslaughter': the ex-mayor of La Faute-sur-Mer, the local officer in charge of urban affairs, her son (who was both a real estate agent and responsible for the dike's maintenance), a civil servant and a local construction businessman. The responsibility of the five defendants was investigated on the basis of several fac-tors: knowledge of risks, crisis management, deficit of information provided to the public, lack of organization of rescue operations, delivery of building permits in flooding zones and insufficiency of dike monitoring.

The small town, where 916 people lived at the time of the storm, is built on the Atlantic coast in an area that has gradually been 'reclaimed from the sea' (*gagnée sur la mer*) by the construction of a dike meant to protect agricultural land from flooding. The town was built on a recent sandy barrier beach, and then expanded, starting in the 1980s, with a boom in seaside tourism. Housing estates have gradu-ally replaced agricultural land and are used mainly as holiday homes (87 per cent in 2010). Entire districts of the municipality were built below sea level, 'protected' by a dike that revealed its deficiencies during the 2010 storm. The neighbourhood with the highest number of storm victims is today referred to as 'the basin' (*la cuvette*), indicating its particular topography. In addition, houses were built on the basis of cheap, single-level urban planning, to respect the 'traditional' local style, which also showed its limits during the storm. People found nowhere high enough to take refuge when faced with the rapid rise of the water during the night of 28 February 2010. Throughout the investigations and the trial, the judges tried to understand whether the granting of building permits in areas designated as dangerous by the risk prevention plans was due to deliberate action, negligence, ignorance or errors on the zoning maps.

During 2010, more than 100 victims and their families instituted civil proceedings in order to demand reparation for the injustices they suffered. The civil proceedings were 'attached' to the legal case and examined together by the criminal court.[6] The first trial took place in September and October 2014, in the courthouse of the coastal town of Les Sables-d'Olonne, which is around 60 kilometres north of La Faute-sur-Mer. The trial was attended by a large number of plaintiffs and members of the local population. During this trial, 50 victims out of the 121 plaintiffs testified in court during a period of six days.[7]

The first judgement was pronounced in December 2014, with relatively significant sentences being given, especially for the ex-mayor of La Faute-sur-Mer and the officer who had been responsible for urban affairs. The court condemned them respectively to four years' and two years' imprisonment. All of the defendants appealed the judgement. A second trial took place in Poitiers, one year later, and the sentences were significantly lowered. The final judgement concluded that the ex-mayor was guilty of having 'deliberately' omitted to inform the population about the risks he was aware of, not having set up the local protection plan, and having issued building permits in flood-risk areas. The ex-mayor's sentence was eventually shortened to two years and suspended and all the others were discharged. Unlike the first court, the appeals court declared its incompetency regarding the civil action and sent it back to the administrative court, arguing that the faults had been committed by the ex-mayor in his capacity of civil servant and not as an individual citizen. In July 2018, the administrative court of Nantes declared the ex-mayor not 'personally' responsible, and his faults not 'detachable' from his function, meaning that he was responsible as a mayor and not as an individual or a simple citizen. This implies that the ex-mayor would not have to pay personally for the compensation of the victims. The court sentenced the municipality of La Faute-sur-Mer, the state and the local association in charge of maintaining the dike (Association Syndicale de la Vallée du Lay) to pay for this compensation.

Reenacting the disaster: the march as a judicial and pedagogical tool

On Thursday 25 September 2014, after lunch, on the ninth day of the trial, under a bright and warm sun, the inhabitants of La Faute-sur-Mer started to gather around the recently inaugurated memorial of the disaster.

Box 9.1   The memorial

Built on a square next to the destroyed districts, near the dike, the sculpture, carved in white stone, represents a stylized wave set on a black base. All around it, a round plaza delimited by a stone wall on which benches are installed allows for contemplation. On a grey stone support, a black marble plaque engraved in gold letters lists the names and ages of the storm victims, and says: 'Let us not forget the victims of storm Xynthia'. A flood marker in the shape of a rectangular pillar informs the visitor that the level reached by the sea that night in the most exposed houses was 2.80 metres (see Figure 9.1).

Figure 9.1   The Xynthia Memorial in La Faute-sur-Mer, 2 March 2014, at the fourth anniversary of the disaster

Source: Jean-Paul Bounine (used with permission)

Around the monument, families of victims and neighbours found each other again, and for some of them it was the first time they had come back to the area since the disaster. Some remembered: 'The sun was shining like this, the day before the storm'. Others shared their feelings about the trial. The victims' testimonies had ended on Tuesday, 23 September. While they were relieved that this difficult period was over, they also waited with anxiety to listen, the following week, to the witnesses and experts, and they especially dreaded the speech of the defense.

Farther on, at the roundabout, police officers and journalists occupied the rest of the scene, wearing sunglasses and patiently waiting for the court and the defendants to arrive. Suddenly, the crowd moved. A stream of vehicles stopped by the dike: police officers on their motorbikes preceded the cars bringing the members of the court, the defendants and their lawyers. Cameras started to come alive, showing a special interest in two figures of the trial: the ex-mayor of La Faute-sur-Mer and his deputy for urban affairs. Two strong yet different person-alities: the paunchy 64-year-old man, with his sunglasses and his moustache – a man sometimes called 'King René' (*Roi René*) before the storm because of his all-powerful relationship with the small town over which he reigned for more than 20 years – and the short and stern-seeming 70-year-old woman, with red hair and a self-confident look. Both were at the centre of the trial: they represented the authority of the town at the time of the storm and they were accused of not having communicated all the information on risks to the inhabitants of La Faute-sur-Mer and of having authorized housing construction in dangerous places. Moreover, the ex-mayor was blamed by many plaintiffs for having lacked empathy toward victims and their families after the disaster. His general attitude – mixing silence, distance and avoidance since the storm – was interpreted by many inhabitants as indicating a lack of sensitivity, and as 'proof' of his culpability. In particular, a tension between the victims' association[8] and the ex-mayor appeared around the building of the memorial of the disaster. The ex-mayor was opposed to its construction for more than three years because he had chosen to evoke the storm through another memorial located at the entrance of the town – a monument that did not mention the victims clearly, nor the storm itself. For the plaintiffs, this dispute reinforced the idea that the mayor wanted to 'hide' the victims and the disaster (Revet 2019).

After everybody had gotten out of the vehicles, the walk started slowly and silently. The president of the court, wearing a grey civilian suit and not the black robe he wears in the courtroom, led the walk, surrounded by the two other judges and followed by the defendants and their lawyers. Further on, separated from the first group by some police officers, were the plaintiffs (some of them carrying flowers), their lawyers and the journalists. The journey followed a circuit going from the dike to the destroyed districts of La Faute-sur-Mer. The one-kilometre-long circuit had been previously marked by a land surveyor mandated by the court, which, according to the appeal judgement, aimed to:

> materialize by all means the dike in its characteristics – width and height – prior to the storm, identify [. . .] the place where the 29 victims died and locate some of the dwellings in which residents of La Faute-sur-Mer died during the storm, with the maximum level reached by the water in regard to the ceiling height[9]

This empty landscape was marked by notices displaying the names and ages of the victims, situated nearby the places where their houses used to stand. Every time the march passed by such a notice, it stopped or slowed down. The walk started to look like a procession or the Stations of the Cross, as the group walked and halted following the rhythm of the notices.[10] After one hour under a heavy sun, the procession ended and the president made the announcement he does after every audience day: 'The hearing is over. It will be resumed next Monday at 2 pm'.

Through the formality of the journey, the silence and this final declaration, the judge insisted on giving a judicial form to the walk and reminded all the participants that they were attending an off-site judicial audience. This 'transportation' *dispositif*, as it was called during the trial, although used only exceptionally in France because of the justice system's lack of financial resources, is provided for by Article 456 of the French code of criminal procedure.[11] The walk concluded the week of plaintiffs' testimonies and introduced the testimonies of the experts and witnesses. For a member of the court, the walk was 'unavoidable':

> I immediately realized that there would have to be an inspection of the site. That it was impossible in a case like this not to have any. And if we didn't anticipate it, it would be asked, because we were 60 kilometres from La Faute-sur-Mer, that there is this no man's land that has been there for years now, and that at some point or another, this question would have emerged during the preparation, so I preferred to anticipate it very early on.[12]

The proximity between the courtroom and the place of the disaster had an impact on the organization of the trial. As mentioned earlier, it allowed a strong presence of plaintiffs and victims' families and a significant media coverage of the trial by local media that were already very active during the disaster. It also allowed the demands expressed by the plaintiffs – or anticipated by the president of the court – to be considered. When organizing the site visit, the court also anticipated another, highly emotional, dimension of the trial. Fearing that the walk would be understood only as a moment of recollection and not in its propitious 'technical' or legal dimension, the judge explained: 'How do we deal with it so that precisely there is no such criticism as I had anticipated, of the recollection dimension, and so that this [inspection] is useful, judicially speaking'?[13]

In order to turn this walk into a 'real' judicial tool, the judge chose to transform the 'no man's land', the destroyed districts and the empty landscape, into a place that 'reenacted' the destroyed zone during the night of the disaster. Therefore, the route was equipped with 'expert' devices and marks.

> There must be an expert, who, based on the documents in the file that refer to the water level and the dike [. . .] can put us in the situation that existed before the deconstruction and before the dike's height was increased, just that.

The walk passed through a landscape filled with a mix of small piles of stones, traces of the destroyed houses, tall and wild weeds and ancient asphalt streets. Red and white ribbons marked the squared surface where the victims' destroyed houses used to stand. Metallic tubes, with two colored symbols (red and yellow) indicated the heights of the ceilings and the levels reached by the water (see Figure 9.2). All along the itinerary, signs with the names and ages of the victims and the distance from their houses were posted (see Figure 9.3).

Figure 9.2 Reenacting the disaster. The house, the ceiling heights (in grey) and the water
levels (in white), September 2014

Source: Jean-Paul Bounine (used with permission)

Figure 9.3 Identifying the victims, September 2014

Source: Jean-Paul Bounine (used with permission)

In such a perspective, the *dispositif* of transportation acted as a judicial reenactment. It staged what happened during the night of the storm, through technical and 'objective' information: Where were the houses built? How large and high was the dike? How old were the victims? How high did the water get? Reenactment is a well-known technique in disaster management, in particular for disaster preparedness programs where simulations are organized on the basis of scenarios aimed at immersing participants in conditions close to reality and which are often based on disasters that have already occurred. Artifacts such as costumes, make-up or scenic elements are then used to reenact the disaster (Davis 2007; Revet 2013; Elie *et al.* 2014). Reenactment techniques are also used in order to build a collective memory of disasters (Zhuang 2014; Weisenfeld 2012).

For the judge in charge of organizing it, the *dispositif* was something 'raw' (*brut*) and merely factual:

> [It's like a reenactment], but at the level of the court, because reenactments only exist at the level of the committing magistrate (*juge d'instruction*) usually and they can take different forms. It can be with or without questioning, there it's really the raw (*brut*), silent transport that the criminal trial allows. [. . .] It's very factual and then we get nothing in terms of responsibilities, that's clear, but that's part of the facts. That's it.[14]

This silent walk in a destroyed landscape equipped with expert devices also opened up the possibility for the expression of other dimensions. After the walk, one of the plaintiffs' lawyers explained to the journalists: 'When you see five centimetres between the roof and the water level, you understand; when you see the dike as it was at the time, with its width and height, you understand' (Field notes, 25 September 2014).

The judge explained that he had organized the 'displacement' of the court to the site of the disaster 'for *it* to speak to everyone'.[15]

In the silence of the walk, then, what was expected to speak was the disaster scene itself, the landscape and elements such as the dike or the water level represented through the colored markers. Even if a trial is usually an oral exercise comprising a corpus of arguments supposed to stop the qualification process and to establish the objective reality that will decide a case, this segment of the trial mobilized dimensions other than mere words or discourses. All of the senses were called in: the sight of the no man's land with broken street lamps that do not light anything anymore, the sight of the names of the victims on the notices, the smell of the sea nearby, the touch of overgrown grass through the walk on the dike and through the empty streets swamped with weeds. The trial, which is usually a scene of description, was rather based on *demonstrations* on that day. It situated the audience beyond description, beyond words. For a former inhabitant of the destroyed district, it is 'better to make up one's mind at the scene than to judge only on paper'.

On this occasion, during the walk, not only did the court convene the plaintiffs, the defendants and their respective lawyers as witnesses, but it also called in other types of artifacts and entities to testify about what happened during that cold night in February. The dike, the sea, the empty streets, the broken lights and the sound of the seagulls all had something to say that day, and the court wanted to listen to them. 'For *it* to speak to everyone', as the judge said. All these artifacts and entities were convened in the course of the silent walk as other forms of witnesses.

The idea, then, was for all the participants in the trial – the members of the court, the plaintiffs, the victims and their families, the defendants, the lawyers and, of course, through the media, the public – to be aware of what had happened during the night of the storm, and why. In this perspective, the transportation *dispositif* can be understood as a material and sensory translation of the judicial data gathered in the paper file during the inquiry, in order to make all the participants 'realize' or 'feel' what happened. In this sense, the trial was thought of by one of the judges as an opportunity to 'restore' something, as he put it during our interview:

The judge:	With regard to the victims, it is quite different, without making it an objective as such, but obviously, given the impact it had on their lives, it was important that the trial as a whole and the displacement be part of it, something that is equal to the event experienced, a question of respect, quite simply . . .
SR:	Only a matter of respect?
The judge:	So that they can understand what happened, this is something that is part, I think, of the purpose of the criminal trial, at a push even more than compensation measures. That is, to go back in time, to give meaning to what they have experienced. [. . .] I mean, you have this kind of psycho-temporal rupture, that the intrusion of an offence into someone's life creates, something that completely amazes you and finally all of a sudden time stops and it can last for months or years. That is why the criminal trial never meets people's expectations, it is obvious, because there is a deep gap. That is true, but I think we must try to work towards that goal anyway. [We must try to] allow them to start their internal clock again, which has stopped at some point.[16]

Thought of as both a judicial and a pedagogical tool by the court, the walk was used both by plaintiffs and by defendants as a symbolic moment, related to the idea of 'repairing' in different ways.

The walk as a memorial journey

For the plaintiffs, the emotional dimension of the walk appeared to be very strong. Some of them walked for one hour with a handkerchief in hand, holding together with their ex-neighbours and families, comforting each other, looking for their lost houses in the empty site. They were dismayed by the lines of color marking the level of the water on metallic tubes, reminding them of the tragic and painful drowning of their loved ones, stuck in cold water against a too-low ceiling. The repeated stops in front of the signs bearing the names of the departed gave the scene a sense of being a religious procession that accentuated its dramatic character. The rear of the procession, where the civil parties were gathered, resembled a funeral march.

In addition to the emotional dimension, the memorial dimension also appeared to be central for the plaintiffs. They assumed it entirely, by starting and ending the march around the memorial. The place was important for their group, since it symbolized their struggle (against the ex-mayor) to have a place of remembrance of the tragedy within the town. In fact, the struggle for the memorial was referred to many times during the week of the plaintiffs' testimonies and was used as a 'proof' of the ex-mayor's lack of empathy. At the end of the march, when the cars transporting the court and the lawyers left, many victims and plaintiffs decided to gather on the small memorial plaza. Some of them placed wreaths under the names of the 29 victims. The local Civil Protection unit stayed around, as if emotion could be so strong that some participants would need special assistance. Journalists and photographers captured the emotional scene with families gathering around the memorial and holding each other as a gesture of solidarity.

By doing so, the plaintiffs transformed the judicial *dispositif* into a memorial journey. Beyond the technical and judicial dimension of the transportation, they used it to express their 'suffering', but also to make this suffering visible to the public. They made the most of the presence of the national press which covered this local event extensively. Furthermore, both the national and regional press spoke intensively about a 'painful' experience or a 'painful' return to the place of the disaster.[17] Hence, through the transportation *dispositif*, and the involvement of the media, the suffering of the victims was made visible. It was publicized. The walk was transformed into one of the scenes during which such suffering could be expressed and shared.

Making amends and repairing the fault: the walk as an act of expiation

The defendants were more constrained by the judicial *dispositif*, the march in particular, and had little leeway to make the best of it. On the contrary, it placed them in a delicate situation, obliging them to walk on a path full of pitfalls. Every notice that signaled the presence of deceased persons, every mark in the landscape figuring how close the houses had been built from the dike, were ordeals they had to overcome. Under the gaze of their accusers and of a significant crowd, whose size was accentuated by the presence of the journalists, the ex-mayor and the other defendants were obliged to walk a long way along the traces of the disaster they were accused of having contributed to.

In this perspective, the transportation of the court proceedings to the site of the disaster placed the defendants in a position of expiation. The *dispositif* functioned as a ritual – a sequence of acts and gestures put in an order that was considered to be performative – with a dimension of reparation. The humiliation imposed by the long walk, marked by regular stops in front of the names of people lost in the disaster, resembled the medieval practice of making amends. Diderot (1778) described this ritual in his *Encyclopaedia* as 'punishment based on dishonor', in order to force criminals to make a 'public reparation of their acts'. It was at the time an infamous punishment used for those 'responsible for scandalous crimes'.[18] The guilty party was taken to their executioner who would make him strip, leaving him only his shirt. A rope was put on his neck and he was given a torch. He was finally driven to a place where he had to ask for forgiveness – from God, from the King and from Justice. Considered a practice of reparation during the Middle Ages, making amends did not prevent other punishments from taking place during the Ancien Régime (Old Regime) and after the ritual, many were executed or sent to the galleys. Making amends was also an act of repentance, however, likely to lead to mercy and pardon (Moeglin 1997). In the last period of the Middle Ages, however, through the public humiliation of the guilty party, a reparation of the victims' honor was possible (*ibid.*). This public dimension is important regarding the 'transportation' *dispositif* examined in this chapter. The expiatory dimension of the walk will better appear when inserted into a larger moment, including the first audience in the courtroom following the court's inspection of the disaster site.

On Monday, 29 September 2014, four days after the walk, the court was back in the Les Sables-d'Olonne courtroom. At the very beginning of the audience, one of the lawyers of the ex-mayor announced to the president that his client wanted to make a declaration. The plaintiffs jittered. The ex-mayor stood and started talking with a slow and apparently moved voice, and a serious look. He held a text in hand, and partially read from it:

> Mister President, I would like to say a few words after these first days of hearings devoted to the victims and the tragedy they have experienced. I didn't recognize myself in the man you were describing. I don't think I'm that man, and yet that's how the plaintiffs see me. It's hard, very hard to hear. Since the beginning of this trial, I have been wondering what I could have done, said, not said, to hurt and shock each and every one of you.
>
> Some may say it's too late. But I still want to tell you that the day after the disaster, I was KO'd, standing in front of the horror of the tragedy that was hitting you. I probably didn't say the right words, I apologize.
>
> I felt responsible for not having understood, surely, what was going to happen that night. I apologize for that.
>
> I also felt there was anger at me, relayed by complaints, interviews, the 'victims' association' blog. I used to blame myself and still blame myself so much that I couldn't, surely, go to many of you.

I am convinced that this disaster made me fall back into silence. I then believed that I had to devote myself to rebuild La Faute (*reconstruire La Faute*), to get this town back on track. That is what I wanted to do, I think, by devoting all my time and energy to it. So did the town's public services, despite what you might have thought. In this respect, I would like to thank the deputies, the city employees, the volunteers, the associations. We cannot but only thank the girls and boys of the town (*les filles et les garçons de la commune*).

I am convinced that I was probably wrong. There was, surely, in the depths of pain and suffering, the time of mourning and compassion. I realize this very strongly today, and for that, I agree to apologize.[19]

By choosing to make this unexpected declaration, the ex-mayor and his lawyers created a continuum between the transportation of the court proceedings to the site of the disaster and the 'declaration of apology', and to link both segments of the trial. Both thus became part of a unique ritual. Humiliated in public by the walk at the scene of the disaster where the citizens he was responsible for died four years ago, the ex-mayor asked for forgiveness afterwards, which is a part of the ritual of reparation.[20]

The ex-mayor asked for pardon for not having understood what was expected from him after the disaster, and for not having understood, before the storm, that such a disaster could happen. Aware that what he was accused of by the plaintiffs was in part a moral fault, an error of judgement and 'wrong' behaviour, he answered to this first. Then he explained that his priority was to 'rebuild La Faute', in a material way, in the way he had 'built' the municipality for the past 20 years. But this time, the building process – according to the victims – should come with or be preceded by a human process of care, of mourning, of accompanying. In French, the town's name 'La Faute' means 'the fault'. So when the mayor said he wanted to '*reconstruire La Faute*', one can also understand that he wanted to 'repair his fault'.

Two ways to understand repairing are interwoven in the former mayor's speech. The first one is material. For the ex-mayor, to repair La Faute meant to be able to 'rebuild' the seaside town and to bring back tourists for the next summer. It implied overcoming the disaster quickly, and not to make too visible what happened in order to recover the tourist appeal the town had before the disaster. By going in this direction, the mayor acted as he was used to: thinking about the material – and economic – future of the municipality, in the perspective of urban development. This first form of repairing was close to 'recovery' since it put the emphasis on material and institutional characteristics.

The second dimension of 'repairing' that was present in the ex-mayor's declaration at the court is the moral one. When the mayor asked for forgiveness, first he did it for having 'hurt' or 'shocked' or 'not having the right words to give to' the victims and their relatives. He then wanted (with this act of contrition) to make amends for a moral conduct that he had been reproached for during the six days hearing of the witnesses' testimony.

Conclusion

While the ex-mayor was pronouncing his discourse, in the courtroom, a rumor emerged from the plaintiffs, as an echo to the scandal provoked by the attempt to solve the moral crisis through begging pardon. It became immediately clear that the pardon would not be granted, at least not publicly. Hence, the president of the victims' association declared to the press, right after the audience of the day: 'We have been waiting four and a half years for this apology; during all this time, the victims were not acknowledged. For us, this apology doesn't change anything'.[21]

One of the members of the victims' association, whose relationships had been tense with the ex-mayor even before the disaster, explained to me, after the audience and still in a state of shock, that after his declaration in the courtroom the ex-mayor 'even tried to shake my hand, as if everything would be forgotten after this reading'. By refusing any contact with the defendant, she refused to grant him the begged pardon, because she was afraid that pardon could mean forgetting.

During the next days, the ex-mayor's speech was closely scrutinized and commented on by the plaintiffs. Some argued that the ex-mayor 'had read a text written by his lawyers'. His repeated excuses were not deemed 'sincere'. One of the words used in the speech, in particular, was deemed a proof of this. The word '*bien*' used in the sentence '*je veux* bien *vous demander pardon*', meant that the ex-mayor agreed or accepted to apologize rather than directly begging for pardon ('I agree/accept to apologize' – rather than 'I apologize') was a way of nuancing the expiation process.[22] On an online forum where they used to interact,[23] one of the plaintiffs cited the psychologist who accompanied them during the trial. She explained that this '*bien*' was probably not written in the text read by the ex-mayor, but certainly 'a manifestation of his unconscious'. '*Je veux bien*' would mean that the lawyers suggested he realized this contrition act, but that the ex-mayor only accepted it with reluctance. As one of the plaintiffs' lawyers pleaded two weeks later: 'The impulses of the heart do not manifest themselves on command. They are spontaneous, immediate'.[24]

A member of the victims' association, interviewed by a local television station during the trial, first argued that he was not convinced by the declaration because it arrived 'too late' in the trial. For him, the ex-mayor should have started the trial by asking for pardon. 'It's a pity he had to listen to all this [the testimonies of the victims] before he asked for pardon', he said. Second, and more interestingly, he compared what the mayor did with a religious confession of sins: 'When I used to go confess my sins when I was a little boy, I first had to admit I had sinned before begging for the pardon of the priest'.[25]

With the trial, the justice system offered a *dispositif* that is supposed – if not to repair – at least to enable the production and stabilization of a narrative of the disaster by qualifying the facts, denouncing the damages and determining the fault, the victims and the perpetrators. Within the trial, though, the transportation of the court proceedings to the site of the disaster offered a specific tool which was not based on the characterization of the fault or financial compensation, but drew on a sequence where different ways of repairing after the disaster could emerge.

As part of the accusatory *dispositif* of the trial, for many the march had a local significance and weight, as much as it was used as an extrajudicial ritual. For the justice and the court, the *dispositif* should be pedagogical; the plaintiffs used it as a way of commemorating the disaster and making their suffering public; and for the defendants and the ex-mayor in particular, the walk was used, together with his declaration in the court, as a way of making amends.

The disaster caused a moral crisis in La Faute-sur-Mer. One of its manifestations was the division of the city into two opposing factions. In one, mostly composed of victims and their supporters, the loss of confidence, both in the ex-mayor's capacity to rule the municipality's public life and in his care for the inhabitants, has added to the crisis caused by the disaster. This loss of confidence was evident during the trial, when the victims were questioning the mayor's management of the town and his lack of empathy after the disaster. Faced with this situation, during the hearings, the victims collectively constructed a figure of the ideal mayor. The ideal figure that gradually took shape was that of a reactive and worried mayor on the evening of the storm, who 'puts on his boots' to be with his citizens, an empathetic mayor, participating after the event in the mourning of his fellow citizens and seeking to establish in the municipality a memory of the disaster through the construction of a memorial. In view of this collectively constructed attitude during the trial as one that would have been morally acceptable, the mayor's behaviour was judged to be 'arrogant', 'indifferent' and 'lacking of empathy', and to have hurt citizens and aggravated his faults (Revet 2019). Despite this, the crisis was not general, and the mayor was still supported by a significant part of the population, who, having elected him without interruption since 1989, saw in him an active entrepreneur, capable of leading the development of the small seaside town, its economic development through tourism in particular. An illustration of this support can be read in the 2014 local elections, in which the former mayor was again elected as a municipal councillor (*conseiller municipal*), with 393 votes.

This moral crisis between the victims and the local authorities was not solved either by the trial or even by the exceptional transportation of the trial to the scene of the disaster and the public demand for pardon that followed. Although positioned in a moral and emotional dimension by most participants, the site inspection ritual failed in repairing the relationship between the ex-mayor and the victims.

Nevertheless, what the ethnography of the judicial *dispositif* makes visible is that all the participants in the trial had the opportunity to use it in different ways, mobilizing a different idea of what it means to 'repair' in each instance. What matters, therefore, for the anthropologist, is not to evaluate the restorative dimension of the *dispositif*, but rather to show how it allows everyone to say *how* to repair after a disaster. For the court, the organization of the trial's transportation to the site of the disaster was understood as a way to repair or 'restore' something broken by the storm, to make sense of what happened to the victims. For the plaintiffs, the march was used as an opportunity to repair themselves through commemorating and mourning. As for the defendants, and the ex-mayor in particular, they used the transportation as a way of trying to repair their faults by making amends and asking for pardon. As the last description of the victims' reactions to his demand showed, however, it seems that some situations can simply not be repaired, no matter how creative the judges are in producing innovative *dispositifs*.

Of course, the march was only one dimension of the trial, and of the whole legal process, since another dimension of repairing emerged in the civil court, from 2018 onwards. In the civil appeal trial of November 2019 in Nantes, the court re-examined the compensation demands of the victims.[26] Although the division of responsibilities and compensation had been fixed by the administrative court in July 2019 (50 per cent for the municipality, 35 per cent for the state and 15 per cent for the association managing the dike), the amounts, contested by all parties, had yet to be fixed. The moral, bodily, financial, psychological or other more symbolic damages such as the loss of family memories washed away by the waves were all assessed by the administrative judge on a case-by-case basis and the decision of 10 December 2019 brought to a close a judicial process of almost 10 years. But did this decision manage to 'repair' anything?

On 1 March 2020, Patrick Jouin, the current mayor of La Faute-sur-Mer, addressed his fellow citizens at the ceremony commemorating the disaster. 'Never again!' he announced in front of the inhabitants and the families of the victims gathered together:

> We must denounce the unacceptable, the irreparable [. . .] yes, we still need compassion and comfort here. [. . .] 10 years later, the ones who are responsible for the disaster have been judged and condemned, but there are still questions of dignity that should be behind us.[27]

Despite the long and winding road travelled by victims over the past 10 years in the search for truth and justice, despite legal innovations and special *dispositifs* introduced in the criminal trial, 'dignity' is still at stake and the irreparable has not been repaired.

Acknowledgements

I would like to thank Laura Centemeri, Sezin Topçu and J. Peter Burgess for their comments and very useful suggestions that allowed me to improve this text. I am also thankful to all the participants in the international workshop Repairing Environments: Post-Disaster Mobilisations, Experiences and Tensions (28 September 2018, ENS Campus Jourdan, Paris) for the rich discussion we had. Thanks to Caitlin Gordon-Walter for her great job in editing the English version of the text.

Notes

1 For a review of the social sciences literature on the 'disaster management cycle' and the circular conception of disaster, see Coetzee and Van Niekerk (2012). For an analysis of

the 'circular' reading of disasters in disaster studies, see Revet (2020). Regarding the use of this circular framing in the humanitarian sphere, see Wörlein (2017).

2 *Dispositifs* are conceived here as 'a prepared concatenation of sequences, intended to qualify or transform a state of affairs through the medium of an assemblage of material or language elements' (Dodier and Barbot 2016: 301).

3 Interviews used in this chapter with members of the tribunal were anonymized.

4 This monitoring work was carried out by Myriam Tazi and Dorian Ryser from the documentation department of CERI-Sciences Po between 12 September 2014 and 26 February 2015, and processed on a dedicated website by Jean-Pierre Masse and Grégory Calès from CERI-Sciences Po as well.

5 Of the 29 victims of La Faute-sur-Mer, 16 were more than 70 years old and 3 were children (13, 5 and 3 years old).

6 In France, the judicial organization confers on criminal courts the competence to judge persons accused of having committed a criminal offence. Only criminal courts can impose fines and/or imprisonment. The civil courts have jurisdiction to settle disputes between private persons. When a private person causes harm to another person as a result of a criminal offence, reparation takes the form of restoration, where possible, or the award of compensation for damages. This reparation is in principle pronounced by a civil court, but it is possible for the victim of a criminal offence to ask the criminal court to rule on their civil interests: in this case, the criminal judge, once the criminal sanction has been pronounced, acts as a civil judge to rule on the civil interests of the victim or victims. This possibility explains the notion of 'plaintiff' (*partie civile*): it is the name given to the victim of a criminal offence who has brought a claim for civil compensation before the criminal court.

7 Fifty plaintiffs (victims and families of victims). Not all victims are plaintiffs. Some choose not to pursue legal action, and others are not considered by the mechanism. The condition to be a plaintiff is either to have been present on the night of the storm or to be able to prove a family relationship with a person who died that night. The mere existence of psychological disorders after the disaster, without the person having been present that night, is referred to the civil court for compensation issues.

8 Following the disaster, in the course of 2010 some of the victims regrouped and formed the Association des Victimes de la Faute-sur-Mer (AVIF): <www.asso-avif.com/>. The AVIF acted as a civil party during the trial.

9 Extract of the appeal judgement, 12 December 2015.

10 The press described the march by employing terms such as 'procession' or 'cortege'. Some of the judicial chroniclers, most attentive to the 'compassionate excesses' of the trial, referred, for instance, to an atmosphere that is at the same time 'a remembrance ceremony, a funeral procession, an institutional tribute, but also, for the five accused [. . .], a public expiation march'. See, *e.g.*, Robert-Diard, P. (2014) 'Au procès Xynthia, la nuit de chaos soudain si concrète', *Le Monde*, 27 September.

11 During the trial, reference was always made to 'transportation from the court to the scene'. The official translation of Article 456 of the Penal Code refers to 'inspection of premises': 'The court, either on its own motion, or upon the application of the public prosecutor, of the civil party or of the defendant, may order any inspection of premises where this is helpful for the discovery of the truth. The parties and their advocates are called upon to attend. An official record is made of such operations'. The official translation of the code of criminal procedure is available at: <www.legifrance.gouv.fr/ Traductions/en-English/Legifrance-translations > (accessed on September 4, 2019).

12 Interview with a member of the court, 1 April 2015.

13 *Ibid.*

14 *Ibid.*

15 'Pour que *ça* parle à tout le monde'. Interview with a member of the tribunal, 1 April 2015, emphasis added.

16 Interview with a member of the court, 1 April 2015.

17 Durand-Souffland, S. (2014); 'Xynthia: Douloureux retour sur les lieux du drame. Douloureux retour à la Faute-sur-Mer', 2014, *L'Est Républicain*, 26 September; 'Retour douloureux sur les lieux du drame', 2014, *Presse Océan*, 26 September; 'Douloureux retour à la Faute-sur-Mer', 2014, *Le Progrès*, Lyon, 26 September.
18 I translate; the exact terms in French were '*une sorte de punition infamante*' and '*faire une réparation publique en justice*'.
19 Hearing report, Fédération Nationale des Victimes d'Attentat et d'Accidents Collectifs (FENVAC), 29 September 2014.
20 On the frequent use of excuses in courtrooms, see Israël (1999).
21 'Procès Xynthia. Les réactions à la demande de pardon de René Marratier', 2014, *Ouest France*, 29 September.
22 In French, the phrase pronounced by the ex-mayor was '*je veux bien vous demander pardon*'. In French '*je veux*' expresses a strong will, whereas '*je veux bien*' introduces a nuance or sometimes even means that one is, in a certain way, forced to accept something.
23 <www.lafautesurmer.net/>.
24 '*Les élans du cœur ne se manifestent pas en service commandé. Ils sont spontanés, immédiats.*' Pleading, Maître G., 13 October 2014.
25 'Flash Journal', *TV Vendée*, 30 September 2014.
26 <http://nantes.cour-administrative-appel.fr/Actualites-de-la-Cour/Actualites-jurisprudentielles/Tempete-Xynthia>.
27 <www.lafautesurmer.net/2020/03/04/ceremonie-de-commemoration-discours-dimanche-1-mars-2020/>.

References

Aldrich, D.P. (2012) *Building Resilience: Social Capital in Post-disaster Recovery*, Chicago: University of Chicago Press.
Barrios, R.E. (2017) *Governing Affect: Neoliberalism and Disaster Recovery*, Lincoln: University of Nebraska Press.
Benadusi, M. and Revet, S. (2016) 'Disaster Trials: A Step Forward', Introduction, special issue *Archivio Antropologico Mediterraneo*, 18(2): anno XIX, 7–16.
Binder, D. (2016) 'The Increasing Application of Criminal Law to Disasters and Tragedies', *Natural Resources & Environment*, 30(3): 1–4.
Chamlee-Wright, E. and Storr, V.H. (2011) 'Social Capital as Collective Narratives and Post-disaster Community Recovery', *The Sociological Review*, 59(2): 266–282.
Coetzee, C. and Van Niekerk, D. (2012) 'Tracking the Evolution of the Disaster Management Cycle: A General System Theory Approach', *Jàmbá: Journal of Disaster Risk Studies*, art. #54, 4(1).
Davis, I. and Alexander, D. (2015) *Recovery from Disaster*, New York and London: Routledge.
Davis, T. (2007) *Stages of Emergency: Cold War Nuclear Civil Defense*, Durham, NC: Duke University Press.
Diderot, D. (1778) *Encyclopédie, ou dictionnaire raisonné des sciences, des arts et des métiers*. <http://gallica.bnf.fr/ark:/12148/bpt6k50533b/f414.item>.
Dodier, N. (1995) *Les hommes et les machines: la conscience collective dans les sociétés technicisées*, Paris: Editions Métailié.
Dodier, N. and Barbot, J. (2016) 'The Force of *Dispositifs*', *Annales. Histoire, Sciences Sociales*, 71(2): 421–448. <www.cairn-int.info/article-E_ANNA_712_0421-the-force-of-dispositifs.htm>.

Durand-Souffland, S. (2014) 'Affaire Xynthia: Retour douloureux à La Faute-sur-Mer', *Le Figaro*, 25 September (online).

Elie, M., Keck, F. and Revet, S. (2014) 'Participating in a Fake Catastrophe: Critique and Engagement in Simulations of Natural Disasters', <hal-01343120>.

Faas, A.J. and Barrios, R.E. (2015) 'Applied Anthropology of Risk, Hazards, and Disasters', *Human Organization*, 74(4): 287–295.

Falconieri, I. (2016) 'Foreseeable Yet Unforeseen Events': Ethnography of a Trial for Unpremeditated Disaster', *Archivio Antropologico Mediterraneo*, 18(2), anno XIX, 83–96.

Fortun, K. (2001) *Advocacy after Bhopal: Environmentalism, Disaster, New Global Orders*, Chicago: University of Chicago Press.

Hastrup, F. (2011) *Weathering the World: Recovery in the Wake of the Tsunami in a Tamil Fishing Village*, New York: Berghahn Books.

Israël, L. (1999) 'La mise en scène d'une justice quotidienne', *Droit et Société*, 42/43: 393–419.

Moeglin, J.-M. (1997) 'Pénitence publique et amende honorable au Moyen Age,' *Revue Historique*, 3(604): 225–226.

Oliver-Smith, A. (1986) *The Martyred City: Death and Rebirth in the Andes*, Albuquerque, NM: University of New Mexico Press.

Quenault, B. (2015) 'De Hyōgo à Sendai, la résilience comme impératif d'adaptation aux risques de catastrophe: Nouvelle valeur universelle ou gouvernement par la catastrophe?', *Développement durable et territoires*, 6(3). <http://journals.openedition.org/developpementdurable/11010>.

Revet, S. (2013) '"A Small World": Ethnography of a Natural Disaster Simulation in Lima, Peru', *Social Anthropology/Anthropologie Sociale*, 21(1): 38–53.

Revet, S. (2019) 'Témoigner au procès de la catastrophe Xynthia. Dimensions juridiques et morales de la parole des victimes', *Droit et société*, 2(102): 261–279.

Revet, S. (2020) *Disasterland: An Ethnography of the International Disaster Community*, London: Palgrave Macmillan.

Weisenfeld, G. (2012) *Imaging Disaster: Tokyo and the Visual Culture of Japan's Great Earthquake of 1923*, Berkeley, CA: University of California Press.

Wörlein, J. (2017) *Gouverner l'humanitaire. Une sociologie politique du monde des acteurs de l'aide en Haïti (2010–2016)*, Doctoral dissertation, Université Paris Ouest Nanterre.

Zenobi, D. (2014) *Familia, política y emociones. Las víctimas de Cromañón entre el movimiento y el Estado*, Antropofagia.

Zhuang, J. (2014) 'Remembering and Reenacting Hunger: Caochangdi Workstation's Minjian Memory Project', *The Drama Review*, 58(1): 118–140.

10 Victims and the ecologies of reparation *dispositifs* in the contaminated growth hormone case

Comparative perspectives on recovery after a health disaster

Janine Barbot and Nicolas Dodier

Translation (from French to English): Nathalie Plouchard-Engel
Trials are an important avenue for people who, considering themselves victims of a disaster, seek redress for what happened. Far from being unequivocal, legal remedy is often viewed by victims as a tangle of criminal, civil and administrative proceedings. What do disaster victims rely on to navigate this complex and specialized world? How do they formulate, by themselves, what allows them to identify, distinguish and assess these various types of proceedings and to weigh them against nonjudicial modes of repairing (medical, psychological, involving support groups, the media, or based on extrajudicial compensation)? In this chapter, we will show how the choice of legal proceedings takes on its full meaning in the context of all the *dispositifs* of reparation mobilized or likely to be mobilized to deal with a disaster consequences.[1] Like Laura Centemeri *et al.* (Introduction), we are interested in the way people envision and enact recovery after a disaster. Indeed, we believe that understanding this process of meaning-making will shed light on the constraints and possibilities disaster victims are faced with when navigating the judicial world. Three main forms of repairing (accusatory, functional and based on care) are distinguished in the introduction of this book. Though the *accusatory* dimension of redress is central to legal proceedings, we need to understand how people also accommodate other forms of repairing (functional and based on care), in order to grasp as a whole the normative work that they carry out around these proceedings. To do so, we will use a two-step comparative approach. First, we will examine the repairing strategies used by the victims of a specific disaster in a given country. We will thus show how differences and conflicts arise between these victims within the same *ecology of dispositifs*. This notion allows us to grasp as a whole the configuration formed by the range of devices that people can mobilize, at a given time, in order to seek reparation as part of recovery from a disaster. It emphasizes that the position on a specific type of legal remedy cannot be dissociated from the work victims jointly carry out around other dispositifs of reparation. The notion of ecology of dispositifs can thus be understood as the realities that fall within the authority of each dispositif, as well as the relations established between these dispositifs. Second, we will compare the national trajectories of redress of the same disaster across various countries. We will thus highlight the respective effects of different ecologies of dispositifs.

DOI: 10.4324/9781003184782-14

This comparative approach centers on a public health disaster that affected several countries, including France, the United Kingdom and the United States: the contaminated growth hormone disaster. In France, this disaster was at the heart of two debates. First, it is one of those 1990s public health scandals that, along with the tainted blood scandal (Feldman 2000; Fillion 2009), 'mad cow' disease (Torny 1998; Barbier 2003) and the asbestos scandal (Henry 2007; Pillayre 2017), drew the attention of a certain number of actors to the need to change the way in which health risks were dealt with. In the intellectual field, it was identified as one of the scandals that epitomized the new role granted to victims and their spokespersons in society and, more specifically, in legal institutions – a new role seen as a sign of progress by some and as a symptom of social regression by others (Dodier and Barbot 2020a).

Our study of the contaminated growth hormone tragedy in France is based on an analysis of *conflicts over reparation* (*conflits en réparation*), that is, instances of disagreement between victims of a disaster over the ways in which one can compensate for what happened. As a result of such conflicts, victims clarify what they are particularly attached to in a specific type of legal strategy. These explanations allow us to recreate their experience of various types of proceedings, how processes of judicial redress end up both bringing them together and dividing them, and how these legal strategies become part of the *ecology of dispositifs of reparation* that these victims are faced with. Several researchers have sought to distinguish the major branches of law by comparing their underlying principles or functions (Durkheim 1893; 1912; Fauconnet 1920; Ewald 1986). But they have provided little information on how non-specialists, in particular victims, compare the various proceedings they are faced with. Other studies have sought to identify the general characteristics of ordinary people's experience of law when they are involved in legal proceedings by studying the place of law in the transformation of disputes (Felstiner *et al.* 1980) or the foundations of legal consciousness (Merry 1990; Ewick and Silbey 1998; Silbey 2005). But they have rarely focused on the respective places given to the various branches of law by individuals and tried to situate them within the range of possible remedies. After examining the normative bases that brought together and divided the victims of a specific disaster in France, we will change scales and highlight the first elements of a comparison of the trajectories of reparation, concerning the same disaster, in three countries particularly affected by it: France, the United Kingdom and the United States.

Victims' normative work

Our case studied is a public health disaster: the iatrogenic contamination of children treated with extracted growth hormone in France. The treatment was intended for children suffering from growth disorders. Until the mid-1980s, it was made from human products (pituitary glands extracted from human cadavers in hospital morgues). These products are the source of transmission of the prion – the infectious agent responsible for Creutzfeldt-Jakob disease (CJD), a rare and fatal neurodegenerative disease. The first cases of iatrogenic CJD occurred in France in

1988. As CJD has a very long incubation period, the latest death was reported in 2021, more than 30 years after the production of human growth hormone (hGH) was suspended.[2] To date, out of roughly 1,000 children treated in the early 1980s, 123 have died.[3]

The tragedy was at the heart of various extrajudicial and judicial proceedings. Early on, after the first CJD cases were reported, civil lawsuits were filed, separately and without success. A preliminary investigation was opened in 1991, after the parents of L., who died of CJD at the age of 15, lodged a criminal complaint. Founded before the contamination occurred, the Association of Parents of children treated with growth hormone was then reluctant to take legal action, whether civil or criminal, hoping that the case would not be publicized and calling for the creation of a victim compensation fund. The Minister of Health and Humanitarian Action, Bernard Kouchner, referred the case to the General Inspectorate of Social Affairs, which issued a report in December 1992, pointing out many 'dysfunctions' within the institutions involved in the various stages of hGH production. In July 1993, this report was used, in the preliminary investigation, to indict (*mettre en examen*) Prof. J. (paediatrician at the Saint-Vincent-de-Paul hospital in Paris and president of the France-Hypophyse association, which was in charge of coordinating the collection of pituitary glands and the distribution of the treatment) and Dr. D. (researcher and former hGH production supervisor at the Pasteur Institute) for manslaughter. In October 1993, after these first indictments, a dispositif of extrajudicial compensation was set up to indemnify CJD victims and their relatives, without their needing to prove any fault on the part of the actors responsible for the production of the treatment. Many families were compensated by this dispositif before taking part in the criminal proceedings. Two victim support groups were formed in the mid-1990s. In a highly conflictual relationship with the existing Association of Parents of children treated with growth hormone, they advocated a strong involvement in these proceedings. In 2008, 17 years after the opening of the preliminary investigation, the initial growth hormone criminal trial was held at the Palais de Justice in Paris. Meanwhile, in the early 2000s, two high-profile civil trials took place, in Montpellier and later in Alès, after deceased CJD victims' relatives, who refused the extrajudicial compensation scheme, filed lawsuits. These civil trials elicited strong reactions from other victims' relatives, individually or through their collectives. They resulted in the conviction of the organizations responsible for producing the treatment, while the criminal trial resulted in the acquittal of all the defendants. This acquittal was upheld on appeal in 2011. In 2014, the Court of Cassation confirmed the conclusion of the criminal proceedings (and the defendants' acquittal).

To analyze these *conflicts over reparation*, we combined several methods of inquiry. We conducted 40 interviews, from 2001 to 2003, with people directly affected by the tragedy. The families involved mentioned the tensions between civil and criminal law. We gathered information on, and from, three support groups: the Association of Parents of children treated with growth hormone, which was founded in 1979 – before the contaminations – in order to promote the distribution of the treatment, to connect families of treated children, and to organize mutual aid; and two victim support groups founded, in 1996 and in 1999, in response to the contaminations (the Association of Parents of Children Victims of CJD (MCJ-APEV),[4] later renamed Contaminated Growth Hormone (MCJ-HCC),[5] and the Association of Growth Hormone Victims, or AVHC).[6] Drawing on this study, we analyzed the normative bases on which victims' legal strategies and conflicts over redress regarding the choice of civil or criminal proceedings relied.[7] We use the term 'victims' to refer to the relatives of children who died of Creutzfeldt-Jakob disease. Sometimes, these relatives speak as people affected by the disaster; at other times, they speak as spokespersons for the victims (their late children). In these conflicts, the victims' families defended various views on how legal proceedings (civil or criminal) could contribute to the aim of redress and be combined with other available dispositifs of reparation (the extrajudicial compensation fund, support groups' mutual aid dispositifs or the media). When discussing these conflicts, victims assessed the benefits, problems and risks associated with each of type of proceeding, as well as other victims' reactions to these proceedings.[8] They tried to explain, defend or stabilize what Ann Swidler (1986) calls a 'strategy of action', that is, a set of goals, values and tools, which, combined with one another, appear, at a given moment, as a whole likely to organize practices. We identified two questions causing disagreement amongst victims over their chosen type of legal proceedings. First, how should people affected by the tragedy manifest an *appropriate attitude toward money*? Second, how should the *targets of the legal action* be conceived? With regard to these questions, the families affected by the disaster interpreted the purposes, constraints and opportunities associated with each type of legal proceedings in different ways.[9]

Victims distancing themselves from money matters

All the families we met presented their involvement in legal proceedings as a fight for truth and justice, which required them to distance themselves from money matters. However, they did so in contrasting ways and developed various strategies to 'moralize' receiving money.[10] They did not disagree on whether they should accept or refuse compensation. Most families were indeed indemnified, either by the extrajudicial fund or through civil or criminal courts. Conflicts over redress were about the benefits of the various dispositifs available and, more specifically, their respective abilities to *present the victims as having no financial interest*. The question was posed as a choice: should the victims be compensated by the extrajudicial fund and take part in the criminal proceedings, or should they take civil action without using the extrajudicial fund?

Some victims thus considered the criminal trial detached from the compensatory logic: a place where their expectations could be seen as genuine expectations of justice, devoid of any financial interest. Mrs. T. told us: 'We don't take part in the criminal trial for the money', but 'simply for the truth'. In contrast, these victims viewed the civil trial as exclusively dedicated to compensation claims: a legal remedy that does not really punish the persons at fault, even though it acknowledges the victims and compensates them, and an option best suited for the families more interested in money than justice. Taking part in the criminal proceedings to 'let the truth simply come out', Mr. S. considered the civil proceedings 'revolting', as they made the legal action undertaken by growth hormone victims seem 'all about the big bucks', both to him and to the public. When filing a civil claim as part of the criminal trial (*se porter partie civile*), the families that had been indemnified by the fund asked for additional compensation. But they considered this the result of a legal battle fought by their lawyers (to contest the small sums allocated by the compensation fund to the victims) rather than a central request on their part.[11] Thus, the president of a victim support group both criticized the primacy of the financial issue in the civil proceedings and warned that the compensatory logic might intrude too much into the criminal proceedings.

For their part, the families that had filed civil lawsuits also wanted to assert their lack of financial interest. Mrs. D., whose civil trial, held in Montpellier, was highly publicized, explained to us that compensation was not at the heart of her legal strategy: 'We filed a civil lawsuit, okay. But it's not about the money, you know.' She was outraged by the lack of understanding and the accusations leveled against her by the families involved in the criminal proceedings and especially by their 'Parisian' lawyers, who she suspected of criticizing 'her' proceedings to keep a stranglehold on the case. She said that, ultimately, the criminal trial was initiated only by parents who had agreed to be indemnified by the extrajudicial compensation fund, regardless of anyone being found guilty. She explained that she refused to be 'amicably' compensated for the death of her daughter and preferred to make those who she deemed responsible for the tragedy 'pay' for their wrongdoings by getting the justice system to convict them. Opting for civil proceedings thus allowed her to avoid compromising herself by accepting the extrajudicial dispositif. Mrs. C., who also filed a civil lawsuit, said that the legal services of one of the implicated institutions, as well as the leader of a victim support group, tried to convince her to turn to the extrajudicial compensation fund:

> Even the support group likes to settle things amicably. But I didn't want to. I said: 'That's it, that's it! I started off like this, and I'll keep going like this. I'm not in for the money. I'm not in for the money.'

The victims as targets of the legal action

The issue of the *scope of the targets of the legal action* was also at the heart of the conflicts over reparation. Some people wanted to take part in proceedings that would 'collectivize' the victims, while others wanted to 'individualize' them.

Many families valued the *collective construction of the victims* in the criminal trial. This process relied on the characteristics of criminal proceedings: the investigating magistrate had decided to examine the cases of all CJD victims, thereby allowing all the families affected by the tragedy, as well as the support groups defending their collective interests, to file civil claims as part of the criminal trial. The families highlighted various elements that made this collective construction of the victims appealing to them. First of all, some considered that the moral truth the legal action was meant to reveal could only be conceived of at a certain level of totalization. It was not merely the truth about each case, with its particular sufferings and circumstances, but the truth about a collective tragedy as a whole. For certain families, the disaster – as well as the tainted blood scandal – even had to be viewed in the broader context of the health care scandals of that time, while its political significance in the history of public health and medicine had to be taken into account. This collectivization of the victims echoed the trajectory of the first families that formed a support group, after progressively 'realizing', in their own words, the similarity of their experiences and the existence of a 'problem' with the production of the treatment. In addition, some families felt that the collective construction of the victims also met the requirements of the legal battle: they would be stronger and would have more chances to win the fight if they came in large numbers and acted in concert – especially as some lawyers urged them to file several complaints, so that winning the case would be, in their words, 'doable'. This fostered a solidarity amongst the families, which took the form of both a beneficial feeling (feeling united in a legal battle fought together) and an incentive (conforming to a legal strategy defined collectively in order to strengthen it). For some families, the collective construction of the victims in the criminal trial was an extension of the close bonds formed with the victim advocacy groups that had helped them when their children were ill. Some expressed this idea in terms of debt: since they felt morally attached to the victim advocacy groups, they wanted to reciprocate the support they had received from them by joining the collective action in the criminal proceedings. Others expressed this idea in terms of trust: they felt that the support groups were able to transform their distress into legal action, and they delegated the choice of the type of proceedings to the support group leaders, assuming that 'their' support group would be the most capable of handling the legal tools as well as the relations with the lawyers. Taking part in the proceedings with (or behind) others, these families appreciated being able to manage their exposure in the criminal trial and in the public sphere. Whether their involvement was a matter of debt or trust, the will to collectively target the victims in the criminal proceedings must be viewed, in this case, as the families' will to rely on the support groups they already felt attached to.

On the contrary, by filing civil lawsuits, some families demonstrated a strong need for individualization, or *re-individualization*, of the victims. While the criminal trial brought together a growing number of victims' relatives, other families sought a legal procedure in which each of them could actually play a central part. From their point of view, as each civil trial revolved around a specific case, civil proceedings constituted a way of re-individualizing legal action, both by exploring the circumstances of the events and by lending presence to their late children in the hearings. Mrs. D. thus claimed that she felt the need to take legal action 'in her own name'. She wanted a trial in which she could be a key player and in which her deceased daughter would take centre stage. She wanted a trial both emotionally and geographically close to 'her' tragedy, so it was held in Montpellier, where her daughter had lived, rather than at the Palais de Justice in Paris, where the criminal trial took place. According to her, in the criminal proceedings, her daughter could be merely one victim amongst others. Associations' leaders would speak on behalf of the victims and their relatives, leaving Mrs. D. little opportunity to make her voice heard, to tell her own story. This is what Mrs. D. said about the legal action that she wanted to dedicate to her daughter:

> "It's P.'s [first letter of the child's name] trial. It's not the trial of all the kids [. . .]. We chose a civil trial, because we wanted it to be done in P.'s name. Whereas the criminal trial would be something we do as a group [. . .]. Because we had promised P. this would be acknowledged. The Pasteur Institute was found liable for P.'s death [. . .]."

The civil court was considered the option that would make it possible to establish liability in a specific victim's case. According to Mrs. D., each family had the right to expect its misfortune to be dealt with individually. The collectivization of the victims in the criminal proceedings was perceived as a problematic source of abstraction, whereby each victim's individuality would vanish in the crowd, in a way.

The individualization of the tragedy through civil trials elicited various reactions from the families involved in the criminal trial. Some were particularly critical, deeming this legal strategy 'individualistic' or describing it as 'selfish'. Mrs. D. was reproached for jeopardizing the collective construction of the victims in the criminal trial – a collectivization that could allow the victims to assert a moral truth befitting a collective tragedy, join forces in the legal battle and perpetuate the bonds formed with beneficent support groups. The individualization of the victims was considered to scatter forces, diminish the general impact of the trial and challenge the solidarity amongst the families, which had been strengthened by their involvement in common legal proceedings. The leader of a victim support group, strongly involved in the criminal trial, even viewed this individualization of the victims as a form of betrayal on the part of families that, at some point or another, had benefited from the help provided by the support group. In the other support group, parents were less critical and more inclined to accept the plurality of legal journeys. This pluralism was defended in two different ways. Some considered that 'coping with' the loss of a child was extremely difficult in itself and that one should 'not judge' the families' choices with respect to redress. They believed that these choices were a 'matter of sensitivity' and depended on personal capabilities, 'character', 'education' or prior involvement in collectives. Everyone would find peace in their own way: by rejecting any type of proceedings, or by taking part in criminal or civil proceedings. Not judging how families 'coped' thus seemed to be a requirement *per se*. The plurality of legal actions could also be assessed with respect to its possible contribution to the efficiency of the legal battle. Far from being contrary to the interests of the criminal trial, the civil lawsuits filed by families seeking re-individualization could help denounce the slowness of the criminal preliminary investigation. The civil trials consolidated the new legal battle that the MCJ-APEV was initiating at the turn of the 2000s, as it was submitting an application to the European Court of Human Rights, alleging the excessive delays of criminal justice.

The persons at fault as targets of the legal action

As with the targeting of the victims, people affected by the tragedy adopted various stances on the relative benefits of individualizing or, on the contrary, of collectivizing the entities taken to court. The families involved in the criminal trial highlighted the *need for individualizing the persons at fault*. The interpersonal confrontation, the 'face-to-face' situation between persons responsible and victims, was highly valued. Some people thus expressed their will to confront such and such accused person, both to 'tell them' what they thought of the case, and to 'hear them' justify their personal actions, acknowledge their wrongdoings, or show remorse. Mrs. H. mentioned that the hearing of the upcoming criminal trial would allow her to speak in front of the defendants: 'I'd like to say some things to their faces'. According to the leader of one of the victim support groups, it would also allow the persons who he deemed responsible for the tragedy to finally express their regrets to the families:

> None of them has ever shown the slightest interest in apologizing. None of them has ever said: 'We fucked up.' Sorry about that [the F-word]. [. . .] They've never felt ashamed. . . . They've never said a single word [. . .]. That's what's unbearable to us.

But this individualization of responsibility was also considered a limit of the criminal trial by the families that, although involved in the criminal proceedings, expressed the *need for collectivizing responsibility*, in order to incriminate 'organizations' or 'systems'. Thus, some parents viewed the individualization of the defendants as a drawback that needed to be overcome, insofar as the criminal trial would likely 'restrict' and 'belittle' the targets. As Mr. O. said: 'That's what's so hard: we went after global institutions, but, actually, we've targeted only a few people'. For many families, the fact that these individuals were 'at the head of' organizations, and could therefore, as targets, embody these collective entities, made it possible to combine the need for individualizing responsibility and that for collectivizing it. The president of one of the victim support groups thus expressed how the 'individuals' implicated in the criminal trial, owing to their social profiles or their functions, represented the collective entities targeted by the criminal proceedings, while being personally held liable. From her viewpoint, in the proceedings, Prof. J. or Prof. D stood for 'France-Hypophyse' or the 'Institut Pasteur' – and even all 'mandarins', a certain 'medical body' whose behaviours she considered deviant. As a result, although sometimes seen as a limit, the individualization of the persons at fault in the criminal trial did not prevent victims' relatives from considering that these persons could also represent collectives.

By filing civil lawsuits, parents wanted, first and foremost, to hold the organizations liable. They defended their decision to start civil action by emphasizing that the Montpellier trial succeeded in holding liable a 'large' entity such as the Institut Pasteur. In keeping with a common figure of social and political critique, Mrs. D., who initiated the proceedings, saw this success as a victory of the 'small ones' against the 'big ones', who would otherwise be safe from any criticism. Ms. D. emphasized that the Institut Pasteur was not 'just anyone' but a 'big name':

> The problem is they [those who criticized the civil trial] didn't understand anything. Above all, we wanted [. . .] everyone to be aware the Institut Pasteur did this. Yes, it's a big name. But even when you're a big name, when you make a deadly mistake, everyone has to right to know about it [. . .]. We are small, but, for the Institut Pasteur, we went big.

Based on an inquiry carried out amongst the victims of a specific disaster, we thus analyzed the normative bases that structured the conflicts amongst these victims over the legal strategies to follow. Two issues were central here: *presenting the victims as having an appropriate attitude toward money, defining the targets of the legal action* (individually or collectively) regarding both the victims and the entities held responsible for the tragedy. These concerns are not specific to the growth hormone scandal; they can also be found in other disasters. Many studies have thus focused on the collective construction of victims (Barthe 2017; Centemeri 2011; Fillion and Torny 2015; Latté 2008; 2012). Fewer have also mentioned victims' efforts to individualize, or re-individualize, the targets of legal action (Jobin 2006). Several studies have highlighted the necessary work that victims carry out to create an appropriate attitude toward financial compensation (Centemeri 2011; Henry 2003; Schuck 1986; Chapter 1). We argue that these issues often arise *jointly* for victims, and the development of legal strategies consists in combining them. Our approach also emphasizes the magnitude of the contrasts and conflicts bringing victims of a specific disaster into opposition, when they try to assess the relative benefits of the various dispositifs that they can mobilize to seek reparation. Conflicts over redress thus seem to both bring victims together and differentiate them.

National trajectories of reparation

The comparison of the modes of reparation of the same disaster across various countries is all the more complex as there are numerous possible lines of inquiry. This is clear from the comparison made by Eric Feldman (2000) between the reparation processes of the tainted blood scandal in the United States, Japan and France. He challenges the usual assumptions about the quasi-deterministic effects of the legal system and culture specific to each country. Indeed, one would expect that, in the United States, where legal remedy is supposedly more readily used and the chances of being compensated are supposedly greater for victims, legal proceedings would be more promptly initiated and more successful than in the other two countries. One would also expect that Japan, where legal remedy is supposedly less readily used when people are faced with misfortune, would offer a limited number of legal strategies. France would thus lie somewhere in between. However, Feldman's study invalidates these assumptions: in the case of tainted blood scandal, legal remedy is more readily used in Japan, and it is more common in France than in the United States. Feldman therefore examines a wide range of reasons that might explain this: national specificities regarding the methods of production of blood products, health authorities' reactions to warnings about the risk of HIV transmission through these products, characteristics of the political and legal contexts, and so on. He concludes that none of these specificities can explain, by itself, the differences in the reparation obtained by victims. He calls for other case studies that will help identify the possible consistencies in the handling of redress regarding scandals related to health products and/or conclude that AIDS is an exceptional case.

Feldman shows the value of questioning culturalist assumptions about legal systems and about the experience of law, and examining in depth the elements that influence the reparation of a disaster in different countries. His work on the circumstances that led to the HIV infections tragedy and on the subsequent reactions highlights an abundance of differentiating elements. Yet it does not result in an analytical framework that makes it possible to organize the comparisons in a controlled manner. We will suggest ways to do so, based on the comparison between the reparation of the growth hormone tragedy in France, in the United States and in the United Kingdom. We will again focus on the ecology of dispositifs of reparation, as it appears through the identification of *national trajectories of reparation*, that is, through the way in which victims were globally identified, considered and treated in these countries.[12] While the victims and their spokespersons made occasional references to what was happening in other countries to support their own strategies of redress, they did not develop transnational coordination, in particular because of the specificity of the ecology of dispositifs in each country. In this case, the comparison of national trajectories does therefore not require us to take into account the transnational dimension of reparation.[13]

In France, in the United States and in the United Kingdom, a national system for the collection of pituitary glands in hospital morgues and for the production and distribution of hGH had been implemented, prior to the contaminations, to alleviate growth disorders in children. In the United States, the National Institutes of Health (NIH) established the National Pituitary Agency (NPA) in 1963. In the United Kingdom, the Medical Research Council (MRC) organized its first clinical trials in 1959 and, in the mid-1970s, the Department of Health (DOH) initiated a national hGH distribution program. In France, France-Hypophyse, an association with similar missions, was founded in 1973. Soon after 1985, when the first British and American CJD cases were reported, the link between CJD and hGH treatment was established because of the atypical profile of the patients affected by the disease (their young age) and the rarity of the treatment. The distribution and prescription of hGH were finally halted in 1985 in the United States and in the United Kingdom. France, whose first CJD case was reported only in 1988, first implemented an additional procedure to inactivate the virus, before replacing hGH treatment with a synthetic growth hormone produced by the pharmaceutical industry, as in the other two countries. For lack of a screening test before the onset of the disease and because of a very long incubation period, the dynamics of the epidemic were delineated gradually. The first cases were reported in the United Kingdom and in the United States, yet over the years, France turned out to be the most affected country. These three countries have the highest number of cases in the world. In 2012, out of 226 cases throughout the world, 119 cases were reported in France, 65 cases in the United Kingdom, and 29 cases in the United States (Brown *et al.* 2012): the remaining 13 cases were recorded in Austria (1), Brazil (2), Ireland (1), Netherlands (2), New Zealand (6), Qatar (1). Before the definitive cessation of the distribution and prescription of hGH, approximately 7,700 patients had been treated in the United States, 1,800 in the United Kingdom and 1,700 in France. The United States is characterized by a small number of legal actions. The legal actions in the US proved unsuccessful for the plaintiffs (a fact that the media reported on discreetly) and resulted in a limited number of out-of-court settlements negotiated on a case-by-case basis, with non-disclosure agreements. In contrast, in France and in the United Kingdom, more legal actions were taken, and they were more publicized. However, significant differences emerged in the national trajectories of reparation in the two countries. We will focus on two major elements of differentiation.

In France and in the United Kingdom, the normative work carried out by the families affected by the tragedy was strongly influenced by the political response to their demand for the creation of an extrajudicial compensation scheme that would indemnify the victims without their needing to prove any fault on the part of the actors responsible for the production or distribution of the treatment. In the United Kingdom, as in France, when the first complaints were filed, families and support groups called on the authorities to act. But the response was quite different. The British authorities refused to implement such a dispositif. They offered several arguments to justify this refusal. First, they stated that it had to allocate available resources toward improving the health care system, rather than dispensing them to people whose misfortunes were not linked to a wrongdoing, but to the risks inherent in the therapies they had benefited from. Second, they asserted their wish not to interfere in legal proceedings already initiated and to leave them to the courts to prove a fault (or lack of thereof) and the methods of compensation of the victims. Lastly, they decided not to introduce a no-fault compensation scheme and, thereby, not to set a precedent, as otherwise any patient suffering from iatrogenic effects linked to other treatments could legitimately request to benefit from such a dispositif.

In contrast, in France, the government created a compensation fund, in the interest of national solidarity: all the families of iatrogenic CJD victims could apply to this fund for indemnification, without needing to initiate legal proceedings or proving a fault. This fund was modeled on the Compensation Fund for Transfused Patients and Hemophiliacs (FITH), set up two years prior as a result of the tainted blood scandal, which was considered an exceptional disaster. This extrajudicial dispositif had a strong impact on the victims' normative work and led most of them to both benefit from the fund and take part in the criminal proceedings. In the United Kingdom, the victims publicly criticized the government's refusal to create a similar dispositif, asserting that this refusal reflected a lack of compassion on the part of the British government. They used the example of France to back up their claims.

Another element of differentiation between the trajectories of reparation in the United Kingdom and in France stems from the nature of legal proceedings. In the United Kingdom, victims can use a civil law dispositif, called 'multi-party action', dedicated to redressing collective tragedies. When the growth hormone tragedy happened, the dispositif was not new. Specialized law firms had used the dispositif many times and were experienced in this technique. Since a similar collective dispositif did not exist in France, after the compensation fund was set up, CJD victim support groups took part in the criminal trial. This difference between French and British judicial dispositifs had important consequences on the emergence of collectives. In the United Kingdom, a multi-party action revolves around a few prototypical cases supposed to represent the variety of situations that victims of a tragedy are faced with. A trial called 'generic trial' then establishes liability (or lack thereof) and defines the conditions of compensation, which will thereafter apply to all persons claiming that their cases are similar. In France, in the criminal trial, collectives of victims formed very differently: they came together into support groups that sought to 'make up the numbers', foster mutual aid and represent victims as a whole. These differences between the French and the British judicial dispositifs had many implications for the way in which the victims seized and criticized them, as well as for the emergence of various victim statuses. This is the case, for instance, of people who, after receiving potentially contaminated treatment, stated that they lived in fear of developing CJD. In the United Kingdom, people suffering from 'post-traumatic stress' were included in the legal proceedings very early on. In France, so-called at-risk children could not benefit from the compensation fund, as it was dedicated to verified contaminations. Some took part in the criminal proceedings later on, with the help of a victim support group.

In the United Kingdom, the first generic trial was held in 1996. The court considered that the health authorities had committed negligence by failing to take into account the warning issued in 1977 about the possible contamination of the treatment. People who had died of iatrogenic CJD, as well as those suffering from post-traumatic stress linked to their exposure to a risk of contamination, were compensated by reason of negligence, provided that they had started their treatment after 1977. For the others, requests for the setting up of a no-fault compensation scheme were reiterated. As part of the generic trial, an appellate judgement extended the benefit of the compensation awarded, by reason of negligence, to people who had received most of their treatment after 1977. In France, the trajectory of redress was quite different: all the people affected by CJD could be compensated by the fund, and the initial criminal trial held in 2008 resulted in an acquittal (confirmed in 2014). Some 'at-risk' children were awarded compensation by a civil court in 2016, nearly 30 years after the first cases of infection occurred in France.

These three *national trajectories of reparation* were therefore strongly influenced by the ecology of dispositifs available and by the way in which actors used them. In the United States, redress was limited, as with the tainted blood scandal. In France and the United Kingdom, redress was more widespread, but with significant differences in the way in which victims were compensated, when they were indemnified and why they were awarded compensation.

Conclusion

Based on the analysis of conflicts over reparation around legal strategies of growth hormone victims in France, we have shown the importance of the ecology of dispositifs that victims are faced with. For victims, reparation means making complex assessments of both judicial dispositifs (civil or criminal) and dispositifs of reparation (in particular support group, compensatory, medical and media dispositifs) that are part of the local ecology of each disaster. We have questioned the influence of this ecology on processes of reparation. By comparing how the same disaster was dealt with in various countries, we have suggested the existence of contrasting national trajectories of reparation, each linked to a specific ecology of dispositifs. The ecology of dispositifs thus emerges as a key variable in the comparison of reparation processes in different countries. However, an ecology of dispositifs does not function mechanically, that is, independently of the normative work carried out by the actors. Examination of conflicts over reparation around the growth hormone tragedy in France has highlighted this. As we have seen, the various legal strategies adopted by the victims were based on intensive normative work, which caused division amongst the victims over two requirements: distancing themselves from money matters and targeting, through legal action, the persons at fault and the victims at the level that seemed more appropriate (collective or individual).

Though it plays an important role, the ecology of dispositifs of reparation is not the only aspect that should be taken into consideration to explain trajectories of recovery after disaster. This becomes clear when comparing how people face different disasters with similar ecologies of dispositifs. Take, for example, the contaminated growth hormone tragedy and the tainted blood scandal. Both involved similar ecologies of dispositifs, with, in each case, an existing patients' association, victim support groups formed following the disaster, a compensation fund set up by the government and civil as well as criminal proceedings (Barbot and Fillion 2007). However, while most families took part in the criminal proceedings of the growth hormone tragedy, far fewer did so in the case of the tainted blood scandal. Two elements in particular explain these variations. First, there were differences in the *degree of financial incommensurability of the harm*. This incommensurability was clearly perceived in the case of the growth hormone tragedy, as it involved parents whose children had died of a still incurable neurodegenerative disease (Barbot and Dodier 2015). In the case of the tainted blood scandal, the situations of the patients treated were more diverse, and experimentation with antiretroviral treatments quickly created the prospect of living with the disease, which implied that compensation could take on an entirely different meaning. In the case of the growth hormone tragedy, involvement in the criminal proceedings was one of the ways in which grieving families could re-moralize their acceptance of the compensation fund, as the money could be reinvested to fight for justice (in particular, to hire 'good lawyers').

The comparison also shows the importance of the *degree of the victims' dependence on the actors incriminated in the disaster*. In the tainted blood case, HIV-infected hemophiliacs remained extremely dependent on the small circle of hemophilia specialists who treated this chronic disease, many of who had prescribed the contaminated products (Fillion 2009). In contrast, in the growth hormone case, CJD was dealt with by means of home help and hospital palliative care, a world in which the physicians blamed for the contaminations – mostly paediatricians with whom the families had severed all contact since the cessation of the treatment – were little involved. This lesser dependence on the incriminated actors may have led the families affected by the growth hormone tragedy to take part in the criminal proceedings.

Using a method based on a *progressive controlled comparison* – first, comparing the situations of victims of a specific disaster in the same country; second, comparing the same disaster across different countries; and third, comparing different disasters in the same country – has helped us better understand disaster redress processes.[14] In our approach, the ecology of dispositifs was pivotal to the progressive comparison carried out. Indeed, it has allowed us to highlight a range of similarities and differences characteristic of such an approach. Relying on a central variable makes it possible to give direction to comparisons. This does not mean adopting a reductionist strategy. The other variables are not considered secondary, but their effects are brought out by a series of comparisons around the central variable.

For each variable thus identified, we can then consider broadening the comparison to include other disasters. Take, for example, the ecology of dispositifs. Based on the case of the growth hormone tragedy, we have shown how the overall ecology (civil and criminal trials + extrajudicial compensation) operated. Comparison allows us to deepen our understanding of the time structure of this ecology – that is, the order in which these various dispositifs were created or implemented. In the case of the growth hormone tragedy, extrajudicial compensation occurred shortly after legal proceedings were initiated and before the trials took place. This time structure was an essential element in the victims' receipt of extrajudicial compensation, since it fostered their suspicion or confusion about accepting money that might divert them from legal action and thus from their interest in seeing justice done. The victims may mobilize extrajudicial compensation quite differently in other time structures, as in the case of nuclear test veterans (Barthe 2017). The nuclear test victims' support group took legal action at a time when there was no compensation scheme. These legal proceedings proved relatively unsuccessful.[15] Faced with what it perceived as the 'failure of the system of reparation', the support group advocated extrajudicial compensation, which it saw as a means of redress that could be based on lower evidentiary standards. Compared to what happened in the case of the growth hormone tragedy, the compensation law enacted a few years later, well after the unsuccessful legal proceedings, was thus received quite differently – it did not involve any moral issues or any efforts to overcome them (in particular, through criminal action).

Comparisons can also focus on the other two variables whose effects on reparation we have observed: victims' degree of dependence on potential defendants, and the financial incommensurability of the harm. Such comparisons could thus provide a better understanding of the *processes of reparation when victims are dependent on potential defendants.* Beyond the cases examined in this chapter, many other studies have shown how victims tend to turn away from legal remedy when prosecution targets actors on whom victims remain dependent. Dependence on the employer has thus often been mentioned for its deterrent effects on trials (Gayet-Viaud 2012; Henry 2003; Pillayre 2017; Latté 2012; Jobin 2006). In some cases, ending the dependence clearly opened the way for legal remedy (Henry 2007). Research has also highlighted the conflicts between dependent and non-dependent victims of the same disaster, the latter being more likely to take legal action. In environmental disasters attributable to a company, conflicts have often arisen between the company's employees (who may be victims of the disaster as well) and the disaster victims outside the company (Jobin 2006; Latté 2012). In addition to these preliminary findings, a more in-depth comparison of the different cases should provide an overview of reparation in a situation of dependence: seeing justice done by means other than judicial? Turning to less accusatory forms of reparation (functional forms, care)?

A similar method could be used to analyze the processes of reparation in a situation of financial incommensurability. Numerous studies have documented denials of compensation on grounds of incommensurability (Zelizer 1979). In this chapter, we have highlighted another approach to incommensurability: some victims accept compensation and then actively take part in criminal proceedings, the compensation money being reinvested in legal action to overcome the moral issues it creates. Other studies have shown how processes of reparation that recognize this incommensurability are created. Jean-Michel Chaumont (1997) showed this in relation to what he calls 'remembrance uniqueness' (*singularité mémorielle*). Certain irreplaceable losses force people to remain in a situation of 'private remembrance uniqueness'. But as Chaumont pointed out, this does not mean that a third party cannot understand the extent of their loss, which is why it is possible to build communities of experience of a particular nature including victims and third parties, who recognize the uniqueness of the victims' experience. To meet the requirement of incommensurability, some victims invent as well new *dispositifs* of reparation. Laura Centemeri (2011) showed that certain victims of the Seveso disaster refused to accept compensation schemes (and legal remedy in general) and created forms of remembrance more in line with their sense of redress. Drawing on work with Inuit people affected by the *Exxon Valdez* disaster and French people affected by the *Amoco Cadiz* disaster, she also showed (Centemeri 2015) how practices eschewing financial compensation aim to maintain what she calls the 'dwelled-in environment' – that is, 'the environment we appropriate forging intimate bonds with human and non-human beings within it, thus creating a place in which interactions occur effortlessly'. To do so, these people establish particular forms of sharing and communication, amongst which empathy plays a crucial part. Thus, comparison makes it possible to broaden the range of possibilities for redressing financially incommensurable harm.

Notes

1 With the notion of dispositif we refer to an assemblage of material or language elements which prepare concatenation of sequences. With regard to repairing processes it might be, for example, judicial trials, extra-judicial compensation systems, media supports, associative help, psychological or medical tools, etc. The concept of dispositif enables thinking about it all together and being more precise than other usual ways: tools, settings, recourse, etc. Dispositif is often translated into English as 'device' but the notion is rather vague, except in the case of 'market device' in the field of economic sociology (see Velthuis 2020), or by words which refer to a Foucauldian approach ('apparatus', 'assemblage') which we have moved away from. This is why we preferred to use the word dispositif in English-language text. For further developments on the genealogy and our use of the notion of dispositif, see Dodier and Barbot (2020b).

2 For lack of a prion screening test, it is impossible to determine, before the onset of the first CJD symptoms, who, amongst the children treated, has been infected by contaminants and is still at risk of developing the disease.

3 <www.santepubliquefrance.fr/maladies-et-traumatismes/maladies-infectieuses-d-origine-alimentaire/maladie-de-creutzfeldt-jakob/donnees/#tabs> (last updated 31 July 2021; last accessed 18 August 2021).

4 Maladie de Creutzfeldt-Jakob – Association des Parents d'Enfants Victimes.

5 Maladie de Creutzfeldt-Jakob – Hormone de Croissance Contaminée.

6 Association des Victimes de l'Hormone de croissance Contaminée.

7 For developments on the study of the normative work of victims, see Barbot and Dodier (2020).

8 For a more extensive discussion of normative work at the crossroads of various dispositifs of redress, see Dodier and Barbot (2017).

9 This section draws on Barbot and Dodier (2017).

10 In the same vein, see Viviana Zelizer's book (1979) on the criticism leveled at life insurance and the ways in which people 'moralize' collecting life insurance.

11 According to the lawyers, the fund did not cover all the harm sustained by the victims and their relatives.

12 In particular, we rely on studies that deal with these disasters: the work of Andrea Boggio (2005), a professor of legal studies, and papers by David Body, the victims' lawyer for the British collective action (Body and Mitchell 2001; Body and Glasson 2005).

13 For opposite cases, see Sandrine Revet (2018) on the emergence of a transnational world built around natural disasters.

14 See also Diane Vaughan (1992) and what she refers to as 'theory elaboration' regarding the sociological explanation of disasters.

15 Out of 100 legal actions taken by veterans, only 10 cases were won.

References

Barbier, M. (2003) 'Une interprétation de la constitution de l'ESB comme problème public européen', *Revue internationale de politique comparée*, 10(2): 233–246.

Barbot, J. and Dodier, N. (2015) 'Victims' Normative Repertoire of Financial Compensation. The Tainted hGH Case', *Human Studies*, 38(1): 81–96.

Barbot, J. and Dodier, N. (2017) 'Se confronter à l'action judiciaire. Des victimes au carrefour des différentes branches du droit', *L'Homme*, 223–224: 99–129.

Barbot, J. and Dodier, N. (2020) 'The Normative Work of Victims of Medical Injuries', in M.-A. Jacob and A. Kirkland (eds) *Research Handbook on Socio-Legal Studies of Medicine and Health, Cheltenham-Northampton*, Cheltenham: Edward Elgar Publishing, 270–286.

Barbot, J. and Fillion, N. (2007) 'La dynamique des victimes. Les formes d'engagement associatif face aux contaminations iatrogènes (VIH et prion)', *Sociologie et Sociétés*, 39(1): 217–247.

Barthe, Y. (2017) *Les retombées du passé. Le paradoxe de la victime*, Paris: Seuil.

Body, D. and Glasson, J. (2005) 'Iatrogenic Creutzfeldt-Jakob Disease: Litigation in the UK and Elsewhere', *Clinical Risk*, January, 11(1): 4–13.

Body, D. and Mitchell, I. (2001) 'The Creutzfeldt-Jakob Disease (hGH) Litigation', in C. Hodges, *Multi-Party Actions*, Oxford: Oxford University Press.

Boggio, A. (2005) 'The Compensation of the Victims of the Creutzfeldt-Jakob Disease in the United Kingdom', *Medical Law International*, 7(2): 149–167.

Brown, P. and Brandel, J.-P. *et al.* (2012) 'Iatrogenic Creutzfeldt-Jakob Disease, Final Assessment', *Emerging Infectious Diseases*, 18(6): 901–907.

Centemeri, L. (2011) 'Retour à Seveso. La complexité morale et politique du dommage à l'environnement', *Annales. Histoire, Sciences Sociales*, 66(1): 213–240.

Centemeri, L. (2015) 'Reframing Problems of Incommensurability in Environmental Conflicts through Pragmatic Sociology. From Value Pluralism to the Plurality of Modes of Engagement with the Environment', *Environmental Values*, 24(3): 299–320.

Chaumont, J.-M. (1997) *La concurrence des victimes. Génocide, identité, reconnaissance*, Paris: La Découverte.

Dodier, N. and Barbot, J. (2017) 'The Force of Dispositifs', *Annales. Histoire et sciences sociales,* English edition, 71(2): 291–317.

Dodier, N. and Barbot, J. (2020a) 'Les raisons des victimes', in B. Cousin and M. Lamont (eds) *La morale des sociologues*, Paris: PUF, 25–44.

Dodier, N. and Barbot, J. (2020b) 'Dispositifs', in J. Bowen *et al.* (eds) *Pragmatic Inquiry: Critical Concepts for Social Sciences*, New York and London: Routledge, 55–67.

Durkheim, E. (2007; 1st edition 1893), *De la division du travail social*, Paris: PUF.

Durkheim, E. (1968; 1st edition 1912) *Les formes élémentaires de la vie religieuse: le système totémique en Australie*, Paris: PUF.

Ewald, F. (1986) *L'État-providence*, Paris: Grasset.

Ewick, P. and Silbey, S. (1998) *The Common Place of Law: Stories from Everyday Life*, Chicago: University of Chicago Press.

Fauconnet, P. (2010; 1st edition 1920) *La responsabilité: étude de sociologie*, Dijon: Éditions Universitaires de Dijon.

Feldman, E. (2000) 'Blood Justice: Courts, Conflict, and Compensation in Japan, France and the United States', *Law and Society*, 34(3): 651–701.

Felstiner, W., Abel, R. and Sarat, A. (1980) 'The Emergence and Transformation of Disputes', *Law and Society Review*, 41: 631–654.

Fillion, E. (2009) *À l'épreuve du sang contaminé. Pour une sociologie des affaires médicales*, Paris: Éditions de l'EHESS.

Fillion, E. and Torny, D. (2015) 'De la réparation individuelle à l'élaboration d'une cause collective. L'engagement judiciaire des victimes du distilbène', *Revue française de science politique*, 65(4): 583–607.

Gayet-Viaud, C. (2012) 'Itinéraires de victimes d'accidents du travail et de maladies professionnelles. Freins et entraves à la mobilisation des droits à la santé et à la réparation', in C. Courtet (ed.) *Risques du travail, la santé négociée*, Paris: La Découverte, 123–142.

Henry, E. (2003) 'Intéresser les tribunaux à sa cause. Contournement de la difficile judiciarisation du problème de l'amiante', *Sociétés contemporaines*, 52: 39–59.

Henry, E. (2007) *Amiante, un scandale improbable. Sociologie d'un problème public*, Rennes: Presses Universitaires de Rennes.

Jobin, P. (2006) *Maladies industrielles et renouveau syndical au Japon*, Paris: Éditions de l'EHESS.

Latté, S. (2008) *Les 'victimes'. La formation d'une catégorie sociale improbable et ses usages dans l'action collective*, PhD thesis in Social Sciences, Paris, EHESS.

Latté, S. (2012) 'La "force de l'événement" est-elle un artefact? Les mobilisations de victimes au prisme des théories événementielles de l'action collective', *Revue française de science politique*, 62(3): 409–432.

Merry, S.E. (1990) *Getting Justice and Getting Even: Legal Consciousness among Working-Class Americans*, Chicago: University of Chicago Press.

Pillayre, H. (2017) *Justice et justesse de l'indemnisation. Acteurs et dispositifs de l'État providence à l'épreuve du scandale de l'amiante*, PhD thesis in Sociology, Paris, EHESS.

Revet, S. (2018) *Les coulisses du monde des catastrophes 'naturelles'*, Paris: Éditions de la Maison des Sciences de l'Homme.

Schuck, P. (1986) *Agent Orange on Trial: Mass Toxic Disasters in the Courts*, Cambridge, MA: The Belknap Press of Harvard University Press.

Silbey, S. (2005) 'After Legal Consciousness', *Annual Review of Law and Social Science*, 1: 323–368.

Swidler, A. (1986) 'Culture in Action: Symbols and Strategies', *American Sociological Review*, 51: 273–286.

Torny, D. (1998) 'La traçabilité comme technique de gouvernement des hommes et des choses', *Politix*, n°44: 51–75.

Vaughan, D. (1992) 'Theory Elaboration: the Heuristics of Case Analysis', in C. Ragin and H. Becker (eds) *What is a Case? Exploring the Foundations of Social Inquiry*, 173–202, Cambridge: Cambridge University Press.

Velthuis, O. (2020) 'Market Devices', in J. Bowen *et al.* (eds) *Pragmatic Inquiry: Critical Concepts for Social Sciences*, New York and London: Routledge, 80–93.

Zelizer, V. (1979) *Morals and Markets: The Development of Life Insurance in the United States*, New York and London: Columbia University Press.

11 Conclusion

Disaster recovery and the repairing perspective – between theory and practice

Laura Centemeri, J. Peter Burgess and Sezin Topçu

Repairing and the irreducible singularity of contexts

A significant body of literature – often focused on the United States – has been developing since the 2000s on the topic of 'disaster recovery indicators' and 'recovery plan quality principles'. Its main objective has been to address evidence of a pervasive failure of recovery processes to reduce vulnerability to future disasters.[1] While the contributors to this volume recognize that these efforts can help policy-makers and actors on the ground in their search for sound operational guidelines for recovery, this has not been the aim of the book. Instead, it has sought to construct a dialogue and create a cross-fertilization between disaster studies and theoretical debates in social sciences. This dialogue is essential if we are to fully measure the challenge that the socio-ecological complexity and cultural/ontological 'multiplicity' of contemporary societies pose to our understanding of disasters (see Mol 1999; De la Cadena and Blaser 2018). In an increasingly interdependent world, which is marked by an awareness of the planetary impact of human activities, disasters are not only on the increase; they are morphing into some sort of 'disastrous condition' that is punctuated by disastrous events.

Taking current theoretical debates into consideration in disaster research is imperative. On the one hand, they allow a better understanding of the overall complexity of multiple systemic crises, including climate change, financial instabilities and the crisis of democratic legitimacy. On the other, we firmly believe that these debates can feed the 'sociological imagination' of the field of disaster studies and contribute to developing the inclusive potential of policies aimed at supporting collective capacities of prevention, preparedness and response to disasters. In return, the dialogue between disaster studies and the theoretical perspectives that surround it can help to clarify and test the operability of approaches otherwise condemned to remain just a paper exercise.

The contributors to this volume all share this view. This book is the result of a dialogue that has been sustained over the past decade between various academic and activist contexts. Each contributor is positioned at the boundary between the specialist field of disaster research and the social sciences, especially sociology and anthropology. A number of them also share some form of engagement with

DOI: 10.4324/9781003184782-15

movements that have emerged in post-disaster situations. This positioning has led to the identification of the theoretical question of 'repairing' as a promising bridge between disaster research and the larger theoretical issues and key political concerns.

To illustrate this potential, the contributors to this volume analyze post-disaster situations as contexts that are particularly conducive to deepening our understanding of the multiple repairing and 'reconstructing' processes that continuously shape societies and their environments. Taken together, the contributions provide an original interpretation of disasters as ongoing and complex processes whose temporal regime is not clearly identifiable, an aspect widely acknowledged in the disaster literature. As several contributors point out (see, in particular, Chapter 7), repairing processes show multiple temporalities. These processes participate in the reproduction and transformation of the social fabric and in the ecologies that human communities shape through the organization of collective life within a particular environment.

The multiplicity of repairing processes reveals different repairing concerns, which can sometimes come into tension, if not open conflict, with each other: defining damages, assigning responsibilities, punishing the guilty, sanctioning activities and behaviours detrimental to the community (as in Chapter 1; Chapter 8; Chapter 9; Chapter 10); ensuring the functionality of the infrastructure that provides fundamental goods and services and preparing for future crises (as in Chapter 2; Chapter 4; Chapter 5); pragmatically taking care of damaged people and places, healing and reconstructing the capacity for collective action and an imagination of possible futures (Chapter 3; Chapter 6; Chapter 7). The evidence from the research collected in the book shows that the unfolding of the different processes of repairing – with a particular focus on the role played by the justice system – is an important element that ultimately contributes to explaining a community's capacity, or lack of capacity, for resilience.

The contributions clearly illustrate considerable diversity in the kinds of disasters. This diversity reflects systemic inequalities that have historically settled into their specific contexts and are produced and reproduced in very different ways. Moreover, the resources (including social capital) that local actors can mobilize in the conflict generated by what we have called the 'what-ness' of the problematic situation are also unequally distributed inside and across specific situations of action.

The various processes of repairing reveal the interconnexion of economic, ecological, technical, political, cultural and symbolic dimensions, which all play a part in the way communities make sense of problematic situations. Precisely because of this complexity, establishing criteria of general validity for intervention and assistance in post-disaster situations with the idea of ensuring successful recovery seems to us a somehow Sisyphean endeavour. A successful recovery emerges at best retrospectively, as a way of putting into narrative form a trajectory that could have not been anticipated. The terms of what can subsequently be defined as a successful recovery are the subject of negotiation and conflict and result from the situated confrontation of different normative expectations and worldviews. Moreover, what is meant by a good recovery varies, depending on the level at which a social actor observes the process and the temporality in which they are situated. In other words, the quality of recovery is to a certain degree in the eye of the beholder.

The active involvement of the communities that have directly suffered the consequences of a disaster remains an essential goal and a non-negotiable standard when decisions are being made about the measures and evaluation criteria that should guide recovery initiatives. This involvement must be accompanied, however, by an acknowledgement of the diversity of the normative presuppositions about recovery that come into play. These are shaped by, amongst other things, the many forms of inequalities and structural violence that emerge in concrete situations (see, on this point, the reflections of Smith and Birkland 2012; Tierney and Oliver-Smith 2012; Johnson and Hayashi 2012).

Consequently, the contributions to this book do not seek to provide a theory of successful recovery, as the very notion of successful recovery is problematic and contentious. This finding does not imply, however, that we should descend into a relativism that condemns us to inaction. Rather, it compels us to support an approach to recovery that does not obscure the structural conditions that produce disasters while giving centrality to the irreducible singularity of contexts.

More precisely, the perspective on recovery embraced by the contributors to this book is one that identifies, within the different processes of repairing that become visible in the aftermath of a disaster (legal, technical/ecological, socio-cultural, experiential), key situations from which to understand how social needs emerge and take shape contextually and how structural conditions of socio-ecological vulnerability are countered or (re)produced (such as those highlighted in Chapter 1 and Chapter 3).

By taking into account voices that are silenced and issues that are excluded from the debate (such as the question of what is beyond repair, like nuclear disasters, discussed in this volume by Topçu in Chapter 2), the repairing prism reveals the intertwining of the material, ecological, structural, moral and interpretive aspects that shape specific situations of action and experience in a disaster. It also contributes to a better understanding of the mechanisms that sustain, in ways that vary according to the context, the reproduction of different forms of injustice, such as distributive injustice, epistemic injustice, environmental injustice and 'narrative injustice' (the latter is extensively discussed by Gorostiza and Armiero in Chapter 4).

Moreover, the fact that this perspective considers the normatively laden interpretive activities in concrete disaster situations is propitious for the 'art of noticing' (Tsing 2015) unexpected forms of response to disaster, such as those analyzed by Keck in Chapter 5 and Thorsen in Chapter 6. Post-disaster recovery is thereby confirmed as a non-linear process, a point highlighted by Chateauraynaud and Debaz in Chapter 7 (but see also Tierney and Oliver-Smith 2012).

The perspective of repairing outlined in the book can thus be understood as a 'sensitizing' tool that invites disaster researchers to pay attention to the interweaving of repairing issues, *dispositifs* and practices in post-disaster situations. In particular, the perspective opened up by Barbot and Dodier in Chapter 10 through the notion of 'ecology of reparation *dispositifs*' is promising in terms of offering an original vantage point for comparing different recovery trajectories.

Accounting for structures: from disaster capitalism to disaster colonialism

Despite an increase in international initiatives aimed at disaster risk reduction, the number of catastrophes on a global scale has risen steeply over the past two decades. At the same time, there has been a worldwide increase in the number of people living in extreme poverty, which is a proven cause of vulnerability and an accelerator of risk and disaster (Oliver-Smith and Hoffman 1999).

At the time of writing, the world is facing the consequences of the ongoing Covid-19 pandemic. Describing it as a 'syndemic', Richard Horton, editor-in-chief of *The Lancet*, called for governments to 'devise policies and programmes to reverse profound disparities' (Horton 2020). A syndemic, or synergistic epidemic, refers to the idea that the virus does not work in isolation but in combination with conditions such as obesity, diabetes and heart disease, which aggravate the damage caused by Covid-19. The distribution of these conditions is closely linked to conditions of poverty and inequality. The 'what-ness' of Covid-19 is a matter of controversy, and the meaning that prevails will guide the response to the global crisis being triggered by the disease. In this context, identifying and analyzing the various emergent claims involving repairing seems to us a promising perspective for understanding to what extent the Covid-19 pandemic/syndemic will or will not operate as a 'reconfigurative' event at the systemic, local and individual levels.

From the point of view of disaster research, the evidence is now overwhelming. Ecological degradation, injustice and social exclusion are the systemic issues that need to be urgently addressed in order to achieve effective disaster risk reduction. At the same time, these structural elements manifest and reproduce in ways that are specific to the culture, history and ecology of particular places. This means that there are no universally valid solutions to the problem. Top-down interventions always generate 'frictions' (Tsing 2005) once implemented locally. We believe that the lack of interest in understanding and working with (and within) these frictions contributes to the fact that recovery programmes become 'confirmatory' – instead of 'transformative' – interventions, that is, interventions that corroborate logics that maintain and reproduce structural conditions of social inequality and ecological degradation (Pellizzoni 2020).

In this sense, there is an urgent need, as Gaillard (2019: 7) argued, to 'relocate disaster studies within the realm of its original political agenda' in order to restore the political and social relevance of the vulnerability perspective that radically transformed this field of study in the 1970s. It is now essential, as Gaillard (2019: 7) also pointed out, to integrate the contributions of subaltern studies into disaster research so as to promote a research agenda that 'builds on the importance of local researchers analyzing local disasters using local epistemologies, especially in the non-Western world'. A similar point was raised by Sun and

Faas (2018: 630): 'One key shortcoming of the political ecology of vulnerability approach is that it preserves and privileges the subjectivity of western science over other ways of seeing and being'. According to these authors, the conceptual challenge that the multidisciplinary study of disasters faces today is that it must link the 'social production' and 'social construction' of disaster perspectives. More specifically, this implies that we 'must contend with multiple ways of knowing – for example, the many people of the world who view nature as including humanity *and* culture, who see landscapes as part of their communities' (Sun and Faas 2018: 630). As Calandra pointed out in her discussion of the category of '*disasta*' in Tongoan discourse, 'grasping the cross-cultural dimensions of disaster requires an appreciation of different theories of causality and moral economies of attribution' (2020: 11). There is nonetheless an enduring 'procedural vulnerability' in disaster research, meaning that the mainstream methods mask important issues and are often blind when it comes to conditions of structural violence (see Veland *et al.* 2013).

Given these problematic issues, the exploration of the disputed 'what-ness' of disaster, the diversity of 'normative expectations' and the meanings of repairing that inform not only the design but also the practical relation to instruments, rules and *dispositifs* of disaster recovery has been our way of responding to the need for a framework that takes into account a plurality of ways of knowing, experiencing and making sense of disaster situations, including perspectives that do not recognize the category of disaster as pertinent.

In this regard, the contributions collected here all adopt, albeit from a range of different perspectives, relational approaches (like pragmatism) to the interpretation of disaster situations as 'problematic situations' in which the moral, epistemic, political and material dimensions are intertwined. As other authors have pointed out (see Go 2016; Doucet 2018), relational approaches in the social sciences allow a fruitful dialogue with perspectives inspired by postcolonial theory and 'ontological politics' that are attentive to how divergent knowledges and practices 'make worlds' (see De la Cadena and Blaser 2018). However, the research in this book shows that the potential for this diversity to really make a difference in the design of disaster policies is limited.

We mentioned in the introduction to the volume the notion of 'disaster capitalism', and we have seen in the chapters that followed how powerful economic actors – often supported by state authorities – contribute to generating 'slow disasters' (see Chapter 1 and Chapter 3) while also conditioning in advance the terms of good recovery (as in the case discussed by Topçu in Chapter 2). The systemic perspective that focuses on the interconnexion of disasters, economic interests, globalization and financialization highlights the implicit adherence of many disaster situation intervention practices to the globally promoted model of neoliberal development.

For example, in their research on 'disaster capitalism' in post-earthquake L'Aquila (Italy), Imperiale and Vanclay (2020: 3) showed how institutional and financial strategies, which were interwoven with the mechanisms that states usually mobilize in disaster situations, such as 'the command-and-control approach, emergency powers and top-down planning', had sustained multiple opportunities to 'capitalize on disasters', not just during the recovery phase but also in relation to the activities of 'imagining and planning' for future disasters. In this sense, future disasters can also be seen as opportunities to orient a society's development in ways that often lie 'outside political accountability' (Fortun *et al.* 2017: 1011).

Moreover, the case of post-earthquake L'Aquila shows that while the usual channels of profit creation are suspended in post-disaster situations, others emerge that are made socially acceptable by the way in which the disaster event and its consequences are framed. As the authors highlighted, the processes of sense-making concerning liability, which is one of the aspects pertaining to what we have called the juridical understanding of repairing, are particularly important in this respect. Social blaming, corruption and the inadequacy of structures are all examples of liability frameworks that contributed to determining the course of recovery in the case of L'Aquila.

As Villanueva and Cobián (2019: 1) rightly pointed out, disaster capitalism is in many cases only 'the latest rendition of a long legacy of colonial capitalism'. Disaster scholars have long recognized that disasters are the result of societal histories and that slow disasters feed fast disasters (see, in particular, Oliver-Smith 2010; Tierney 2014). The important research that has denounced the existence in the United States of an enduring racial divide in disaster relief (see Bullard 2008; Wright 2011) has also highlighted the fact that disaster situations not only amplify but *produce and reproduce* structural inequalities. In this respect, Danielle Zoe Rivera spoke of an ongoing 'disaster colonialism', that is, a colonialism that operates through disasters, where the term 'colonialism' points to 'the procedural vulnerabilities operating through pre-disaster and post-disaster response' (2020: 8).

Repairing against 'defuturing': design activism for recovery

One topic that this book only marginally addresses (see Chapter 9), but which is increasingly central in explaining the transformations that this very same notion of disaster is undergoing in our societies, is the specific challenges raised by climate change. Together with the erosion of biodiversity, climate change presents us with the looming possibility of a planetary catastrophe. In particular, we want to emphasize the value, for our discussion on recovery and repairing between theory and practice, of the literature on the role of urban planning in recovery processes and adaptation to climate change (see Kim 2021).

In the space of just a few years, cities have gone from being one of the main ecological problems to the central players in the development of climate change mitigation and adaptation policies (Angelo and Wachsmuth 2020). However, the numerous 'redemptive approaches to cities (sustainable city, liveable cities, smart cities, resilient cities, and the like)[. . .] do not have the corrective force to deal with the critical situations cities are increasingly facing' (Fry 2017: vii).

The academic discussion on how to think about urban planning in relation to the challenge of climate change has seen the emergence of a repairing framework that could usefully inspire planning for disasters (and disaster recovery) more generally. From this point of view, a framework that echoes our concern for complexity and multiplicity in addressing disasters recovery is that of 'metrofitting', elaborated by Tony Fry, which is based on an approach to urban spaces as 'broken' and 'ruined' (Fry 2017).

'Brokenness' was seen by Fry as the precondition of disaster. Brokenness – as the author explained – is not (only) a condition 'reducible to built fabric or infrastructure in visible need of repair. It can be equally evident in a failing operational metabolism, social ecology, system of governance and inability to manage a crisis of structural unsustainability' (Fry 2017: 4). In this sense, 'every city is structurally implicated in an unsustainable metabolism (via its economy and population's way of life)' and consequently 'all cities, by degree, are broken and in need of repair – this is not to reinstate their past but to cope with the future' (*ibid.*: 60). 'Metrofitting' is presented by the author as 'redirective, reparative and reconstructive action to transform what relationally exists (materially, operationally and socio-culturally)' in such a way as to counteract 'the convergence of numerous "defuturing" impacts (like climate change, population pressures, geopolitical instability, resource stress, and social and individual technologically linked cultural transformations)' (*ibid.*: viii). Within this framework, Fry invited us to think of the 'process of repair' as a process that does not just mend and reinstate 'what things originally were but futurally redirects them to be able to deal or adapt to emergent conditions' (*ibid.*: 4).

We do not have the space within the confines of this contribution to present Fry's perspective in detail; however, we would like to highlight the fact that Fry also rejected 'the promise of a "how-to book of answers"' and embraced the complexity of the task of the socio-ecological transformation of human settlements, which implies a radical 'remaking' of planning. Planning has to become 'more socially relationally engaged, perceptive and dialogical and less bureaucratic, instrumental, developmentally orientated and gesturally consultative' (*ibid.*: 139).

A similar approach emerged in the reflections of the urban sociologist Richard Sennett (2018), who also recognized that the notion of repair could be key in the way we think about cities faced with the challenge of resilience in the context of climate change. In particular, Sennett distinguished three practical ways to 'make a repair': restoration, remediation and reconfiguration. In restoration, the goal is to erase the trace of damage and remake everything as new. In remediation, the goal is to intervene in such a way that there is an improvement in performance but without changing form or function. In reconfiguration, the condition of brokenness and ruin is an opportunity for recreation, starting from what exists, in terms of both form and function. According to Sennett, the perspective of repairing takes us 'closer to understanding resilience' (Sennett 2018: 289). In his opinion, when repairing processes include a 'reconfigurative' purpose, they make the need for a change in the established frameworks of making the city visible and open to public discussion.

Both of these studies invite us to think about recovery through the prism of a 'design-based approach', where design refers to 'a particular approach to organizing experts and publics in planning for complex, large-scale infrastructural projects' (Collier *et al.* 2016). Post-disaster decision-making processes can then be approached in terms of 'wicked problems' that require 'a series of improvised decisions and choices rather than those based on proven solutions': 'wicked problems form an integral part of the society that generated them, thus their resolution requires change at societal level' (Lee 2015: 110).

As discussed by Manzini (2015: 1), this perspective stems from the idea that a world facing multiple systemic crises is

> a world in which everybody constantly has to design and redesign their existence, whether they wish to or not, a world in which many of these projects converge and give rise to wider social changes, a world in which the role of design experts is to feed and support these individual and collective projects – and thus the social changes they may give rise to.

This perspective encourages due attention in disaster research to the various grassroots forms of 'design activism' (Fuad-Luke 2009) that can emerge in post-disaster situations, which are understood as forms of practical engagement in repairing and reconstruction processes that take shape in affected communities.

This type of activism came to the fore, for example, in the case of the Central Apennine earthquake in Italy, a series of high-intensity seismic events that began with the earthquake of 24 August 2016 and that resulted in the destruction of the town of Amatrice and the loss of 235 lives. In this region, a movement called the Active Solidarity Brigades (*Brigate di Solidarietà Attiva*), which had emerged in the aftermath of the disastrous earthquake in L'Aquila in 2009, promptly took action in this new crisis situation. These 'brigades' are grassroots groups that intervene in emergency situations by actively promoting solidarity initiatives and self-management support activities amongst the population in question based on the model of the early twentieth-century mutual aid organizations. In the aftermath of the Amatrice earthquake, this grassroots mobilization supported the design and self-construction of emergency housing solutions suited to the mountain context to allow farmers in the area to continue to take care of their fields and animals, which would otherwise have been abandoned. More generally, in an already critical situation of rural abandonment in the Italian territory, this mobilization counteracted the further abandonment of the mountains of this region that was being precipitated by the handling of the emergency. These groups also promoted a collective, self-managed research experiment, called the Emidio di Treviri Project, aimed at the bottom-up production of critical knowledge on the management of the post-earthquake situation (see Olori and Menghi 2019). This research, which has received no external funding, involves a broad national community of social scientists, architects, psychologists, urban planners, anthropologists, engineers and employment lawyers giving their time on a voluntary basis. Most importantly, the research directly involves researchers living in or near the disaster area. It has not been given an expiration date but continues in the form of a permanent observatory. This experiment, although not truly replicable in other contexts and not without criticality, is a worthy example of how research on disasters can be conducted in a way that actively includes local populations in the design not only of practical interventions of repairing but also of research activities on recovery.

We have already discussed, in the introductory chapter, the limitations of interpreting resilience as an individual capacity to respond to change in a creative way. Similarly, from the perspective of design activism which we are discussing here, if the structural conditions of vulnerability and subalternity are disregarded, the call for bottom-up practices of reconstruction and repair are at risk of turning into just another empty slogan.

An increase in these design activism initiatives is desirable, if only to serve as proof of the real possibility of turning recovery processes into processes of democratic empowerment, social change and socio-technical innovation. However, the rise of these 'beautiful islands of applied cultural and socioeconomic wisdom' (Manzini 2015: 26) would not be enough to promote a change towards more just societies and more liveable environments for all, humans and non-humans alike.

From this point of view, the reflection elaborated by Arturo Escobar (2018), which was based on Latin American examples, concerning the possibility of 'design under the conditions of repression and violence' deserves careful consideration. At the heart of Escobar's reflection is the idea of 'autonomy-oriented design' as an expression of a 'design from the South' (see also Kalantidou and Fry 2015), which was understood as design 'stemming from communal worlds, where each community would practice the design of itself on the basis of local, decolonial knowledges' (Escobar 2018: 206).

More research as well as experimental practices to test a repairing perspective are needed to further develop the approach that has been outlined in this book. It points to an understanding of recovery as oriented towards creating (if needed) and supporting the capacities of communities to repair and 'reconfigure' broken socio-ecosystems through autonomy-oriented design. These capacities, however, should be promoted within a broader framework of commitment to facilitate the structural transformations that are needed to counter the 'defuturing' (Fry 1999) systemic processes that continue to feed fast and slow disasters.

Note

1 See, for a synthesis of this literature, Smith *et al.* (2018); see also Mayer (2019).

References

Angelo, H. and Wachsmuth, D. (2020) 'Why Does Everyone Think Cities Can Save the Planet?', *Urban Studies*, 57(11): 2201–2221.
Bullard, R.D. (2008) 'Differential Vulnerabilities: Environmental and Economic Inequality and Government Response to Unnatural Disasters', *Social Research*, 75(3): 753–784.
Calandra, M. (2020) 'Disasta: Rethinking the Notion of Disaster in the Wake of Cyclone Pam', *Anthropological Forum*, 30(1–2): 42–54.

Collier, S., Cox, S. and Grove, K. (2016) 'Rebuilding by Design in Post-Sandy New York', *Limn 7: Public Infrastructure/Infrastructural Publics*. <https://limn.it/articles/rebuilding-by-design-in-post-sandy-new-york/> (accessed 08 February 2021).

De la Cadena, M. and Blaser, M. (2018) *A World of Many Worlds*, Durham and London: Duke University Press.

Doucet, A. (2018) 'Shorelines, Seashells, and Seeds: Feminist Epistemologies, Ecological Thinking, and Relational Ontologies', in F. Dépelteau (ed.) *The Palgrave Handbook of Relational Sociology*, Cham, Switzerland: Palgrave Macmillan.

Escobar, A. (2018) *Designs for the Pluriverse: Radical Interdependence, Autonomy, and the Making of Worlds*, Durham and London: Duke University Press.

Fortun, K., Knowles, S.G, Choi, V., Jobin, P., Matsumoto, M., de la Torre III, P., Liboiron, M. and Murillo, L.F.R. (2017) 'Researching Disaster from an STS Perspective', in U. Felt, U., R. Fouche, C.A. Miller and L. Smith-Doerr (eds) *The Handbook of Science and Technology Studies*, 4th edition, Cambridge, MA: The MIT Press, 1003–1028.

Fry, T. (1999) *A New Design Philosophy: An Introduction to Defuturing*, Sydney: New South Wales University Press Ltd.

Fry, T. (2017) *Re-Making Cities: An Introduction to Urban Metrofitting*, London: Bloomsbury Publishing.

Fuad-Luke, A. (2009) *Design Activism: Beautiful Strangeness for a Sustainable World*, London; Sterling, VA: Earthscan.

Gaillard, J.C. (2019) 'Disaster Studies Inside Out', *Disasters*, 43(S1): S7–S17.

Go, J. (2016) *Postcolonial Thought and Social Theory*, Oxford and New York: Oxford University Press.

Horton, R. (2020) 'Offline: COVID-19 Is Not a Pandemic', *The Lancet*, 396(10255): 874.

Imperiale, A.J. and Vanclay, F. (2020) 'The Mechanism of Disaster Capitalism and the Failure to Build Community Resilience in Post-Disaster Situations: Learning from the L'Aquila Earthquake', *Disasters*, (April 2009): 1–26.

Johnson, L.A. and Hayashi, H. (2012) 'Synthesis Efforts in Disaster Recovery Research', *International Journal of Mass Emergencies and Disasters*, 30(2): 212–238.

Kalantidou, E. and Fry, T. (eds) (2015) *Design in the Borderlands*, London: Routledge.

Kim, K. (2021) *Learning from Disaster: Planning for Resilience*, London: Routledge.

Lee, A.J. (2015) 'Wicked Problems Framework: Architectural Lessons from Recent Urban Disasters', in A. Masys (ed.) *Disaster Management: Enabling Resilience*, Cham, Switzerland: Springer.

Manzini, E. (2015) *Design, When Everybody Designs: An Introduction to Design for Social Innovation*, London and Cambridge: MIT Press.

Mayer, B. (2019) 'A Review of the Literature on Community Resilience and Disaster Recovery', *Current Environmental Health Reports*, 6(3): 167–173.

Mol, A. (1999) 'Ontological Politics: A Word and Some Questions', *The Sociological Review*, 47(1_suppl): 74–89.

Oliver-Smith, A. (2010) *Defying Displacement: Grassroots Resistance and the Critique of Development*, Austin, TX: University of Texas Press.

Oliver-Smith, A. and Hoffman, S. (eds) (1999) *The Angry Earth: Disaster in Anthropological Perspective*, Abingdon and New York: Routledge.

Olori, D. and Menghi, M. (2019) 'Ricerca, attivismo e trasformazione sociale nel post-sisma: L'esperienza di una ricerca collettiva, pubblica e dal basso tra criticità e prospettive [Research, Activism and Social Transformation in the Post-Earthquake Period: The

Experience of a Collective, Public Research Project from Below, between Criticality and Prospects]', *Cambio*, 9(17): 95–107.

Pellizzoni, L. (2020) 'The Time of Emergency. On the Governmental Logic of Preparedness', *AIS Journal of Sociology*, 16: 39–54. <https://doi.org/10.1485/2281-2652-202016-3>.

Rivera, D.Z. (2020) 'Disaster Colonialism: A Commentary on Disasters Beyond Singular Events to Structural Violence', *International Journal of Urban and Regional Research*. <https://doi.org/10.1111/1468-2427.12950>.

Sennett, R. (2018) *Building and Dwelling: Ethics for the City*, New York: Farrar, Straus and Giroux.

Smith, G. and Birkland, T. (2012) 'Building a Theory of Recovery: Institutional Dimensions', *International Journal of Mass Emergencies and Disasters*, 30(2): 147–170.

Smith, G., Martin, A. and Wenger, D.E. (2018) 'Disaster Recovery in an Era of Climate Change: The Unrealized Promise of Institutional Resilience', in H. Rodríguez, W. Donner and J.E. Trainor (eds) *Handbook of Disaster Research*, 2nd edition, New York: Springer, 595–618.

Sun, L. and Faas, A.J. (2018) 'Social Production of Disasters and Disaster Social Constructs: An Exercise in Disambiguation and Reframing', *Disaster Prevention and Management*, 27(5): 623–635.

Tierney, K. (2014) *The Social Roots of Risk: Producing Disasters, Promoting Resilience*, Stanford, CA: Stanford University Press.

Tierney, K. and Oliver-Smith, A. (2012) 'Social Dimensions of Disaster Recovery', *International Journal of Mass Emergencies and Disasters*, 30(2): 123–146.

Tsing, A.L. (2005) *Friction: An Ethnography of Global Connections*, Princeton: Princeton University Press.

Tsing, A.L. (2015) *The Mushroom at the End of the World: On the Possibility of Life in Capitalist Ruins*, Princeton and Oxford: Princeton University Press.

Veland, S., Howitt, R., Dominey-Howes, D., Thomalla, F. and Houston, D. (2013) 'Procedural Vulnerability: Understanding Environmental Change in a Remote Indigenous Community', *Global Environmental Change*, 23(1): 314–326.

Villanueva, J. and Cobián, M. (2019) 'Intervention – Beyond Disaster Capitalism: Dismantling the Infrastructure of Extraction in Puerto Rico's Neo-Plantation Economy', *Antipode ONLINE*. <https://antipodeonline.org/2019/06/25/beyond-disaster-capitalism/> (accessed 08 February 2021).

Wright, B. (2011) 'Race, Place, and the Environment in the Aftermath of Katrina', *Anthropology of Work Review*, 32(1): 4–8.

Index